The Ongoing Feast

Arthur A. Just Jr.

The Ongoing Feast

Table Fellowship and Eschatology at Emmaus

A PUEBLO BOOK

The Liturgical Press   Collegeville, Minnesota

A Pueblo Book published by The Liturgical Press

Design by Frank Kacmarcik. "Emmaus" by Email von Egino Weinert, Cologne.

1	2	3	4	5	6	7	8	9

Library of Congress Cataloging-in-Publication Data

Just, Arthur A., 1953–
    The ongoing feast : table fellowship and eschatology at Emmaus / Arthur A. Just, Jr.
        p.   cm.
    "A Pueblo book."
    Includes bibliographical references.
    ISBN 0-8146-6013-4
    1. Bible. N.T. Luke XXIV—Criticism, interpretation, etc. 2. Dinners and dining in the Bible. I. Title.
    BS2595.2.J88 1993
    226.4'06—dc 20   93-595
                                                                CIP

To Linda, with love and gratitude

Contents

Abbreviations

AnBib	Analecta biblica
ANQ	Andover Newton Quarterly
AsSeign	Assemblées du Seigneur
ATR	Anglican Theological Review
BibBhas	Bible Bhashyam
BibTrans	The Bible Translator
BR	Biblical Research
BSac	Bibliotheca sacra
BTB	Biblical Theology Bulletin
BW	Biblical World
BZ	Biblische Zeitschrift
CBQ	Catholic Biblical Quarterly
CR	Clergy Review
CTM	Concordia Theological Monthly
CurrTM	Currents in Theology and Mission
DunRev	Dunwoodie Review
EstBíb	Estudios Bíblicos
EstEcl	Estudios Eclesiásticos
EBib	Études bibliques
EvQ	Evangelical Quarterly
EvT	Evangelische Theologie
Expos	Expositor
ExpTim	Expository Times
FRLANT	Forschungen zur Religion und Literatur des Alten und Neuen Testaments

Greg	Gregorianum
IDB	Interpreter's Dictionary of the Bible
Int	Interpretation
ITQ	Irish Theological Quarterly
JAAR	Journal of the American Academy of Religion
JBL	Journal of Biblical Literature
JES	Journal of Ecumenical Studies
JETS	Journal of Evangelical Theological Society
JQR	Jewish Quarterly Review
JSNT	Journal for the Study of the New Testament
JTC	Journal for Theology and the Church
JTS	Journal of Theological Studies
KJV	King James Version
LTS	Lutheran Theological Seminary
LumVit	Lumen Vitae
LXX	The Septuagint
NB	*New Blackfriars*
NEB	*New English Bible*
NovT	*Novum Testamentum*
NRT	*La nouvelle revue théologique*
NTA	Neutestamentliche Abhandlungen
NTS	*New Testament Studies*
RB	*Revue Biblique*
RevExp	*Review and Expositor*
RevistB	*Revista bíblica*
RevQ	*Revue de Qumran*
RHPR	*Revue d'histoire et de philosophie religieuses*
RR	*Review for Religious*
RSV	*Revised Standard Version*
SBT	*Studies in Biblical Theology*
ScEsp	*Science et Esprit XXX, 1*
SE 1	*Studia Evangelica I*

SJT	*Scottish Journal of Theology*
SNTSMS	*Studiorum Novi Testamenti Societas, Monograph Series*
TBT	*The Bible Today*
TB	*Tyndale Bulletin*
TDNT	Kittel G. and G. Friedrich (eds.) *Theological Dictionary of the New Testament* (10 vols.; Grand Rapids: Eerdmans, 1964–1976).
TDNT Abridged	Kittel G. and G. Friedrich (eds.) *Theological Dictionary of the New Testament* Abridged in One Volume by G. Bromiley (Grand Rapids: Eerdmans, 1985).
TJ	*Trinity Journal*
TRTR	*The Reformed Theological Review*
TS	*Theological Studies*
TWOT	Harris, R. L., G. L. Archer, and B. K. Waltke (eds.) *Theological Wordbook of the Old Testament* (Chicago: Moody Press, 1980) I-II.
ZNW	*Zeitschrift für die neutestamentliche Wissenschaft*

All English translations are taken from the *RSV* unless otherwise noted.

Preface

My interest in Luke 24 was sparked by two studies. Paul Schubert's "The Structure and Significance of Luke 24"[1] placed the Emmaus story in the center of Luke's literary development. Paul Minear's "Some Glimpses of Luke's Sacramental Theology"[2] provided an overview of Lukan table fellowship as a manifestation of the eschatological kingdom. This interest was reinforced by an analysis of the theological significance of meals and meal parables in the New Testament, presented in Geoffrey Wainwright's *Eucharist and Eschatology*.[3] All three studies brought together Emmaus, table fellowship, and eschatology as a workable theme. This led to my submission of a doctoral thesis to the University of Durham, England, entitled "Table Fellowship and the Eschatological Kingdom in the Emmaus Narrative of Luke 24," which was accepted by the faculty of theology on July 4, 1990. This study preserves the essential argument of that thesis, although I have reduced it considerably, particularly in the footnotes.

Recent Lukan studies see the evangelist as a thematic writer exhibiting a unique literary character in comparison with the other evangelists. For example, Jerome Neyrey's *The Passion According to Luke* (1985) and Joseph B. Tyson's *The Death of Jesus in Luke-Acts* (1986)[4] develop the theme of Jesus' death by tracing several motifs

[1] P. Schubert, "The Structure and Significance of Luke 24," *Neutestamentliche Studien für Rudolf Bultmann*, ed. W. Eltester (Berlin: Alfred Töpelmann, 1954) 165–186.

[2] P. Minear, "Some Glimpses of Luke's Sacramental Theology," *Worship* 44 (1970) 322–331.

[3] G. Wainwright, *Eucharist and Eschatology* (New York: Oxford University Press, 1981).

[4] J. Neyrey, *The Passion According to Luke* (New York: Paulist Press, 1985), and J. Tyson, *The Death of Jesus in Luke-Acts* (University of South Carolina Press, 1986).

developed by the evangelist throughout Luke-Acts. Neyrey and Tyson illustrate that the Gospel of Luke anticipates the further development of such motifs in Acts, a literary analysis characteristic of current Lukan scholarship.

By means of the Emmaus meal and Lukan eschatology, I trace the table fellowship motif[5] in Luke. I seek to demonstrate the way in which the evangelist develops this motif throughout the Gospel and brings it to fulfillment in the Emmaus account. As the Emmaus account epitomizes Luke's table fellowship of teaching and eating, it becomes a vehicle for interpreting the entire Gospel, while Luke's eschatology provides a limitation for evaluating his table fellowship matrix.

My goal is to trace Luke's development of the table fellowship matrix in the Gospel *without consulting Acts*, a departure from most current Lukan scholarship. This methodology is justified in view of the climactic nature of Luke 24 with its emphasis on Emmaus.[6] A detailed analysis of table fellowship in Acts has already been initiated by other scholars and is simply assumed.[7]

My study is limited to a literary critical analysis of the Lukan motif of table fellowship in view of the Emmaus story, an approach differing from other Emmaus studies with their interest in form, source, and redaction criticism. Form, source, and redaction critical perspectives have been served by three excellent monographs on Emmaus: J. Wanke's *Die Emmauserzählung. Eine redaktionsgeschichtliche Untersuchung zu Lk 24,13-35*,[8] R. J. Dillon's *From*

---

[5]A number of scholars have discussed Lukan meals, e.g. W. Bösen, *Jesusmahl, Eucharistisches Mahl, Endzeitmahl: Ein Beitrag zur Theologie des Lukas* (Stuttgart: Katholisches Bibelwerk, 1980); E. C. Davis, "The Significance of the Shared Meal in Luke-Acts," (Ann Arbor: Xerox University Microfilms, 1967); R. J. Karris, *Luke: Artist and Theologian* (New York: Paulist Press, 1985); D. E. Smith, "Table Fellowship as a Literary Motif in the Gospel of Luke," *JBL* 106 (1987) 613–638; and J. Wanke, *Beobachtungen zum Eucharistieverständnis des Lukas auf Grund der lukanischen Mahlberichte* (Erfurter theologische Schriften 8; Leipzig: St. Benno-Verlag, 1973).

[6]Cf. C. Talbert, *Reading Luke* (New York: Crossroad, 1982) for an example of this approach.

[7]Cf. P. F. Esler, *Community and Gospel in Luke-Acts* (Cambridge University Press, 1987) 91–109 on table fellowship in Acts.

[8]J. Wanke, *Die Emmauserzählung. Eine redaktionsgeschichtliche Untersuchung zu*

Eyewitnesses to Ministers of the Word: Tradition and Composition in Luke 24,[9] and J. Guillaume's *Luc interprète des anciennes traditions sur la résurrection de Jésus.*[10] These three works complement one another by considering Emmaus in the context of Luke 24 and anticipating Acts. As form, source, and redactional critical studies, the character of their approach differs somewhat from my literary critical analysis. In his redactional assessment of Emmaus, Wanke does extensive language and motif analysis as these relate to the origins of the tradition. Dillon builds on Wanke's redactional work, but develops a method "to probe his [Luke's] *selection, coordination, and enlargement of source-material.*"[11] Guillaume looks at the traditions behind Luke's resurrection narrative from a "Form, Traditions et Redaktionsgeschichte" methodology,[12] but also devotes a section to biblical, Hellenistic, and genre parallels. I am gratefully dependent on the insights of these three scholars.

Since submitting my thesis to the University of Durham, two significant works have appeared that are not noted in this study since they had no bearing on its development. David Moessner's *Lord of the Banquet: The Literary and Theological Significance of the Lukan Travel Narrative*[13] is a literary critical analysis of Luke's travel narrative. It complements my work by tracing in Luke's travel section (Luke 9:51 to 19:44) many of the same themes I develop. Jan Wojcik's *The Road to Emmaus: Reading Luke's Gospel*[14] offers a gnostic understanding of Emmaus. It is more a hermeneutical text than an interpretative one. Both books are insightful and serve as commentaries on my study.

Lk 24,13-35 (Erfurter theologische Studien 31; Leipzig: St. Benno-Verlag, 1973).

[9]R. J. Dillon, *From Eyewitnesses to Ministers of the Word: Tradition and Composition in Luke 24* (Analecta biblica 82; Rome: Biblical Institute, 1978).

[10]J. Guillaume, *Luc interprète des anciennes traditions sur la résurrection de Jésus* (EBib; Paris: Gabalda, 1979). Guillaume does not make use of Wanke's or Dillon's study.

[11]Dillon, *From Eyewitnesses*, X (emphasis Dillon).

[12]Guillaume, *Luc interprète*, 8.

[13]D. P. Moessner, *Lord of the Banquet: The Literary and Theological Significance of the Lukan Travel Narrative* (Minneapolis: Fortress Press, 1989).

[14]J. Wojcik, *The Road to Emmaus: Reading Luke's Gospel* (West Lafayette, Ind.: Purdue University Press, 1989).

Since this book is the culmination of my graduate studies, there are many people who have contributed to this work. To all of them I am deeply grateful and acknowledge here their special contribution: my professors at Yale Divinity School who initiated this Lukan journey—Abraham Malherbe for his marvelous course that opened my eyes to Luke 24 and Emmaus, and Aidan Kavanagh who expanded my horizons and inspired the topic of this study; my colleagues at Concordia Theological Seminary who offered invaluable support and insight—David Scaer for introducing me to theology and carefully reading the various stages of my manuscript with insight and wit, Dean Wenthe for his pastoral encouragement, William Weinrich for his conversations on the Fathers and his learned advice, and James Voelz for his assistance in the initial doctoral proposal; those who made my doctoral work possible—John Stephenson whose introduction to the University of Durham paved the way, and the Aid Association for Lutherans and Concordia Theological Seminary for making it financially possible; those who helped in the formation of the text—Michael Hollman, Richard Resch, and Mark Twomey and the editors at The Liturgical Press; my examiners James Dunn and John Court who read my thesis and found it worthy; and my students for their support and encouragement as I learned from them what makes a good teacher of exegesis. Finally, I give my deepest thanks to the Reverend Canon John McHugh, my doctoral father and friend. His careful and gentle supervision taught me the art of exegesis and a deeper love for the biblical text, and his warm hospitality and table fellowship made the research and writing of "our Emmaus" an experience of a lifetime.

I dedicate this work to my wife, Linda, for her unwavering support and encouragement which made it possible for me to work in the midst of our three children, Abigail, Nicholas, and Jacob.

July 25, 1991
St. James the Elder, Apostle

Acknowledgments

The publishers are grateful to the following for permission to quote from copyright materials:

Baker Book House for *The Resurrection Narratives: A Redactional Study* by Grant R. Osborne copyright © 1984. By permission.

Earl Clinton Davis for "The Significance of the Shared Meal in Luke-Acts" in Ann Arbor: Xerox University Microfilms copyright © 1967. Used by permission.

Editrice Pontificio Istituto Biblico for *From Eyewitnesses to Ministers of the Word: Tradition and Composition in Luke 24* by Richard J. Dillon in Analecta Biblica/82. By permission.

E. J. Brill for *Mass and the Lord's Supper* by Hans Lietzmann copyright © 1979. By permission.

Epworth Press for *Eucharist and Eschatology* by Geoffrey Wainwright copyright © 1971, 1981. By permission.

Georges Borchardt, Inc. for *Sharing the Eucharistic Bread* by Xavier Léon-Dufour copyright © Editions du Seuil, 1982. Originally published as *Le Partage Du Pain Eucharistique* by Les Éditions du Seuil, Paris. English translation copyright © 1987 by The Missionary Society of St. Paul the Apostle in the State of New York. Used by permission.

Gillian Feeley-Harnik for *The Lord's Table: Eucharist and Passover in Early Christianity* copyright © 1981 by Gillian Feeley-Harnik. Used by permission.

From THE GOSPEL ACCORDING TO LUKE I–IX (ANCHOR BIBLE) by Joseph A. Fitzmyer. Copyright © 1981 by Doubleday, a division of Bantam Doubleday Dell Publishing Group, Inc. Used by permission of Doubleday, a division of Bantam Doubleday Dell Publishing Group, Inc.

From THE GOSPEL ACCORDING TO LUKE X–XXIV (ANCHOR BIBLE) by Joseph A. Fitzmyer. Copyright © 1985 by Doubleday, a division of Ban-

Chapter 1

The Passion Statements in Luke 24

The twenty-fourth chapter of the Gospel of Luke is pivotal to the two volume work of Luke-Acts. It makes possible an understanding of the purpose of the Gospel and the purpose of Acts, for the evangelist's final word in the Gospel looks back upon the ministry of Jesus to give meaning to what had happened, while at the same time it looks forward to the Acts of the Apostles and sets the stage for what is about to unfold. Without Luke 24, it would be very difficult to comprehend the plan that the evangelist has so elaborately set forth. But with Luke 24, the literary genius of Luke the evangelist becomes evident.[1]

The literary style of Luke-Acts is orderly and deliberative, displaying structure and form. As Paul Schubert says of Luke's literary technique, "His literary methods serve his theology as his theology serves them. In short, Luke's theology of history has a grandeur all its own."[2] This is evident in the theme of Jesus' table fellowship in Luke as a manifestation of the eschatological kingdom. As Robert Karris observed, "the theme of food occurs in every chapter of Luke's Gospel . . . the motif that God in Jesus provides for a hungry creation occurs in all significant contexts in the Gospel of Luke: infancy narrative, Galilean ministry, journey to Jerusalem, last days of Jerusalem."[3]

The climax of Luke 24 is not the Jerusalem resurrection appearances, as one might expect, but the meal at Emmaus; and the

[1] J. Fitzmyer, *The Gospel According to Luke X-XXIV* (New York: Doubleday, 1985) 1533–1543. See D. E. Smith, "Table fellowship," 613 n. 1 for a bibliography on Luke's literary style.

[2] Schubert, "The Structure and Significance," 185. Cf. also C. Talbert, *Literary Patterns, Theological Themes, and the Genre of Luke-Acts* (Missoula: Scholars Press, 1974).

[3] Karris, *Luke: Artist and Theologian,* 5–6. This is an overstatement, but it does highlight the prominence of Luke's food motif.

structure of Luke 24 is centered on the revelation of Christ, not in Jerusalem to the eleven, but to the other two disciples at Emmaus in the breaking of the bread.[4] I shall endeavor to demonstrate this *from a literary point of view.* If one sees the Emmaus meal as the climax of Luke's Gospel, then it is possible to recognize *at the end* that the table fellowship of Jesus with his people was *from the first* a manifestation of the eschatological kingdom. For if one looks carefully at the evangelist's references to food, one may perceive in them an eschatological significance. This suggests that the first Christian meals were an anamnesis, not just of Jesus' Last Supper with his disciples, but of the entire table fellowship that Jesus engaged in from his baptism to his ascension.

Since the Emmaus meal is so important to Luke 24, it must be carefully considered within the context of this pivotal chapter. Some have argued that Luke 24 is an apologetical attempt to establish Christianity as a legal religion and to remove any stumbling blocks that would prevent the Gentiles from accepting it as a religion with a long and trustworthy history.[5] This position is based on the fact that Luke's understanding of the death of Jesus seems consistently to emphasize that he was in no way a criminal, and that the death of Jesus was a profound mistake by the Jews, who acted in ignorance (Luke 23:34, 39-43, and 47).[6] In Luke 24, the death and resurrection of Jesus Christ are part of a divine plan of salvation in fulfillment of the Scriptures. The significance of the cross, then, is shown only after the resurrection. Thus it could be argued that the theological purpose of Luke 24 is to offer an explanation for the political embarrassment that the suffering and death of Jesus the Messiah caused the Church as it sought acceptance in the Roman world as a licit religion.

Such a thesis becomes reasonable when it is observed that Luke 24 contains four passion statements: 24:7, 19-21, 25-27, and 44-49.

[4]Cf. Schubert, "The Structure and Significance," 177, and Dillon, *From Eyewitnesses,* 167, 168-169, 204, 207-208, 220, and 223 for other suggestions on a climax in Luke 24 (e.g. Luke 24:46f. or 24:52).

[5]Cf. Fitzmyer, *X-XXIV,* 1534, 1557; Schubert, "The Structure and Significance," 165-186; and Esler, *Community and Gospel,* 16-23.

[6]See J. Fitzmyer, *The Gospel According to Luke I-IX* (New York: Doubleday, 1981) 22-23, 219-221 and Dillon, *From Eyewitnesses,* 29-31, 278-281 on the controversy over the death of Jesus in Luke-Acts.

These kerygmatic statements provide a perception into Luke's concept of the death of Jesus in both the Gospel and Acts, and each must now be examined in turn to see how the kerygma of Luke 24 fulfills the passion predictions of the Gospel itself.[7] Luke 24 is composed of three scenes before the account of the ascension: the women at the tomb (24:1-11, [12?]), the Emmaus journey (24:13-35), and Jesus' appearance in Jerusalem to the disciples (24:36-49). In each of these there is a statement about the passion.

LUKE 24:7

The first passion statement in Luke 24 occurs within the story of the empty tomb. In the Synoptic Gospels, the purpose of the three narratives of the empty tomb is to prepare the reader for the assertion that Jesus is risen, but none of the Synoptics or John gives an account of the resurrection itself. Only the Gospel of Peter relates such information.[8] The focus of Luke's final chapter is on what J. Fitzmyer calls, "the *praeconium paschale*, the essential Easter proclamation in the Synoptics."[9] It is worthwhile comparing Luke's version with those of Mark and Matthew:

a) *Mark 16:6*   "Do not be amazed; you seek Jesus of Nazareth, who was crucified. He has risen, he is not here . . ."
(*Êgérthê, ouk éstin hôde . . .*).

b) *Matthew 28:5-6*   "Do not be afraid; for I know that you seek Jesus who was crucified. He is not here; for he has risen, as he said."
(*Ouk éstin hôde, êgérthê gar kathôs eípen*).

c) *Luke 24:5-6*   "Why do you seek the living among the dead? He is not here, but has risen."
(*Ti zêteíte ton zônta metá tôn nekrôn: ouk éstin hôde, allá[10] êgérthê*).

---

[7]See R. Tannehill, *The Narrative Unity of Luke-Acts* (Philadelphia: Fortress Press, 1986) 277-278.

[8]Cf. Schubert, "The Structure and Significance," 167; Fitzmyer, *X-XXIV*, 1534.

[9]Fitzmyer, *X-XXIV*, 1537.

[10]Cf. Dillon, *From Eyewitnesses*, 32.

In the *praeconium paschale,* Matthew (28:6) and Luke (24:6) agree: "He is not here for he has risen"; whereas Mark states, "He has risen, he is not here!" Matthew adds to his *praeconium paschale* the words, "as he said," and Luke is more emphatic when he first says, "Why do you seek the living among the dead?," focusing on the resurrected Christ as alive.[11] This establishes the resurrection as an important theme of Luke 24. Both Matthew and Luke understand the resurrection in terms of what Jesus said, but where Matthew makes the simple statement, "as he said," Luke includes in 24:6-7 a complete kerygmatic statement about the passion and resurrection of Jesus that recalls what Jesus said while he was in Galilee:[12]

"Remember how he told you while he was still in Galilee,
  that the Son of man must be delivered into the hands of sinful
    men,
  and be crucified,
  and on the third day rise."

This passion statement is significant for various reasons. First, it is only found in Luke. Second, its cool formality makes a dramatic contrast with the bewilderment of the women. This is emphasized by the aorist imperative "remember" (*mnêthête*). This verb is used in Luke only six times, five of which refer to God's promises (Luke 1:54; 1:72; 23:42; 24:6, 8). This imperative may therefore have implied to Luke's readers that Jesus' words in Galilee were the words of God. Third, this passion statement immediately transposes the reader to 9:22 where Jesus, *during his ministry in Galilee (éti ôn en tê Galilaía),* makes the first prediction of his passion.[13] Fourth, the language used by Luke in this verse appears throughout Luke-Acts with reference to the passion. For example, the title "Son of Man" is used in Luke's three passion predictions: 9:22, 9:44, and 18:31; and it also occurs in the context of a

[11]Cf. Fitzmyer, *X-XXIV,* 1545: " 'Life' is one of the effects of the Christ-event in Lucan theology; this is a fitting way to depict the risen Christ." Cf. Romans 14:9.

[12]Cf. Schubert, "The Structure and Significance," 167–168, 174; Dillon, *From Eyewitnesses,* 16–20.

[13]Dillon, *From Eyewitnesses,* 26, also notes a connection in 24:7 to the transfiguration.

passion allusion at 17:24-25. The term of divine necessity, *dei*, links 24:7 with 9:22 (cf. 17:25) and is used three times in Luke 24 at verses 7, 26, and 44. Luke clearly perceives the death of Jesus as a divine necessity.[14] Other important passion words are "delivered" (*paradídōmi*—Luke 9:44; 18:32; 24:20; Acts 3:13), "hands of sinful men" (*cheíras anthrṓpōn*—Luke 9:44), "crucified" (*stauróō/staurós*—Luke 9:23), "rise" (*anístēmi*—Luke 9:22; 18:33; 24:46), and "on the third day" (*tȇ trítȇ hēméra*—Luke 9:22; 18:33; 24:21, 46; Acts 10:40).[15] Fifth, the reaction of the women to the words of the angels recalls the passion predictions. In 24:8, Luke's phrase, "and they remembered his words" (*kai emnȇsthȇsan tȏn hrȇmátōn autoú*), is similar to one used in 9:45 and 18:34, the second and third predictions of the passion. Sixth, the lack of understanding and disbelief at the passion and resurrection by the apostles in 24:11 is characteristically and uniquely Lukan within the resurrection narrative itself.[16] Although in Matthew 28:1-10 and Mark 16:1-8 astonishment and fear are expressed by the eyewitnesses, there is no report given by the evangelist concerning the reaction of the disciples to the resurrection. In Luke 24:11, the report of the empty tomb is considered by them to be "an idle tale."[17] Seventh, the concept of the twelve or the eleven (v. 9) and

[14]Cf. H. Conzelmann, *The Theology of St. Luke* (New York: Harper, 1967) 153 and n. 3 on *dei* as part of Luke's salvation vocabulary and his motif of the fulfillment of Scripture. Also Tannehill, *Narrative Unity*, 278; Dillon, *From Eyewitnesses*, 24 n. 71, 44 nn. 128, 129, and 130.

[15]See Guillaume, *Luc interprète*, 69–73 on Lukan and non-Lukan vocabulary in the Emmaus narrative.

[16]Cf. Dillon, *From Eyewitnesses*, 19, 26. He writes on p. 19: "If the whole tomb experience is now to become a contrasting episode to the risen Lord's own instilling of the Easter faith (24:25ff.), then the painstaking establishment of all the *bruta facta* of the experience will serve only as the foil *ex parte hominis* to the risen One's activity! . . . The *fact* of the empty tomb begets *perplexity* and requires the *interpreting word* of the angels. Here we encounter the first of three combinations of *unintelligible facts* versus *elucidating word* which will constitute the controlling pattern of this chapter's design (vv. 2-3 *vs.* 5-7; 19-24 *vs.* 25-27; 36-43 *vs.* 44-49)" (emphasis Dillon).

[17]Matthew 28:17 and John 20:25 suggest a lack of understanding and disbelief at the passion and resurrection of Jesus. It is only Luke, however, who includes this reaction in the first resurrection appearance of Jesus. In fact, John 20:8 says "the other disciple . . . saw and believed." Cf. Tannehill, *Narrative Unity*, 262–263.

the use of the word "apostles" (v. 10) is typical of Luke. It serves as a connection between Luke 9, 24, and Acts 1.

Thus, by including this first passion statement into the story of the empty tomb, Luke affirms that the sufferings and the resurrection of Jesus are part of the divine plan as foretold by Jesus in Galilee.

LUKE 24:19-21 AND 24:25-27

The next passion statement occurs within the Emmaus story at Luke 24:19-21 and 24:25-27. The Emmaus account, unique to Luke, is a story of the appearance of the risen Lord. But it is not simply another appearance story; on the contrary, it develops Luke's *proof-from-prophecy* motif, a theme Paul Schubert considers to be central to Luke 24.[18]

The conversation of the two travelers on the road to Emmaus is described by Luke in great detail. When Jesus approaches them on the road, they are discussing the event of Jesus' death. Luke noticeably says that "their eyes were kept from recognizing him." Luke 24:19-21 describes the disciples' expectations of Jesus' Messiahship before he died and their perception of Jesus' death while their eyes were closed and before he opened the Scriptures to them. In 24:19, Jesus of Nazareth is described as, "a prophet mighty in deed and word before God and all the people." The idea of a prophet is a positive theme for Luke. Jesus is also described as a prophet by himself or others (Luke 4:24; 7:16; 7:39; 9:8, 19; 13:33 and Acts 3:22-23; 7:37). He is compared favorably with Elijah and Elisha (Luke 4:24-27),[19] John the Baptist and other prophets (Luke 9:7-8, 19), and Moses himself in fulfillment of Deuteronomy 18:15 (Acts 3:22; 7:37).[20] Strangely, the disciples do not seem to recollect that the prophets are persecuted for the sake of the kingdom (Luke 6:23; 11:47-51; 13:33-35, and Acts 7:52).

[18]Schubert, "The Structure and Significance," 176. D. L. Bock, *Proclamation From Prophecy and Pattern: Lucan Old Testament Christology* (*JSNT*, Supplement Series 12; Sheffield: JSOT Press, 1987) 274–275 offers a modification of Schubert's formula. Cf. below on Bock's thesis.

[19]Cf. Fitzmyer, *I-IX*, 213–215.

[20]In Acts 7:22 where Moses is described as "mighty in his words and deeds" (plural), the same words used of Jesus in Luke 24:19 (*dunatós en érgō kai lógō*—singular).

The mention of a prophet takes us back to Luke 9. In 9:7-9, Herod questions the identity of Jesus. In 9:18ff., Jesus asks the question of the disciples: "Who do the people say that I am?"[21] Both Herod and the disciples answered that he was either John the Baptist or Elijah or one of the old prophets. In the transfiguration (Luke 9:28-36), the two great prophets of old, Moses and Elijah, appear with Jesus. As Fitzmyer points out:

"Luke casts Jesus in the role of the prophet like Moses promised in Deut 18:15-18 . . . where he converses with Moses (and Elijah) about his 'departure' to be accomplished in Jerusalem and where the instruction given to the disciples by the heavenly voice, 'Listen to him,' (9:35), echoes that of Deut 18:15. The role is even more explicitly given to him in Peter's speech in the Temple, where a form of Deut 18:15,18-19 is quoted (Acts 3:22-23), and again in Stephen's speech, where Deut 18:15 is cited (Acts 7:37)."[22]

This discussion of the identity of Jesus in Luke 9 leads up to Peter's confession that Jesus is the Christ of God, and to Luke's first passion prediction affirming for the disciples that the Son of Man must suffer and die. Luke uses the divine *dei* to introduce his passion prediction, and thus places Jesus in solidarity with all the prophets before him who gave up their lives for the kingdom. In Luke 13:33, Jesus reaffirms to the Pharisees that he must (*dei*) die in Jerusalem, for Jerusalem has been guilty of killing the prophets.[23] It appears that Luke wants his readers to understand Jesus as one of a long line of prophets who came to Jerusalem and was killed by the inhabitants of the city (13:34). If it had not been for Luke 24, however, the reader might have thought that Jesus simply suffered the same fate as the rest of the prophets. For even though Jesus himself had predicted his resurrection, it is only the

[21]See Tannehill, *Narrative Unity*, 218.

[22]Fitzmyer, *I-IX*, 213. Cf. also J. D. G. Dunn, *Christology in the Making* (Philadelphia: The Westminster Press, 1980) 139.

[23]Acts 3:18ff. and 7:37 are quotations from Moses in Deuteronomy 18:19 that describe Jesus as the prophet like unto Moses but greater than Moses. This occurs in the context of a statement that accuses the Jews of putting Jesus to death in their ignorance, but "what God foretold by the mouth of all the prophets, that his Christ should suffer, he thus fulfilled" (v. 18).

risen Christ in Luke 24 who opens the eyes of the disciples and interprets the Scriptures so that both the reader and the disciples understand the death of this prophet.[24]

In Luke 24, the problem that perplexes the disciples on the road to Emmaus is not that Jesus is a prophet, or even that he had been put to death, but rather that he had been put to death by crucifixion. He was mighty in deed and word like Moses, but "our chief priests and rulers delivered him to be condemned to death, and crucified him" (v. 20). These two disciples use the same language as the two angels in 24:7, that Jesus was delivered (*paradídōmi*) and crucified (*stauróō*), except they describe the events without understanding the meaning behind them. They did not *remember* the words that Jesus had spoken to them in Galilee. There is shock and embarrassment in their words, and Luke heightens the horror of what happened by saying in essence, "not only was it bad enough that our own chief priests and rulers delivered him up to the judgment of death, but they even went so far as to execute him by crucifixion, the most shameful and embarrassing of deaths."[25] Obviously, this was not the disciples' plan nor their hope, for they confess that they had set their hopes on Jesus as the one to "redeem Israel."

The redemption of Israel is a theme Luke mentions very early in the Gospel, for Zechariah praises God for his salvation in 1:68-75 (*lútrōsin* in 1:68), in the context of his prophecy concerning the special role of his son, John the Baptist, in Israel's redemption (1:76-79), and Anna sees in the child Jesus the redemption of Yahweh (*lútrōsin* in 2:38). Luke completes his statement in Luke 24:19-21, which is essentially an imitation of 24:7, by adding this third element to go along with *paradídōmi* and *stauróō*, namely, "But we had hoped that he was the one to redeem (*lutroústhai*) Israel. Yes, and besides all this, it is now the third day since this happened" (v. 21). These words of the disciples show that they are resigned

[24]Cf. Fitzmyer, *I-IX*, 213–215 and Dillon, *From Eyewitnesses*, 114–132 on the prophet-Christology of Luke.

[25]This problem concerning the crucifixion arises in Galatians 3:13 where Paul quotes Deuteronomy 21:23 saying: "Christ redeemed us from the curse of the law, having become a curse for us—for it is written, 'Cursed be every one who hangs on a tree.' " Cf. also 1 Corinthians 1:23: ". . . but we preach Christ crucified, a stumbling block to Jews and folly to Gentiles. . . ."

to the fact that it is too late for anything to happen that might reverse the tragedy of Christ's death. Thus, Luke 24:19-21 shows the complete lack of understanding of the disciples concerning the purpose of Jesus' death and heightens the offense that such a death caused the Jewish community that followed Jesus.

Luke 24:22-24 confirms the disciples' ignorance and lack of understanding of the divine necessity of the death and resurrection of Jesus. All they seem to grasp is the singular fact of the empty tomb, but they cannot believe that Jesus is alive. Luke elaborates here upon 24:11, thus drawing attention not only to their lack of belief, but to the extent of their incredulity at the resurrection and their negative judgment of those women who had seen the empty tomb. Luke's purpose, then, is to create in 24:19-24 a bold contrast to the passion statement of the risen Christ which is now to follow.

The passion statement by the risen Christ in 24:25-27 is set in opposition to the disciples' ignorance in 24:19-24. It begins with a rebuke by Jesus of the disciples: "O foolish men, and slow of heart to believe all that the prophets have spoken!" They are "foolish men" (anóêtoi—24:25) because of their foolish judgment in 24:11, since both verses speak of the unbelief of the disciples. The disciples are rebuked because they did not believe the prophets. The risen Lord points out the first great mistake of the disciples— that they did not perceive that Jesus had to be "delivered up according to the definite plan and foreknowledge of God" (Acts 2:23) in fulfillment of the Scriptures.

The passion statement by Jesus in 24:26-27 is typical of Luke's passion predictions. It uses language similar to the first passion prediction at 9:22 where the theme of suffering before glory is developed. But it is not surprising that the disciples had failed to see this theme of suffering before glory as foretold in the Scriptures, for in Luke's Gospel there are only a few references to the passion fulfilled in Scripture. In Luke 18:31, there is an explicit reference to the death of Jesus as fulfilled in the Scriptures, occurring right before the third passion prediction. There is an indirect reference to the rejection of Jesus in the parable of the tenants in Luke 20:17, and another significant reference in 22:37. Otherwise, the only place where this concept is clearly developed is in chapter 24 where it is mentioned five times in 24:27, 32, 44, 45, and 46. The death of Jesus in fulfillment of the Scriptures is much more common in Acts (2:22-28; 3:13-18; 4:10-11; 8:30-35; 10:39-43; 13:26-35; 17:2-3; and 26:17-23).

Luke's theology in the Gospel is very much a *proof-from-prophecy* theology,[26] but the emphasis on the death of Jesus as proven through prophecy is not evident in the Gospel until the last chapter. In fact, without Luke 24, there would be very little evidence to demonstrate that Jesus' death fulfilled Scripture. But with Luke 24, the concept can be read backwards into all the Old Testament prophecies and allusions which Luke has employed.[27] In the light of the rest of his Gospel, Luke 24:27 is an extraordinary statement. From Moses through the prophets, Jesus opens the Scriptures, presumably because it was hidden from their eyes (v. 16). The mention of Moses, the prophets, and "in *all* the scriptures" (*en pásais tais graphaís*) is a reference to the entire Old Testament canon.[28] But it is significant that the Scriptures were opened with respect to "the things concerning himself" (*ta perí heautoú*). The word "concerning" (*perí*) is common to Luke 24 and is always used of things concerning Jesus (24:4, 14, 19, 27, 44). Luke 24 portrays a Jesus who interprets the Scriptures messianically, demonstrating that he, the Christ, must die and rise according to the Scriptures, that he must suffer first before he enters into his glory. This passion statement stands out as *one of the climaxes* of the Emmaus story.

Luke's last reference to the open Scriptures (24:32), a uniquely characteristic theme for him, is placed in the recognition scene of Jesus by the Emmaus disciples after his breaking of the bread. This is key with respect to the theme of table fellowship and the eschatological kingdom. But it is important to note that the reaction

[26]Cf. Schubert, "The Structure and Significance," 176ff. Cf. also C. Talbert, *Reading Luke*, 234–240; and "Promise and Fulfillment in Lucan Theology," in *Luke-Acts: Perspectives from the Society of Biblical Literature Seminar* ed. C. Talbert (New York: Crossword, 1984) 91–103; and Tannehill, *Narrative Unity*, 23 on prophecy and fulfillment serving Luke's apologetical concerns.

[27]Cf. Bock, *Proclamation from Prophecy and Pattern*, 47–53. J. McHugh, "A Sermon for Easter Sunday," *CR* LXXI (March, 1986) 92 suggests the line of argument I will use in my discussion of 24:27.

[28]I. H. Marshall, *The Gospel of Luke* (Grand Rapids: Eerdmans, 1978) 897.

of the disciples shows Luke's readers the power behind what occurred in 24:25-27. When the Scriptures are opened up concerning the necessity of the suffering and glory of Christ, hearts will burn. But Jesus is not recognized except in the breaking of the bread.

LUKE 24:44-47

The third passion statement in Luke 24 occurs at 24:44-47. In each of the passion statements, there is a gradual progression.[29] The first one, by the angels, commands the women to remember Jesus' words in Galilee, but does not connect it with the fulfillment of the Scriptures; the second one, by the risen Christ, repeats the theme of suffering before glory, but now explicitly connects Christ's death with the fulfillment of the Scriptures; the third statement of the passion continues the theme of the risen Christ opening up the Scriptures but adds a new dimension, namely, "that repentance and forgiveness of sins should be preached in his name to all nations, beginning from Jerusalem" (v. 47). This final passion statement is the most structurally perfect of the three. It connects the death and resurrection of Christ in fulfillment of the Scriptures with the mission of the Church. As Schubert says, "These stages together represent a literary climax of considerable effectiveness, resting upon and giving 'heart-warming' expression to Luke's dominant theological conviction."[30] Luke 24:44-47, therefore, is an appropriate introduction to the theme of Acts and provides a smooth transition to Luke's second volume.[31]

Luke 24:44-47 is similar to the other passion statements in Luke. For example, Luke uses "fulfill" (plêróô) in Luke 9:31 to refer to Jesus' éxodos in Jerusalem during the transfiguration (cf. Acts 3:18; 13:27). The use of dei has already been noted as Luke's way of speaking of divine necessity (Luke 2:49; 9:22; 13:33; 17:25; 24:7, 26, 44; Acts 17:3). All three major passion statements in Luke 24 use dei, but each one uses it differently. At 24:7, dei is followed by

[29]Schubert, "The Structure and Significance," 176–177. Cf. Tannehill, Narrative Unity, 293–298 on 24:44-47.

[30]Schubert, "The Structure and Significance," 177.

[31]Cf. D. Juel, Messianic Exegesis (Philadelphia: Fortress Press, 1988) 82–83; Dillon, From Eyewitnesses, 284–290.

three aorist passive infinitives, "to be delivered . . . crucified . . . and raised" (*paradothênai, staurôthênai,* and *anastênai*), that give exquisite symmetry to this kerygmatic formula. At 24:26, *dei* is followed by a shorter but more comprehensive statement, emphasizing the necessity of suffering as a prelude to glory. At 24:44, Luke's final word concerning the divine *dei* also includes the kerygma.[32]

Some of the other familiar phrases and words in 24:44-47 are Moses and the prophets (24:27), the opening of the Scriptures (24:27), "suffering" (*páschô*—Luke 9:22; 17:25; 24:26; Acts 1:3; 3:18; 17:3; 26:23), "the Christ" (*ton christón*—Luke 9:20; 24:26; Acts 3:18; 17:3; 26:23), "rise" (*anístêmi*—Luke 9:22; 18:33; 24:7; Acts 2:24, 32; 10:41; 13:33, 34; 17:3), and "on the third day" (*tê trítê hêméra*—Luke 9:22; 18:33; 24:7, 21; Acts 10:40). But there are some new additions to Luke's passion statement that introduce themes in preparation for Acts: "preaching" (*kêrússô*—Acts 10:37, 42), "in his name" (*epí tô onómati autoú*—Acts 2:21; 3:16; 4:10; 5:28; 10:43), "repentance" (*metánoia*—Acts 2:38; 3:19; 5:31; 8:22; 13:24; 26:20), "forgiveness" (*aphíêmi*—Acts 5:38; 8:22), and "nations" (*éthnê*—Acts 10:35, 45; 26:23). Thus this last statement looks back to the Gospel and forward to Acts.

Luke's structuring of this final passion statement is theologically instructive. As mentioned, Luke 24:44 refers back to the three passion predictions in Luke 9:22; 9:44 and 18:33. This is accomplished by means of the words "while I was still with you" (*éti ôn sun*

---

[32]Most scholars observe that Luke's understanding of the death of Christ does not embrace the Pauline notion of vicarious atonement. But the divine necessity for suffering may be seen from the perspective of the obedience of Christ to God. Jesus was obedient even to death on the cross, and having displayed "total obedience," he had to be raised. Cf. J. D. G. Dunn, *Baptism in the Holy Spirit* (Philadelphia: The Westminster Press, 1970) 42–43, on the death of Jesus in Luke in his discussion of Jesus' baptism: "For Luke this work ['the messianic office of Servant and Representative of his people'] culminated in the cross where Jesus accepted and endured the messianic baptism in Spirit-and-fire *on behalf of his people* . . . Thus we may say that for Luke Jesus' ministry as Servant and Representative is consummated by his suffering the messianic baptism of fire *on behalf of his people* . . . Jesus, as Servant, suffers *on their behalf;* the fire is kindled on him; he is baptized with the messianic baptism of others; he drains the cup of wrath which was the portion of others" (emphasis mine). Cf. also Dillon, *From Eyewitnesses,* 278–290.

12

umín).[33] The beauty of Luke's structure is more evident if the text is organized in the following manner:

"Everything written about me
 in the law of Moses and the prophets and the psalms
 must be fulfilled.
(Then he opened their minds to understand the scriptures and
 said to them,)
Thus it is written,
 that the Christ should *suffer*
  and on the third day *rise* from the dead, and
 that repentance and forgiveness of sins
 should be *preached* in his name to all nations,
  beginning from Jerusalem."

The grammatical framework of these verses demonstrates the developing kerygma of Luke 24. There are four infinitives: "fulfill" (*plêrôthênai*—aorist passive), "suffer" (*patheín*—aorist), "rise" (*anastênai*—aorist), and "preach" (*kêruchthênai*—aorist passive). The first infinitive, "to be fulfilled" (*plêrôthênai*), is dependent on *dei*, and there may be reason to believe that the last three infinitives are dependent on the phrase "must be fulfilled" (*dei plêrôthênai*).[34] Textual variants demonstrate an attempt to include another *dei* in verse 46 to convey this dependence. The evidence favors the text, but the variant readings suggest that the final three infinitives are "theologically" dependent on "must be fulfilled," i.e. it must be fulfilled that the Christ suffer, rise, and it must be fulfilled that repentance and forgiveness be preached in his name. For the emerging Church, Luke prepares the kerygma in a compact formula in 24:44-47 that includes both the divine necessity of the death and resurrection of Jesus Christ in fulfillment of the Scriptures and the preaching of repentance and forgiveness to all nations.[35] This kerygma is now not only a part of the Church's mission, but as Luke will demonstrate in his second volume, it is already a part of the Church's history.

[33]Cf. Marshall, *The Gospel of Luke*, 905. Note the similarity between 24:6 (*éti ôn en tê Galilaía*) and 24:44 (*éti ôn sun umín*).
[34]See Acts 2:23, 31 where *dei* does not occur but the notion that it represents does. Cf. Tannehill, *Narrative Unity*, 294.
[35]Cf. Dillon, *From Eyewitnesses*, 45.

Chapter 2

The Function of Chapter 24 in the Gospel of Luke

In the center of each of the three sections of Luke 24, there is a passion statement in which Luke progressively affirms that there are now three necessary elements in the kerygma that are important to the Church of Acts: 1) the necessity of the death and resurrection of the Christ, 2) in fulfillment of the Scriptures, and 3) the proclamation of this to all nations. Luke 24 confirms the *proof-from-prophecy* motif as one of the dominant themes of the Gospel. If this theme is read back into Luke and forward into Acts, Luke's theological purpose in chapter 24 becomes evident, for his climax is foreshadowed at pivotal places throughout his Gospel, particularly in Luke 9. By reading back into Luke from the perspective of the Emmaus meal, one may see how this meal is the culmination of Luke's theology of table fellowship as an expression of the eschatological kingdom.

LUKE 1-9

Paul Schubert makes a persuasive argument that the first nine chapters of Luke offer evidence for his *proof-from-prophecy* theology. He considers this necessary in view of the statement of 24:6, ''Remember how he told you while he was still in Galilee . . .'' Since Luke urges the women to remember, he also urges the reader to go back to the *in-Galilee* chapters (i.e. up to 9:50) and see how this has developed.[1] Schubert cites three examples from the first eight chapters of Luke that clearly demonstrate Luke's *proof-from-prophecy* theology. He points out many ''messianic'' prophecies in Luke 1 and 2 and notices ''structural and material

---

[1]Cf. Schubert, ''The Structure and Significance,'' 178–186. Note that Luke 9:18 has *katá mónas*. Contrast this to Matthew 16:13 = Mark 8:27 that specifies *eis . . . Kaisareías tês Philippou*, i.e. *not* in Galilee!

similarities" between Luke 1-2 and Luke 24. His other examples are 4:14-32 and 7:18-23.[2] Schubert demonstrates in Luke's first eight chapters that the *proof-from-prophecy* motif establishes the identity of Jesus as the Messiah. But all these examples deal solely with the prophecy of Jesus as the Messiah, with none specifically referring to his death. Furthermore, in none of these are the disciples involved, and in some of them, there are only allusions to the Old Testament. It is not until Luke 9 that there is any mention of the passion and resurrection.

D. L. Bock has expanded upon Schubert's *proof-from-prophecy* motif based upon his *proclamation from prophecy and pattern* perspective.[3] The significance of the addition of the words "and pattern" is that Bock maintains that Jesus not merely fulfills prophetical texts, but also lives according to the pattern of prophetical activity. By Luke 9, the identity of Jesus as both prophet (9:19) and Messiah (9:20) has developed so that Peter is able to make the confession that Jesus is the "Christ of God."[4] In 24:19ff., the two disciples say that they had hoped that Jesus would be the redeemer of Israel. But in spite of his deliverance into the hands of the chief priests and rulers, his condemnation to death, and his crucifixion, they still believed that he had been "a prophet mighty in deed and word before God and all the people." The *proclamation from prophecy and pattern* motif in Luke 24 implies that there is nothing extraordinary in the suggestion that the Messiah might die, since that was the fate of many prophets. For Luke, the resurrection is the suffering Jesus' great vindication, and it is this that

---

[2]Ibid., 178-179.

[3]Bock's methodological approach is more literary and therefore his formulation is preferred to that of Schubert's. His book will provide groundwork for my discussion of the death of Jesus in fulfillment of the Scriptures. Cf. also L. C. Crockett, "The Use of the Old Testament in Luke: with Emphasis on the Interpretation of Isaiah 61.1-2" Volumes I and II, (Ph.D. diss., Brown University; Ann Arbor: University Microfilms, 1966); W. Larkin, "Luke's Use of the Old Testament in Luke 22-23" (Ph.D. diss., University of Durham, 1974); and "Luke's Use of the Old Testament as a Key to His Soteriology," *JETS* 20 (1977) 325-335; and D. J. Moo, *The Old Testament in the Gospel Passion Narratives* (Sheffield: The Almond Press, 1983).

[4]Dillon, *From Eyewitnesses*, 114-132 argues that Luke develops a "prophet-christology" until Luke 9 where there is a shift in emphasis.

confirms his identity as the Christ (24:26, 46). But let us return to chapter 9.

LUKE 9

Luke 9, like Luke 24, is a watershed chapter.[5] The evangelist includes here the mission of the twelve to preach and heal (9:1-6), a reference to the resurrection from the dead (9:7-9), the feeding of the five thousand (9:10-17), Peter's confession of Jesus as the Christ of God (9:18-21), the first passion prediction (9:22), a summons to follow Jesus by taking up one's cross daily (9:23-26), an assertion that the kingdom of God is not far distant (9:27), and the transfiguration (9:28-36).[6] All these themes are reflected in Luke 24.

But that is not all. For there is, in fact, a surprising chiasmatic correspondence evident when the structure of Luke 9 and 24 is compared:

Luke 9:1-36	*Luke 24*
9:1-6 Jesus sends forth the Twelve with power and authority.	24:44-49 Jesus commands the Eleven to be witnesses to all nations once they are clothed with power from on high.
9:7-9 Herod hears that some are questioning whether Jesus is John the Baptist risen, Elijah, or one of the old prophets risen from the dead.	24:36-43 The disciples question in their hearts whether the Jesus who has appeared to them is truly risen and not just a ghost.

[5]Talbert, *Literary Patterns*, sees both Luke 9 and 24 as important to the Gospel of Luke. He notes that Luke 9 and 24 are structurally related to other sections of Luke-Acts (Luke 9:1-48 and 22:7–23:16; Luke 24 and Acts 1; Luke 9 and Acts 1), but he does not comment on a structural relationship between the two. Cf. also E. E. Ellis, "The Composition of Luke 9 and the Source of Its Christology," *Current Issues in Biblical and Patristic Interpretation: Studies in Honor of Merrill C. Tenney* (Grand Rapids: Eerdmans, 1975) 120–127; J. Fitzmyer, "The Composition of Luke, Chapter 9," *Perspectives on Luke-Acts*, ed. C. H. Talbert (Danville, VA: Association of Baptist Professors of Religion, 1978) 139–152 on the structure of Luke 9; and Dillon, *From Eyewitnesses*, 37ff.

[6]Cf. Tannehill, *Narrative Unity*, 98–99, 214–228 on the significance of the juxtaposition of pericopes in Luke 9.

9:10-17 The feeding of the five thousand and the breaking of the five loaves and the two fish.

9:18-22 Peter's confession that Jesus is the "Christ of God" and the first passion prediction. Jesus commands them to tell no one.

9:23-27 Jesus speaks of the cost of discipleship, the daily taking up of the cross to follow him—suffering before glory.

9:28-36 The Transfiguration: the vision of Christ in glory. A passion reference in 9:31 (Luke alone), closing with the imperative: "Listen to him!"

24:28-35 Jesus sitting at table with the two disciples and the breaking of the bread.

24:25-27 Jesus' passion statement that the Christ should suffer before entering glory. He opens up the Scriptures to them.

24:13-24 The disciples show their complete lack of understanding of the cross and the cost of discipleship. They wanted a prophet mighty in deed and word, not a crucified Messiah—glory without suffering.

24:1-11 The Resurrection: "Why seek the living among the dead?" A passion reference at 24:7, containing the imperative: "Remember how he told you while he was still in Galilee . . ."

In comparing the language of these parallels, some striking similarities exist. In 9:1-6 and 24:44-49, the Twelve (9:1) and the Eleven (24:9, 33) are given power (*dúnamis* 9:1; 24:49) and are sent (*apostéllô* 9:2; 24:49) to preach (*kêrússô* 9:2; 24:47). In 9:6, they are preaching the gospel (*euaggelízô*); in 24:46-47, they are preaching the content of the gospel—suffering, resurrection, and "repentance and forgiveness of sins."[7] These similarities are not found in Mark or Matthew, but only in Luke. Both Luke 9:1-6 and 24:44-49 are commissioning stories.

There are no striking verbal similarities between Luke 9:7-9 and 24:36-43.

The feeding of the five thousand in Luke 9:10-17 and the table scene on the road to Emmaus in 24:13-35 are remarkably alike. Both take place when the day was wearing away (*hêméra* and *klínô* in 9:12; 24:29).[8] Both have Jesus speaking prophetically (*laléô*). In

[7] Cf. Luke 9:6 to the Markan parallel (6:12) where preaching repentance replaces *euaggelízô*.

[8] Cf. Luke 22:14, the hour = evening.

17

9:11, Jesus speaks of the kingdom of God; in 24:32, the disciples report how he spoke to them on the road and opened the Scriptures to them. Both use Luke's phrase for the select group who follow Jesus, the Twelve (9:12) and the Eleven (24:33). The scene, therefore, is very much the same. This provides the setting for the miracle that is to take place in both scenes. In 9:10-17, it is the multiplication of the loaves and the fish; in 24:13-35, it is the revelation of Christ in the breaking of the bread. The language in 9:15-16 and 24:30 is almost identical, for Luke wants his readers to recall the miracle of the feeding of the five thousand when they read that at Emmaus, Jesus revealed himself in the breaking of the bread (cf. Luke 22:19). In both chapters 9 and 24, Luke uses the same constellation of words: reclining, taking, and blessing (*kataklínô,*[9] *lambánô,* and *eulogéô*).[10] There is nothing Lukan about the language of 9:16, so Luke is recalling a Synoptic miracle. But both passages conclude with the image of broken bread. In 9:17, the disciples gather together twelve baskets of broken bread (*klasmátôn kóphinoi dôdeka*); in 24:35, the Eleven are gathered together to hear how Jesus was made known to the two disciples in the breaking of the bread (*en tê klásei tou ártou*). Therefore, both 9:10-17 and 24:28-35 have Jesus teaching his disciples, then eating with them, and finally revealing himself miraculously in broken bread.[11]

Luke 9:18-22 and 24:25-27 have the following words and phrases that are similar and refer to the death or the resurrection: "Christ" (*christós*—9:20; 24:26), dei (9:22; 24:26), "suffering" (*páschô*—9:22; 24:26), "on the third day" (*tê trítê hêméra egerthênai*—9:22, cf. Luke 24:7, 21, 26), and "enter into his glory" (*eiselthein eis tên dóxan autou*—24:26). But one dissimilarity between

[9]Cf. Luke 22:14, *anepésen.* Cf. Tannehill, *Narrative Unity,* 289.

[10]The other similar words are from the same root: *kataklâô* (9:16) and *kláô* (24:30); *dídômi* (9:16) and *epidídômi* (24:30).

[11]Cf. B. P. Robinson, "The Place of the Emmaus Story in Luke-Acts," *NTS* 30 (1984) 490: "In the first place the narrative [9:10-17] is quite close linguistically to the Emmaus story (day is declining; all reclined; he took, blessed, broke, and distributed bread). We may further note that Luke has taken liberties with the order of Mark's material in order to place the Confession of Peter immediately following the Feeding story. I think it highly likely that this is because he saw *in the feeding-confession sequence of Luke 9 a foreshadowing of the feeding-recognition sequence in Luke 24*" (emphasis mine).

these two passages points to a significant difference in the correspondence between Luke 9 and 24. In 9:21, Jesus charges and commands his disciples to tell no one that he is the Christ who must suffer, die, and rise.[12] But in 24:27, Jesus opens up the Scriptures to reveal to them that his suffering and glory are in fulfillment of the Scriptures. In chapter 9, Luke gradually heightens the messianic-passion secret; but in chapter 24, Luke gradually demonstrates that the disciples finally understand the passion and resurrection because the risen Christ has opened up the Scriptures to them.

The verbal parallels between 9:23-27 and 24:13-24 are few. Both mention the cross (9:23; 24:20) and salvation (9:24; 24:21). These

[12]The comparison between Luke 9:21 and Mark 8:30 is significant. In 9:21, Luke heightens the messianic secret, which is prominently developed in Mark, by adding *parêggeilen* to *epitimêsas*. Mark 8:30 has simply *kai epetímêsen autoís*, but Luke reads *o de* (nb. the emphasis) *epitimêsas autoís parêggeilen*. (Cf. Bauer, Arndt, and Gingrich, *Greek-English Lexicon of the New Testament* (Chicago: University of Chicago, 1957) 618: *paraggélô* "*to give orders, command, instruct, direct* of all kinds of persons in authority, worldly rulers, Jesus, the apostles." This double command of silence will be reversed in Luke 24:48 when the disciples become witnesses of the suffering and rising Christ. Also Fitzmyer, *I-IX*, 775. Further, this messianic secret is now tied inextricably to Christ's passion by the participle *eipôn*. Where Mark has (8:31) *kai êrxato*, Luke continues in the same sentence: *o de . . . eipôn* (Nestle, 25th edition). After Peter's bold confession that Jesus is "the Christ of God," Jesus charges and commands his disciples to tell no one. Luke syntactically connects Peter's confession to the first passion prediction at Luke 9:22 where Jesus says that "the Son of Man must suffer many things . . ." Mark's messianic secret is now Luke's passion secret (cf. Dillon, *From Eyewitnesses*, 23ff.; Conzelmann, *The Theology of St. Luke*, 56; J. Fitzmyer, "The Composition of Luke, Chapter 9," 145–146). This is unique to Luke, for in the second and third predictions of the passion (9:45 and 18:34), Luke also ties the messianic secret to the passion. This theme is not found in the passion predictions of Matthew and Mark. In their first passion prediction, Peter's denial overshadows the passion prediction (Matt 16:21-23 and Mark 8:31-33); in the second, there is a display of distress by the disciples and a lack of understanding, but Jesus does not command the silence of the disciples (Matt 17:23 and Mark 9:32); in the third, no response is given at all (Matt 20:9 and Mark 10:34). Luke 9 shows a gradual movement towards total misunderstanding and silence. By the end of the Gospel, Luke has demonstrated that the disciples are completely confused concerning the purpose of Jesus' messiahship and consider the prospect of an empty tomb and a risen Christ to be utter nonsense.

two passages are similar in their views on discipleship. In 9:23-27, discipleship is spoken of in terms of its cost—taking up one's cross, losing one's life. Those who are ashamed (*epaischúnomai*) of Jesus and his words, the Son of Man will be ashamed of that person when he comes in his glory and the glory of the Father.[13] But in 24:13-24, when Jesus does come in glory, the example of discipleship demonstrated by the two disciples on the road to Emmaus is that of embarrassment at the cross. *They are perfect examples of what discipleship is not.* In fact, none of the disciples fit Jesus' criteria for discipleship until Luke 24 when the risen Christ reveals everything to them. Thus, due to their reaction, the two disciples receive the rebuke of Jesus, "O foolish men," and hear the passion statement that the Christ must suffer before entering into his glory. Instead of denying themselves by taking up their cross and following Jesus, they have even denied the cross by failing to believe all that the prophets have spoken.

Perhaps the most obvious parallel between Luke 9 and 24 is that of the transfiguration and the resurrection. Marshall describes the transfiguration as "an anticipatory vision of the glory of Jesus at his resurrection or his parousia."[14] Many have observed a similarity between these two stories. Luke opens the scene of the transfiguration in 9:28 by saying: "Now about eight days after these sayings . . . ." Schubert points out that the expression "after these sayings" (*metá tous lógous toútous*) refers back not only to Peter's confession, but is "very deftly linked to the prediction of the passion, death, and resurrection (v. 22) and to the attending saying about the nature of true discipleship (vs. 23-27)."[15] This preserves a Lukan theme that suffering must always precede glory (cf. Luke 24:26).

Even more arresting in Luke's approach is the "eight days" which is first introduced in the transfiguration narrative. Only here does Luke use this phrase, and its only other occurrence in the New Testament is John 20:26 where Jesus appears to Thomas eight days after the resurrection. Luke speaks of eight days

[13]Cf. Tannehill, *Narrative Unity*, 222–223.
[14]Marshall, *The Gospel of Luke*, 381.
[15]Schubert, "The Structure and Significance," 181. Cf. also Dillon, *From Eyewitnesses*, 26.

whereas Mark and Matthew speak of six. Many early Christian communities understood Sunday as the eschatological eighth day, the day of resurrection, the day of the new creation.[16] The parallel between the transfiguration and the resurrection suggests that Luke is subtly tying these two passages together by the eight days. In Luke 24:1, he simply says "the first of the sabbath," which is Sunday. But is not Sunday also the eighth day?[17]

This analogy between the transfiguration and the resurrection is reinforced by the two men appearing in glory at Luke 9:30 and the two men at the tomb at Luke 24:4 (*kai idoú ándres dúo* in both chapters). The dazzling nature of Jesus' clothing is described by *exastráptô* (9:29), and the dazzling apparel of the angels by a cognate, *astráptô* (24:4). (Does the former—hapax legomenon in the New Testament—indicate that Jesus' clothing was even brighter than that of the angels?) Luke uses *éxodos* in the transfiguration narrative to predict the passion (9:31), which Jesus fulfills in Jerusalem (chapters 22–24).[18] The story of the empty tomb with its passion statement (24:7) looks back to Galilee, and specifically to chapter 9 with its prediction. As Peter, John, and James entered the cloud, they were afraid (9:34). As the women entered the tomb, they were perplexed and afraid (24:2-5). A voice from the cloud commands the disciples to obey Jesus (9:35), "This is my Son, my Chosen; listen to him!" (*akoúete*, a present imperative,

[16]E. E. Ellis, *The Gospel of Luke* (London: Thomas Nelson, 1966) 276 writes: "*That very day*: each of the resurrection episodes opens with a time reference to the 'eighth day' (24.1, 13, 33). See on 9.28; 24:1-12; cf. Barnabas 15:8f.; Justin, *Dial.* 138; Farrer, *Matthew*, p. 87. The symbolism identifies Jesus' resurrection as the beginning of a new creation" (emphasis Ellis). Cf. also M. Searle, *Sunday Morning: A Time for Worship* (Collegeville: The Liturgical Press, 1982). The "eight days" may, however, indicate simply the Greek way of reckoning time.

[17]Marshall, *The Gospel of Luke*, 382 rejects the notion that the eight days refer to the day of the new creation.

[18]Cf. Bock, *Proclamation from Prophecy and Pattern*, 116 on the eschatological perspective of 9:31: "It is in this total glorification context that the 'exodus' comment of Luke must be seen. For Jesus' departure points not just to his death, nor even his resurrection or ascension; but it is a departure, an exodus, that ultimately will lead to the demonstration of glorious authority (Acts 10.34-43). Thus, *the exodus refers to his departure into the whole eschatological programme that is tied to Jesus*" (emphasis mine).

i.e. *always* listen to him!). The words of the angels to the women (24:5), "Why do you seek the living among the dead? Remember . . ." (*mnêsthête*, an aorist passive imperative), presuppose the command of 9:35. The connection is this: my Son, my Chosen, he is the living one—listen to him—remember his words.[19]

The conclusions in each of these passages also are similar. In the transfiguration Luke says, "And they kept silence and told (*apêggeillan*) no one in those days anything of what they had seen" (9:36). This puts a tight lid on the messianic-passion secret. From 9:1 to 9:36, there is a progression from openness to complete silence. Luke 9 begins quite openly with the disciples preaching the Gospel and healing everywhere. But as the passion, death, and resurrection are introduced, there is the command to keep silent (9:21), and the subsequent obedience of the disciples (9:36). On the other hand, from 24:1 to 24:49, there is a progression from silence and misunderstanding to a command to make the gospel known to all nations. Luke 24 begins with the women returning from the tomb and telling (*apaggéllô*) everything to the Eleven who do not believe them and consider the report utter nonsense. In Luke 24 there is a gradual opening of the eyes of the disciples to the necessity of the passion, death, and resurrection of Jesus. Through Luke 24 there is this continuing revelation to the disciples that the crucified Christ has risen. By 24:49, not only have all things been exhaustively revealed to them, but they are commanded to preach and to be witnesses of this kerygma.

This comparison between chapters 9 and 24 has yielded some instructive insights into how Luke structurally, linguistically, and thematically has framed his Gospel. The chiasmus between 9 and 24 appears to move two ways: as Luke 9 builds towards the transfiguration, there is a gradual silence and concealment of the passion and resurrection; as Luke 24 builds towards the ascension, there is a gradual movement from puzzlement and disbelief to openness and understanding. The movement in Luke 24 towards faith in the passion and resurrection reverses the movement in Luke 9 towards disbelief. The reason for each movement is different. In Luke 9, the regression into silence and concealment is because the disciples are unable to understand the prediction of the

[19]Cf. Tannehill, *Narrative Unity*, 224–225; Dillon, *From Eyewitnesses*, 22–26.

passion, death, and resurrection. In Luke 24, the gradual opening up is to show, from the very beginning of the chapter, that the resurrection overcomes the embarrassment of the cross and that the passion and resurrection are part of a divine plan in fulfillment of the Scriptures. In both Luke 9 and 24, the death of the Messiah is the critical issue addressed.

Luke 9 is also the end of Jesus' Galilean ministry and the beginning of his journey to Jerusalem, the place of destiny where the passion will be accomplished.[20] Many scholars have remarked on the critical nature of Luke 9:51 to Luke's Gospel.[21] There are good reasons to consider 9:51 *the turning point*. Luke 9 is the place where Jesus' death and resurrection explicitly become part of Jesus' messianic destiny and where Jesus begins the journey towards his death in Jerusalem. As Schubert says of Jerusalem, "Somehow Jerusalem is for Luke the place of the full manifestation of Jesus as the Christ."[22] And of Luke 9:51 he says, "9:51 is closely linked to what precedes and by virtue of this fact it sets the stage for what is to follow."[23] Similarly in chapter 24 we have a journey from Jerusalem back to Jerusalem, and it is not without significance that in 9:51 the evangelist writes "the days drew near for him to be *received up*" (*análêmpsis*—cf. the words *analambánô* to denote the ascension in Acts 1:2, 11, 22).[24]

There are four other passages in Luke that deal with the death of Jesus and relate to Luke 24. They will be discussed only briefly.

LUKE 9:44-45

This second passion prediction in Luke also occurs in chapter 9 alongside the first one, emphasizing again the importance of this chapter. Luke makes some additions to this second prediction that prepare for Luke 24. The introductory statement is Lukan and heightens the significance of this second prediction: "Let these words sink into your ears." The passion prediction is short and

[20]Dillon, *From Eyewitnesses,* 113 n. 127 notes that Luke frames his journey with passion instruction (Luke 9:18-45 and 18:31-34).

[21]Cf. Fitzmyer, *I-IX,* 830–832 for an extensive bibliography on 9:51.

[22]Schubert, "The Structure and Significance," 183–184. Also J. Sanders, *The Jews in Luke-Acts* (Philadelphia: Fortress, 1987) 24–36, on Jerusalem in Luke.

[23]Schubert, "The Structure and Significance," 184.

[24]Cf. Dillon, *From Eyewitnesses,* 177 n. 60, 224.

truncated: "for the Son of man is to be delivered into the hands of men." The language corresponds with chapter 24—the Son of Man is used in Luke 9:22; 24:7 (18:31); "deliver" (*paradídōmi*) is used in Luke 18:32; 24:7, 20; "hands of men" (*cheíras anthrôpôn*) is used in Luke 24:7. Luke leaves out the fact that Jesus will be killed and will rise after three days (cf. Matthew 17:23; Mark 9:31). This creates suspense and misunderstanding, especially in light of the clean triad of 9:22. In 9:45, the messianic-passion secret is heightened by the disciples' lack of understanding. The necessity of suffering, death, and resurrection as part of God's plan is hidden from them and they do not perceive it. "This saying" (*to hrêma touto*) refers to his suffering and is used by Luke in a similar way in 18:34 and 24:8, 11.

LUKE 13:33

This passage has already been mentioned in connection with the word "prophet" in Luke 24:19. In 13:33, Jesus says that a prophet cannot perish outside of Jerusalem. Jesus will die there, but he will do what none of the prophets did before him—he will rise. This material is unique to Luke, showing his particular concern for Jerusalem. This is also part of Luke's "pregnant use of *poreúesthai* [to journey] . . . [where] the context is one of opposition and hostility, and the implication is that his destiny is to be reached despite such opposition"[25] (cf. 9:51, 52, 53, 56, 57; 10:38; 13:22, 33; 17:11; 19:12).

LUKE 17:25

In this pericope, Luke places a passion allusion within the context of an eschatological discourse. First there must be suffering, and then the parousia will come. The placement of a passion prediction in this context is peculiar to Luke, and the language inextricably ties it to Luke 24 (cf. *dei*, 9:22; 24:7, 26, 44; and *páschô*, 9:22; 24:26, 46). The statement that Jesus "must . . . be rejected by this generation" prepares for the destruction of Jerusalem and the rejection of the gospel by the Jews in Acts (e.g. chapters 13 and 28).[26]

[25]Fitzmyer, *I-IX*, 169.
[26]Cf. Tannehill, *Narrative Unity*, 257–258.

Luke's third passion prediction is tightly structured and also prepares the reader for Luke 24. It is addressed to the Twelve. In Luke 24, the disciples will finally understand the plan of salvation when the risen Christ opens the Scriptures to them. In Acts, they will be the leaders of the Church. Luke is the only Synoptic evangelist to include the phrase ''and everything that is written of the Son of man by the prophets will be accomplished.'' This is a major theme in Luke 24, and thus, by this third and final passion prediction, the reader is prepared for Luke 24 and the focus on the death and resurrection of Jesus *in fulfillment of the Scriptures*. The expanded description of the passion and death in Mark (mocked, shamefully treated, spit upon, scourged, killed) is picked up by Luke (and not by Matthew). As Luke progresses toward chapter 24, the shame and embarrassment of the crucifixion is heightened. He is the only Synoptic evangelist to include the reaction of the disciples: ''But they understood none of these things; this saying (*to hrêma touto*) was hid from them, and they did not grasp what was said.''[27]

Therefore, in all three passion predictions, the concealment and the inability to comprehend the plan of salvation is present.[28] The themes of Luke 24, the resurrection as the vindication of the crucifixion and the fulfillment of the Scriptures as the accomplishment of the divine plan, are developed in Luke's Gospel in anticipation of their climax in Luke 24. In this final chapter of the Gospel, the stage is set for Acts and the acceptance of Christianity as a legal religion. Luke 24 is the final affirmation that ''everything written about me in the law of Moses and the prophets and the psalms'' has been fulfilled. Jesus has realized in himself the destiny of the prophet who after suffering is vindicated by God. In the next chapters my interpretation of the Emmaus story will be based on this principle.

---

[27]Ibid., 226–227.

[28]Cf. Tannehill, *Narrative Unity*, 54, 127, 193, 199, 220–222, 226–227, 253–254, 258–259, 271–274; and Dillon, *From Eyewitnesses*, 42–44, 113–114, 134, 196–197 on the hiddenness of the plan that is revealed to the disciples in Luke 24.

Chapter 3

The Genre and Structure of the Meal at Emmaus

We now turn to the Emmaus meal as the climax of Luke 24 and also the climax of the Gospel. This chapter will investigate the nature of the Emmaus meal and consider its place within the table fellowship of Jesus with his disciples, demonstrating that the meals of Luke-Acts and the climactic meal at Emmaus form a matrix of events that have theological significance. This table fellowship of Jesus that climaxes in Luke 24 is part of Jesus' ministerial style that is a manifestation of the eschatological kingdom present among the people.

This activity of Jesus eating with his disciples is common to his ministry,[1] an activity that he continues in his post-resurrection appearances. Luke records not only the meal at Emmaus, but also the fact that Jesus eats a piece of broiled fish before the Eleven to prove that he is not a spirit, but one possessing flesh and bones (Luke 24:41-42). In John's Gospel too, Jesus has breakfast on the beach with his disciples as one of the final opportunities he has to communicate to them his parting wishes (John 21:9-14). In Acts 10:41, Peter includes in his sermon to Cornelius that a significant demonstration of his status as a witness to God's Anointed One is the fact that he was among those "who ate and drank with him after he rose from the dead."[2] Thus in this table fellowship matrix, the meals after the resurrection are significant in apostolic preaching as an attestation that the disciples were present with the risen Lord.

In considering this matrix of events in Luke-Acts, one must decide how the Emmaus meal fits into the entire table fellowship of

[1] Cf. Karris, *Luke: Artist and Theologian*, 47–78; Smith, "Table Fellowship," 613–638; and J. Navone, *Themes of St. Luke* (Rome: Gregorian University Press, 1970) 11–37 on the theme of food in Luke.

[2] Cf. also *sunalizómenos* in Acts 1:4.

Jesus. As one of the post-resurrection meals, is it to be classed with the other post-resurrection meals between Jesus and his disciples, or is it in a special category of its own? Is it part of God's continuous table fellowship with his people that stretches back to the creation story and continues through Jesus in these last days in the Church? The meal at Emmaus is significant because it is the first post-resurrection meal described in Luke-Acts, and thus its nature could be determinative of all meals before and after the resurrection.

As indicated earlier, Luke 24 is a watershed chapter in Luke-Acts where many of the themes that Luke develops in his Gospel find their fulfillment. The Emmaus narrative is not only the climax of the theme of table fellowship in Luke, but is also the place where other themes such as Luke's geographical, revelatory, and *proclamation from prophecy and pattern* motifs[3] are shown to be subordinate to Luke's table fellowship matrix.[4] This view is not commonly accepted,[5] but the very structure of the Emmaus narrative justifies a consideration of this suggestion.

[3]Cf. Fitzmyer, *X-XXIV*, 1557–59. The four motifs that he sees operating in the Emmaus narrative are: 1) Geographical, 2) Revelatory, 3) Christological as fulfilling Old Testament prophecy, and 4) Eucharistic. Dillon, *From Eyewitnesses*, 78 asserts that Luke 24 brings together themes that are developed in Luke and carried out in Acts, showing the clear continuity between the two books. R. H. Fuller, *The Formation of the Resurrection Narratives* (New York: The Macmillan Company, 1971) 110–111 sees three theological motifs: "1. Jesus as a prophet; 2. a summary of the passion tradition; and 3. a scriptural proof of the suffering-glory pattern."

[4]Cf. Dillon, *From Eyewitnesses*, 69–155 who argues that v. 35 recapitulates the major theme of the Emmaus story, namely, the mission of the Church will be centered in the table fellowship of the apostolic community that involves both the words of Jesus and the meal of Jesus; J. Dupont, "The Meal at Emmaus," *The Eucharist in the New Testament* (ed. J. Delorme; Baltimore and Dublin: Helicon Press, 1964) 105–121 who maintains that the focus of the story is the breaking of bread where Jesus distributes the Eucharist to the Emmaus disciples; and Robinson, "The Place of the Emmaus Story," 493–494 who sees converging the Lukan themes of journey, fulfillment of prophecy, recognition, and hospitality, but gives special attention to the hospitality theme, concluding that "all Christian fellowship meals [are] proleptic celebrations of the coming Kingdom."

[5]G. R. Osborne, *The Resurrection Narratives: A Redactional Study* (Grand Rapids: Baker Book House, 1984) 118 asserts that "the dominant theme here

The genre of Luke 24:13-35 complements Luke's theological purpose. The Emmaus appearance of Jesus differs from many of the other resurrection appearances.[6] According to J. Dupont, the main goal of the Emmaus story is not to provide another objective proof for the resurrection of Jesus; in fact, he claims the opposite is true. The whole account is governed by the closed eyes of the disciples who are, by the hand of God, kept from seeing Jesus (the theological passive *ekratoúnto* in 24:16). If Luke's intention was to provide eyewitnesses of the resurrected Christ, he begins the narrative from an opposite angle. It appears that Luke's primary motive is not to present another proof of the risen Christ nor to offer an apologetic for the humiliating death of Jesus, but to appeal to the heart and emotions of the reader.[7]

---

is the reality of the resurrection;" I. H. Marshall, "The Resurrection of Jesus in Luke," *TB* 24 (1973) 82–83 states that the main theme of the story is to demonstrate "a guarantee of the reality of the resurrection and of the identity of the risen One with Jesus, and the application of the means of grace is secondary;" H. D. Betz, "The Origin and Nature of Christian Faith According to the Emmaus Legend," *Int* 23 (1969) 45–46 sees the Emmaus story as legend where "the Christian faith has its origin and nature in the specific conviction that the absurdity of faith in Jesus is again and again overcome by the Christian's experience of the salvation-event connected with Jesus of Nazareth," and Schubert, "The Structure and Significance," 174 who claims that the Emmaus story "was an appearance-story which was dominated wholly and exclusively by the motif of a recognition scene which is so familiar from ancient mythology, legend and literature."

[6]Dupont, "The Meal at Emmaus," 106–112.

[7]Even though the Emmaus story is not like other appearance-stories, this does not mean that it fails to provide proof of the resurrection or offer an apologetical claim that God has vindicated Jesus by raising him from the dead. Dupont, "The Meal at Emmaus," 111 argues that the Emmaus story, with its dramatic structure and climactic moment of recognition, is in the category of "the edifying or moving story" that is aimed at our emotions and not at our reason. If Dupont is right, then Luke has constructed a story that is much more persuasive than a mere presentation of the facts. This genre of story is more than an intellectual exercise for the hearer and serves better as an apologetic since it "penetrate[s] into the depths of his soul." Dupont is correct in his evaluation of the dramatic and emotional nature of the Emmaus story, but his conclusions that this does not serve apologetical purposes is without warrant.

If one now considers the three categories of post-resurrection appearance-stories postulated by C. H. Dodd,[8] the Emmaus story is not in the first category of the *concise narrative* where the bare facts are in focus. According to Dodd, such resurrection appearances present the facts in order to prove that Jesus is risen from the dead, coinciding with Dupont's category of the appearance-story as objective proof of the resurrection. The Emmaus story does not fit into this category since there are no facts presented about the resurrection of Jesus, even though the disciples' recognition of him is the climax of the story; for the moment Jesus is recognized, he disappears.

But the Emmaus story does fit into Dodd's second category, the *circumstantial narrative*, where the concern is more for the development of a plot with a dramatic climax that is anticipated throughout the narrative.[9] In this genre of appearance-story, Luke is able to weave into the narrative his theological motifs and build toward one grand moment. The actual structure of the Emmaus story is the vehicle for Luke's theological purpose, recapitulating in this final chapter the narrative style of the entire Gospel. All of Luke's skill as a storyteller and as an artist are revealed in this genre. Luke writes to touch the deep memory, to awaken the faith that he has subtly nourished throughout his Gospel. This is the language of faith, the language of parable, the language of symbol.[10] And it is also the language of apologetic. As I proceed further into the Emmaus story, the dominant image will be the table fellowship of Jesus as he reveals his eschatological kingdom to his dis-

[8]C. H. Dodd, "The Appearances of the Risen Christ: An Essay in Form-Criticism of the Gospels," *Studies in the Gospels: Essays in Memory of R. H. Lightfoot*, ed. D. E. Nineham (Oxford: Blackwell, 1957) 9–35. Fitzmyer, *X-XXIV*, 1556–1557 discusses Dodd's categories in connection with Emmaus. Cf. also Dillon, *From Eyewitnesses*, 74–78.

[9]Dodd's third category entitled *mixed narratives* is a combination of concise and circumstantial narratives. Cf. also Fitzmyer, *X-XXIV*, 1557.

[10]Cf. Dupont, "The Meal at Emmaus," 112: "He is not content simply to tell us about the paschal message, he wants to make it sink into our hearts." D. A. Losada, "El episodio de Emaús: Lc 24, 13–35," *RevistB* 35 (1973) 4–7 discusses the genre of the Emmaus story and comments on Dupont and Dodd. Guillaume, *Luc interprète*, 83–92 discusses the genre of Luke on the basis of both biblical and non-biblical parallels. He proposes the following representative genres: "Wandersage," "reconnaissance," and "épiphanie."

ciples by means of the exposition of Scripture and the breaking of
the bread.

THE STRUCTURE OF LUKE 24:13-35

The genre of the Emmaus story is a vehicle for Luke's theology,
but so also is its structure,[11] which has undergone considerable
analysis in recent years.[12] Some scholars question such a structural
analysis,[13] but in light of the previous chapters on the structure
and function of Luke 24, and Luke's penchant for a thematic
presentation of the material, a structural analysis is essential to
determining Luke's theological purpose.

The evangelist has postulated a group of concentric circles in
Luke 24:13-35. This is consistent with Luke's structure, for in both
Luke and Acts he seems fond of "circular journeys," sometimes
called "the ring structure."[14] X. Léon-Dufour has proposed the
following schema in five circles that shows movement from the
outer circle to the center and back, e.g. in the fifth circle the two

---

[11]See Talbert, *Literary Patterns,* and D. E. Smith, "Table Fellowship," 613 n.
1.

[12]See the structural studies of X. Léon-Dufour, *Resurrection and the Message of
Easter,* trans. R. N. Wilson (London: Geoffrey Chapman Publishers, 1974);
J. D'Arc, "Catechesis on the Road to Emmaus," *LumVit* 32 (1977) 62–76; "Un
grand jeu d'inclusions dans 'les pèlerins d'Emmaüs,' " *NRT* 99 (1977) 143–
156; *Les pèlerins d'Emmaüs,* (Série "Lire la Bible" 47; Paris: Éditions du Cerf,
1977); R. Meynet, "Comment établir un chiasme: A propos de 'pèlerins d'Emmaüs,' " *NRT* 100 (1978) 233–249; and F. Schnider and W. Stenger, "Beobachtungen zur Struktur der Emmausperikope (Lk 24,13-35)," *BZ* 16 (1972)
94–114. My structural analysis of the Emmaus story is indebted to these foundational studies.

[13]See Dillon, *From Eyewitnesses,* 81–82 and Osborne, *The Resurrection Narratives,* 117.

[14]This observation was first brought to my attention by my thesis supervi-
sor, Dr. J. McHugh, who suggested the "circular journey" or "ring structure" for the Emmaus meal. He pointed out in correspondence that "when
travel is involved, you often end up where you start. E.g. the Infancy Gospel
begins, and ends, in Jerusalem, indeed in the Temple; the entire Gospel
begins, and ends, in Jerusalem, and in the Temple. Paul, on his journeys,
gets back to his starting point (except for his final journey, but cf. Ac 1:8). So
also Emmaus: the pair go back to Jerusalem." This insight gave rise to the
following structural study of Luke 24:13-35.

disciples are journeying from Jerusalem and returning to Jerusalem:

5) v. 13 "That very day (*autê tê hêmera*) two of them were going . . . from Jerusalem"

4)   v. 14 ". . . and talking with each other (*pros allêlous*) . . ."

3)   v. 15 ". . . Jesus himself (*kai autós*) drew near and went with them."

2)   v. 16 "But their eyes (*ophthalmoí*) were kept (*ekratoúnto*) from recognizing him (*epignônai autón*)."

1)   vv. 17-30 (the center circle) "*the colloquium and breaking of the bread*"

2)   v. 31a "And their eyes (*ophthalmoí*) were opened (*diênoíchthêsan*) and they recognized him (*epégnôsan autón*)."

3)   v. 31b ". . . and he (*kai autós*) vanished (*áphantos*) out of their sight."

4)   v. 32 "They said to each other (*pros allêlous*) . . ."

5) v. 33 "And they arose that same hour (*autê tê ôra*) and returned to Jerusalem."

The conclusion: vv. 34-35

The correspondence between the events preceding the colloquium and those following it may be more easily perceived in the following scheme:

a) The fifth circle:	v. 13	"That very day (*autê tê hêmera*) two of them were going . . . from Jerusalem"
	v. 33	"And they arose that same hour (*autê tê ôra*) and returned to Jerusalem."
b) The fourth circle:	v. 14	". . . and talking with each other (*pros allêlous*) . . ."
	v. 32	"They said to each other (*pros allêlous*) . . ."
c) The third circle:	v. 15	". . . Jesus himself (*kai autós*) drew near and went with them."
	v. 31b	". . . and he (*kai autós*) vanished (*áphantos*) out of their sight."
d) The second circle:	v. 16	"But their eyes (*ophthalmoí*) were kept (*ekratoúnto*) from recognizing him (*epignônai autón*)."

v. 31a   "And their eyes (*ophthalmoí*) were opened
          (*diênoíchthêsan*) and they recognized him
          (*epégnôsan autón*).
e) The center circle: vv. 17-30 *"the colloquium and breaking of the bread"*
f) The conclusion: vv. 34-35[15]

There have been attempts to determine a similar structure to the
center circle, but most of them appear to be artificial and uncon-
vincing.[16] It is counterproductive to superimpose a structure on
this central portion of the Emmaus story. This section must be
seen as one complete thought, for here Luke sets forth most carefully the theme of table fellowship. Therefore, my interpretation of
the Emmaus story will consider the relationship between 24:13-16
and 24:31-33 (the four outer circles), and between 24:17-30 (the
center circle) and 24:34-35 (the conclusion). The first matrix of
verses (the four outer circles) frames the pericope as to *time, place,
and persons.*[17] This schema recognizes Luke's propensity for framing his accounts carefully. The next matrix of verses (the core of
the pericope and the conclusion) gives the central theme of the
Emmaus story—the table fellowship that includes both the words
on the road (v. 32) and the breaking of the bread (v. 30). Luke
24:35 states the theme that the evangelist wants to communicate
to the developing Church: "And they expounded the things he
taught on the road and how he was known to them in the break-

[15]Cf. Léon-Dufour, *Resurrection* 160–164 and Dillon, *From Eyewitnesses*, 81 n.
34 who reconstructs Léon-Dufour's argument. Also Tannehill, *Narrative Unity*,
292.

[16]Cf. Osborne, *The Resurrection Narratives*, 117 and Dillon, *From Eyewitnesses*,
81 n. 34.

[17]Dillon, *From Eyewitnesses*, 82 provides a framework of time, place, and persons in the Emmaus story that gives us a valuable insight into the way in
which Luke weaves his themes together under the overall theme of table fellowship. Dillon's motivation here is to determine the compositional characteristics of the pericope and his methodology serves his purpose. Since his
concern is not to assert the priority of the theme of table fellowship, his
redactional and compositional study proceeds from "the framework passages
(vv. 13f. 33-35. 21b-24) to the travelers' colloquium (vv. 17-27), and finally to
the narrator's exposition (vv. 15f.) and meal scene (vv. 28-32)." I will adopt
portions of his approach and that of Léon-Dufour, but will deviate from them
in order to show the theological significance of the table fellowship matrix in
the ministry of Jesus in the Gospel.

ing of the bread'' (my translation—*kai autoí exêgoúnto* **ta en tê odô** *kai hôs egnôsthê autoís* **en tê klásei tou ártou**).

In proceeding from here I will develop this structure exegetically in the following order: the time, place, and persons framework of the meal at Emmaus and the four outer circles (vv. 13-16; 31-33) in chapters IV and V; and the dialogue on the road, the meal at Emmaus (the center circle vv. 17-30), and the conclusion of the pericope (vv. 34-35) in chapters VI through XII.

Chapter 4

The Framework of the Meal at Emmaus

A consideration of the time-, place-, and persons-framework of
Luke 24:13-35 is the first step in a detailed analysis of the ring
structure of the Emmaus story that highlights Luke's table fellowship matrix as an expression of the eschatological kingdom.[1] The
fifth or outermost circle of the narrative, both before and after the
meal, refers to the same time ("that very day" in 24:13 and "that
same hour" in 24:33), the same place ("from Jerusalem" in 24:13
and "to Jerusalem" in 24:33),[2] and the same persons (the Emmaus
disciples, "two of them," in 24:13 and "they arose . . . and
returned" in 24:33). This framework affects Luke's table fellowship
matrix since he uses references to time, places, and persons to
frame pericopes that constitute part of this matrix.

THE TIME-FRAMEWORK

The Three Day Sequence:
Day of Preparation, Sabbath, First Day of the Week
   In Luke 24, time is a significant part of Luke's structure which
he uses to express his theological ideas.[3] Beginning with 23:54,

---

[1]Cf. Dillon, *From Eyewitnesses*, 83–90 on the persons, time, and place of
24:13.

[2]Ibid., 84 where Dillon notes that the antecedent of *autôn* is not the eleven
apostles in 24:9, 10 but the *loipoí* of v. 9. Luke's intention is to expand the
circle in this pivot between the two volumes of Luke-Acts. The two disciples
appear among "the corps of paschal observers." The two are thought by the
early Church Fathers to be members of the seventy-two. In Luke 9:1ff., Jesus
sends out the twelve; in Luke 10:1ff., he sends out the seventy, two by two.

[3]Ibid., 85: ". . . the *time*-framework functions for Lk as an *idea*-framework
since the events woven together into the *chronological* integrity of the 'third
day' also fit together into the *theological* integrity of Lk's Easter panorama"
(emphasis Dillon).

Luke is setting apart the day of the resurrection from all other days, a reflection of his literary style and his theological program. As the passion and resurrection of Jesus unfold, the days are marked very carefully. In 22:7,[4] Luke describes the day on which the Last Supper is celebrated as "the day of Unleavened Bread, on which the passover lamb had to be sacrificed" (*édei thúesthai to páscha*).[5] The parallel between the time-framework of the Last Supper and of the Emmaus meal helps shape Luke's theme of table fellowship.

The Day of Preparation. Luke 22:1 affirms that *the feast* of Unleavened Bread, called the Passover, is drawing near. In 22:7, the evangelist asserts that *the day* of Unleavened Bread on which the passover lamb is slain has come. In 22:14, *the hour* has come, indicating the beginning of the first of our three days. Among the Synoptics, Luke alone has the reference to the hour. His intention is to set apart this meal and the hour of reclining at table with the disciples. This time-reference is critical to Luke's table fellowship matrix. Luke calls it an "hour" of passion (22:14) to designate the beginning of the final Passover that Jesus will observe with his disciples, a significant statement within his table fellowship matrix.[6] Matthew 26:20 and Mark 14:17 simply indicate that "it was evening," whereas Luke designates both the time of day *and* the theological hour when the fundamental meal of the table fellowship matrix is about to be eaten, an eschatological meal that has as

---

[4]Luke anticipates 22:7 with 22:1 where he sets the context for the narrative of the Last Supper by telling the reader that the feast of Unleavened Bread was drawing near, which is also called the Passover. He connects with this declaration of time the curious announcement that the chief priests and scribes were plotting Jesus' death. In the next verses (22:3-6), the betrayal of Judas is announced. Luke wants the reader to make the connection between the feast of Unleavened Bread, the Passover (the sacrifice of the passover lamb), and the death of Jesus. His reiteration of the time context in 22:7 indicates that the time sequence is important to his theological intent.

[5]Contrast Mark 14:12, "when they sacrificed the passover lamb" (they— active) with Luke 22:7, "on which the passover lamb had to be (*dei*) sacrificed" (the impersonal passive). By his use of *dei* and the passive, Luke suggests the divine purpose of this sacrifice as it fits into God's time-framework.

[6]Cf. Neyrey, *The Passion*, 12; Fitzmyer, *X-XXIV*, 1384, 1396-7.

its focus the death of Jesus. Like Luke, John refers in 13:1 to the hour when the whole passion history begins to unfold: ". . . when Jesus knew that his hour had come to depart out of this world to the Father . . . ."

This movement from the day to the very hour indicates the urgency of the moment that is affirmed by Jesus' words in 22:15-16. Jeremias argues that Jesus observes the passover with his disciples but does not partake of the food, fasting in anticipation of the eschatological banquet.[7] For in 22:16 when Jesus says, "I tell you I shall not eat it until it is fulfilled in the kingdom of God," the reference is forward to his next meal, still a meal of unleavened bread, namely, the meal at Emmaus, for then the kingdom has come.[8]

In the narrative of this last Passover meal, Luke refers both to the suffering of Jesus (22:15: "before I suffer") and the fulfillment of Scripture. It is necessary (dei) that the Scriptures be fulfilled which prophesies: "And he was reckoned with transgressors; for what is written about me has its fulfillment" (22:37).[9] This reference to Jesus' death in fulfillment of the Scriptures refers back to 22:7, where the same word for necessity (édei) is used of the necessity of the sacrifice of the Passover lamb.[10] Already at the Last Supper, Luke mentions the necessity of Christ's death in fulfillment of the Scriptures, the first time dei is used with the fulfillment of Scripture concerning the sufferings of the Christ, foreshadowing 24:26 and 24:44-47.

The narrowing from the day to the hour of the Passover meal is heightened by Luke in 22:53b when Jesus is arrested in the gar-

[7]J. Jeremias, *The Eucharistic Words of Jesus* (London: SCM Press, 1974) 208. X. Léon-Dufour, *Sharing the Eucharistic Bread* (New York: Paulist Press, 1987) 306–308, 371 n. 8 disagrees with Jeremias. Cf. below.

[8]R. de Vaux, *Ancient Israel*, Volume 2: Religious Institutions; trans. J. McHugh; (New York: McGraw-Hill Book Company, 1961) 490–492 claims that the feast of unleavened bread lasted eight days.

[9]Luke 22:35-38 is unique to Luke's Gospel, accenting the death of Jesus as a necessity in fulfillment of the Scriptures.

[10]Among the Synoptics, only Luke indicates the necessity (édei) of sacrificing the Passover lamb, highlighting the necessity of Jesus' death in his Gospel and anticipating both 22:37 and 24:7, 26, 44. Luke frames the Last Supper with references to the death of Jesus (22:7 and 37). (Cf. dei in Matt 26:35, 54).

den. Jesus responds to the chief priests, temple officers, and elders[11] with the words: "But this is your hour (ê hôra), and the power of darkness." The hour of the Passover meal has now turned into the hour of darkness, and the passion officially has begun. This is the climactic moment, and Luke again uses "the hour" to describe its arrival.[12] Thus just as Luke frames the narrative of the Last Supper with two references to the suffering of Jesus (22:15 and 37), so he frames the entire sequence of the actual sitting at table for the Passover (22:14) to the arrest of Jesus (22:53b), with a time-reference to the hour.[13]

The question arises: does Luke include the Last Supper within the overall time-framework of the passion—the Day of Preparation, the Sabbath day, and the first day of the week? Luke's reference to "the hour" places this day within the framework of the passion. If one argues that Day 1, the Day of Preparation, begins at sundown on Thursday, Day 2, the Sabbath day, begins at sundown on Friday, and Day 3 begins at sundown on Saturday, then Jesus *does* rise "on the third day," on Sunday morning, the first day of the week.[14] In a sense, therefore, Luke frames the entire

[11]Cf. Luke 22:2, "the chief priests and the scribes"; 22:4, "the chief priests and captains"; and 22:52, "the chief priests and captains of the temple and elders." Fitzmyer, X-XXIV, 1451 rightly observes that this identifies the crowd in 22:47. The numerous references to the Jerusalem authorities in Luke 22 (chief priests, scribes, captains of the temple, and elders) shows that the entire Jerusalem establishment is plotting the death of Jesus. Its fulfillment comes with the arrival of "the hour" in 22:53b. See chapter VIII on Jesus' opposition in Jerusalem.

[12]Among the Synoptics, only Luke uses "the hour" here. Both Matthew and Mark use "hour" in the context of Gethsemane and not in the arrest of Jesus (Matt 26:45; Mark 14:41). Luke's placement of this time reference sets off the narratives of the Last Supper, Gethsemane, and the arrest of Jesus from the rest of the passion narrative.

[13]Cf. Neyrey, *The Passion*, 12.

[14]The reference in 22:7 to the day on which the passover lamb had to be sacrificed refers to the Thursday afternoon. Cf. Fitzmyer, X-XXIV, 1382: "For the 'necessity' stemming from the pentateuchal prescription, see Exod 12:6, the MT of which reads, 'and the whole assembly of Israel shall kill it between the two evenings,' which came to mean 'at twilight,' and then roughly from 2:30-5:30 P.M." Exodus 12:18-22 states that the Passover meal took place after sunset. Cf. F. Brown, S. R. Driver and C. A. Briggs, *A Hebrew and English Lexicon of the Old Testament* (Oxford: Clarendon Press, 1979) 787.

passion and resurrection of Jesus with two meals: the Last Supper, the last Passover of the old age (22:14-38), and the Emmaus Supper, the first meal of the new age (Luke 24:13-35).[15]

The Sabbath. The Sabbath is marked by Luke in his time-sequence of passion and resurrection by noting the transition from the Day of Preparation to the beginning of the Sabbath in 23:54 ("it was the day of Preparation, and the sabbath was beginning").[16] The first day in the grave (Friday afternoon) is the day of the death of Jesus, the eschatological hour of darkness. But in 23:54, Luke juxtaposes the Day of Preparation and the Sabbath which "was about to begin" (note the *New English Bible's* translation of the imperfect), to show the time-sequence which is not recognized by Joseph of Arimathea and the women who come to the grave. Good Friday is simply another Day of Preparation for the Sabbath and has no eschatological dimension. This foreshadows the misunderstanding of the Emmaus disciples concerning the death of Jesus, his Sabbath rest in the tomb, and his resurrection on the third day. They are marking time according to the old order and do not recognize that a new order has dawned.[17] This will change completely in Luke 24 when the significance of the events that occurred during this time-sequence is opened up to the disciples by the risen Lord. Luke 23:54 therefore serves as an introduction to Sunday, the final day in Luke's sequence, but the first day of the week (24:1).

---

[15]In the forthcoming discussion of the time of the Emmaus meal it will be necessary to show that it occurs *before* sundown on Sunday.

[16]In comparing the Synoptic Gospels, it is hard to determine whose time-framework is more "theological." Mark makes a clear connection between the Day of Unleavened Bread and the burial of Jesus. Mark and Luke clearly demarcate the Day of Unleavened Bread, the Day of Preparation, and the Sabbath day (Matthew does not). Luke's time agenda is carefully shaped to preserve the three day sequence. He places the reference to the Day of Preparation and the Sabbath day at the end of the burial of Jesus for emphasis. His time references are as theological as Matthew's and Mark's, although he does not draw a parallel between the burial of Jesus and the Last Supper with "when it was evening." He will draw the parallel between the Last Supper and the Emmaus meal in 24:33, showing continuity in the table fellowship matrix.

[17]Cf. Osborne, *The Resurrection Narratives*, 102.

The First Day of the Week. The introduction to the first day of the week, the eighth eschatological day, the first day of the new creation, Sunday, is contrasted by Luke in 23:56b to the last day of the week, the seventh day, the last day of the old creation, the Sabbath[18]: "On the sabbath they rested according to the commandment." Luke does not use the word "commandment" (*entolê*) very often in his Gospel (1:6; 15:29; 18:20), but he juxtaposes it here with "Sabbath" to demonstrate that the followers of Jesus were still operating according to the old Law.[19]

In some Greek New Testament editions, 23:56b is closely associated with 24:1,[20] indicating that there is a close relationship between these two verses and between the transition from Luke 23 to 24: "On the sabbath they rested according to the commandment, but on the first day of the week . . ." (*kai to* **men** *sábbaton hêsúchasan kata tên entolên, tê* **de** *miá tôn sabbátôn* . . .—note the **men** . . . **de** construction that links these two days together grammatically and gives us reason to consider a theological link). This double use of "Sabbath" and the distinct character that Luke gives to each use shows that there is both a shift in time and a shift in the theological implications that these days now mark.

The first use of "Sabbath" is combined with "commandment," reminding us that the observance of this day was according to the Law, marking it as the seventh day of the sequence—the day of rest, the fundamental day of worship according to the old covenant.[21] The second use of "Sabbath" is used in the phrase "on

[18]Cf. Ellis, *The Gospel of Luke*, 275; Osborne, *The Resurrection Narratives*, 102.

[19]Cf. G. Schrenk, *entolê*, TDNT II 548 on 23:56b and the old provisions under the Law that are abolished with Christ's death and resurrection (cf. Heb 10:5-10).

[20]In the twenty-fifth edition of Nestle, Luke 23:56b forms a new paragraph that begins Luke 24. It is separated from 24:1 by a comma. In the twenty-sixth edition, it has been separated from Luke 24 and ends with a period. At one time, this close association was considered a grammatical possibility by the manuscript witnesses.

[21]Luke appears to have a Sabbath theology that is fulfilled in the burial of Jesus and the transition to the resurrection. Cf. Osborne, *The Resurrection Narratives*, 102: "*sábbaton* appears three times here (23:54, 56; 24:1), showing Luke's emphasis on Jesus' authority over the 'Sabbath.' He uses Mark's two references on Jesus and the Sabbath (4:31f.; 6:1f.), and adds two more: the healing of the crippled woman (13:10-17) and the man with dropsy (14:1-4).

the first day of the week," to denote Sunday. All the Synoptics distinguish between these two days. But Luke seems to separate the Sabbath from the first day of the week more emphatically by saying that the women kept the Sabbath according to the commandment. The complete unanimity of the four canonical Gospels as to the wording of this day points to its significance as the first day of the week.

There are various explanations for this time-note. Some have suggested that this is a reflection of the liturgical practice of the early Christian communities "which fixed the commemoration of Christ's resurrection at the time of eucharistic worship."[22] Others see this as a reference to "the eighth day."[23] Still others see Semitic influence, the "stereotyped usage for Sunday (Acts 20:7; John 20:19; I Corinthians 16:2)."[24] None of these explanations precludes a theological reading of this time-note. In fact, they suggest that such a reading is possible and should be carefully considered.

There is another dimension to the time-framework of the resurrection narratives. Although all the canonical Gospels refer to this as "the first day of the week," the time of day when this occurs varies between the Synoptics and John. Matthew 28:1 refers to the dawn as does Luke 24:1 (*órthrou bathéôs*, a genitive of time); Mark 16:2 indicates that it is early dawn when the sun had risen; and John 20:1 says that it was early, while it was still dark. Although the Synoptics and John seem to contradict each other, some have attempted to resolve them by noting that these references to the time of day have primarily theological ramifications.[25] The emphasis of Matthew, Mark, and Luke is on the coming of light as opposed to John who includes the transition from darkness. In a sense, none of these contradict each other, but each is viewing the time of appearance at the tomb on the first day of the week either

---

For this author Sabbath healings are a prelude to the greatest Sabbath miracle of all, the resurrection."

[22]Léon-Dufour, *Resurrection*, 107 who also says: "Even if the data is not firm enough for us to be certain, the narrative has a liturgical flavour."

[23]Ellis, *The Gospel of Luke*, 271.

[24]Marshall, *The Gospel of Luke*, 883. Cf. also Fitzmyer, *X-XXIV*, 1544 who notes that this expression is used of Sunday in Psalm 24 in the LXX.

[25]Cf. Osborne, *The Resurrection Narratives*, 198–99.

from the perspective of darkness or from the perspective of light. One's temporal perspective could certainly indicate one's theological intent. In Luke's time sequence, by viewing the resurrection from the perspective of light in 24:1, he is also introducing the eighth, eschatological day which ushers in the new creation.[26] The shameful embarrassment of crucifixion and the horror of the death of Jesus are now erased by the coming of this new day, the first day of the week, the day of resurrection.[27]

It may be helpful to draw one parallel between Luke 24 and Genesis 1. If, as I argued above, Luke begins the day at sundown, then the eschatological day—Easter—begins in darkness (as in Genesis 1:2) and blazes into light (as in Genesis 1:3). From Genesis 1:1 to 2:4a, six days of creation are described, each having an evening and a morning except for the Sabbath in which there is no evening. In the Hebrew text and the LXX, there is a major break at the end of Genesis 1, setting the seventh day apart from the other six days. The seventh day is a day that has no evening. Although Genesis 2:3 reads, "So God blessed the seventh day and hallowed it, because on it God rested from all his work which he had done in creation," God did not cease to be constantly working in his creation. Jesus affirms this in John 5:17 where, in a Sabbath controversy over his healing on the Sabbath, Jesus says: "My Father is working still, and I am working." In view of the eschatological nature of Sunday in Luke's time-sequence, it appears that the work that the Father and the Son are still doing is the recreation of the world on the Sabbath that has no evening or morning, the eighth day, the first day of the new creation.[28]

[26]Cf. B. B. Rogers, *The Wasps of Aristophanes* (London: G. Bell and Sons, 1915) 32 n. 216 on *órthros bathéôs*: "The dim twilight that precedes the dawn . . . the thick dullness of night [that] has not yet yielded to the clear transparency of day."

[27]See Osborne, *The Resurrection Narratives*, 99: ". . . resurrection is not only the vindication of Jesus' death but also a sign of the new life that results from it."

[28]Such an eschatological view of the Sabbath forms the conclusion of Augustine's *Confessions*, XII 35–37:

"35 O Lord God, grant us peace, for all that we have is your gift. Grant us the peace of repose, the peace of the Sabbath, the peace which has no evening. For this worldly order in all its beauty will pass away. All these things

As soon as Sunday, the first day of the week, is introduced by Luke in 24:1, there is a shift in focus on how this day is to be perceived. Matthew and Luke use the expression "on the third day" to designate the day of resurrection within the passion predictions (cf. Matt 16:21; 17:23; 20:19; Luke 9:22; 18:33; 24:7, 21, 46). Mark does not use this expression, but the words "three days" (cf. Mark 8:31; 9:31; 10:34).[29] The use of "three days" seems to refer

---

that are very good will come to an end when the limit of their existence is reached. They have been allotted their morning and their evening.

36 But the seventh day is without evening and the sun shall not set upon it, for you have sanctified it and willed that it shall last for ever. Although your eternal repose was unbroken by the act of creation, nevertheless, after all your works were done and you had seen that they were very good, you rested on the seventh day. And in your Book we read this as a presage that when our work in this life is done, we too shall rest in you in the Sabbath of eternal life, though your works are very good only because you have given us the grace to perform them.

37 In that eternal Sabbath you will rest in us, just as now you work in us. The rest that we shall enjoy will be yours, just as the work that we now do is your work done through us. But you, O Lord, are eternally at work and eternally at rest. It is not in time that you see or in time that you move or in time that you rest: yet you make what we see in time; you make time itself and the repose which comes when time ceases."

Cf. also P. J. Bernadicou, "Christian Community According to Luke," *Worship* 44 (1970) 207–208: "Each of the resurrection episodes opens with a time reference to the 'eighth day' (24:1, 13, 33). The symbolism identifies Jesus' resurrection as the beginning of a new creation. Perhaps too Luke wishes to indicate why Christians celebrate their liturgical gathering on the eighth day or Sunday, the day they joyfully commemorate Christ's resurrection and exaltation. Since Luke is also aware of a considerable period of time during which the resurrected Christ made other appearances (cf. Acts 1:3), he clearly intends to present a theme rather than a chronicle when he limits the appearances about which he speaks to the eighth day and the environs of Jerusalem."

[29] "Three days" is also used in Matthew 26:61 and Mark 14:58 before Caiaphas in Jesus' prediction that he will destroy and rebuild the temple in three days, and in Matthew 27:40 and Mark 15:29 at the cross by the crowds who quote the same prediction. Luke does not include these references to the resurrection in his passion narrative. Matthew 12:40 also uses "three days and three nights" twice concerning the sign of Jonah. This passage is unique to Matthew. One would expect Luke to have this pericope in his Gospel, with his emphasis on the three-day sequence of passion events. In fact, Luke does not use "three days" in reference to the resurrection anywhere in his Gospel.

to the totality of the passion event involving the three day process, whereas the use of "on the third day" seems to refer to the final day of the three-day sequence in which Jesus rises from the dead. Luke shows his interest in the three-day sequence of passion and resurrection by clearly demarcating the days. In Luke 24, however, he repeats the passion formula three times, each time using "on the third day," the only Synoptic to do so. It is this third day that is significant to Luke because it is the day of resurrection and the day in which the Christian community now gathers to celebrate the eschatological meal.[30] The first day of the week in Luke 24:1 has now become the third day in Luke 24:7, linking together the predictions of the passion of Jesus in the Gospel (particularly the passion prediction in 9:22) and the fulfillment of those predictions on this first day of the week.[31] The two other uses of "on the third day" in Luke 24 also reflect Luke's intention of portraying Sunday as the final, climactic day in the three-day sequence. The reference to the third day in Luke 24:21 by the Emmaus disciples betrays their lack of understanding of the passion and resurrection time-sequence, and the final reference in 24:46 places the third day within the commissioning passion instruction. Thus, this third day that was anticipated by Luke throughout his Gospel now reaches fulfillment and shifts from being a stumbling block (24:21) to being a fundamental part of the Lukan kerygma that is to be proclaimed by the emerging Church in Acts (Luke 24:46).[32]

[30]Cf. Luke 13:32 in the context of an eschatological discourse in support of "the third day" as the eschatological day of resurrection: ". . . the third day I finish my course." It seems reasonable that 13:32 is another proleptic demonstration in the ministry of Jesus of the eschatological fulfillment of his work "on the third day." Thus, Luke 13:32 foreshadows Luke 24.

[31]Cf. Dillon, *From Eyewitnesses*, 14: "Its particular value to Luke [the women's sabbath rest], however, is that it sets the stage, chronologically, for the subsequent phases of the paschal happenings: 'the first day of the week' (24,1 = Mark), when the action can continue, and the distinctively Lucan kerygmatizing thereof: '*the third day*' (24,7.21b.46). In short, here is the carefully constructed *time-framework* in which the Lucan Easter story will be told. The imposition of an exact chronological schema on his narrative is one of Lk's devices for bringing out the theological significance of the events recounted" (emphasis Dillon).

[32]Luke's use of "on the third day" may recall Hosea 6:2, the only reference in the LXX to "the third day." Cf. N. Walker, "After Three Days," *NovT* 4

The Five Time-Notices of the Meal at Emmaus

Luke's overall time-framework from 22:1 to 24:12 as a means of expressing his theological ideas now may instruct us on his use of time in the Emmaus pericope. There are five time-notices in Luke 24:13-35 to be considered.

Luke 24:13. The first time-notice in 24:13, "that very day," is part of the outer circle and emphatically states that the day on which Jesus rose from the dead is the same day that the Emmaus disciples made their journey to Emmaus. This day has been described already in 24:1 as "the first day of the week" and in 24:7 as "the third day." It has also been distinguished in the passion narrative from the Day of Unleavened Bread, the Day of Preparation, and the Sabbath day. Whatever activity happens on this day will be of eschatological significance since it is an eschatological day.

Luke 24:18. The second time-notice in 24:18, "in these days," is part of the center circle and refers to the activity of Jesus during the past week in Jerusalem, going back either to Jesus' entrance into Jerusalem (19:28) or to the Passover meal (22:1).[33]

There appears to be a parallel to 24:18 in 19:41-43 where Jesus laments over the city of Jerusalem for not knowing the time of its visitation:

(1960) 261-262 who argues that Hosea 6:2 inspired Luke to change Mark 8:31 from "after three days" to "on the third day." In Hosea, "after two days" means the third day, and thus in Mark 8:31, "after three days" would indicate the fourth day. Marshall, *The Gospel of Luke,* 371 suggests that Mark's reckoning of "after three days" is simply a reflection of the Hebrew reckoning of three days as "a short time." Luke may have had Hosea in mind, but his use of "on the third day" instead of Mark's "after three days" highlights Sunday as the eschatological day for theological reasons. Cf. also Dillon, *From Eyewitnesses,* 47-48 on the Old Testament background of "the third day."

[33]The clue to this reference may be found "in Jerusalem," i.e., the only visit to Jerusalem in the ministry of Jesus. This would suggest the entrance of Jesus into Jerusalem on Palm Sunday as the reference. The Emmaus disciples also speak of "these days" without any idea of their significance in salvation history. This is in contrast to 19:42 where Jesus, in the singular, refers "to that day," a significant time-reference for salvation history.

24:18   "Are you the only visitor to Jerusalem who does not know the things (*égnôs ta*) that have happened there in these days (*en autê taís hêmérais taútais*)?"

19:41-42 "And when he drew near and saw the city (*tên pólin*) he wept over it, saying, 'Would that even today you knew (*égnôs en tê hêméra taútê*) the things (*ta*) that make for peace! But now they are hid from your eyes."

Notice, however, in 24:18, the disciples speak about the things that happened in Jerusalem from the perspective of total misunderstanding. They speak of "these days" not yet realizing that "this is the day that the Lord has made." Within the time-framework of the Emmaus story, this second time-notice moves us from a focus on Sunday (24:13) to the broader perspective of what is happening during the whole passion-resurrection time-sequence (24:18). Thus Luke is able to keep both the third day and the three days in focus within the Emmaus story.

Luke 24:21. The third time-notice in 24:21, "the third day," is also part of the center circle and is, like 24:13, another reference to the day of resurrection.[34] The expression "on the third day" is never used by the Emmaus disciples (i.e. its non-use expresses their complete misunderstanding, since to use this formula would be a demonstration of their understanding of the significance of "the third day"). The key to understanding this phrase is most likely found in determining the meaning of *ágei*. There are two common understandings—either with Jesus as the subject, "He is passing;" or impersonally, "one is keeping the third day, we are at the third day."[35] Thus though the disciples do not understand the significance of this reference, there is a direct link in this verse to 24:18 concerning the events that happened in Jerusalem and the

[34]See above on the third day.
[35]Cf. A. Plummer, *Gospel According to St. Luke* (Edinburgh: T. & T. Clark, 1913) 554; H. K. Luce, *The Gospel According to St. Luke* (Cambridge: At the University Press, 1933) 361; J. M. Creed, *The Gospel According to St. Luke: The Greek Text, with Introduction, Notes, and Indices* (London: Macmillan, 1930) 296; F. Blass and A. Debrunner, *A Greek Grammar of the New Testament*, trans. R. W. Funk (Chicago and London: The University of Chicago Press, 1961) 72 §129; A. T. Robertson, *A Grammar of the Greek New Testament in the Light of Historical Research* (Nashville: 1923) 392; Guillaume, *Luc interprète*, 71.

time-sequence that has now been reached. At this point in the narrative, Luke's time-framework has prepared the reader for the colloquium and anticipates the fourth time-notice that introduces the climactic section of the Emmaus story.

Luke 24:29. The fourth time-notice in 24:29, "for it is toward evening and the day is now far spent," is the climax of Luke's time-framework in the Emmaus story.[36] It introduces the final act—the breaking of the bread when the eyes of the Emmaus disciples are opened to the presence of Jesus.

The time of day is important in terms of all the meals that Jesus has taken with his disciples during his ministry. There is a close parallel between this description of the declining day[37] and the description given in 9:12 concerning the day when Jesus fed the five thousand in the wilderness.[38] The relationship between the time of day for the Emmaus meal and other meals in the table fellowship matrix is significant, linking them together to achieve a climax at the breaking of the bread at Emmaus. R. D. Richardson comments:

"First, in a setting of teaching on *the Kingdom of God* at the hour *when the day was far spent*, it is recorded that Jesus took five *loaves of bread* (with fishes as a subsidiary) and *blessed and brake and gave*

[36]Cf. Fitzmyer, *X-XXIV*, 1567: "In Jewish calendaric reckoning this would mean that 'the first day of the week' (24:1) has come to an end; but Luke disregards that, considering the hours after sundown as part of the same day." Luke is not disregarding Jewish custom but heightening the climax of the day, the meal at Emmaus, by placing it at the very end of the first day of the week. The reader wonders if the first incident of the post-resurrection table fellowship of Jesus with his disciples will occur on the first day of the week, the first "Lord's day." The third day is *almost* over, but they still have time to return to Jerusalem.

[37]Note the distinction here between "evening" and "night." In March or April the Emmaus meal might have occurred between 4:00 and 6:00 p.m. In Jewish reckoning, there is no afternoon, just morning or evening. If the meal occurred at 4:00 p.m., this would be before the evening or at the beginning of the evening.

[38]Cf. above where I first observed this similarity. Cf. also Davis, "The Significance of the Shared Meal," 106 on the late afternoon setting for the Emmaus meal, characteristic of Jesus' healing and meals (Luke 4:38-40; 5:29-38; 7:36-50; 9:10-17; 11:37-41; 14:1-24; 22:14ff.; 24:36ff.); Dillon, *From Eyewitnesses*, 85.

to the disciples to set before the multitude (Lc. ix. 11ff.). Subsequently, at a Sabbath-*supper* (one that was incepted, we may understand, with a hallowed cup, and the blessing, breaking and sharing of bread when evening had ushered in the holy day of the week), Jesus urges hospitality for the unprivileged, and in so doing inspires a transition of thought to a non-exclusive Messianic banquet, so that another guest exclaims "Blessed is he that shall *eat bread* in *the Kingdom of God*" (xiv. 1-24). Next, at the Last Supper, when *the hour* is come (i.e. the evening, as well as the predestined, hour), Jesus *blesses a cup*, bidding *the disciples take and share it*, and likewise he *blesses, breaks and gives them bread*. In so doing he appears to forecast, as we have seen, a future similar rite that will anticipate the Messianic banquet of which he himself will partake with his disciples when they *eat and drink at (his) table in (his) Kingdom* (xxii. 14-30). And as if to make these forward implications more explicit, to 'open the eyes' of those who were not present at the Last Supper (of which, as the type of all subsequent Supper-rites before the coming of the Kingdom, he is represented as not himself partaking), his first action upon 'enter(ing) into his glory'—after he had sat down at table with two disciples at Emmaus, *on the first day of the week, the day being* already *far spent*—is to *take bread, bless, break and give it*, himself again not partaking (xxiv. 13-35). Moreover, this last section of the Gospel emphasises by a twofold repetition that the Lord is *made known in the breaking of the bread*. So we come naturally to the *breaking of bread* described in Acts, with which are associated discourses on *the Kingdom of God* and faith in Jesus (Acts xx. 7, 21, 25)."[39]

Luke achieves this climax by carefully crafting the time context for the Emmaus meal. The first day of the week is not quite over when this action of Jesus occurs. The lateness of the day adds to the drama: will the risen Lord be recognized on the third day? The moment in which the bread is finally broken and the risen Lord is first recognized is the denouement of the Gospel.

---

[39]R. D. Richardson in his supplementary essay in H. Lietzmann's *Mass and the Lord's Supper* (Leiden: E. J. Brill, 1979) 311–312 (emphasis Richardson). Cf. also O. Cullmann, *Early Christian Worship* (London: SCM Press, 1953) 9–12 on time and place of worship in Acts.

Luke ties together the description of the time of day and the activity of breaking bread in 24:30 with a typical Lukan expression, "*kai egéneto* . . . followed by a temporal clause," using a temporal clause common to him, "the dative of the articular infinitive with *en,* [used] especially in a temporal sense."[40] There may be some theological significance to this expression in this particular place. Most commentators acknowledge that this is a Hebraism or a Septuagintism, and as such, it demonstrates Luke's interest in writing a history in keeping with Old Testament histories. Specifically, *kai egéneto* is thought to imitate the *waw* consecutive.[41] In other words, we have here an example of an act of God in salvation-history. If this is true, then there is an intimate connection between the time of day and the breaking of the bread: God does fulfill his promises before the ending of the third day.

Luke 24:33. The fifth and final time-notice in 24:33, "that same hour," takes us back to the first time-notice which is also in the outer circle. The movement in this time-frame in the Emmaus story is from the day to the hour. As we observed in the Last Supper account, Luke frames his narrative in the same way, moving from the day in 22:7 to the hour in 22:14. In both Luke 22 and Luke 24, this movement conveys an urgency of the moment and a focus on a particular event.[42] In Luke 22, the movement of time helps the reader to see that it is the Passover meal that is the essence of this day. But the hour of the Passover meal in 22:14 soon turns to the hour of darkness in 22:53b. As we have noted above, this is when the passion officially begins. After Jesus is arrested, darkness covers this whole passion scene, symbolized most vividly in the darkness that covers the earth at the death of Jesus in 23:44-45. This darkness is also expressed by the total incomprehension on the part of the disciples to the significance of the death of Jesus, symbolized in the words of the Emmaus disciples in 24:19-24. From 22:53b to 24:31, the world was plunged into darkness both literally and figuratively.

---

[40]Cf. Fitzmyer, *I-IX*, 118–119. This may be another example of Luke's use of Greek in imitation of the Septuagint to convey a "Biblical style."

[41]See F. Büchsel, *gínomai, TDNT* I 682.

[42]Cf. Dillon, *From Eyewitnesses*, 92.

What a contrast between the hour and the power of darkness in 22:53b and the return to Jerusalem with open eyes in 24:33. In Luke 24, the movement of time does not focus on the meal but on the activity of the disciples who return to Jerusalem with opened eyes in order to meet and explain to the waiting Eleven and those with them about the events that had happened on the journey to Emmaus. The focus on "the hour" is not only the closing off of the Emmaus narrative, but also an introduction to the conclusion of the narrative where Luke gives us the meaning behind the events that happened on the road. The crucial hour has now come for the Church to recognize, as it is huddled together in Jerusalem as the Eleven and those with them, that first, the Lord has risen and appeared to Simon (24:34) and that second, the Lord has opened up the Scriptures and made himself known in the break-ing of the bread (24:35).

These two revelations recapitulate two of the great themes in Luke-Acts and function as the turning point of Luke's two volumes. The first theme concerns the preparation of the disciples throughout Luke to be apostles. Now in Luke 24, they have access to the kerygma of a crucified and risen Christ and will carry that kerygma into the world, beginning from Jerusalem (cf. Luke 24:44-49). Peter is *the* representative of the apostolic community. The resurrection of Jesus becomes official when the Eleven can say: "the Lord has risen indeed and appeared to Simon."[43] The sec-ond theme concerns the table fellowship of Jesus with his disciples that has manifested itself throughout his ministry as a teaching and eating fellowship (cf. Luke 22:14-38). The Church will now continue this table fellowship with Jesus, for Jesus will be present in the Church through his teaching and his meals (cf. Acts 2:42). Within Luke's time-framework, the narrowing from the day to the hour sets 24:34-35 apart as a climax. The hour of return is signifi-cant because it is in this hour that the disciples recognize and un-derstand that Christ has risen, that the kerygma has come to

---

[43]Luke uses the designation of the disciples as the Twelve and later as the Eleven more than the other Gospels. *apóstolos* occurs six times in Luke and twenty-eight times in Acts, whereas it occurs once in Matthew and twice in Mark.

completion, and that the continuing presence of the embodiment of the kerygma, the risen Lord, is now in their midst.

What strikes the reader at this point is the lack of time-notices in the rest of the Gospel. The evangelist does not mark time as carefully as before, for the climax of the Gospel has been reached—the old aeon has passed away and the new aeon has dawned. Once the risen Lord is recognized, time is now measured with respect to his resurrection.

Thus, Luke has preserved a careful time-framework of three days that begins with the Day of Preparation, Good Friday, when the hour of the passion begins and the power of darkness arrives. The Day of Preparation moves into the Sabbath Day of rest in the tomb, with the darkness clouding the understanding of Jesus' disciples. Finally, the Sabbath Day moves into the first day of the week, the day of resurrection, the eschatological day. This day begins at deep dawn, in darkness, but when it was toward evening and the day was now far spent, the darkness of ignorance turns to the light of open eyes and the disciples have access, for the first time, to a total understanding of the plan of salvation. This movement from darkness to light occurs during a three day period with great emphasis on the third day when, as the passion predictions foretold, the Christ rose from the dead.

THE PLACE-FRAMEWORK

The place-framework for the outer circle is Jerusalem. In 24:13, "from Jerusalem" prepares the way for "to Jerusalem" in 24:33. R. J. Dillon's argument, that Luke uses Jerusalem here as the geographical locus for the passion and resurrection events, is persuasive. But it does raise a problem. If Jerusalem is the place of the sacred events of passion and resurrection, why does the Emmaus meal occur *not in Jerusalem* but in a village that was some distance away from Jerusalem, "about seven miles"? And why is Luke so careful to say in 24:33 that the disciples *returned to Jerusalem*? How is it possible, according to Luke's geographical perspective, for the first post-resurrection meal to take place outside Jerusalem?

According to Luke's table fellowship matrix, the significant meal in Israel's history was the Passover that had to take place in Jerusalem. The new Passover, the Last Supper of Jesus with his disciples, also takes place in Jerusalem, consistent with Luke's geographical perspective. But the first meal that the resurrected Lord has with his disciples, the Emmaus meal, takes place outside of Jerusalem. This placement of the meal outside of Jerusalem also conforms with Luke's geographical perspective. For if the Emmaus meal is proleptic of the meal fellowship of the early Christian communities, then the location of the Emmaus meal is also proleptic of the primary geographical location where meal fellowship will be celebrated in the Church, i.e. outside Jerusalem.[44]

But where was Emmaus? Traditionally there are three proposed possibilities: Amwas (near the modern Latrun), the village of Qubeibeh, and Kolonieh.[45] The last, located nearly four miles (i.e. thirty stadia) northwest of Jerusalem, seems the most likely candidate, and therefore the sixty stadia of Luke may represent a round-trip from Jerusalem and back. This would be a one-hour walk each way, just sufficient to establish clearly that the meal was taken well outside the boundaries of the city.[46]

[44]Cf. Dillon, *From Eyewitnesses*, 86, 93–94. Although Dillon sees the significance of Jerusalem differently than I do, his words help support my position that Jerusalem is significant to the Emmaus story, not because the meal takes place in Jerusalem, but because it takes place outside Jerusalem and thus points to the Church's mission and life in Acts. Cf. also J. D. G. Dunn, *Unity and Diversity in the New Testament* (London: SCM Press, 1977) 354.

[45]There has been a great deal written on the location of Emmaus. Wanke, *Die Emmauserzählung*, 37–42 discusses the location of Emmaus and provides a thorough bibliography on the subject. P. A. Arce, "Emmaús y algunos textos desconocidos," *EstBíb* 13 (1954) 53–90 offers an exhaustive analysis of the issue through history and the various locations that have been cited as possibilities for the biblical Emmaus. Guillaume, *Luc interprète*, 96–109 looks at the textual critical problems concerning sixty/a hundred-and-sixty stadia, and the archaeological evidence. See also R. M. Mackowski, "Where is Biblical Emmaus," *ScEsp* 32 (1980) 93–103; Fitzmyer, *X-XXIV*, 1561–1562.

[46]Cf. P. Benoit, *The Passion and Resurrection of Jesus Christ* (New York: Herder and Herder, 1969) 273–274: "Where then is Emmaus? Qubeibeh is certainly 60 stadia away, but it was picked out for exactly that reason, and its tradition does not appear until the thirteenth or fourteenth century. Kolonieh, it is objected, is no more likely since it is only 30 stadia away. This is true, but there could be a slight confusion in the physical data here without offending against scriptural inerrancy. Luke does not belong to the country, he merely noted down the information he had gathered: they went to Emmaus, came

The two other place references in Luke 24 come after the end of the Emmaus story in 24:47 and 52. In 24:47, repentance and forgiveness of sins are to be preached "beginning from Jerusalem." In 24:52, Jesus leads them out to Bethany for the ascension, and after the ascension the disciples returned "to Jerusalem." The Venerable Bede comments that just as the Gospel began in Jerusalem in the temple so it ends with the apostles returning to Jerusalem and gathering together not to shed the blood of animal victims, but to praise God:

" 'And after many similar remarks, Luke at the end of his gospel gathers the disciples in the Temple to praise God.' More eloquent still are the words with which he closes his great commentary: 'Luke has expounded the priesthood of Christ more fully than the others, and his ending is striking in its beauty. Having begun his gospel with the ministry of the priest Zechariah in the Temple, he ends it with a story of Temple devotion. There he depicts the apostles (that is, the future ministers of the new priesthood) gathered together not to shed the blood of animal victims, but to praise and to bless God.' "[47]

Thus an analysis of the place-framework of Luke 24:13-35 indicates that the Emmaus meal foreshadows the new meal of the new age, a meal that has its source in the death and resurrection of Jesus Christ and its fulfillment in the Church which now serves as the locus for the presence of the crucified and risen Christ. Therefore, the Emmaus meal is the climax of Jesus' table fellowship with his disciples in the Gospel and the beginning of his table fellowship with the Church in Acts.

THE PERSONS-FRAMEWORK

The framework of persons in Luke 24:13 and 33 is suggested by the following phrases: "two of them" in v. 13, "and they found

---

back the same evening, 60 stadia. Later, using these notes for the writing of his gospel, he makes Emmaus 60 stadia away, forgetting that the figure referred to the double journey. This is a possible explanation. In general, critics adopt Kolonieh as the Emmaus of the gospels. There is no real evidence, but in a case like this we have to be content with probabilities."

[47]Quoted from J. McHugh, *The Mother of Jesus in the New Testament* (Garden City, New York: Doubleday, 1975) 121.

the eleven gathered together and those who were with them" in
v. 33. A number of questions concerning the identification of these
groups has direct bearing upon the table fellowship matrix.

In 24:13 there seems to be no doubt that the "two of them"
refers to the two disciples at Emmaus.[48] As Dillon observes, the
problem centers on the antecedent of *ex autôn*: is it the inner circle
of the disciples in 24:11 (*autôn*) or the broader circle of disciples in
24:9 (*toís héndeka kai pásin toís loipoís*)? Dillon is correct in pointing
us to 24:18, where Cleopas is identified as one of them, for this
makes it clear that the antecedent is not the inner circle but "all
the rest" of 24:9.[49] Luke's purpose here not only maintains continuity with the preceding narrative of the resurrection, but it also
preserves a Lukan theme of "the Eleven and the rest."[50] In terms
of the table fellowship matrix, one wonders if there is any significance to the fact that Luke centers the Emmaus story around
two disciples out of the broader circle and not around two disciples out of the Eleven.

This is heightened by 24:33 where the two Emmaus disciples return to Jerusalem in order to consult with the Eleven and those
with them. All of these disciples constitute the paschal witnesses,
but who are the ones who first have the Scriptures opened up to
them and recognize the Lord in the breaking of the bread? It is
not the Eleven, but two out of the rest, and Luke carefully makes
this distinction clear in 24:33-35. One does not expect the first witnesses to the resurrected Christ in Luke's Gospel to be the Emmaus disciples who are not included among the Eleven. We

[48]See Guillaume, *Luc interprète,* 77 on the Lukan theme of "two witnesses."
[49]But cf. Fitzmyer, *X-XXIV,* 1561: ". . . one cannot exclude the possibility
that the unnamed disciple is one of the Eleven." In 24:33, however, Luke
says that the two returned to the Eleven which seems to rule out the possibility that the unnamed disciple was one of the Eleven. See chapter VI on
Cleopas.
[50]Cf. Dillon, *From Eyewitnesses,* 83–84 for the above observations. He also
writes: "The important thing about the travelers is that they belong to the
corps of paschal observers. That is what *ex autôn* means to express, and it
prepares the reader for the return of the two to the full assembly at the conclusion of the story (v. 33)." Dillon also notes on p. 277 that "it may not be
inappropriate to consider the travelers to Emmaus representatives of the
'Seventy-two,' thus participants in the proleptic world-mission of Luke
10. . . ."

would expect Luke to relate the narrative of the risen Christ's appearance to Peter, something he refers to in 24:12. In fact, the entire Emmaus account is framed by Luke with a reference to the appearance of the Lord to Peter (24:12, 34), but these references only state that such an appearance occurred. Luke's underlying purpose is to offset this testimony of Peter with a detailed and climactic narrative in which the Lord not only appears to the two disciples, but opens up the Scriptures concerning himself and reveals himself in the breaking of the bread.[51] The Church's agenda in Acts, although beginning with the Eleven, will soon include a greater circle of followers whose access to his presence is foreshadowed by his appearance to the Emmaus disciples.

[51]Ibid., 65–67, 94–99 where Dillon's observations indirectly support my position that the apostolic declaration of the Lord's appearance to Simon is set off against the Emmaus disciples' testimony and pales in comparison.

Chapter 5

The Outer Circles of the Meal at Emmaus

THE FIFTH CIRCLE

v. 13 "That very day two of them were going to a village named Emmaus, about seven miles from Jerusalem."

v. 33 "And they rose that same hour and returned to Jerusalem . . . ."

Our analysis of the outer four circles in the Lukan framework of the meal at Emmaus begins with the fifth circle. Luke 24:13 opens with "and behold" (*kai idoú*), a typical Lukan construction[1] and one that also occurs in Luke 24:4 and 49. In *24:4*, this construction introduces the two men in dazzling apparel who come to the perplexed women. It is combined with another Septuagintism and common construction in Luke's Gospel, *kai egéneto* + *kai* + a finite verb. Taken together, these two constructions not only point to Lukan authorship but underline the biblical history that Luke is writing.

The resurrection narrative of Luke and the transfiguration story are purposely paralleled by the phrase in 9:30, "and behold, two men" (*kai idoú ándres dúo*). In the transfiguration, *kai idoú* introduces Moses and Elijah who appear in glory discussing "his departure, which he was to accomplish at Jerusalem." Among the Synoptics, only Luke mentions the glory of Moses and Elijah (9:31) and the glory of Jesus (9:32); and he alone uses *éxodos* to

---

[1]Cf. Fitzmyer, *I-IX*, 121. He considers *kai idoú* a Septuagintism since this phrase is very common in the Septuagint. If, as some have claimed, Luke is interested in writing a history in keeping with Old Testament histories, the use of *kai idoú* to introduce significant sections of his Gospel shows a continuity with the LXX. It is a Lukan phrase (26 times), introducing significant passages related to the table fellowship motif, e.g., 2:25; 7:12; 9:30; 23:50; and 24:4, 13, and 49.

describe what Jesus is about to fulfill in Jerusalem. Considering the passion themes in these short verses of the transfiguration,[2] it is difficult not to see a direct parallel to the resurrection narrative in 24:4. Now that Jesus has accomplished in Jerusalem what he set out to do, Luke reflects back upon both the prophecy of Jesus in Galilee in Luke 9 and the prophecy of the Scriptures that foretold of Jesus' passion and resurrection, since only Luke refers to the death and resurrection of Jesus in the transfiguration account.[3] Thus *kai idoú* ties together 9:30-32, where Moses and Elijah see Jesus in glory, 24:4, where the angels, appearing in glory, know that Jesus is now in glory, and 24:13, where the two disciples are about to see Jesus revealed in glory.

Luke also uses *kai idoú* in *24:49*, although *idoú* may not be original.[4] If it is an authentic part of the text, then it forms a triad in Luke 24, introducing the final words of Jesus in the Gospel when he sends the promise of the Father (i.e. the Holy Spirit) upon the eleven disciples. This concludes the entire chapter and foreshadows Acts. It also looks back upon the commission of the twelve in 9:1-6 and the seventy(-two) in 10:1-12. Luke 24:49 also recalls the passion instruction of 24:4-8.

Thus, in considering the framework of the Emmaus pericope, Luke uses *kai idoú* to hold together Luke 24 and to show the continuity between the three major pericopes of this chapter.[5]

[2]Luke's use of *éxodos* recalls the exodus of the Israelites out of Egypt, a type of Christ's redemption which he accomplishes in the holy city of Jerusalem. As prophets of the old covenant, Moses and Elijah testify that the Old Testament speaks of the Messiah who must suffer and die before entering into his glory, foreshadowing Luke 24.

[3]Cf. Fitzmyer, *I-IX*, 794.

[4]Ibid., 1584 where Fitzmyer notes that "most mss. (A, B, C, Q, Y, 063, *f* 1,13, and the Koine text-tradition) have *kai idoú egô*, which is preferable." Cf. also B. Metzger, *A Textual Commentary on the Greek New Testament* (London: United Bible Societies, 1975) 188–189.

[5]Another example of Luke's use of *kai idoú* may be seen in paralleling 23:50 with 2:25 where Simeon is introduced in the same way as Joseph of Arimathea. Both sections begin with *kai idoú*; both men are identified with similar phrases (2:25; 23:50); both are described in the same way (2:25; 23:50); and both are waiting for the redemption of the world in the Christ event (2:25; 23:51). Both Simeon and Joseph of Arimathea are devout representatives of those in Israel with messianic expectations. Perhaps Luke connects

v. 14 ". . . and *talking with each other* about all these things that had happened."

v. 32 "They *said to each other*, 'Did not our hearts burn within us while he talked to us on the road, while he opened to us the scriptures?' "

As one proceeds into the narrative, the content of the conversation of the disciples on their journey to Emmaus is recounted. Léon-Dufour sees a parallel between 24:14 and 32 because of the similarity of the nature of the activity between the Emmaus disciples: "they conversed."[6] By his literary style in 24:14, Luke creates continuity with what went before and heightens the paschal facts that will be the focus of the Emmaus pericope. As part of the framework of Luke 24:13-35, verse 14 introduces the reader to the topic of the colloquium of 24:17-30—"all the things that have happened"—which is a fundamental part of Luke's table fellowship. The proper understanding of the facts of the passion is at issue here. The disciples' failure to understand the facts and the opening up of those facts to them by the risen Christ are two of the main topics of the Emmaus story. The meal alone is not enough, but the meal must be seen in terms of the kerygma which entails a proper understanding of the passion facts according to the Scriptures.

This leads us to Luke 24:32, the other part of this fourth circle that has direct parallels to 24:14, particularly *pros allêlous* ("with each other") with its verbs of speaking, and a reference to the conversation with Jesus on the road that causes the disciples' hearts to burn ("while he talked to us on the road"). Between 24:14 and 24:32 a complete change has come over the disciples concerning the passion facts. As they began the journey conversing about all the things that had happened, it is apparent from 24:17-24 that they completely failed to understand the passion facts. This is highlighted by 24:17, the beginning of the colloquium

---

these two events to show that what was foreshadowed in the infancy narrative is now coming to completion. Considering the connection between the burial of Jesus and Luke 24, there is a gradual unfolding of the full dimension of God's eschatological salvation from the beginning to the end of his Gospel.

[6]Cf. Léon-Dufour, *Resurrection*, 161-162.

between Jesus and the Emmaus disciples, where the risen Christ now enters into the discussion of the passion facts: "What is this conversation which you are holding with each other as you walk?" The disciples' conversation in 24:14 and 17 shows that they did not understand the passion facts, i.e. these facts were not understood among the apostles.

Their progress towards light is heightened by Luke's traveling motif. The disciples are conversing about the things that happened in Jerusalem as they make their way towards a village in 24:13 (*poreuómenoi*); they are questioned by Jesus concerning their conversation about the things that happened in Jerusalem "as they are walking toward Emmaus" in 24:17 (*peripatoúntes*); and they speak to one another concerning their burning hearts as Jesus spoke to them and opened up the Scriptures for them "while he was on the road" in 24:32 (*en tê hodô*). The reader is reminded of the teaching of Jesus to his disciples on the road to Jerusalem (9:51–19:44). In 24:32, the two things that caused the hearts of the disciples to burn were Jesus *speaking* to them on the road and *opening up* for them the Scriptures. In both speaking and opening up, the topic of the conversation on the road was the passion facts.

At this point, a dramatic change has come over the disciples. The mystery concerning "the things that had happened" as they began the journey has now been opened by the risen Lord in his conversation with them on the road. But even though the Lord has spoken to them and opened up the Scriptures to them, they still do not have open eyes. Within the table fellowship matrix, the colloquium with Jesus on the road and the exegetical lesson are not enough *by themselves* to enable them to recognize the presence of the risen Lord. They are necessary preconditions, but Luke demonstrates in his conclusion in 24:35 that they must be taken together with the breaking of the bread: "And they expounded the things he taught on the road and how he was known to them in the breaking of the bread" (my translation). Thus, Luke 24:14 and 32 are both concerned with "the things he taught on the road."[7]

[7]At this point in my investigation, it is possible to say that the Emmaus disciples are walking *away* from Jerusalem with incomprehension, knowing

v. 15 "While they were talking and discussing together, *Jesus himself drew near and went with them."*

v. 31b "*. . . and he vanished out of their sight."*

The purpose of this third circle is to introduce Jesus into the narrative. Léon-Dufour forms the third circle within the framework of 24:13-35 around the appearance of Jesus in 24:15 ("Jesus goes with them") and his departure in 24:31b ("Jesus vanishes out of their sight").[8] Between these verses, the presence of Jesus will be crucial to the direction of the narrative. This third circle lifts the narrative to a higher level.

There are a number of Lukan characteristics about 24:15. He makes the transition from verse 14 to verse 15 with two typical and familiar Lukan constructions that are often used together: "*kai egéneto + kai + a finite verb"* in the indicative (*suneporeúto*) and "the dative of the articular infinitive with *en*, especially in a temporal sense," (two infinitives here, *en tô homileín autoús kai suzeteín*).[9] Luke not only resorts to Septuagintisms in this verse to cast it in the mold of a familiar biblical story, but his choice of introduction connects verse 15 with the fourth and fifth circles. But Luke's use of *kai egéneto* may reflect even more than an imitation of a biblical style. Dillon, in quoting Wanke, offers the observation on Luke 24:4 and 15 that "Lk seeks to evoke the atmosphere of the earthly appearance of heavenly beings, a particularly sacred occasion which the Old Testament always cloaked in numinous glow and solemn language." Thus Luke is not simply imitating the literary style of the Old Testament, but shaping his language to imitate the character of a narrative that is about heavenly beings (angels) in 24:4 and the Messiah in 24:15.[10]

---

only passion facts. The question to be answered is whether or not it is full knowledge that brings them back to Jerusalem.

[8]Cf. Léon-Dufour, *Resurrection*, 162.

[9]Cf. Fitzmyer, *I-IX*, 119–120; *X-XXIV*, 1563. Dillon, *From Eyewitnesses*, 89 thinks that this construction denotes "attendant circumstance of heavenly visions and appearances."

[10]Dillon, *From Eyewitnesses*, 21, quoting Wanke, *Die Emmauserzählung*, 29.

As Luke introduces Jesus into the pericope in 24:15, he reiterates in the opening phrase the three elements of the Lukan framework: 1) the time-framework is recalled by "in that very day . . . it came to pass . . ."; 2) the place-framework is intimated by the temporal phrase, "while they were conversing and discussing," implying that this activity was going on while they were leaving Jerusalem and proceeding to Emmaus (note the use of *homiléô* as in 24:14 to describe the same activity); and 3) the person-framework is reiterated by *autoús*, the antecedent being the two Emmaus disciples who were conversing with each other about the things that happened in Jerusalem.[11]

In the second half of 24:15, Jesus is set apart as he is introduced into the narrative by the participial phrase "Jesus himself drew near" (*kai autós Iêsoús eggísas*, which is dependent on *suneporeúto*). Fitzmyer translates this "Jesus himself happened to draw near and began to walk with them."[12] Luke uses *eggízô* in connection with *suneporeúto*, a part of Luke's geographical perspective.[13] As the Emmaus disciples proceed towards their destination, Jesus draws

---

[11]Dillon, *From Eyewitnesses*, 145 writes: "v. 15 effectively expresses the evangelist's plan for the story's composition as a whole: the association between *the mystery of the passion* (*homileín . . . kai suzêteín perí pántôn ktl.*, v. 14) and the *journey* shared with Jesus (*suneporeúto autoís*). This picture—passion instruction framed in a 'journey'—is the structure of the central gospel chapters all over again! The unknown Emmaus disciples are being caused to recapitulate the path already charted by the evangelist, evidently because they are put forth as representatives of the vast body of believers gathered about the nucleus of the historic Twelve" (emphasis Dillon).

[12]Fitzmyer, *X-XXIV*, 1553; cf. p. 120; *X-XXIV*, 1563 on the intensive use of *kai autós*.

[13]Cf. Fitzmyer, *I-IX*, 168–169 on *poreúesthai* and Luke's geographical perspective. On pp. 1557–1558 Fitzmyer writes: "The disciples are en route to Emmaus, 'making their way' (*poreuómenoi*, v. 13) and Christ comes to 'walk with them' (*suneporeúeto autoís*, v. 15). Note the double use of *en tê hodô*, 'on the road' (vv. 32,35). It is precisely the geographical setting in which Christ instructs them about the sense of the Scriptures. Thus at the end of the Lucan Gospel the appearance-story *par excellence* takes place, not only in the vicinity of the city of destiny, toward which Jesus' entire movement in the Gospel has been directed, but his final and supreme instruction about the relation of his destiny to that which Moses and the prophets of old had announced is given 'on the road.' The subtle, yet highly deliberate, use of this Lucan motif is not to be missed."

near to them. Luke also uses *eggízô* in 24:28 in connection with *eporeúonto* as all three together draw near to their destination. The word "draw near," *eggízô*, may have some significance in the Emmaus story since it carries theological weight in other places in Luke, i.e. Jesus drawing near to Jerusalem, his city of destiny.[14]

Luke uses *eggízô* eighteen times in his Gospel and six times in Acts,[15] compared to seven times in Matthew, three times in Mark, and never in John. This word carries with it an eschatological dimension,[16] and therefore, it is helpful to review those places in Luke and Acts where *eggízô* carries with it eschatological connotations either in connection with Luke's geographical perspective or with his table fellowship matrix.

In Luke 15:1, the tax collectors and sinners draw near (*eggízontes*) to hear him. In 15:2, Luke's classic statement—"this man receives sinners and eats with them"—sums up Jesus' table fellowship ministry. This introduces the three parables of forgiveness in chapter 15 that illustrate the nature of the kingdom, culminating in the parable of the prodigal son where the kingdom is a feast for sinners prepared by the Father himself. This is confirmed in 15:25 as the elder son draws near (*êggisen*) and hears the music and dancing of the messianic feast. He is not like the sinners and tax collectors but like the Pharisees who do not recognize the kingdom when they see it (cf. Luke 13-14). In both cases, *eggízô* is used for those who come into the presence of the kingdom: in 15:2, the tax collectors and sinners draw near to Jesus who receives them, eats with them, and tells them a parable about the eschatological feast; in 15:25, the brother of the prodigal son draws near to the feast only to reject the eschatological witness of his father, a reaction similar to the Pharisees.

In Luke 18:35, Jesus draws near (*eggízein*) to Jericho, the scene of two eschatological events: the healing of the blind man in fulfillment of Luke 4:18 and Isaiah 61, and the declaration to Zacchaeus the chief tax collector that "today salvation (*sôtêría*) has come to this house . . . (19:9)." The significance of these events is height-

---

[14]Cf. W. G. Kümmel, *Promise and Fulfillment* (Naperville: Alec R. Allenson, Inc, 1957) 19–25 on *eggizô* in the NT.

[15]In Acts, an eschatological sense is conveyed in 1:12; 7:17; 9:3; 22:6.

[16]Cf. H. Preisker, *eggús*, *TDNT* II 331.

ened by Luke's statement immediately following the Zacchaeus account in 19:11, that Jesus "proceeded to tell them a parable, because he was near to Jerusalem (*diá to eggús eínai Ierousalêm*), and because they supposed that the kingdom of God was to appear immediately."

In Luke 19:29, *eggízô* is used in a geographical sense of drawing near to a city, as is the case of 7:12, 18:35, and 19:11. Jesus draws near to Bethphage and Bethany at the Mount of Olives to give instructions to his disciples concerning his entrance into Jerusalem. It has particular theological significance in this geographical context. In 19:37, Jesus draws near (*eggízontos*) to the Mount of Olives and the disciples begin to rejoice at his entrance into Jerusalem. In the next verse, Jesus is called the King who brings peace in heaven and glory in the highest (cf. Luke 2:14). In 19:41, Jesus draws near (*êggisen*) to the city and, seeing it, weeps over it's rejection of the suffering Messiah's death. The passion setting for *eggízô* gives it an eschatological connotation.

In Luke 21:8, 20, and 28 in the eschatological discourses, *eggízô* is used in connection with the kingdom of God and the approaching new age. In 21:8, the time is drawing near (*êggiken*); in 21:20 the desolation of Jerusalem is drawing near (*êggiken*); in 21:28, the redemption is drawing near (*eggízei*). In 21:30 and 31, the adverb *eggús* is used in the eschatological sense where the signs that summer is drawing near are compared to the signs that the kingdom of God is drawing near.

In Luke 22:1, *eggízô* is used of the approach of the feast of Unleavened Bread on which the Passover lamb is slain. This sets the stage for the Last Supper where Jesus institutes the eschatological feast of the Church. In 22:47, Judas draws near (*êggisen*) to Jesus to kiss him. Both these references frame the meal that occurs on the night in which he is given up into death.

The next reference is in the Emmaus story at 24:15 where Jesus draws near to the disciples. In Jesus, the kingdom of God draws near to them. Up until Luke 24, *eggízô* is used of a gradual movement towards the consummation of the kingdom in Jerusalem with the death and resurrection of Jesus. Now that the kingdom has come in Jesus, Jesus draws near to the Emmaus disciples (*eggísas suneporeúeto autoís*) to reveal the essence of the kingdom by opening up the Scriptures to them and making himself known in the breaking of the bread. The kingdom is present but not yet seen by them. In 24:28, the disciples draw near to Emmaus (*kai êggisan eis tên kômên hoú eporeúonto*) where, in Luke, the kingdom is first unveiled to the world. In both 24:15 and 28, Luke continues his geographical motif of movement towards a place of revelation by his continued use of *poreúomai* (once in 24:15; twice in 24:28). Thus by means of the verb *eggízô*, Luke signals that Emmaus is a place of eschatological significance.

This returns us to the second part of the third circle in 24:31b. The parallels to 24:15 are obvious. Just as Luke introduced Jesus to the Emmaus story with the intensive use of *kai autós*, he now gives Jesus leave from the Emmaus disciples with the same phrase.[17] In 24:15, Jesus draws near to the disciples from out of nowhere; in 24:31b, he "vanished out of their sight" (*áphantos*)[18] as soon as he is recognized. Both verses give the sense of the miraculous, supernatural appearance and disappearance of Jesus to the Emmaus disciples. Fitzmyer translates this verse "and he became (someone) disappearing from them," saying that with this phrase "the goal of the story has been reached."[19]

[17]Cf. Fitzmyer, *I-IX*, 120 on the unstressed use of *kai autós* in 24:31b. Since Luke uses this same expression for Jesus in 24:15 and 31b as he enters and exits the narrative, both uses are the same, namely the intensive use. This is Luke's favorite expression for Jesus in the Emmaus account (24:15, 25, 28, and 31). Cf. A. Ehrhardt, "The Disciples of Emmaus," *NTS* 10 (1963–64) 184: "In general it may be said that in our story *autós* takes the place of the personal pronoun, something which is typical for the Septuagint, and in the New Testament especially for Luke."

[18]This is the only appearance of *áphantos* in the NT. Dillon, *From Eyewitnesses*, 153 n. 239 also notes that "the expression *áphantos egéneto* is *hapax legomenon* in the NT but belongs to the most frequently used vocabulary in hellenistic sources depicting heavenly 'translations.'" Marshall, *The Gospel of Luke*, 898 notes that "it is as a supernatural visitor that the risen Jesus is portrayed" and gives us the following references: Euripides, Or. 1496; Hel. 605f.; Virgil, Aen. 9:657; 2 Macc. 3:34. Fitzmyer, *X-XXIV*, 1568 describes this as a construction commonly used in the Septuagint, e.g. Judges 21:16 and Job 2:9b. He also cites 2 Maccabees as a parallel and states that "in classical Greek the adj. is used of disappearing gods." This may be another example of Septuagintisms in Luke 24 that shows Luke is attempting to write a biblical history.

[19]Fitzmyer, *X-XXIV*, 1568.

The full theological significance of 24:15 and 31b to the table fellowship matrix will not be known, however, until the colloquium and the breaking of the bread. But the third circle provides the Emmaus story with the framework of Jesus' appearance and disappearance, raising the possibility of interpreting the opening of Scripture and the opening of the disciples' eyes as an eschatological moment that has its focus in the breaking of the bread.

THE SECOND CIRCLE

v. 16   "But their *eyes* were kept from *recognizing* him."
v. 31a "And their *eyes* were opened and they *recognized* him. . . ."

Léon-Dufour linked these two verses together for obvious reasons: in 24:16, "Their eyes are kept from recognizing him," and in 24:31a, "Their eyes are opened and they recognize him."[20]

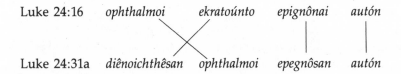

Luke 24:16   *ophthalmoi   ekratoúnto   epignônai   autón*

Luke 24:31a   *diênoichthêsan   ophthalmoi   epegnôsan   autón*

The language in these verses is almost the same and the chiasmus is remarkable, striking at the heart of the narrative itself and preparing us for the colloquium and the breaking of the bread. The purpose of this second circle in Luke's framework is to describe the condition of the disciples before and after the opening up of the Scriptures and their recognition of him in the breaking of the bread. The motif of minds closed to the kerygma of a crucified and resurrected Jesus and the rejection of that kerygma has been woven throughout the Gospel, but here that motif is reintroduced and overcome by the motif of openness to God's plan of salvation and recognition of the risen Christ.[21]

Luke uses the metaphor of closed and opened eyes for this condition in both 24:16 and 31a. In the Gospel, "the eyes" may describe the understanding or misunderstanding of God's revelation

[20]Léon-Dufour, *Resurrection*, 162.
[21]Cf. Dillon, *From Eyewitnesses*, 146–147 on a foreshadowing of Luke 24:16 in Luke 9:45, supporting the close relationship between these chapters.

64

in Jesus. In *Luke 2:30*, Simeon takes the infant Jesus in his arms, blesses God by saying that he may now depart in peace "for mine eyes have seen thy salvation." Luke connects the eyes here to the understanding of Simeon that the infant Jesus embodies God's salvation. In *Luke 4:20*, all the eyes of the synagogue were on Jesus after he read from Isaiah, a programmatic text for the theme of Jesus' rejection by his own people. The eyes that are fixed on him in Nazareth are so closed to his messianic character and the eschatological salvation he brings that they are driven to attempt to throw him headlong over a cliff.

In *Luke 6:39-42*, Jesus tells a parable he introduces with the phrase: "Can a blind man lead a blind man?" (Luke uses *ophthalmós* six times in these four verses.) If the disciples are to lead the world to see that God's kingdom is present in Jesus, they first must be those who can *see*. Until the Emmaus story, it appears as if everyone in Luke is blind to the words of the teacher Jesus. Jesus says in 6:40: "A disciple is not above his teacher, but every one when he is fully taught will be like his teacher." In the Emmaus narrative, the risen Christ now teaches the disciples, by means of the Scriptures, concerning the truth of the kerygma of his suffering, death, and resurrection.

In *Luke 10:23*, Jesus says: "Blessed are the eyes which see what you see!" (Luke differs from Matthew here, emphasizing "seeing" by repeating twice, "see what you see"; whereas Matthew balances the seeing with hearing: "Blessed are your ears, for they hear." Matthew does, however, precede this with a quotation from Isaiah that includes the statement, "and their eyes they have closed, lest they should perceive with their eyes.") Luke's context is that of Jesus sending out the seventy and rejoicing in the Holy Spirit that the Father has hidden (*apékrupsas*) "eschatological secrets"[22] from the "wise and understanding and revealed them to babes." The disciples are the eyewitnesses to these things, a vision of the eschatological kingdom that many prophets and kings before them had desired to see and hear but were not able.[23] Luke 10:23 anticipates the opening of the eyes of the dis-

[22]Cf. Fitzmyer, *X-XXIV*, 868–869.

[23]Luke 10:21 begins with a familiar time-framework, *en autê tê hôra*, used in 24:33 when the eyes of the disciples are opened and they see the eschatologi-

ciples by the risen Lord in Luke 24:31a after Luke's heightening of the hiddenness of the kingdom in 24:16.

In *Luke 11:34,* another reference to eyes is located within the context of an eschatological saying about light: "Your eye is the lamp of your body. . . ." Luke works with the classic eschatological antinomy of light and dark. Jesus is pictured as the one who brings light to a generation that is seeking signs. The eye is the means by which a person is illuminated into seeing that the new age has come in Jesus Christ.[24] Luke uses the eyes as the means of illumination in Luke 24. The enlightened disciples of Luke 24 will walk in the light in Acts. Acts ends with a reference to the closed eyes of the Jews (28:26-27).

In *Luke 18:35-42,* he opens the eyes of a blind man immediately before he dines with Zacchaeus in Jericho.

In *Luke 19:42,* Jesus speaks to Jerusalem and says: "Would that even today you knew the things that make for peace! But now they are hid from your eyes." Luke 19:41-42 is proleptic of the theme of closed and opened eyes in 24:16 and 31b.

This Lukan motif of closed and open eyes refers, not to physical vision, but to an eschatological understanding of the work of Jesus.[25] This motif of opened eyes stretches back beyond the Lukan writings to the very beginning of salvation history in Genesis chapter 3. The phrase used in Luke 24:31 for "their eyes were opened" is the same phrase used in the LXX in Genesis 3:7 (*autôn diênoíchthêsan oi ophthalmoí*) where the eyes of Adam and Eve are opened to the knowledge of good and evil and they recognize their nakedness. There is a striking parallel here. The open eyes of Adam and Eve are the first expression of the fallen creation that now sees the image of God clouded by disobedience; the open eyes of the Emmaus disciples are the first expression of the new

---

cal kingdom in its fullness because the risen Lord has revealed it to them. Cf. Ellis, *The Gospel of Luke,* 158 on this time reference in 10:21: "*hour:* like 'season' or 'today,' a technical eschatological expression and not a chronological yardstick. It is the 'hour' of 'these things,' i.e., of the manifestation of the power of the new age (10:17,19)" (emphasis Ellis).

[24]Ibid., 167.

[25]Cf. W. Michaelis, *ophthalmós,* TDNT V 378; Tannehill, *Narrative Unity,* 281–282.

creation that now sees the image restored in the new Adam, the crucified and risen Christ.[26] This is a clear link between the old and new creations, establishing the Emmaus meal as an eschatological event. The meal of broken bread at Emmaus reverses the first meal of the fruit of the tree of the knowledge of good and evil. By partaking of the meal of the risen Christ, the eyes of all creation are now open to see in Jesus the seed of the woman promised in Genesis 3:15. The table at which they now sit is the messianic table. Just as Adam and Eve's eating of the forbidden fruit was the first meal of the fallen creation, so this meal at Emmaus is the first meal of the new creation on the first day of the week.[27]

The two words used to contrast the condition of the eyes "to be kept" (ekratoúnto) in 24:16 and "to be opened" (diênoíchthêsan) in 24:31a, are theological passives that imply that God is the agent of the closing and opening of their eyes.[28] "To be kept" (kratéô) is rare in Luke,[29] and in 24:16 it means that the disciples' eyes were prevented from recognizing Jesus,[30] the exact opposite of the expression in 24:31a. This meaning fits with the messianic-passion secret of Luke where the divine plan of salvation is either hidden from the disciples or they do not understand it. The incomprehensibility of God's secret ways and the overpowering sense of joy when they are seen is underlined by the contrast of closed and open eyes. "To be opened" (dianoígô) is also rare in Luke. Except for 2:23, it is found only in Luke 24 where it refers to the opening of the eyes in 24:31a,[31] the opening of Scriptures in 24:32, and the

[26]See Neyrey, *The Passion*, 165–184 on Luke's Adam typology.

[27]Cf. also Robinson, "The Place of the Emmaus Story," 484–485 who, along with M. D. Goulder [*The Evangelist's Calendar* (London: S.P.C.K., 1978)], argues that there are other passages from Genesis that are associated with the holding of the eyes (e.g. Gen 18-22).

[28]Cf. Fitzmyer, *X-XXIV*, 1563 and 1568; Wanke, *Die Emmauserzählung*, 35; Guillaume, *Luc interprète*, 77–79; Tannehill, *Narrative Unity*, 282; Dillon, *From Eyewitnesses*, 104–105.

[29]It occurs only here and in 8:54, and in Acts 2:24; 3:11; 24:6; 27:13. In every case it means to hold or seize, with the exception of Acts 27:13 where it means obtaining one's purpose and here in 24:16 where it refers to the eyes.

[30]W. Michaelis, *kratéô, TDNT* III 911.

[31]It occurs three times in Acts: in 7:56 Stephen describes the opening of the heavens; in 16:14 Lydia's heart opens to the words of Paul; and in 17:3 the

opening of the mind to understand the Scriptures in 24:45. In all three instances the meaning is essentially the same.

The final parallel to be considered between these two verses is the use of the same word for recognition: *epiginôskô*.[32] There may be a significant parallel here with Luke 1:4. The fact that Luke chooses *epiginôskô* instead of *ginôskô* in the prologue suggests a special meaning of this word.[33] Luke wants Theophilus to know the certainty of the things about which he has been informed (a reference to the sacred events?). This is hidden from the eyes of the Emmaus disciples until 24:31, when a similar certainty is imparted to them when they recognize Jesus. The entire pericope is framed by this "knowledge," and perhaps, we may say, the entire Gospel too. If so, then both Theophilus and the Church will know the truth concerning the things that have been taught in the breaking of the bread.

Scriptures are opened by Paul in Thessalonica. In all three instances, there is a precedent in Luke 24.

[32]R. Bultmann, *gínôskô ktl.*, *TDNT* I 703 says it "is often used instead of *ginôskô* with no difference in meaning." Cf. J. H. Moulton and G. Milligan, *The Vocabulary of the Greek Testament* (London: Hodder and Stoughton, 1930) 236 on Dean Robinson's conclusion that in the papyri: ". . . the verb *epiginôskô* denotes not so much fuller or more perfect knowing, as knowing arrived at by the attention being directed to (*epí*) a particular person or object . . ."

[33]Cf. Fitzmyer, *I-IX*, 300 who claims the literal translation of *epiginôskô* is "may come to know," and notes that "the verb *epiginôskô* in Lucan usage means either 'to recognize' an object or fact, or 'to learn' or 'acquire knowledge' (see Acts 19:34; 22:24; 23:28; 24:8,11). Being a compound verb in *epí-*, it may imply the acquiring of profound knowledge. If so, it would stand in contrast to the rest of the verse."

Chapter 6

The Center Circle—The Dialogue Setting

The center circle of the meal at Emmaus, Luke 24:17-30, describes the two fundamental motifs that make up the table fellowship matrix of Jesus: the colloquium and the breaking of the bread. The next seven chapters focus on the center circle of the Emmaus meal to show the climactic nature of the words of Jesus and the meal of Jesus within Luke's table fellowship matrix.

To repeat, Luke divides the center circle into two very distinct sections: the colloquium and the breaking of the bread.[1] I will adopt this simple division, but also will consider how Luke prepares the reader to interpret this circle narrative by carefully describing its setting. I will divide and analyze this setting according to three subsections: the narrative as dialogue, the dialogue participants, and the dialogue content.

THE NARRATIVE AS DIALOGUE

After the introduction of Jesus into the Emmaus narrative in 24:15-16, while the eyes of the disciples are closed, the transition to the center circle occurs as the participants engage in a lively dialogue. Within the next three verses (24:17-19), the conversation goes back and forth at rapid pace. After the initial flurry of conversation, the dialogue settles down into two main statements: that of the disciples in 24:19-24 (introduced by "and they said to him" in v. 19) and that of Jesus in 24:25-27 (introduced by "and he said to them" in v. 25). But before Luke launches into the con-

---

[1]Cf. E. A. LaVerdière, *Luke* (Wilmington: Michael Glazier, 1980) 285: "The body includes two distinct subunits, a dialogue narrative, which is situated on the way to Emmaus (24:17-27) and a meal narrative, which is located at Emmaus itself in the home of the disciples (24:28-30). These two units reflect the general structure of the early Christian assembly for the breaking of the bread, which included both a discussion and a meal (Acts 20:7-12)."

tent of the colloquium, he first establishes, by the shape of his narrative, that this *is a dialogue* between the Emmaus disciples and Jesus.

The establishment of this narrative as a dialogue is important for a number of reasons.[2] First, the words of Jesus to the Emmaus disciples form one of the two major sections of this narrative and link the center circle with the outer circles of the Emmaus narrative. Luke skillfully accomplishes this link by means of the question that Jesus asks the disciples in 24:17: "What is this conversation (*oi lógoi hoútoi*) which you are holding with each other as you walk?" The link within the framework of the narrative is accomplished by the words "with each other" (*pros allêlous*). In both 24:14 and 32, where Luke also uses this phrase, the character of the narrative is that of dialogue concerning the passion facts. As I observed earlier, there is a progression in the Lukan framework from complete blindness toward complete openness.

Second, although the Emmaus narrative does not fit all the criteria of a "controversy dialogue," there are some similarities. The passion facts create a problem for the Emmaus disciples concerning Jesus. According to R. Bultmann, "the *starting-point* of a controversy dialogue lies in some action or attitude which is seized on by the opponent and used in an attack by accusation or by question."[3] In the Emmaus story, Jesus is the opponent of the two disciples because he closes the eyes of the disciples and seizes on the passion facts as a means of questioning the disciples about their Christology. Bultmann also states that "the *reply* to the attack follows more or less a set form, with special preference for the counter-question or the metaphor, or even both together. Nevertheless—like the attack—it can also consist of the scripture quotation."[4] In the Emmaus dialogue, the two disciples respond to Jesus by presenting two different Christologies, both of which

[2] Cf. Léon-Dufour, *Sharing the Eucharistic Bread*, 362 n. 22 on the Last Supper as dialogical: "By 'dialogical' I do not mean that there is an exchange of words but rather that the situation is a *relational one*: here Jesus is in a reciprocal relation with his disciples" (emphasis mine).

[3] Bultmann, *History of the Synoptic Tradition* (New York: Harper, 1963) 39 (emphasis Bultmann).

[4] Ibid., 41 (emphasis Bultmann).

they do not understand. Their response is in the form of a confession and a lament. Jesus replies to them with Scriptural proof, and the controversy is resolved with the breaking of the bread. This dialogue at Emmaus is not a traditional controversy dialogue, but it is a dialogue that has as its center a Christological conflict over the interpretation of the death of Jesus.[5] As I will observe, controversy at meals is a Lukan motif.[6]

Third, the Emmaus narrative as dialogue reflects the genre of the Last Supper which is also dialogical. E. A. LaVerdière suggests that this dialogue narrative may reflect early Christian liturgies. The dialogical character of the Emmaus narrative establishes the structural components of word and meal in the liturgy used in the early Christian communities, showing the eschatological nature of the colloquium and the meal of Emmaus in Luke's table fellowship matrix.[7]

Fourth, the Emmaus dialogue may anticipate the story of Philip and the Ethiopian eunuch in Acts 8:26-39. The similarities between these two passages have been observed by many.[8]

---

[5]Ibid., 41. Bultmann also indicates that these controversy dialogues are "typically rabbinic," which suggests that the issue is one of interpretation. Cf. also Benoit, *Passion and Resurrection*, 277–278; Betz, "The Origin and Nature of Christian Faith," 40.

[6]See chapters IX. and X. on "Lukan Meals and Meal Metaphors."

[7]LaVerdière, *Luke*, 285 suggests that Jesus' "role in the introductory dialogue is simply to draw out the disciples." This may be too simple a conclusion. The dialogue form is employed by Luke to accomplish more than this.

[8]Cf. Dillon, *From Eyewitnesses*, 112 who suggests that this parallel "is meant to press a point of continuity between the Easter *wayfarers'* experience and the exposure of the nascent Gentile churches to the comings and goings of wayfaring missionaries. Philip, like the risen Lord, comes on the scene as a stranger. His questions lead to a travelers' dialogue, and the dialogue builds to his *christological exposition of the scriptures*, with focus on the mystery of the *messiah's passion* (Acts 8:32ff.; cp. Is 53:7-8 LXX). A sacramental action, baptism, and the strange expositor's disappearance conclude the scene, just as the sacramental repast and the Lord's disappearance close the Emmaus episode" (emphasis Dillon). See also Losada, "El episodio de Emaús: Lc 24, 13-35," 11f.; J. Dupont, "Les pèlerins d'Emmaüs (Luc xxiv, 13-35)," *Miscellanea biblica Bonaventura Ubach* (Scripta et documenta 1; Montserrat, 1953) 349–374; J. A. Grassi, "Emmaus revisited (Lc 24, 13-15 and Acts 8, 26-40)," *CBQ* 26 (1964) 463–467; Robinson, "The Place of the Emmaus Story," 483–484; Wanke, *Die Emmauserzählung*, 122; Guillaume, *Luc interprète*, 80–81, 131–132.

Once the significance of the narrative as dialogue has been established, the next step is to look at the dialogue participants. This raises the difficult question as to the identity of Cleopas. Many scholars have been more interested in determining the identity of the other disciple.[9] But the real interest should not be focused on the other disciple, for there is no convincing argument that specifically identifies him.[10] For some reason, Luke has chosen to include Cleopas in his story. Is this just a part of Luke's narrative drapery, or does it contribute to his theological intent?

There are essentially two opinions concerning the identity of Cleopas. One connects Cleopas with Alphaeus, making him the husband of Mary the mother of James and Joses. The support for this position from both modern and ancient commentators is sketchy.[11] The more prevalent position is that Cleopas is the uncle

[9]Cf. Fitzmyer, *X-XXIV*, 1563–1564 who discusses the other disciple more than Cleopas. He makes a brief comment about the possibility that *Klôpas* may be "the name of the husband or father of Mary who stands at the cross of Jesus in John 19:25," but Fitzmyer dismisses this and discusses the literature that argues for the identity of the other disciple as Peter. He then raises the question: "For Luke the companion is unnamed; and this raises the question why he names Cleopas at all. There is no need for it; and so the best explanation is that it was already part of the pre-Lucan tradition." Fitzmyer's question needs to be extended and addressed more fully. Why is Cleopas part of the the pre-Lukan tradition and why has Luke chosen to keep him in his narrative? In addition to Fitzmyer's bibliography, cf. also N. Huffman, "Emmaus among the Resurrection Narratives," *JBL* 64 (1945) 221–226 on the arguments surrounding the identity of Cleopas' companion as Peter.

[10]However, there have been some fascinating suggestions. Peter is the most common choice on the basis of 24:34, but some have suggested that "Emmaus" was not a town but the other disciple (cf. Fitzmyer for the literature on this). Marshall, *The Gospel of Luke*, 894 cites other suggestions such as the wife of Cleopas or his son (Metzger, *A Textual Commentary*, 185; K. Bornhäuser, *The Death and Resurrection of Jesus Christ* [Bangalore, 1958] 221f.), and Philip the deacon (Benoit, *Passion and Resurrection*, 275). Still others suggest James the brother of Jesus (E. Schweizer, *The Good News According to Luke* [Atlanta: John Knox Press, 1984] 370), Nathanial or Luke (E. Klosterman, *Lukas* [*Handbuch zum Neuen Testament*, ed. Lietzmann], 12 auflage [Tübingen, 1929] 234). Origen suggests that the second person was Simeon, the son of Cleopas, who became the second bishop of Jerusalem.

[11]Cf. H. H. Platz, "Cleopas," "Clopas," *IDB* I 649–650 who suggests that "Cleopas is sometimes identified with Clopas." Concerning Clopas, Platz

of Jesus, the brother of Joseph, Jesus' foster-father. This was first proposed by Hegesippus and cited by Eusebius.[12] There are two reasons why such an identification may be important. First, if Cleopas is the uncle of Jesus, then his son is Simeon, the second bishop of Jerusalem, the leader of the Church of Jerusalem after A.D. 70. Such a man may have been easily recognizable to Luke's readers and a prominent figure in Church politics at the time when Luke's Gospel was beginning to circulate. This would have lent authority to the Emmaus narrative and been a source of continuity between the meals of the Church and the meal of Jesus at Emmaus, i.e. the father of the bishop of Jerusalem ate with Jesus on the road to Emmaus and now his son eats the meal of Jesus with the Church.[13] Second, if Cleopas is part of the family of Jesus, then the Emmaus narrative may have been handed down as part of Jesus' family history.[14] The existence of a family tradition is

---

writes: "The connection with Alphaeus can be established only if MARY the wife of Clopas is the same person as Mary the mother of James and Joses (Mark 15:40 = Matt. 27:56; cf. Luke 23:49; 24:10), and if the James mentioned here is the same as JAMES (2) son of Alphaeus (Mark 3:18 = Matt 10:3 = Luke 6:15; Acts 1:13). Mary the wife of Clopas may thus be recognized as the wife of Alphaeus, and it is possible to suppose that Alphaeus and Clopas are the same person."

[12]Eusebius, *Hist. Eccl.* iii, 32. Cf. McHugh, *The Mother of Jesus*, 212–216, 244–245 who discusses Hegesippus as cited by Eusebius with respect to the relationship within Jesus' family between Clopas and Joseph and their sons. McHugh's conclusions as to the relationships in Jesus' family are significant, particularly his emphasis from Hegesippus that Cleopas was the father of Simeon, the second bishop of Jerusalem. McHugh gives two translations of Hegesippus which I conflate into one: "After the martyrdom of James the Just (*nephew of Joseph and of Clopas*) on the same charge as the Lord, his [*i.e. Jesus'*] uncle's child Simeon, the son of Clopas is next made bishop. He was put forward by everyone, he being yet another cousin of the Lord" (emphasis McHugh).

[13]There are some who suggest that Cleopas's companion on the road to Emmaus was his son Simeon, since Origen in *Contra Cels.* ii. 62, 68 gives the name of Simon to this companion. Cf. Creed, *The Gospel According to St. Luke*, 295: "Zahn connects the tradition (Orig. *C. Cels.* ii. 62, 68) that Cleopas's unnamed companion was Simon with the statement in Eus. *H. E.* iii. II that the apostles appointed *Simeon, the son of Clopas*, cousin to the Lord, to succeed James as Bishop of Jerusalem" (emphasis mine).

[14]Cf. Ellis, *The Gospel of Luke*, 276: "If Eusebius is correct, the Emmaus story was originally a tradition of Jesus' family. Cf. Ac. I.14." At the very least, the

suggested more by Luke than any of the other Gospels, since Luke himself states in the prologue (1:2) that he consulted with eyewitnesses (*autóptai*). Ellis' cross reference to Acts 1:14 is helpful insofar as it indicates that Luke includes Jesus' family within the apostolic community before Pentecost.[15]

There are a number of reasons why the Emmaus story, as the climax of Luke's table fellowship matrix, could be considered a part of the family tradition. First, it would heighten the drama surrounding the closed eyes of the disciples. If Jesus' uncle did not recognize him, then there must be a good theological reason why their eyes were prevented from seeing him. This would help explain why Luke includes the strange statement in 24:17 that "they stood still, looking sad." H. Conzelmann observes in Luke's Gospel a polemic against the relatives of Jesus, first introduced in 4:16-30 and continued in 8:19-21.[16] This is contrasted to those who are called to discipleship, particularly the disciples gathered around Peter and the sons of Zebedee. The relatives are spoken against because they want to "see" Jesus (8:20), a reference to their desire to see the miracles of Jesus. Jesus' response is to say that "My mother and my brothers are those who hear the word of God and do it" (8:21). The contrast here is between seeing miracles and hearing (believing) the word. Conzelmann states concerning 8:19-21: "The very position of the scene indicates that the relatives are excluded from playing any essential part in the life of Jesus and therefore the life of the Church."[17] Jesus' rela-

---

Emmaus story should be considered part of the Jerusalem tradition. Cf. B. Reicke, *The Roots of the Synoptic Gospels* (Philadelphia: Fortress Press, 1986) 49–52 who, although making no mention of Emmaus story as part of the Jerusalem tradition, presents a strong case for the existence of this tradition. In reference to Luke 1:2, he writes: "By this reference to the beginning of Christian preaching and teaching, Luke meant the Jerusalem church."

[15]Acts 1:14: "All these with one accord devoted themselves to prayer, together with the women and Mary the mother of Jesus, and with his brothers."

[16]Conzelmann, *The Theology of St. Luke*, 42–43, 47–48.

[17]Ibid., 48. See chapter IX where I refer to G. Feeley-Harnik, *The Lord's Table: Eucharist and Passover in Early Christianity* (Philadelphia: University of Pennsylvania Press, 1981) 40–54, and J. Jeremias, *Jerusalem in the Time of Jesus* (Philadelphia: Fortress Press, 1969) 269–380 in "Part Four: The Maintenance of Racial Purity" on the kinship laws in the New Testament era.

tives do, in fact, take a very prominent role in the Church in Acts. Perhaps Conzelmann's observation lends weight to the argument that the Emmaus narrative is a family tradition. Luke may be using Emmaus as a way of restoring Jesus' relatives to the fellowship of the Church. If "to see miracles" is what causes them to fall out of fellowship, then the motif in the Emmaus story of closed and opened eyes would serve Luke's purpose of illustrating how even Jesus' relatives, who rejected him because he did not work miracles in their hometown (4:23), are capable of being restored by having their eyes opened to the word of Jesus as he opens to them the Scriptures and reveals himself in the breaking of the bread (24:35). Thus, Jesus' relatives become the paradigm for the effects of Jesus' words on those who only wanted to see miracles. Now, the real miracle is to see him in the breaking of the bread.

Second, it would tie together more closely Acts 1-2 and Luke 24. The breaking of the bread is important to the first chapters of Acts since the first post-resurrection meal at Emmaus included the family of Jesus which is a part of the apostolic community before and after Pentecost.

Third, it explains one of the reasons why Christian meals were readily accepted as the focal point of early Christian liturgies, since James, the brother of Jesus, and Simeon, the cousin of Jesus, were the first two bishops of Jerusalem. A continuation of the table fellowship of Jesus in the Church would have had both ecclesiastical and familial overtones for these leaders of the Church. If the early Christian community viewed Emmaus as an eschatological meal, then the continuation of that table fellowship in the Church, encouraged and led by the family of Jesus, would have also been viewed eschatologically. Thus the identity of Cleopas as part of the family of Jesus could have possible ecclesiastical and liturgical overtones.

The other participant in the Emmaus dialogue is Jesus, who was introduced in 24:15. His identification by Cleopas in this dialogue setting sets the tone for the entire Emmaus dialogue. Cleopas asks Jesus if he is the only stranger in Jerusalem who does not know the things that have happened there in these days. To live as a (resident) *alien* (*pároikos*) has possible theological overtones within

Luke's table fellowship matrix. The verbal form—*paroikéô*—and its derivatives occur only eight times in the New Testament, once in the Gospels (Luke 24:18). In Acts *paroikéô* occurs three times within the context of the Old Testament where it is used primarily of Israel, especially with regard to its sojourn in Egypt.[18] The Israelites' status as aliens in Egypt was part of the redemptive story. But there were also individuals like Moses and Abraham who were accorded this status. In Acts, Luke taps into this rich history, where "alien" or "exile" (*pároikos*) occurs twice within Stephen's speech in 7:6, in reference to Abraham,[19] and in 7:29, in reference to Moses; and in 13:17, in Paul's sermon to the Jews in Antioch of Pisidia where it is a reference to Israel.

Other New Testament references take on a new significance, for the term now applies to the Christian and to the Church. In Ephesians 2:19, Christians are "no longer strangers and sojourners, but fellow citizens with the saints and members of the household of God." In 1 Peter 1:17, the Christian's sojourn in the world is described as a time of exile, and in 2:11, Christians are called aliens and exiles. In Hebrews 11:9, Abraham is said to have sojourned in the land of promise by faith. Although it appears as if both the Church and the Christian are being described as aliens and fellow citizens, this is not contradictory, for in the New Testament the Church has an alien status with regard to the world but a holy status with regard to God. Christians have two countries of

[18]Cf. K. L. and M. A. Schmidt, *pároikos, TDNT* Abridged, 789: "Israel views its alien residence in Egypt not just as a historical fact but also as an occasion for theological reflection. In God's sight all peoples are resident aliens (cf. Is. 19). This does not cancel out possession of the land but it is a reminder that there must be humility before God."

[19]Cf. Genesis 15:13 where God says to Abraham: "Know of a surety that your descendents will be sojourners (LXX - *pároikon*) in a land that is not theirs, and will be slaves there, and they will be oppressed for four hundred years." This is a "promise" to Abraham that his descendents will be aliens in the land for generations and generations. Cf. K. L. and M. A. Schmidt, *pároikos ktl., TDNT* V 846: "[the] patriarch as resident alien is a *túpos* in whom the people of Israel sees its own true nature reflected." Cf. Heb 11:8ff. where Abraham serves as the example of alien status which is now transferred and confirmed in the New Testament community.

residency: the world, where they are strangers, and the household of God, where they are citizens.[20]

Thus the New Testament references have an eschatological focus since they recognize both a temporal status in the world and an eschatological existence as citizens of a heavenly place. The Old Testament references are also eschatological since they too refer to a promised land and a future deliverance. The Passover, as the major cultic meal among the Israelites, celebrated the tension of Israel's alien/citizen status, represented by their deliverance from Egypt and the expectation of full release from worldly bondage. Although no longer aliens in Egypt, they were constantly struggling with their status in the "promised land."[21]

Of the eight occurrences of *paroikéô* and its derivatives in the New Testament, Luke 24:18 and the reference to Christ as the stranger in Jerusalem is the only place where *paroikéô* refers to Christ. This is often dismissed as having no theological significance, unrelated to the other uses of the word in the New Testament.[22] From the perspective of the Emmaus disciples, Jesus is perceived as a Passover pilgrim who somehow avoided any news of the crucifixion. But does Luke have a cryptic allusion in his reference to Jesus as a stranger in Jerusalem?

As the Son of the Most High (1:32), Jesus is the *true* alien and Cleopas' question of him is, in some ways, a confession of his true identity. A major theme of the Emmaus story is that Jesus,

[20]Cf. K. L. and M. A. Schmidt, *TDNT* Abridged, 790: "Like ancient Israel, the saints were strangers and sojourners but are now fellow citizens (Eph 2:19) . . . . Proleptically Christians are *already* fellow citizens even while they are *still* resident aliens, but only because *one day* they will be citizens even in the full sense. A term of honor, *paroikía* lays on them the responsibility of befitting conduct (1 Pet 2:5ff.)" (emphasis Schmidt).

[21]Cf. R. C. D. Jasper and G. J. Cuming, *Prayers of the Eucharist: Early and Reformed* (New York: Oxford University Press, 1980) 10 for the eschatological direction of the embolism for Passover in the *Birkath Hammazon*. Compare this to the prayer of *Didache* 10, a Christian reformulation of the *Birkath Hammazon*. The heightened eschatological flavor of this prayer has shifted the focus of the *Birkath Hammazon* from Jerusalem to the Church. Many believe that the *Birkath Hammazon* is a source for early Christian Eucharistic prayers (cf. Jasper and Cuming, 9).

[22]Cf. K. L. and M. A. Schmidt, *TDNT* Abridged, 790 on Luke 24:18 and *paroikéô*; and *TDNT* V 853: "*paroikeín* might simply mean 'to live.' "

the visitor in Jerusalem, is really no stranger at all. He comes from a far country to secure for himself a kingdom (cf. 19:12), to bring Israel home, identifying himself with his people (cf. 2:32) and fulfilling Israel's ancient hopes. The context of Luke 24, with its emphasis on the death and resurrection of Jesus in fulfillment of the Scriptures, is Luke's climax to Jesus' identification with Israel. If the people of Israel are strangers, then Jesus, as Son of Man, embraces in his very person the same tension that Israel experienced and Luke's church now experiences. As Son of God and Son of Man, he is both stranger in the world and redeemer of the world. Crucial for Luke's Gospel is the manner in which he receives the world and the way in which the world receives him.

In so many table scenes,[23] Jesus shows the hospitality of God to the rejected of the world. He is known for eating with sinners and publicans, the disenfranchised of life. The redemption of the world through Jesus Christ and his divinely ordained suffering and death show God's hospitable attitude towards his creation. Jesus, as the one who comes from afar, opens up the Scriptures to show the disciples the divine hospitality which would come to full expression in the messianic kingdom. What is at stake for the disciples and all Israel is the manner in which they will receive this stranger, i.e. will they receive him with the same open hospitality as Jesus showed to strangers during his earthly life or will they receive him with hostility and rejection?[24] The two disciples become

[23]Cf. D. R. Dumm, "Luke 24:44-49 and Hospitality" in Sin, Salvation, and the Spirit, ed. D. Durken (Collegeville: The Liturgical Press, 1979) 231-239 whose insights concerning this theme in Luke were instrumental in the formulation of this argument. Cf. also J. Koenig, New Testament Hospitality (Philadelphia: Fortress Press, 1985), particularly his chapter on Luke entitled "Guests and Hosts, Together in Mission (Luke)" 85-123. Robinson, "The Place of the Emmaus Story," 485-487 describes Luke's hospitality motif in his Gospel and in the Emmaus story. Robinson also points us to the chapter entitled "Some Secular Interests" in H. J. Cadbury, The Making of Luke-Acts (London: SPCK, 1958) 239-253 which documents "Luke's fondness for descriptions of entertainment and hospitality."

[24]Cf. Dumm, "Luke 24:44-49 and Hospitality," 236: "At Emmaus, it was only after the disciples had offered hospitality to the stranger that he was revealed to them (Luke 24:29-31) . . . The ultimate hospitality is, then, an entertainment of divine mystery in human life. Table hospitality is but a sign and sacrament of this" (emphasis Dumm).

foundational for the new Israel in their acceptance of what is in fact a divine invitation to banquet eschatologically with the Son of God. The historical narrative takes on parabolic proportions. The common ground where the Divine meets humankind and humankind meets the Divine will be at the table, for it is in this fellowship that God offers his hospitality and his forgiveness in the presence of Jesus in bread and wine. Humankind has the opportunity to reciprocate that hospitality by receiving in this meal the "divine mystery" of God's redemptive action in Jesus Christ. This hospitality at the fellowship of the table is therefore eschatological, a sign pointing to and participating in the ultimate table fellowship at the messianic banquet where God's hospitality reaches its final fulfillment.[25]

Luke uses the dialogue participants in the Emmaus colloquium to focus on table fellowship. Cleopas, if indeed he is the uncle of Jesus, does not recognize a member of his own family, but considers him a stranger to Jerusalem and to the passion facts. Luke's identification of Jesus as the alien sets up the theme of hospitality in which Cleopas and the other disciple demonstrate their willingness to have the Scriptures opened by showing hospitality to Jesus. In turn Jesus will show God's hospitality by revealing his true identity in the breaking of the bread. The theme of hospitality blends directly into the themes of recognition and table fellowship, both of which come to a climax when Jesus breaks bread.[26] This sets the stage for interpreting the entire Emmaus story eschatologically because Luke introduces the participants of the dialogue into an eschatological context.

---

[25]Ibid., 238: "Man's best hospitality, however, is only a meager preparation for the lavish hospitality of God, first in the resurrection and Lordship of the Messiah, and finally in the heavenly banquet, where table-fellowship becomes a sign of definitive fulfillment and ultimate freedom."

[26]H. Flender, *St Luke: Theologian of Redemptive History* (Philadelphia: Fortress Press, 1967) 80–81 unites the hospitality and journey motifs of Luke: "Alongside the journey motif the hospitality accorded to Jesus is a characteristic of Luke. He treats the two motifs as parts of a single whole. In Jesus 'God himself visits the people, hidden in the guise of the wanderer refreshing himself as a guest in their home.' In the Emmaus story (Luke 24.13-35) this twofold motif of wanderer and guest comes out clearly."

In the setting of the dialogue, Luke also directs our attention towards its content. The actual content is the subject of 24:19-27, but Luke leaves no doubt as to its essence in the dialogue setting. His introduction of the content is subtle, coming from the question of Jesus and the response of Cleopas. It fits cleanly into the dialogue genre and maintains the integrity of the narrative.

An indication of the dialogue content comes from the first words spoken by the risen Christ in Luke: "What is this conversation which you are holding with each other as you walk?" The content of the conversation of the Emmaus disciples before Jesus met them was the passion facts. Now with his first words, Jesus enters into the disciples' conversation concerning the recent events in Jerusalem. Jesus seems to refer to the passion facts with his question of them.

Is Luke suggesting by the phrase "what is this conversation" (*oi lógoi hoútoi*) that a *word motif* is being introduced into the narrative? Such a suggestion would accommodate the theory that an essential part of table fellowship is an exposition of the Scriptures that entails a proper interpretation of the passion facts. This implies that Scripture and passion facts are presuppositional to table fellowship. Still another of Luke's themes is that these passion facts are in fulfillment of the Scriptures (cf. Luke 24:27, 44-46). Does Luke anticipate these themes in his Gospel from beginning to end so that a distinct word motif concludes here in Luke 24 or does he introduce it here as a *novum*?

The prologue first states Luke's intentions, not Luke 24. It may imply a word motif, since Luke emphatically states that he is writing a narrative (*diêgêsis*) of the things that have been accomplished, that ministers of the word (*hupêretai . . . tou lógou*) delivered this to him, and that the purpose of his Gospel is certainty (*aspháleia*) concerning the words (*lógôn*) with which Luke's readers have been instructed. The nature of this narrative, the content of the message of the ministers of the word, and the words already used in catechesis (*katêchêthês*) seem to introduce a word motif to Luke's narrative. But this hypothesis is not possible without Luke 24, for the prologue's intentions are not realized until the risen Christ lays out for the apostles the kerygma of the emerging Church. In actuality, the prologue itself recapitulates the progression of Luke's word motif from the narration of the events of Jesus' life and ministry (*perí tôn . . . pragmátôn*),[27] to the creation of certainty concerning the words they have been taught (*perí hôn katêchêthês lógon*).[28] The prologue intimates a word motif in Luke-Acts that comes to fruition as a *preaching of the kerygma* in Luke 24. Luke refers to his Gospel in Acts 1:1 as the first word (*prôton lógon*), suggesting that the Gospel itself fits under the genre of "word."

A juxtaposition of "the words" of Jesus and the passion facts in Luke further suggest a word motif in his Gospel. The pivotal Luke 9 has three passages where this juxtaposition occurs. In 9:26, Jesus speaks of being ashamed of "my words," a reference back to the first passion prediction in 9:22; in 9:28, the transfiguration follows upon "these words" of Jesus, another reference to the first passion prediction in 9:22; and in 9:44, just before the second passion prediction, Jesus says: "Let these words sink into your ears; for the Son of man is to be delivered into the hands of men." Likewise in 24:44, Jesus refers back to these sayings of Luke 9 as "these my words."

Luke also uses the phrase "this saying" (*to hrêma toúto*) twice in 9:45 to indicate that the disciples did not understand the saying of Jesus and were afraid to ask him about it. The "saying" of 9:44 concerning the passion is highlighted by Luke through the misunderstanding and fear of the disciples. *hrêma* is also used by Luke after the third passion prediction in 18:34: ". . . this saying [concerning the passion of Jesus] was hid from them and they did not grasp what was said." In Luke 24, *hrêma* is used in verse 8 to refer back to the sayings in Galilee concerning the passion and resurrection, and in verse 11 concerning the report of the women about the kerygma expounded by the angels that the Eleven considered nonsense.

Thus, Jesus' simple question in 24:17 suggests that the content of the dialogue will be the kerygma of a crucified and risen Christ.

[27]Cf. Fitzmyer, *I-IX*, 292.

[28]Cf. Dillon, *From Eyewitnesses*, 270–272 for his conclusion concerning the purpose of Luke's prologue; Dunn, *Christology*, 231–232 on "the word" in Luke.

This is supported by the disciples' reaction to Jesus' question: "And they stood still, looking sad."[29] This kerygma is already being referred to by the early Christian communities as "the word."

A second indication of the dialogue content comes from Cleopas' response to Jesus' question: "Are you the only visitor to Jerusalem who does not know the things that have happened there in these days?" The focus of concern is on *ta genómena*, a reference to the sacred things that happened in Jerusalem, i.e. the passion and resurrection of Jesus. This same formula (the neuter *ta*) will be used throughout Luke 24 as a shorthand for the three-day sequence of passion, death, and resurrection (cf. 24:19: "the things concerning Jesus of Nazareth"—*ta perí Iêsoú tou Nazarênoú*; 24:27: "the things concerning himself"—*ta perí heautoú*; 24:35: "the things he taught on the road"—*ta en tê hodô*). The use of this formula also looks back to the prologue and confirms that the narration of the things that have been fulfilled among us must be the sacred facts that occurred in Jerusalem ("a narration of the things which have been accomplished among us"—*diêgêsin perí tôn peplêrophorêmenôn en hêmín pragmátôn.*—Note the use of *perí* and the neuter *pragmátôn*). Thus Cleopas' response, though misguided, affirms that the core of the dialogue will concern the kerygma of a dying and rising Messiah.

It is also possible to discern the goal of the dialogue within the context of the setting of the colloquium. Luke anticipates his conclusion in 24:35 by means of the word "to know" (*ginôskô*). Knowledge of the kerygma is set forth as the purpose of the Gospel in the prologue of Luke ("that you may know the truth concerning the things of which you have been informed"—*hína*

[29]Cf. Dillon, *From Eyewitnesses*, 113: ". . . We hear that the travelers stood still, *skuthrôpoí* ('with gloomy looks'); and rather than imagining the actual psychological state of the followers after Good Friday which might be authentically captured here, let us ask again, insistently: what does our author understand by it? Does he not intend to portray the travelers *still under the pall of the passion-mystery*? . . . All three descriptions [*skuthrôpoí* (24:17), *anóêtoi*, and *bradeís tê kardía* (v. 25)] belong to the motif of the disciples' bewilderment and incomprehension under the pall of the great *mysterium*" (emphasis Dillon). Cf. also Ehrhardt, "The Disciples of Emmaus," 186 who sees an Old Testament parallel to Job.

epignôs perí hôn katêchêthês lógôn tên aspháleian). The lack of knowledge or understanding is a problem continually confronted by the
disciples (Luke 18:34—"they did not grasp what was said"—*ouk
egínôskon ta legómena*; and Luke 24:18—"does not know the things
that have happened there in these days"—"*ouk égnôs ta genómena
en autê en taís hêmérais taútais*); and the inhabitants of Jerusalem
(Luke 19:42—"would that even today you knew the things that
make for peace"—*ei égnôs en tê hêméra tautê kai su ta pros eirênên*;
and Luke 19:44—"because you did not know the time of your
visitation"—*anth' hôn ouk égnôs ton kairón tês episkopês sou*); and the
true knowledge of the presence of the risen Christ in their midst
that comes to the Emmaus disciples through the breaking of the
bread (Luke 24:35—"and how he was known to them in the
breaking of the bread"—*hôs egnôsthê autoís en tê klasei tou ártou*).

Thus the setting of the dialogue, like the framework and outer
circles, already contains, by anticipation, the essence of what the
colloquium and breaking of the bread will reveal. Luke's continual
reiteration of his themes becomes a powerful literary device to
persuade the reader to accept his narrative as certain, the very aim
he set forth in the prologue.

Chapter 7

The Center Circle—
The Christology of the Emmaus Disciples

The colloquium on the road to Emmaus dominates the narrative by virtue of the amount of material that Luke allocates to this dialogue between Jesus and the disciples. Although Luke has already introduced all his themes into the Emmaus story in the outer circles (24:13-16), it is during the colloquium that he now enfleshes them.

The colloquium continues the genre of dialogue. It begins with Jesus asking "What things?" and the Emmaus disciples responding with their own interpretation of the events of Jesus' life. The dialogue juxtaposes three opposing Christologies. At stake in this colloquium is the correct perception of who Jesus is.[1] First, the Emmaus disciples give their Christology in 24:19, "the things concerning Jesus of Nazareth," (*ta perí Iēsoú tou Nazarēnoú*), and then in 24:20 they give their understanding of the Christology of the religious leaders in Jerusalem. The climax of the colloquium comes in 24:25-27 when Jesus presents his Christology, "the things concerning himself," (*ta perí heautoú*), based on the evidence of the Old Testament Scriptures. Luke's presentation of these three competing Christologies is the perfect format for him to encapsulate the previous twenty-three chapters that are dedicated to the portrayal of the life and teaching of Jesus of Nazareth. Every major group in the Gospel is represented here, and the definitive word concerning the proper Christology is given by the risen Lord by means of an exegetical lesson on Old Testament messianic prophecy.

The goal of the colloquium, however, is not simply a rhetorical debate over the proper interpretation of prophecy and the events

[1]Cf. Betz, "The Origin and Nature of Christian Faith," 39 about Emmaus: "The problems reflected in the story are primarily christological."

of Jesus' life, death, and resurrection. Rather, Luke takes the reader from the level of historical data to a faith engendered by Jesus' interpretation of these events against the backdrop of the Old Testament. Therefore, the goal is faith—faith to believe all that the prophets had spoken about the suffering of the Christ which precedes his entrance into glory. Thus for Luke, faith in the proper Christology is the goal of this dialogue, setting the pattern for all Christian dialogue within the worshipping assembly.[2] The colloquium is Christological and functions within the table fellowship matrix as *preparation for the meal*.

The entire colloquium is dominated by the question of the risen Christ: "What things?" (*poía*). As the colloquium begins in earnest, the things of the passion are clearly the issue (Luke's use of the neuter to refer to the passion events). The colloquium is framed by the question of Jesus in 24:19, and his interpretation of the Old Testament of the things concerning himself in 24:27. By having Jesus begin and end the colloquium, Luke demonstrates that Jesus' Christology is the norm for Luke's Gospel and the norm for the Church. It also highlights the change that takes place in Jesus' position within the colloquium. Jesus begins the dialogue as the questioner and, reversing the roles, ends up as the teacher.[3] This is Luke's clear intention, for in the section on the breaking of the bread, Jesus begins the meal as the guest and ends as the host at the table.[4] Thus Jesus dominates the whole pericope by his words and deeds.

[2]Ibid., 38–39.

[3]Cf. Dillon, *From Eyewitnesses*, 111: ". . . the Stranger's questions build pathos and anticipation towards the point where he himself, the questioner, will become the teacher uttering the final answer (v. 25: *kai autós eípen pros autoús*)." Here is one of Luke's important emphases in his Christology—Jesus the teacher.

[4]Cf. Robinson, "The Place of the Emmaus Story," 486: "The remarkable thing about the Emmaus story . . . is the fact that Jesus changes roles in the middle of it. In 24.29 we hear of his entering in order to stay as the the disciples' guest (*eisêlthen tou meínai sun autoís*); but in the very next verse he is taking the host's role and breaking and distributing the bread. This indicates that in a sense the Kingdom is already a present reality, in the person of Jesus. In Jesus the Kingdom is made present, and the meal at Emmaus with Jesus suddenly taking over as host is an *eikôn* of the Kingdom; the disciples are indeed now feasting at his table in the Kingdom."

In order to highlight Jesus' interpretation of "the things concerning himself" (24:25-27), Luke leads up to it by the Emmaus disciples' unabashed *confession of their Christological hope* (24:19) and their *Christological lament* (24:20-24). These two dimensions of the Emmaus disciples' confession form the two levels of Christology that Luke has developed in his Gospel: (1) the prophet mighty in deed and word before God and all the people who, they had hoped, would redeem Israel (24:19, 21); and (2) the prophet delivered up by the chief priests and rulers, condemned to death, and crucified (24:20).[5] The first one represents the disciples' hope; the second one represents their lament. In this chapter, I shall read back into Luke's Gospel from the perspective of Luke 24:19 to see how Luke has developed his Christological concerns that climax here in the Emmaus meal. In the next chapter, regarding the opponents of Jesus, I shall read back into Luke's Gospel from the perspective of Luke 24:20 to observe the charges against Jesus by his opponents that led to his death.[6]

The confession of the Emmaus disciples in 24:19 presents Jesus with their Christology. There are three dimensions to their Christological statement: first, the title *"Jesus of Nazareth"*; second, the identity and work of the one bearing the title, *"a prophet mighty in deed and word"*; and third, the two audiences who witness the work of the one bearing the title, *"before God and all the people."* In essence, this is the Christology of the Emmaus disciples. The Christology of the chief priests and the rulers articulated in 24:20 is not part of their Christology because it does not fit into their view of Jesus as a prophet mighty in deed and word. The death of Jesus is such a new phenomenon for the disciples that they have yet to incorporate it into their Christology and make it fully their own. It is antithetical to their beliefs about Jesus. Therefore, Luke 24:20 is not a part of the confession of the disciples to Jesus of their Christology, but is a recitation of the facts that indicate how badly their Christology has gone awry. It is the beginning of their lament in Luke 24:20-24 that is based on their hope for Jesus (the confession of 24:19) and the reality of his crucifixion and death (the dashed hopes of 24:20). Thus the

[5]See Juel, *Messianic Exegesis*, 24.
[6]Cf. Tannehill, *Narrative Unity*, 96–99, 279–280.

Christological statement of the Emmaus disciples may be confined to these three areas of consideration.

JESUS OF NAZARETH

Both the titles *Jesus of Nazareth* and *prophet* are technical terms in the Christology of Luke-Acts that have bearing upon my discussion of the Emmaus disciples' Christology.[7]

The title *Jesus of Nazareth* and the place of Nazareth are foundational in Luke's exposition of Christology.[8] The title itself is used only three times in the Gospel. In 4:34, Jesus is teaching with authority in Galilee and a man with an unclean spirit cries out to Jesus: "Ah! What have you to do with us, Jesus of Nazareth? Have you come to destroy us? I know who you are, the Holy One of God"; in 18:37, a blind man is told by the crowd that "Jesus of Nazareth is passing by," and the blind man cries out "Jesus, Son of David, have mercy on me";[9] and in 24:19, Jesus is called *Jesus of Nazareth* by Cleopas. The place of Nazareth is prominent in Luke's infancy narrative as the place of the annunciation (1:26), the hometown from which Mary and Joseph travel to Bethlehem (2:4), and the place of Jesus' nurture (2:39, 51). The only other

---

[7]Fitzmyer, *I-IX*, 213–215 places "prophet" under Luke's Christological titles but says nothing of "Jesus of Nazareth;" Navone, *Themes of St. Luke*, 132–140 shows that Luke "depicts Jesus especially as a prophet;" F. Hahn, *The Titles of Jesus in Christology* (London: Lutterworth Press, 1969) 352–406 discusses the eschatological prophet in the Christological traditions of Judaism and primitive Christianity; Dillon, *From Eyewitnesses*, 117–126 sees Luke's use of prophet as the significant Christological title for Jesus in the Emmaus story; Dunn, *Christology*, 137–138 discusses Jesus' understanding of himself as an inspired eschatological prophet. I will argue here that Jesus of Nazareth is as significant a title as prophet and synonymous to it.

[8]Nazareth is designated in three different ways in the NT, and Luke has all three. See Bauer, Arndt, Gingrich, *Greek-English Lexicon*, 534.

[9]Cf. Fitzmyer, *X-XXIV*, 1215–1216 on four possible meanings of *ho Nazôraíos*. He concludes that "probably the best explanation of *Nazôraios* at the moment is to regard it as a gentilic adj. meaning 'a person from Nazara/Nazareth,' but with the possible added nuance of either *nâzîr*, 'consecrated one,' or *nêser*, 'sprout, scion' of Davidic lineage." Cf. H. H. Schraeder, *Nazarênós, Nazôraíos*, *TDNT* Abridged 625: "the term *Nazôraíos* derives from the city of Nazareth as the hometown of Jesus. Neither linguistic nor material objections to this view are convincing."

reference to the place of Nazareth occurs in 4:16 where it introduces Jesus' visit to the synagogue in his hometown.

Is there any theological significance to the use of the designation *Jesus of Nazareth* by the Emmaus disciples? For one thing, it forces the reader to go back and consider Jesus' roots in the Gospel. This is part of the methodology in Luke 24, for in 24:6, the women are to remember Jesus' words in Galilee, and now in 24:19, the Emmaus disciples, recalling the origins of Jesus by the title "Jesus of Nazareth," point the reader back to 1:26-38 where we are told of his virginal conception by the power of the Holy Spirit. There are three other references to Nazareth in 2:4, 39, and 51, but the next scene at Nazareth is in Luke 4:16-30.

The Nazareth Episode: Luke 4:16-30

Luke sees the Spirit as the active divine factor in the life of Jesus as early as his conception (1:35) where the angel announces to Mary that "the *Holy Spirit* will come upon you"; in his baptism (3:22): "and the *Holy Spirit* descended upon him in bodily form, as a dove"; and in his temptation (4:1): "and Jesus, full of the *Holy Spirit*, returned from the Jordan, and was led by the *Spirit* for forty days in the wilderness." So also Jesus must begin his ministry in 4:14 "in the power of the *Spirit*."

The importance of the Spirit in Jesus' ministry is stressed in his sermon to his hometown in Nazareth, described by many as a programmatic text for Lukan Christology.[10] Jesus, being anointed with the Spirit in baptism, now manifests himself in his teaching in the synagogue where he assigns to himself messianic characteristics by quoting Isaiah: preaching of good news to the poor, proclamation of release to the captives, recovery of sight to the

---

[10]Cf. Fitzmyer, *I-IX*, 529; Dillon, *From Eyewitnesses*, 119; Marshall, *The Gospel of Luke*, 178. Many others consider Luke 4:16-30 programmatic, e.g. D. L. Tiede, *Prophecy and History in Luke-Acts* (Philadelphia: Fortress, 1980) 19-63; J. B. Combrink, "The Structure and Significance of Luke 4:16-30," *Neotestamentica* 7 (1973) 27-47; H. Anderson, "Broadening Horizons: The Rejection at Nazareth Pericope of Luke 4:16-30 in Light of Recent Critical Trends," *Int* 18 (1964) 259-275; and D. Hill, "The Rejection of Jesus of Nazareth (Luke iv 16-30)," *NovT* 13 (1971) 161-180.

blind, freedom to the oppressed, and proclamation of the acceptable year of the Lord.[11]

Many consider Luke 4:16-30 to be programmatic because it defines one crucial dimension of Lukan Christology, "the charismatic, *thaumaturgical* feature of both the ministry of Jesus and the mission of the church."[12] Conzelmann perceives the miracles of Jesus to rank higher in Luke's Christology than his teaching, not only in this pericope, but throughout Luke 4:16–9:51.[13] This seems to ignore Luke's real emphasis on the teaching of Jesus in the first part of his ministry, and the balance that he maintains between Jesus' teaching and his miracles.[14] The reason Jesus returned in the power of the Spirit into Galilee (4:14) was to teach in the synagogues, resulting in his "being glorified by all" (4:15).[15] This summary statement of 4:14-15, in which he introduces the whole of the Galilean ministry,[16] does not mention miracles at all, only teaching in the synagogues, and the major emphasis of the Nazareth episode is to give a paradigmatic example of Jesus'

[11]Fitzmyer, *I-IX*, 532 considers this a prophetic anointing and A. R. C. Leaney, *A Commentary on the Gospel According to St. Luke* (London: Adam and Charles Black, 1958) 118, a messianic one. Jesus' reference to himself as a prophet in 4:24 supports Fitzmyer. But within the context of this programmatic text and Luke's developing Christology, this anointing may be messianic. The forthcoming analysis of Luke 24:19 will argue that the designation of Jesus as a prophet by Luke is a messianic designation.

[12]Dillon, *From Eyewitnesses*, 115 (emphasis Dillon). See Dunn, *Jesus and the Spirit*, 69-76 on "Jesus as a miracleworker."

[13]Cf. Conzelmann, *The Theology of St. Luke*, 37.

[14]Cf. P. J. Achtemeier, "The Lucan Perspective on the Miracles of Jesus: A Preliminary Sketch," *JBL* 94 (1975) 550-551; Tannehill, *Narrative Unity*, 77-99 on "Jesus as Preacher and Healer"; Dillon, *From Eyewitnesses*, 127-128 n. 172.

[15]The teaching of Jesus is an important part of the table fellowship matrix and will form a major section of chapters IX. and X. The first use of *didáskô* is here in 4:15, and its last use is in 23:5 that specifically points back to the beginning of Jesus' teaching in Galilee as a reason for his arrest and crucifixion. For Jesus as the teacher see Luke 4:31; 5:3, 17; 6:6; 11:1; 13:10, 22, 26; 19:47; 20:1, 21; 21:37; 23:5. Jesus teaches in places of Jewish worship: in synagogues, 4:15, 31; 6:6; 13:10, and in the temple, 19:47; 20:1; 21:37. The shift, of course, takes place after Jesus' entrance into Jerusalem. Jesus also teaches at the home around the meal (5:29-35; 7:36-50; 11:37-52; 19:1-10). Teaching at the table in the home is one accent of my analysis of Jesus' table fellowship.

[16]Conzelmann, *The Theology of St. Luke*, 30.

teaching that sets the stage for the rest of his teaching in the Gospel.[17]

The parallels to Luke 4:15 in the other Synoptists are quite different: Matthew reports that Jesus began to preach, "Repent, for the kingdom of heaven is at hand"; Mark says that Jesus was "preaching the gospel of God, and saying, 'The time is fulfilled, and the kingdom of God is at hand; repent and believe in the gospel.'" Luke has been accused of offering a "bland summary statement" in contrast to Matthew and Mark,[18] or a "shift in emphasis" where the proclamation of the proximity of the kingdom is replaced by the proclamation of the content of that kingdom (4:18-21).[19] But the question that arises is whether or not Luke is really engaging in a shift in emphasis, or whether he describes the preaching of the gospel of God and the nearness of the kingdom in a different way which more closely fits his Christology. Luke 4:16-30 illustrates the Christological statement of the Emmaus disciples in 24:19. As Jesus unrolls the scroll in the synagogue at Nazareth, he opens the meaning of Isaiah,[20] thus illustrating the first or introductory phase of Lukan Christology: "a prophet mighty in deed and word." The rejection of his message at Nazareth points to the second phase of Luke's Christology, for

[17]Cf. H. Rengstorf, *didáskô, TDNT* II 139: "The form in which Jesus teaches is that of a Jewish teacher of the period . . . We do at least have information about what happened in the synagogue at Nazareth (Lk. 4:16 ff.). After the reading of the Scripture portion (Is. 61:1f.), which took place standing, Jesus seated Himself like other expositors of the time and based His address on the passage just read (Lk. 4:21 ff.). This handling of a text is 'teaching' for later Judaism . . . The same practice of sitting to teach is mentioned by Mt. in 5:1 at the beginning of the Sermon on the Mount . . . and by Lk. in 5:3 at the beginning of the the discourse by the lake. It is thus with good reason that Jewish tradition concerning the teaching of Jesus also speaks in terms *limmûd.*" Cf. W. C. Kaiser, *limmûd, TWOT* I 480: "The taught ones in Isa 8:16 are the Lord's disciples who know his law. The Servant of the Lord, however, has the tongue and ear of the learned (Isa 50:4). Therefore all Israel's children await the messianic era with joy, for all will be taught by the Lord (Isa 54:13)."

[18]Fitzmyer, *I-IX*, 522.

[19]Conzelmann, *The Theology of St. Luke*, 114.

[20]Fitzmyer, *I-IX*, 532 rightly observes that Luke gives us "a conflation of 61:1a, b, d; 58:6d; 61:2a."

both Elijah and Elisha were prophets, rejected by their own people (cf. 4:28-30).[21] The Nazareth episode and the Isaiah prophecy hardly seem to stress deeds over words. In fact, the context indicates that it is the teaching of Jesus that takes precedence: "to preach good news to the poor (*euaggelísasthai*), to preach (*kêrúxai*) release to the captives, and recovery of sight to the blind, to set free (*aposteílai*) those who are oppressed, to proclaim (*kêrúxai*) the acceptable year of the Lord."

It is uncertain whether the four infinitives are dependent on "sent" (*apéstalken*), or whether "to preach good news" (*euaggelísasthai*) is dependent on "he has anointed me" (*échrisen*).[22] In either case, the intent is the same. Three of the four infinitives have to do with teaching or proclamation,[23] and only one involves

[21]Cf. Neyrey, *The Passion*, 70 on Luke's "richer meaning" of Jesus' prophet title as compared to Mark: "Jesus' inaugural appearance at the Nazareth synagogue contains three key elements of what 'prophet' means for Luke: (a) prophets are rejected in their homeland (4:24); (b) prophets minister to Gentiles, as Elisha and Elijah did (4:25-27); (c) prophets are killed by those to whom they are sent (4:28-29). The rejection and maltreatment of prophets, which is heralded at the beginning of the Gospel, is repeated at the end of the story in the account of Jesus' maltreatment in 22:63-65."

[22]Combrink, "The Structure and Significance of Luke 4:16-30," 31 suggests a chiastic arrangement of the four infinitives dependent on *apéstalken*. Marshall, *The Gospel of Luke*, 183 writes: "The punctuation is disputed. Most editors place a stop after *ptôchoís* so that *euaggelísasthai* is dependent on *échrisen* (*UBS*). Others put a stop after *me*, so that *euaggelísasthai* is dependent on *apéstalken* . . . The latter punctuation agrees with that of MT and LXX, and fits in with Luke's interpretation of the quotation of 4:43, which is to be preferred." Marshall gives a full bibliography on this grammatical point.

[23]There does not seem to be a great difference in Luke's thinking between teaching (*didáskô*) and preaching (*kêrússô*). Concerning 4:15, Marshall, *The Gospel of Luke*, 177 writes that "*didáskô* is frequently used to indicate the work of Jesus in all the Gospels and has much the same meaning as *kêrússô*." G. Friedrich, *kêrússô*, TDNT III 713 comments: "In the NT, especially the Synoptists, we often find *kêrússein* and *didáskein* together, Mt. 4:23; 9:35; 11:1; Ac. 28:31 (cf. R. 2:21). Teaching is usually in the synagogue, whereas proclamation takes places anywhere in the open . . . But the NT also speaks of a *kêrússei* in the synagogue. Jesus did not give theoretical teaching when He spoke in the synagogue. He did not expound Scripture like the rabbis. He did not tell people what they must do. His teaching was proclamation. He declared what God was doing among them to-day: This day is this scripture fulfilled (Lk. 4:21). His exposition was a herald's cry. His teaching concerning

a direct thaumaturgical task, although the meaning of "setting free those who are oppressed" may simply mean to forgive their sins.[24] The sense of forgiveness may want to be pressed here since it is used twice in 4:18 and because of Luke's use of "forgiveness" (*áphesis*) in 24:47 where, in conjunction with "to preach" (*kêrúxai*), it constitutes Jesus' parting words to the disciples in the Gospel: "and that repentance and forgiveness of sins (*áphesin hamartiôn*) should be preached (*kêruchthênai*) in his name to all nations, beginning from Jerusalem."[25] This would link together the first and last proclaimed words of Jesus. The only real thaumaturgical phenomenon in the Isaiah quotation is the "recovering of sight to the blind." This could be spiritualized, but there is reason to consider it literally, especially in light of Luke 7:21-22 where the blind receiving their sight is fundamental in Jesus' testimony to John that he is the coming one.[26]

Luke's use of the title *Jesus of Nazareth* in his Gospel is linked to the healing of a man with an unclean spirit and a blind man, confirming the thaumaturgical character of the Galilean ministry of Jesus. Both in 4:34 and 18:37, those who call out to *Jesus of Nazareth* fit within the messianic categories of Isaiah that are read by Jesus in the synagogue of Nazareth. Both the man with the un-

---

the coming of the kingdom of God was an address demanding decision either for it or against it. Hence His preaching was very different from that of the scribes at synagogue worship."

[24]Cf. Dillon, *From Eyewitnesses*, 136–137: "The conflation of the Isaian statements results in a doubled *áphesis*-proclamation; and whatever 'liberation' the post-exilic prophet might have been prophesying, there is only *one sense* this noun ever has in NT usage (10x out of 17x in Lk-Acts!): it always means God's 'liberation' of men *from sin's bondage,*—his *forgiveness*. Understood in this way, *áphesis hamartiôn* in Lk-Acts can be simply equivalent to 'salvation' (Lk 1, 77) or 'being justified' (Acts 13, 38f.) *simpliciter*" (emphasis Dillon); cf. also Dillon on p. 273: ". . . the gift of forgiveness announced at Nazareth as the substance of the eschatological prophecy . . . ."

[25]Whereas the forgiveness of sins occurs at the inauguration of John's ministry with the proclamation of the kingdom in Mark 1:4 (*kêrússôn baptisma metanoías eis áphesin hamartiôn*), Luke systematically develops the proclamation of the forgiveness of sins that climaxes at the conclusion of Jesus' ministry with the inauguration of the apostolic mission in 24:47.

[26]Talbert, *Reading Luke*, 55 structures Luke 4:18 to place "sight to the blind" in the center of the quotation.

clean spirit (release to the captives, set at liberty those who are oppressed) and the blind man (recovery of sight to the blind) identify Jesus in further messianic terms, calling him the "Holy One of God" (4:34) and the "Son of David" (18:38). Jesus of Nazareth is perceived as a miracle-worker with messianic qualities by those who receive the benefits of his messianic deeds. He is indeed a prophet, mighty in deed in the two places where he is called *Jesus of Nazareth.*

Luke's placement of the healing of the blind man is significant as it occurs immediately following his final passion prediction and his last marking of Jerusalem as the city of Jesus' destiny in 18:31-34. The teaching and miracle-working phase of Jesus' ministry is coming to an end, and in 19:28, he will arrive in Jerusalem for the final events of his life. The final miracle of Jesus in Luke's Gospel frames the thaumaturgical phase of Jesus' ministry from 4:16 to 19:28.[27] It is a direct fulfillment of 4:18 that announces Jesus the Messiah's preaching of recovery of sight to the blind. This is confirmed by Jesus in deeds and words in 7:21-22; for the blind along with the poor, the maimed, and the lame become paradigmatic for those who deserve and receive the benefits of the miracles of Jesus (14:13, 21). Luke emphasizes the recovery of sight to the blind man in 18:35-43 by using "to receive sight" (*anablépô*) three times in 18:41-43. The reason given for the healing is the faith of the blind man. The entire miracle is marked by the faith of this man who, on hearing that Jesus of Nazareth, the miracle-worker, was passing by, twice calls him by the messianic name "Son of David" and asks for mercy, believing that Jesus is able to restore his sight. In Luke 18:35-43, physical and spiritual wellness overcome physical and spiritual blindness. This reflects that same juxtaposition of Luke 4:18-19 where the restoration of physical blindness coincides with spiritual salvation ("the acceptable year of the Lord").[28]

---

[27]This is also the last miracle for Matthew and Mark prior to Jesus' entrance into Jerusalem. However, both Matthew and Mark have the miracle of the withered fig tree during Jesus' Jerusalem ministry, something which Luke replaces with the parable of the fig tree in 21:29-33.

[28]Cf. Fitzmyer, *I-IX*, 533: "The Isaian description of a period of favor and deliverance for Zion is now used to proclaim the Period of Jesus, and the new mode of salvation that is to come in him."

Perhaps Luke's emphasis on the recovery of sight by the blind, at the beginning and end of Jesus' ministry (4:18–18:43), is to be seen in light of the closed and opened eyes of the Emmaus narrative. Before his death in Jerusalem, Jesus was a teacher who restored physical sight. Afterwards, in fulfillment of Isaiah 61 and Luke 4, the resurrected Lord opens the eyes of his disciples to see him in the breaking of the bread, the new miracle of the new age.[29] The healing of the blind man concludes the miracles of Jesus in his ministry, but after the great miracle of the resurrection, there is offered to all the possibility of seeing through the eyes of faith that recognize the presence of Jesus in the breaking of the bread.

The remainder of Luke 4:16-30 confirms, not that the kingdom of heaven simply is near, but that it has indeed already come and is present in Jesus.[30] Thus, after reading Isaiah, Jesus can say in 4:21: "Today this scripture has been fulfilled in your hearing."[31] Lukan scholars differ on whether this refers to salvation in the past or salvation in the present/future. Conzelmann began the discussion with his statement that "Paul identifies his own time as the eschatological one [2 Cor 6:2], but Luke sees salvation already as a thing of the past."[32] But the use of the perfect "has been ful-

---

[29]Fitzmyer, *X-XXIV*, 1568 describes this as seeing "with the eyes of faith."

[30]Note the similarity between Luke 4:18 and 4:43 (*kai taís hetérais pólesin euaggelísasthai me deí tên basileían toú theoú hóti epí toúto apestálên*). Cf. Ellis, *The Gospel of Luke*, 89: "Unlike Matthew (3:2), Luke (4:43) begins the proclamation of the kingdom of God with the mission of Jesus. For Luke the 'proclamation' of the kingdom is nothing less than its 'presence'. Only Jesus will effect this."

[31]Matthew's interest in fulfillment is reflected in his quotation of Isaiah 9 in 4:15-16 that highlights Jesus' ministry to the Gentiles. Luke does the same thing in his quotation of Isaiah 61/58 in which he reflects a more Christological perspective. The significance of "Galilee of the Gentiles" as the place of the Church's future mission will be handled by Luke in 4:16-30 through the prophets Elijah and Elisha so as to encompass Matthew's emphasis and anticipate his own concerns in Acts. Cf. also E. Lohmeyer, *Galiläa und Jerusalem*, FRLANT 52, (Göttingen: Vandenhoeck und Ruprecht, 1936) who first suggested that there was a different Christological perspective during the apostolic period between Christian liturgical communities in Galilee and Jerusalem.

[32]Conzelmann, *The Theology of St. Luke*, 36.

filled" (*peplêrôtai*)[33] implies that salvation is a present and continuing reality.[34] Luke intends the Nazareth episode to be a profound Christological statement.[35]

Therefore, the agenda for Luke in this first teaching of Jesus in Nazareth is the same as that in Emmaus: both narratives present legitimate Christologies, and as Christologies they are complementary. Taken together, they form the full Lukan Christology.

Luke's intent here is to show that there are two phases to the revelation of the Christ: a thaumaturgical phase and a rejection phase, both of which are in accordance with Scripture.[36] The rejection phase is the second section of the Nazareth episode, Luke 4:22-30, where Luke introduces the title of Jesus as the prophet: ("Truly, I say to you, no prophet is acceptable in his own country"). He follows up this statement of Jesus with two Old Testament prophets who, as teachers and miracle workers, were rejected by the people. Luke's development of the rejection phase. of his Christology begins after a positive reaction to his words in 4:22: "And all spoke well of him (*emartúroun autô*), and wondered at the gracious words which proceeded out of his mouth." There is disagreement whether *emartúroun autô* is a positive statement,

[33]Cf. Blass and Debrunner, *A Greek Grammar*, 341; J. Horst *oús*, *TDNT* V 554, n. 108: "The perf. *peplêrôtai* denotes a state: is fulfilled, lives in the present in fulfillment of what was promised earlier;" Marshall, *The Gospel of Luke*, 185: "The perfect tense (*peplêrôtai*) is almost equivalent to a present."

[34]Esler, *Community and Gospel*, 56: ". . . the message of salvation which Jesus quotes from Isaiah (4.18-19) is regarded by Luke as being fulfilled in the 'today' of his own community, not just in that of the congregation of Nazareth."

[35]Whereas Matthew and Mark announce that the kingdom of heaven is near, Luke identifies the kingdom with Jesus, showing that the Old Testament messianic hopes now find their fulfillment in Jesus.

[36]Cf. Fitzmyer, *I-IX*, 529: "The Lucan story, transposed to this point in the Gospel, has a definite programmatic character. Jesus' teaching is a fulfillment of OT Scripture—this is his kerygmatic announcement . . . . But that same teaching will meet with success and—even more so—with rejection. Luke has deliberately put this story at the beginning of the public ministry to encapsulate the entire ministry of Jesus and the reaction to it. The fulfillment-story stresses the success of his teaching under the guidance of the Spirit, but the rejection-story symbolizes the opposition that his ministry will evoke among his own. The rejection of him by the people of his own *patris* in the larger sense."

i.e., "they testified to him" (*autô* as dative of advantage), or a negative statement, i.e., "they testified against him" (*autô* as dative of disadvantage).[37] The controversy arises to help explain the change in the attitude of the people of Nazareth to Jesus' words. The shift in attitude from a positive statement in 4:22a-22b to a negative one in 4:22c seems abrupt. Something seems to come over Jesus when they ask: "Is not this Joseph's son?"

In response, Jesus quotes the proverb, "Physician, heal yourself," and concludes that the miracles he performed in Capernaum are now expected in his hometown.[38] Such demands indicate that his very own people do not understand his mission as "interpretation of Scripture and proclamation of God's period of salvation."[39] The people who want wondrous deeds instead of teaching, reject Jesus the teacher, and demand Jesus the miracle-worker.

Jesus replies to this by pointing to the example of Elijah and Elisha. Both men were great prophets which meant that they were great teachers; but both of them were known more for their miracles than their teaching, two of which are included here by Luke (Elijah's miracle at the home of the widow of Zarephath; Elisha's miracle to Naaman the Syrian, a leper); yet both these prophets, in spite of their miracles, were rejected by Israel and were sent to the Gentiles.[40] All these things are fundamental to Luke's Christology: Elijah and Elisha serve as patterns of the prophet. Luke highlights the rejection of Jesus in a graphic way in

[37]The negative reaction was first proposed by J. Jeremias, *Jesus' Promise to the Nations*, SBT 24 (Naperville: Allenson, 1958) 44–46 who also suggested that "*thaumázein* can express both admiring astonishment, and opposition to what is strange."

[38]Cf. Conzelmann, *The Theology of St. Luke*, 31–38 on Luke's reversal of Nazareth and Capernaum.

[39]Fitzmyer, *I-IX*, 535.

[40]L. C. Crockett, "Luke 4:25-27 and Jewish-Gentile Relations in Luke-Acts," *JBL* 88 (1969) 177–183 discusses the relation between Luke 4:25-27 and Acts 10-11, highlighting the table fellowship between Jew and Gentile. He concludes that "Luke 4:25-27, then, must be seen as a prolepsis not simply of the gentile mission, and certainly not of God's rejection of Israel and turning to the gentiles, but rather of Jewish-gentile *reconciliation*, the *cleansing* of the gentiles which makes it possible for Jews and gentiles to live and eat together in the new age" (emphasis Crockett).

4:28-29, filling up the synagogue with wrath against Jesus' allusions to Elijah and Elisha and bringing the people of Nazareth to the point where they are ready to send him headlong over the cliff. This not only foreshadows Jesus' rejection in Jerusalem, but even "foreshadows the locale of the crucifixion itself (23:6)."[41] Jesus escapes miraculously "passing through the midst of them," the only miracle he performs in Nazareth. His escape here reminds us of his sudden appearance to the disciples after the Emmaus story in Luke 24:36 where "Jesus himself stood among them."

Luke's appeal to the prophets Elijah and Elisha is a commentary on Jesus' words that a prophet is without honor even in his own country. It prepares the way for 7:16 and 7:18-35, where wisdom's children, John and Jesus, stand in a long line of rejected prophets; and Luke 9, where the identity of Jesus is in question and he is placed in the category of prophets like John the Baptist or Elijah (9:8, 19). It is in Luke 9:18-22 where the kerygma of a rejected Christ is first explicated by Luke in the passion prediction. Luke shapes his material in chapter 9 so that Jesus is seen as John the Baptist risen from the dead or Elijah reappeared, thereby placing him in the category of rejected prophet. In Luke 9:28-36, it is Moses and Elijah, the prophets *par excellence* in the Old Testament, who appear with Jesus at his transfiguration. Both Moses and Elijah are particularly known for their miracles and their rejection by Israel. Jesus' introduction of Elijah and Elisha into his response to the people of Nazareth anticipates the theme of rejection that Luke will later develop as Jesus comes to the close of his Galilean ministry (Luke 9) and sets his face toward Jerusalem. Thus, the sermon at Nazareth is programmatic for Luke in that it lays down the chief elements of Luke's Christology: Jesus of Nazareth, a prophet mighty in deed and word, rejected by his own people.

---

[41]Fitzmyer, *I-IX*, 538. Cf. also Ellis, *The Gospel of Luke*, 98: "*out of the city*: foreshadowing the day of his crucifixion. Executions were not carried out within the walls. Cf. Lev. 24:14; Ac. 7:58. By their action they excommunicate Jesus and, in effect, make him a Gentile." Esler, *Community and Gospel*, 57 notes that Luke 4:28-30 "is the only occasion in the Synoptic Gospels where the Jews try to do away with Jesus, apart from their plotting which leads to crucifixion." Esler cites parallels in John 8:59 and 10:31.

Jesus of Nazareth in Acts

The title *Jesus of Nazareth* is more prominent in Acts, occurring seven times in 2:22, 3:6, 4:10, 6:14, 10:38, 22:8, and 26:9. Once Jesus' followers are called "Nazarenes," in 24:5.[42] Most of these references confirm that this title describes the thaumaturgical nature of Jesus' messianic character. The parallel in Acts 2:22 to Luke 24:19 is clear, even down to the Greek vocabulary:

Luke 24:19   "Concerning *Jesus of Nazareth,* who was a prophet (*anêr prophêtês*) *mighty in deed* and word (*dunatós en érgô kai logô*) before God and *all the people . . . ."*

Acts 2:22   "*Jesus of Nazareth,* a man (*anêr*) attested to you by God with *mighty works and wonders and signs (dunámesi kai térasi kai sêmeíois*) which God did through him *in your midst . . . ."*

In both accounts, what is significant is the title *Jesus of Nazareth* and his function as a "man" (*anêr*) mighty in miraculous deeds before the people of Israel. Peter's Pentecost sermon begins with the first Christological phase, "the ministry of wondrous deeds," a ministry that would be familiar to the men of Israel. In 2:23, Peter moves from one Christological level to another in speaking of Jesus' "destination to violent rejection," a reference to the crucifixion and death of "this Jesus." To be sure, *Jesus of Nazareth* is the worker of mighty works, wonders, and signs, but in addition, *this Jesus* was offered up on a cross.[43]

---

[42]See C. F. D. Moule, "The Christology of Acts," *Studies in Luke-Acts* (Philadelphia: Fortress Press, 1966) 165–166 on the use of Galilee and Nazareth in Acts, giving the various opinions as to its meaning and significance. Moule points out the continuity between Luke and Acts through the designation of Jesus the man as a product of Nazareth. His followers are immediately identified as "men of Galilee" in Acts 1:11 and as "Galileans" in Acts 2:7, demonstrating "the Galilean and Nazarene origin of the church."

[43]Dillon, *From Eyewitnesses,* 125–126 also comments on the connection between "the wonder-worker and sufferer" in the Pentecost sermon of Peter, drawing it together with Cleopas' speech in 24:19f. He rightly observes that "the construction of the passage [Acts 2:22-23] shows that its main assertion is the accusation of the Jerusalem audience: *prospêxantes aneílate,* whereas the preceding reference to the accrediting wonders, like the subsequent resurrection statement, is only a subordinate clause to that main assertion."

Some occurrences of this title *Jesus of Nazareth* in Acts confirm that it is a reference to his miracles, but nevertheless also part of a broader kerygmatic construction that includes both phases of Christology: the "wondrous deeds" and the "destination to violent rejection."[44] In 3:6, Peter heals a lame man at the temple gate called Beautiful by saying "in the name of Jesus Christ of Nazareth, walk." The addition of "Christ" to the title more fully embraces the kerygma surrounding Jesus in Acts, for the miracle is done in the name of Jesus *Christ* of Nazareth—Jesus of Nazareth the teacher/miracle-worker and Christ the rejected prophet. In 4:10, Peter speaks before the Sanhedrin in defense of his healing of the cripple in 3:6. The question put to him concerning the miracle was "by what power or by what name did you do this?" Peter responds by saying: "Be it known to you all, and to all the people of Israel, that by the name of *Jesus Christ of Nazareth*, whom you crucified, whom God raised from the dead, by him this man is standing before you well." Peter is confronted with two possible ways of explaining the healing: either by what power or by what name. Peter chooses to answer that the healing was "in the name of Jesus Christ of Nazareth."[45] Acts 4:10 is a parallel to 3:6, confirming that all dimensions of Lukan Christology are included in the recitation of the healing: *Jesus of Nazareth* the miracle-worker has now become more completely "Jesus *Christ* of Nazareth whom you crucified, whom God raised from the dead." The two Christological levels are merged into one and thus completed.

This development and completion reaches its climax in Acts 10:38, one of the most characteristic kerygmatic statements of Luke in Acts. In Peter's sermon to Cornelius, there is a clear delineation between the two levels of Luke's Christology. First, Peter introduces the significance of the "word motif" to Jesus' ministry that *begins from Galilee* ("the word [*ton lógon*] which he sent to Israel, preaching good news of peace by Jesus Christ" in 10:36, and "the word which was proclaimed [*to genómenon hrêma*] throughout all Judea" in 10:37). Then, in 10:38-39 he presents the thaumaturgical dimension by taking us back to the baptism of

44Ibid., 35–36, 119.

45Neyrey, *The Passion*, 142–143 argues that in Acts, faith in the name of Jesus saves (Acts 2:21; 3:6, 16; 4:10; 9:14, 21; 10:43; 22:16).

Jesus and the first sermon Jesus gave in Nazareth where he claims for himself the messianic qualities of Isaiah 61: "How God anointed Jesus of Nazareth with the Holy Spirit and with power; how he went about doing good and healing all that were oppressed by the devil, for God was with him. And we are witnesses to all that he did both in the country of the Jews and in Jerusalem." This is a description of Jesus' Galilean ministry that is represented by the title *Jesus of Nazareth*. Second, in 10:39-41, Peter includes in this formula the suffering dimension of Christology: "They put him to death by hanging him on a tree; but God raised him on the third day and made him manifest; not to all the people but to us who were chosen by God as witnesses, who ate and drank with him after he rose from the dead." Acts 10:38-43 figures prominently in the table fellowship matrix of Luke-Acts because of the attestation of those who "ate and drank with him after he rose from the dead." Those who participated in these post-resurrection meals are able to carry on the Christological tradition of both a miracle-working and suffering Christ in the table fellowship of the early Christian communities. This passage also reflects the final kerygmatic statement in Luke 24:44-47 where both the divine necessity of the death and resurrection of Jesus Christ in fulfillment of the Scriptures and the preaching of repentance and forgiveness to all nations (cf. Acts 10:42-43) are part of the apostolic message.

A PROPHET MIGHTY IN DEED AND WORD

There is a close relationship in Luke's writings between the title *Jesus of Nazareth* and his "prophet-Christology" that reflects the thaumaturgical character of Jesus' messiahship.[46] However, there is a second phase of Lukan prophet-Christology, the rejected

---

[46]Cf. Dillon, *From Eyewitnesses*, 122: "His [Cleopas] characterization of Jesus as wonder-working prophet—*anêr prophêtês ktl.*—is not the survival of some primitive and flawed christological viewpoint, it is specifically and recognizably Lucan, depicting the first phase of Jesus' mission and the first step in understanding him." Some, however, see the title "prophet" as reflecting an incomplete Christology, e.g. Wanke, *Die Emmauserzählung*, 60–62, and Schürmann, *Das Lukasevangelium: Erster Teil: Kommentar zu Kap. 1, 1–9, 50* (Herders theologischer Kommentar zum Neuen Testament III/1; Freiburg: Herder, 1969) 402f., 507f.

prophet. The essence of the prophet is that he is both miracle-worker and suffering servant. In Luke 24:19-20, the Emmaus disciples express this double-Christology: first in 24:19, the prophet of mighty wonders, and then, in 24:20, the prophet rejected—but they never put the two ideas together. The complete Christology begins with Jesus the prophet mighty in word and deed and ends with Jesus rejected by the chief priests and rulers, condemned to death, and crucified.

The Moses Typology

These two successive phases of the prophet first being recognized and later being rejected apply not only to Jesus, but also to Moses,[47] and to all those who stand in the prophetic tradition, such as Elijah, Elisha, and John the Baptist. This parallel is drawn most explicitly in Acts 7:22 within Stephen's account of salvation history. Just like the Emmaus disciples' confession of Jesus as a "prophet mighty in deed and word," Moses is described in the same way ("mighty in his words and deeds"). But Jesus, like Moses, is rejected by his own people, a fundamental part of the Mosaic pattern in Acts 7:35-40. The placement of Moses in the account of salvation history in Acts 7 engages in the same kind of "step-parallelism" utilized in the infancy narrative between John the Baptist and Jesus,[48] only here the comparison is between

[47]Hahn, *The Titles of Jesus*, 372–388 has a subdivision entitled "Jesus as the New Moses" in his appendix on "The Eschatological Prophet." Dillon, *From Eyewitnesses*, 132 traces the relationship between Jesus and Moses as the mighty rejected prophets, the deliverers of the people, the workers of wonders and signs. He draws a parallel between Jesus and Moses concerning the journey motif as a means of deliverance, especially since this is so much a part of the framework of Luke's Christology (cf. Luke 9:31, 51). Dillon writes: "We are convinced that a *positive Mosaic-prophet typology* is intended by the evangelist in the words of Cleopas. These are not mistaken or inadequate phrases but the very basis of the scriptural 'necessity' which the risen One is about to expound in v. 26. Nor will it be by accident, of course, that his exposition will be made *arxámenos apó Môüséôs* (v. 27), for Moses, as *prototype of the rejected prophet*, is the key to the passion mystery that is about to be broken" (emphasis Dillon).

[48]Cf. Fitzmyer, *I-IX*, 315 on John and Jesus in the infancy narrative: "Luke has not used parallelism just for the sake of parallelism. There is more. The parallelism does not merely suggest that John and Jesus are twin agents of

Moses and Jesus. In Acts 7:37, Moses, the rejected miracle-worker, points to Jesus who is the greater prophet: "This is Moses who says to the Israelites, 'God will raise up for you a prophet from your brethren as he raised me up.' "[49] Where one might expect that the figure of Moses would be used only as a parallel to Jesus the miracle-working prophet, this parallel also stresses that Moses was rejected: "Our fathers refused to obey him [Moses], but thrust him aside, and in their hearts they turned to Egypt . . . ." (Acts 7:39). Jesus is the final prophet in a rich tradition of those who were rejected by a "stiff-necked people, uncircumcised in heart and ears . . . always resist[ing] the Holy Spirit" (Acts 7:51). The prophets were killed because they "announced beforehand the coming of the Righteous One" (Acts 7:51-53).

The motif of the rejected prophet continues throughout Acts as the apostles carry out their mission. The first rejected prophet is Stephen himself who, like Jesus, is full of the Holy Spirit (7:55) when he is stoned to death because of his teaching (Acts 7). Dillon carefully shows how this schema of miracles and passion continues in Acts, first with the apostles, then with the deacons Stephen and Philip, and finally with Paul. He suggests that Acts 19 is the beginning of Paul's journey to Jerusalem and subsequent passion that comes after his most complete work of miracles and wonders. The divine *dei* even appears in Acts 23:11 and governs both the journey of Paul to Jerusalem and to Rome. Dillon also argues for this understanding of the apostles who stand in the tradition of the prophets and Jesus (cf. Joel's prophecy in Acts 2).[50] This prophecy announces the theme that the prophets are both miracle-workers and suffering servants.

God's salvation on the same level. Rather, there is a step-parallelism at work, i.e. a parallelism with one-upmanship. The Jesus-side always comes off better." Luke also engages in one-upmanship in his comparison between Moses and Jesus in Acts 7 as the reader would see from his knowledge of Luke's "first word" about Jesus.

[49]Robinson, "The Place of the Emmaus Story," 482, and Dillon, *From Eyewitnesses*, 122–123, also see Acts 7:22 as a parallel of Luke 24:19 and a development of the prophet Christology.

[50]Cf. Dillon, *From Eyewitnesses*, 126: "By repeating *kai prophêteúsousin* in his transcription of the prophet's words, directly prior to the promise: *kai dôsô térata . . . kai sêmeía ktl.* (vv. 18f.), our author seems to associate the apostles'

A Prophet Rejected—Luke 13:31-35

But this idea of the great prophet being rejected by the people, which is stated in Luke 24 and developed in Acts, is by no means absent from Luke's Gospel. Indeed, the theme is constantly fore-shadowed, not merely in Luke 4, but particularly in Luke 13. Luke 13:31-35 serves as yet another statement on the rejection of Jesus the miracle-working prophet, and it also establishes Jerusalem as the city of destiny and the place of rejection. It has already been observed that there is a relationship between Luke 13:31-35 and Luke 24, especially with the time reference in 13:32, "and the third day I finish my course," another proleptic demonstration in the ministry of Jesus of the eschatological fulfillment of Jesus' work on the third day.

There is, however, another time connection with Luke 24 that illustrates the crucial role Luke 13 plays in Luke's thematic develop-ment. Luke 13:31 begins, "at that very hour," the same way Luke begins his conclusion of the Emmaus narrative in 24:33, demon-strating there, as in chapters 22 and 24, a sense of urgency and focus-ing on a particular event (e.g. in Luke 22, on the Passover meal as the essence of the day, and in Luke 24, on the moment of the meal).

The parallels here between Luke 13 and Luke 24 cannot be avoided. Luke's use of *dei* in 13:33 places chapter 13 within his passion matrix and provides a direct link to 24:7, 26, and 44. But the important fact about Luke 13 is the example in 13:10-17 of Jesus' teaching and miracle in the synagogue on the Sabbath. This miracle provokes a controversy in which the ruler of the syna-gogue says: "There are six days on which work ought to be done;

---

miracle with those of Jesus (v. 22) as *accrediting signs of the eschatological proph-ecy.* This observation, besides confirming the relationship of Peter's statement to that of Cleopas, shows how important Lk's (Mosiac) prophet-christology is to his understanding of the necessity of the Lord's passion (and the suffer-ing of his witnesses as well). Prophecy, as a principal form of communion between God and man, is inevitably also a volatile ground of contention be-tween the two realms. Precisely the one whom God *accredits,* man *repudiates;* thus it is that divine forgiveness and human conversion become the prerequi-sites of God's rule, and thus is the bitter course charted for all who stand in the prophets' tradition,—principally, of course, the *summus propheta* and his emissaries" (emphasis Dillon). Dillon also notes on p. 124 the schema of miracles and rejection in Acts (Acts 3-4, 5, Stephen, Philip, and Paul).

come on those days and be healed, and not on the sabbath day"
(13:14). Here is Luke's classic juxtaposition between teaching and
miracles, with teaching taking precedence over miracles. Jesus'
Sabbath healing gives him an opportunity in the synagogue for
his Sabbath theology that finds its fulfillment in Luke 24. "Sabbath healings are a prelude to the greatest Sabbath miracle of all,
the resurrection."[51] The teaching of Jesus on the Sabbath in the
synagogue foreshadows the teaching of the Church on Sunday,
the eschatological day, where it teaches the kerygma of the new
age, the kerygma of a crucified and risen Christ in Jerusalem, as
Jesus did on the road to Emmaus. Thus, the prophet-Christology
of Luke 13 foreshadows and prepares for the completion and perfection of that Christology in Luke 24.

Luke 13:22 is a major division for Luke in his journey-to-
Jerusalem motif, and 13:35 indicates the necessity for the prophet
to die in Jerusalem. Luke 13:22-35 is framed in 13:22 by Luke's
description of Jesus' activity of "teaching and journeying toward
Jerusalem," and in 13:35 by Jesus' foreshadowing of the proclamation of the crowd when he arrives in Jerusalem, "Blessed is he
who comes in the name of the Lord!"

The significant element in Luke 13 is the comparison between
miracles and suffering. This is further developed by Jesus' response to Herod, a statement of the two phases of Luke's
Christology: "Behold, I cast out demons and perform cures today
and tomorrow, and the third day I finish my course . . . for it
cannot be that a prophet should perish away from Jerusalem. O
Jerusalem, Jerusalem, killing the prophets and stoning those who
are sent to you!" (13:32-34). Jesus is not only referring to himself,
but to all the prophets who were rejected by unbelieving Israel
and all the apostles who will be rejected, recalling especially the
stoning of Stephen in Acts 7. Thus, Luke 13:31-35 reiterates the
Christology of the Nazareth episode in 4:16-30 and foreshadows
the preliminary acknowledgement by the Emmaus disciples in
24:19-20 that Jesus the prophet, mighty in deed and word, is rejected by the religious establishment. The Emmaus disciples have
hardly advanced in their Christology beyond that which was commonly held by the people before Jesus' death.

[51]Osborne, *The Resurrection Narratives,* 102.

Luke concludes his statement about Jesus' prophetic character with the unusual designation that Jesus is the prophet mighty in deed and word "before God and all the people." It is not unusual for Luke to acknowledge that Jesus' deeds and words were done before the people (*laós*), but it is unusual to acknowledge that Jesus was this kind of prophet before God.

The preposition "before" (*enantíon*) is exclusively Lukan. It may convey the sense of "in the presence of" or "before" (Luke 20:26; Acts 8:32), or "in the sight or judgment (of)" (Luke 1:6; 24:19; Acts 7:10).[52] The other references in the Lukan corpus do not seem to be very helpful in coming to an understanding of Luke's meaning of "before God" in 24:19. The commentators are generally silent concerning this expression, recognizing that it may simply indicate that "Jesus had the stamp of divine authority upon him."[53]

However, this does not take into consideration Luke's propensity for developing themes in his Gospel that reach their fulfillment in Luke 24. Throughout his Gospel, Luke's intention is to demonstrate that Jesus the "prophet mighty in deed and word" was a part of God's redemptive plan (*boulê*). Therefore, the expression in 24:19, *before God*, is a significant statement of Luke's Christology from the divine perspective as it reflects the messianic expectations of the Old Testament. It is not simply a flawed Christology from the perspective of the people. For example, Jesus' prophetic character, as it fits into the divine plan of redemption, is already anticipated in the infancy narrative. In Luke 1:6, Zechariah and Elizabeth stand in the judgment of God as "righteous" (*díkaioi*),[54] "walking in all the commandments and ordinances of the Lord blameless." As faithful Jews, these ances-

[52]Moulton and Milligan, *The Vocabulary of the Greek Testament*, 211 state that the sense of "in the presence of" is "peculiar to the Lukan writings in the NT;" cf. also Bauer, Arndt, and Gingrich, *Greek-English Lexicon*, 261.

[53]G. H. P. Thompson, *The Gospel According to Luke* (Oxford at the Clarendon Press, 1972) 278.

[54]Marshall, *The Gospel of Luke*, 52 comments that *díkaios* "in combination with *enantíon toú theoú* implies a religious rather than a purely ethical character, seen in obedience to God's commands and going beyond a merely external legal righteousness."

tors of Jesus lived in accordance with God's Old Testament covenant. In the judgment of God, they were what he expected in the lives of his people, for they lived in accordance with his plan for them. According to Luke, Zechariah and Elizabeth as "righteous" people would be judged before God in the same way as he judged the prophets and martyrs in the Old Testament. Jesus' sermon at Nazareth would be addressed to them, and Luke would have fully expected that, as "righteous," they would have understood Jesus' messianic fulfillment of Isaiah's words, including both his wondrous deeds and his rejection by the people.[55]

In the same way, the Emmaus disciples see in Jesus the mighty prophet, righteous in the judgment of God because his deeds and words were in conformity with their messianic expectations and in keeping with the prophetic tradition. He was like Moses, Elijah, and Elisha in his messianic accomplishments, thereby in complete fulfillment of their expectations of God's plan for his Messiah. The Emmaus disciples were so convinced that Jesus exhibited messianic characteristics that they go on to say that "we had hoped that he was the one to redeem Israel" (24:21). For Luke, the Christology expressed by the Emmaus disciples in 24:19 is not a flawed Christology, but one looking for completion. The Emmaus disciples were incapable of incorporating into their Christology a confession of the scandal of the crucifixion.[56] But like Zechariah and Elizabeth, they recognized that the work of a prophet mighty in deed and word was a fundamental part of God's salvific plan.

[55]Cf. Neyrey, *The Passion*, 143–144: "The holiness of these towering saints of Luke's infancy narratives rests primarily on their faith, viz., their belief in God's immediate fulfillment of his promises to Abraham and David." Neyrey concludes on p. 154 that "Luke includes Jesus among the righteous figures in Luke-Acts who believe in God's fulfillment of his promises of salvation . . . righteousness, then, might be said to consist in belief in God's promise of salvation. As such, Jesus would be portrayed as a singularly righteous figure, one full of faith." Cf. also R. E. Brown, *The Birth of the Messiah* (New York: Doubleday, 1977) 451–454 on the faith of Simeon.

[56]Zechariah and Elizabeth may have responded as the Emmaus disciples did. It appears as if all the followers of Jesus, although fully aware of the necessity for Jesus' rejection and death, find it hard to accept the crucifixion until after the risen Lord opens up the Scriptures to them and shows them how this fulfills the Old Testament prophecies.

Zechariah, Elizabeth, and the Emmaus disciples reflect the expectations of the Lukan Old Testament saints as illustrated in the reaction of the people (*laós*) in Luke 7 where the evangelist anticipates the Emmaus disciples' statement that Jesus is a prophet mighty in deed and word before God and all the people.[57] Luke's use of *laós* in connection with his prophet Christology in Luke 7:16 presents Jesus as the miracle-worker who continues the messianic ministry of miracles announced at Nazareth (Luke 4:16-30), and elicits a faithful response of fear and praise from the people to Jesus the eschatological prophet like Moses. For the people at Nain, Jesus' miracles demonstrate God's visitation of his people, anticipated by Luke in the Benedictus (1:68) where the Lord God of Israel is blessed "for he has visited and redeemed his people." Miracles announce that the visitation has begun.

Luke contrasts his description of the people's reaction to Jesus' miracles with a description of their reaction to the rejected prophet in 7:18-35, where the evangelist describes Jesus' prophetic character *before God*.[58] Before the people and John, Jesus appears as the coming one through his miracles; but before God, Jesus is the one who must (*dei*) face rejection in fulfillment of the divine plan predicted by Isaiah. Jesus' prophetic ministry of deed and word "before God" is accepted by the people who are baptized by John (7:29), but rejected by the religious leaders who are not baptized by him (7:30).

[57]The Lukan use of *laós* has been noted in detail. Cf. J. Kodell, "Luke's Use of *Laos*, 'People,' Especially in the Jerusalem Narrative (Lk 19, 28-24, 53)," *CBQ* 31 (1969) 327-343. Kodell distinguishes between the Jewish leaders and the people in 19:28-24:53 and offers nine examples of this distinction, the last one being 24:19-20. Fitzmyer, *X-XXIV*, 1217 writes concerning its use in Luke 18:37 (and 24:19): "*Laos* is the Septuagintal word for God's people, and the frequency with which Luke uses it from now to the end of his Gospel is striking (it will appear nineteen times) and it is often used in contrast to the leaders of Jerusalem (esp. from 19:47-48 on)." See also J. B. Tyson, *Luke-Acts and the Jewish People* (Minneapolis: Augsburg, 1988); Tannehill, *Narrative Unity*, 143-144 on *laós* in Luke; and Sanders, *The Jews in Luke-Acts*, 37-83 in his chapter "The Jewish People," and pp. 304-317 on his conclusions.

[58]Cf. Dillon, *From Eyewitnesses*, 118-119 who also observes this important contrast between acceptance and rejection in Lukan Christology that manifests itself in the Nain story and the subsequent testimony of Jesus to John the Baptist.

Chapter 8

The Center Circle—The Opponents of Jesus

The second part of the confession of the Emmaus disciples in Luke 24:20-24 is their lament to Jesus about the fate of this prophet mighty in deed and word. Within the dialogue, the Emmaus disciples now contrast their Christology with the passion facts that are reflected in 24:20, demonstrating their complete misunderstanding of what had taken place in Jerusalem. Their recitation of the facts is in the form of a lament over dashed hopes. Luke 24:20 begins with the disciples asking themselves how it was possible that the chief priests and rulers of the people could have delivered Jesus into the judgment of death and crucified him. Their sorrow is emphasized in 24:17, "and they stood still, looking sad"; in 24:21, where they confess that "we had hoped that he was the one to redeem Israel"; and in 24:22-24, where they are so blinded by grief that even the news from the women and the report of the angels that Jesus is alive is not enough to convince them that Jesus is risen. The Emmaus disciples, by virtue of their own questioning, are interested in the Christological perspective of the Jerusalem authorities. One cannot speak of the Christology of the chief priests and rulers, however, but only of their perception of Jesus as they assessed him and his activities.

THE CHIEF PRIESTS AND RULERS IN LUKE-ACTS

The first step in determining this perception is to identify the chief priests and rulers in contrast to the other religious leaders in Jerusalem.[1] All the Synoptics list the following groups as members

---

[1]Tyson, *The Death of Jesus*, 48–83 uses the conflict between Jesus and his religious opponents as a means of identifying them. My discussion of the chief priest and rulers in Luke 24:20 is indebted to Tyson's and Sanders' (*The Jews in Luke-Acts*) careful analysis of the different religious groups and their relationship to Jesus.

of the Jewish religious establishment: Pharisees, chief priests, Sadducees, elders, and scribes. Matthew and Luke also include lawyers, while teachers of the law, rulers, and soldiers are exclusively Lukan categories.[2] These groups fit within a category that Joseph Tyson calls "the people of this generation [*tous anthrôpous tês geneás taútês*—Luke 7:31] . . . a technical term that Luke used to refer collectively to those who responded negatively to Jesus."[3] "The people of this generation" are divided by Tyson into two categories:

"The various groups may in turn be gathered into two larger complexes, for Luke's tendency is to divide the groups into two blocks—one whose major constituents are the Pharisees, and the other headed by the chief priests. Moreover, the priestly block is exclusively associated with the city of Jerusalem and the temple, while the Pharisaic block is primarily associated with Galilee and certain undesignated places."[4]

The Chief Priests

Tyson's perception that the Pharisees operate outside of Jerusalem is significant for Jesus' table fellowship in Luke. But an analysis of Luke 24:20 must begin with the chief priests, or what Tyson calls, "the priestly block." The singular "chief priest" is used only three times in Luke's Gospel to refer to the individual high priest in 3:2; 22:50; and 22:54. All other references are in the plural, "to denote members of the Sanhedrin who belonged to

[2]"Leading men" may be another Lukan category. It occurs in various constructions at Luke 19:47; Acts 13:50; 25:2; 28:7, 17. G. Bornkamm, *présbus ktl.*, *TDNT* VI 659 n. 45 equates them with the elders (*presbúteroi*) in 19:47, describing them as "lay nobility."

[3]Tyson, *The Death of Jesus*, 63. He lists Luke 9:41; 11:29-32, 47-51; 13:26-27; 17:25, and Acts 2:40 to support his contention. In Luke 7:18-35, Tyson also identifies on p. 62 those who respond positively to Jesus as " 'all the listening people,' tax collectors, and wisdom's children." This distinction is valuable to my study.

[4]Ibid., 63. Tyson states on pp. 63–64: "With the Pharisees are associated lawyers, teachers of the law, and *scribes*. Chief priests appear to be associated with *scribes*, elders, Sadducees, *stratêgoi*, and first citizens . . . . With the exception of the *scribes*, the lines that mark off the two blocks of opponents are clean" (emphasis mine). Cf. also J. T. Carroll, "Luke's Portrayal of the Pharisees," *CBQ* 50 (1988) 605.

high-priestly families: ruling high priests, those who have been deposed, and adult male members of the most prominent priestly families."[5] With the exception of Luke 3:2, all the references occur while Jesus is in Jerusalem, or refer to Jesus' betrayal in Jerusalem (Luke 9:22). Tyson's analysis of the role of the chief priests during Jesus' teaching in Jerusalem is exhaustive:[6]

"This block, in contrast to the Pharisaic block, is uniformly presented in a bad light. The overall designation of these groups as violently hostile to Jesus is the same throughout Luke's gospel. There are controversies between them and Jesus, and there are attacks on them by Jesus. Their purpose is never hidden from the reader: they seek to have Jesus put to death. Their tactics are gradually revealed, but we learn that they involve sending spies, trying to trap Jesus verbally, conspiring with a traitor, isolating Jesus from the populace, and turning him over to the political authorities. Consequently they engineer his arrest, formulate charges against him, and bring the charges before Pilate and Herod. The reluctance of these two rulers to condemn Jesus finally withers away before the insistent pleadings of the priestly block of opponents, who, in the trial scenes, have the backing of the Jewish public. The chief priests are pictured as thoroughgoing villains."[7]

The Rulers

In Luke 24:20 the evangelist's designation of the religious authorities in Jerusalem also includes "the rulers." Luke is the only Synoptic Gospel to use "rulers" (*árchontes*) to refer to Jerusalem religious authorities. John uses the word to refer to the Sanhedrin in John 3:1; 7:26, 48; and 12:42.[8] In looking over the evidence, the question has to be asked: Who are the "rulers?" W. Bauer, W. F. Arndt, and F. W. Gingrich define them as "authorities, officials," specifically as "Jewish authorities," and

[5]Bauer, Arndt, and Gingrich, *Greek-English Lexicon*, 112.
[6]Tyson, *The Death of Jesus*, 73–74.
[7]Ibid., 76–77.
[8]Cf. R. E. Brown, *The Gospel According to John I-XII* (New York: Doubleday and Company, Inc, 1966) 325; and C. K. Barrett, *The Gospel According to St John* (London: SPCK, 1967) 170, 268.

include Luke 24:20 under the category "members of the Sanhedrin," (along with Luke 18:18; 23:13, 35; John 3:1; 7:26, 48; 12:42; Acts 3:17; 4:5, 8; 13:27; 14:5). Included in this category is Luke 14:1 where "a ruler who belonged to the Pharisees" is described as "a member of the Sanhedrin who was a Pharisee."[9] G. Delling defines the rulers as follows:

"In the NT *árchôn* . . . denotes Roman and Jewish officials of all kinds, often without specifying the particular office. In Jn. and Lk. the *árchontes* are groups in the Jewish people, distinguished by Lk. from the *presbúteroi, grammateís, archiereís*, and by Jn. from the Pharisees (and sometimes even opposed to them, 12:42), though they may be fellow-members of the religious *archaí*. Occasionally *archôn* may simply mean 'respected.' "[10]

G. Schrenk makes this pertinent comment about *archiereís* in Luke 24:20: "The *hoi archiereís kai hoi árchontes* of Lk. 23:13; 24:20 is unusual, since the *árchontes* are normally the chief priests."[11]

These definitions raise a number of questions about Luke 24:20. Is it a reference to the chief priests, the scribes, the Pharisees, or the Sanhedrin? Is it a carefully crafted designation or a Lukan redundancy? Does it have any bearing on the death of Jesus and the reasons for his death? If Luke sums up one level of his Christology in Luke 24:19 by the simple statement that "Jesus of Nazareth . . . was a prophet mighty in deed and word before God and all the people," might he also be summing up the opposition to Jesus by means of the designation "our chief priests and rulers?" This suggests that "our chief priests and rulers" refers to the Sanhedrin, and since the chief priests were Sadducees, then "the rulers" would refer to the remainder of the Sanhedrin, including the Pharisees. A close look at these categories in Luke-Acts will determine whether or not there is support for this.

The Pharisees and Scribes

To begin, one needs to evaluate Tyson's contention that the Pharisees do not figure into the death of Jesus since they are not

[9]Bauer, Arndt, and Gingrich, *Greek-English Lexicon*, 113.
[10]G. Delling, *árchôn*, TDNT I 489.
[11]G. Schrenk, *archieréus*, TDNT III 271. Cf. Tannehill, *Narrative Unity*, 187.

mentioned within Jesus' Jerusalem ministry, i.e. 19:45–24:53.[12] The Pharisees' last appearance is in Luke 19:39 just before Jesus enters into the city of Jerusalem. Tyson considers "the Pharisees" as the title for one of the two major blocks of Jesus' opposition. Included in the Pharisaical block are lawyers, teachers of the law, and scribes.[13] Although the lawyers (Luke 7:30; 10:25; 11:45, 46, 52, [53]; 14:3) and the teachers of the law (Luke 5:17; Acts 5:34) do not appear during Jesus' Jerusalem ministry, the scribes do (Luke 19:47; 20:1, 19, 39, 46; 22:2, 66; 23:10). In fact, the scribes are the only religious authorities who appear with both the Pharisees (Luke 5:21, 30; 6:7; 11:53; 15:2; Acts 23:9) and the chief priests (Luke 9:22; 19:47; 20:1, 19; 22:2, 66; 23:10).[14]

Who are the scribes? In Luke, they appear either with the Pharisees or the chief priests except in Luke 20:34-47 where they appear alone within the context of Jesus' temple teaching. In 20:39, they agree with Jesus' answer to the Sadducees about marriage. Surprisingly, Jesus then launches into a warning against them in 20:45-47. In the only pericope where the scribes appear in isolation from the Pharisees and chief priests, Jesus says they will receive the greatest condemnation.

The scribes are the only religious figures who appear with Jesus in all three localities of his teaching: in Galilee, in his journey to Jerusalem, and in Jerusalem itself.[15] Their first appearance in Luke

[12]Tyson, *The Death of Jesus*, 68.

[13]Ibid., 63. Cf. Tannehill, *Narrative Unity*, 169–172, and Sanders, *The Jews in Luke-Acts*, 84–94, 101–110 on scribes and Pharisees in Luke.

[14]Tyson, *The Death of Jesus*, 64 dismisses this by saying: "The association of scribes with both Pharisees and chief priests may appear to present a problem. But when we recognize their minor role in the narrative, the problem becomes inconsequential. It should be emphasized, however, that Luke is very careful to associate all of the other minor groups with either Pharisees or chief priests, but not with both. With the exception of the scribes, the lines that mark off the two blocks of opponents are clean." Tyson may be correct here, but if Luke is careful in drawing the lines between Jesus' opponents, then his use of the scribes as a crossover group may be a significant statement about those bearing responsibility for Jesus' death. Certainly the role of the scribes in the Jerusalem narrative (8 occurrences) does not seem to be a minor one, especially since the chief priests are mentioned only 13 times, the rulers 3 times, the elders 2 times, the Sadducees once, and the Sanhedrin once.

[15]The Pharisees are confined to his ministry outside of Jerusalem and the

5:21 defines their role within the Gospel. In this healing of the paralytic, the scribes and the Pharisees question Jesus' ability to forgive sins and accuse him of blasphemy. Earlier in 5:17 they are referred to as "the teachers of the law."

"The term *nomodidaskaloi* occurs only here in the gospel tradition; in Acts 5:34 it is used of Gamaliel, identified as a Pharisee in the Jerusalem Sanhedrin. They are probably to be understood as a specific group within the Pharisees and probably are the same as the 'Scribes' of v. 21, leaders of the Pharisaic group, the 'rabbis' of later tradition."[16]

Fitzmyer suggests a close relationship between the scribes and the Pharisees. This seems to be confirmed in Luke 5:30 at the feast of Levi where Luke introduces these religious leaders as "the Pharisees and *their (autôn)* scribes," i.e. the scribes as a subgroup of the greater Pharisaical block. The rest of the occurrences in Luke between these two groups do not preserve such a distinction, for in 5:21, 6:7, and 11:53 the scribes are listed first, and in 15:2 the Pharisees precede the scribes. Luke 5:30 seems to be the clue that unlocks the mystery of the relationship between the scribes and the Pharisees.

This observation, however, may not be consistent with the traditional view on the relationship between the scribes and Pharisees. For one thing, Pharisees and scribes are not one and the same group.[17] This is borne out by Luke who, in the woes of Jesus

---

chief priests to his Jerusalem ministry. The other major group in the Sanhedrin, the *presbúteroi*, appear outside Jerusalem only in 7:3 in the miracle of the healing of the centurion's servant, and in 9:22, which is a passion prediction of what will take place in Jerusalem. For all intents and purposes, the elders are attached to Jesus' Jerusalem ministry: in 20:1, they appear with the chief priests and scribes in questioning Jesus' authority; in 22:52, they are in the company of the chief priests and captains of the temple at the arrest of Jesus; and in 22:66, they assemble as part of the Sanhedrin to try Jesus.

[16]Fitzmyer, *I-IX*, 581.

[17]Cf. J. Jeremias, *grammateús, TDNT* I 741 on scribes: "To understand the judgment of Jesus on the theologians of his age, we must distinguish them sharply from the Pharisees, whose societies were mostly composed of small people with no theological mastery"; or Jeremias, *Jerusalem in the Time of Jesus*, 254.

against scribes and Pharisees, distinguishes between the scribes (Luke 11:45-52; 20:46) and the Pharisees (Luke 11:37-44). *But the leaders (árchontes) of the Pharisees were scribes, and these Pharisaical scribes represented the Pharisees in the Sanhedrin.*[18] The nomenclature for the Sanhedrin in the Synoptics tends to include the three religious groups of the chief priests, scribes, and elders, although there are variations on this tripartite designation.[19] The designation to ''be rejected by the elders and chief priests and scribes'' in Luke 9:22, although occurring outside of Jerusalem, is programmatic for the Sanhedrin in Luke. In my observation of the close relationship between Luke 9 and 24, the focus was on the relationship between 9:22 and 24:25-27. The similarities may now be extended to include 24:20 in reference to the Sanhedrin. The reader must read Luke's passion history in view of Luke 9:22, cognizant that those responsible for the death of Jesus were elders, chief priests, and scribes.[20] This is confirmed by looking at the four trials of Jesus.

[18]Cf. Jeremias, *Jerusalem in the Time of Jesus*, 236: ''Apart from the chief priests and members of the patrician families the scribe was the only person who could enter the supreme court, the Sanhedrin. *The Pharisaical party in the Sanhedrin was composed entirely of scribes''* (emphasis mine). Jeremias also writes on p. 254: ''One point is true: that the *leaders* and the influential members of Pharisaic communities were *scribes''* (emphasis Jeremias). Cf. also Kodell, ''Luke's Use of *Laos*,'' 329 n. 13 on the religious leaders in Luke's Jerusalem narrative: ''*Hoi archiereis* and *hoi grammateis* are coupled in these chapters (19,47; 20,1.19; 22,2.66; 23,10), but earlier it was *'hoi grammateis kai hoi pharisaioi'* (5,21.30; 6,7; 11,53; 15,2). The Pharisees are still present, though now as members of the Sanhedrin.''

[19]Cf. E. Lohse, *sunédrion, TDNT* VII 864 on the various designations in the Synoptics as to the makeup of the Sanhedrin. Luke chooses to distinguish the members of this council as chief priests/scribes in Luke 19:47; 22:2; 23:10; as chief priests/elders in Acts 4:23; 23:14; 25:15; as simply chief priests in Luke 22:4; [23:4]; and Acts 22:30; as elders/chief priests/scribes in Luke 9:22; as *rulers*/elders/scribes in Acts 4:5; as *rulers* of the people and elders in Acts 4:8; and as elders/scribes in Acts 6:12.

[20]Cf. Fitzmyer, *I-IX*, 780 on elders, chief priests, and scribes in 9:22: ''[These] three groups . . . made up the Great Sanhedrin in Jerusalem. This threesome is met here for the first time in Luke.'' Marshall, *The Gospel of Luke*, 370 observes that ''Luke stresses the unity of the three groups by omitting the article with the second and third nouns.'' Tannehill, *Narrative Unity*, 188 notes that ''this group's appearance [chief priests, scribes, and elders] on

The Jewish Religious Authorities at the Trials of Jesus.[21]

THE JEWISH TRIAL (22:66).[22] This is Luke's only reference to the Sanhedrin. Jesus appears here before the fullest representation of Israel: "the assembly *(to presbutérion)* of the elders of the people gathered together, both chief priests and scribes; and they led him away to their council" *(eis to sunédrion autôn)*. The "assembly" *(presbutérion)* is different from the "elder" *(presbúteros)*, referring to "the highest Jewish council in Jerusalem . . . called *sunédrion*."[23] For Luke, there is also a difference between the "assembly" *(presbutérion)* and the "council" *(sunédrion)*. The first refers to the assembly of the Sanhedrin itself, while the second refers to the council-chamber.[24] In any event, the trial of Jesus is before the official religious establishment of Israel, the Sanhedrin, composed of chief priests and scribes. Only Luke has *presbutérion*, and for him, it is made up of *both* chief priests and scribes. Matthew and Mark construct the participants of this trial a little differently. Matthew 27:1 does not have *sunédrion* or scribes, but only "all the chief priests and the elders of the people"; Mark 15:1 has the fullest accounting: "the chief priests, with the elders and scribes, and the whole council" *(sunédrion)*.

PILATE'S FIRST TRIAL (23:1). Luke describes the group that brought Jesus to Pilate as "the whole company *(plêthos)*[25] of them." The

---

the scene in 19:47, with the specific intent of destroying Jesus, makes clear that Jesus' prophecy in 9:22 is nearing fulfillment."

[21]See Sanders, *The Jews in Luke-Acts*, 5–15, 221–226 on the Jewish leaders in the trial of Jesus.

[22]The titles for the four trials of Jesus are taken from Neyrey, *The Passion*, 81.

[23]Bauer, Arndt, and Gingrich, *Greek-English Lexicon*, 706. Cf. also G. Bornkamm, *présbus ktl., TDNT* VI 654.

[24]D. R. Catchpole, *The Trial of Jesus* (Leiden: E. J. Brill, 1971) 191–192 offers the following arguments for this position: 1) A reference to the council already occurred in *presbutérion*; 2) *sunédrion* is used in a local sense in Acts; 3) *eis* does not mean "before"; 4) a change in locale must be indicated by *apégagon* and necessitated by Jesus being first taken in 22:54 to the high priest's house.

[25]Fitzmyer, *X-XXIV*, 1474 notes that *plêthos* "is uniquely Lucan," indicating that the crowd moving Jesus from trial to trial is made up of the Sanhedrin.

nearest referent is Luke 22:66 that includes the Sanhedrin, both chief priests and scribes, and the men in 22:63 who were holding Jesus in custody. The representatives of the Jewish religious establishment in 23:1 are the same as those in 22:66. In the course of the trial in 23:4, Pilate asks a question of the chief priests and the crowds. "The chief priests" is most likely Lukan shorthand for the Sanhedrin. As Jesus moves from trial to trial, more people are involved than just the Sanhedrin. The crowds here are closely associated with the chief priests, and Luke wants the reader to see that they are one and the same group. The responsibility for the death of Jesus is now spreading beyond the Jewish religious establishment to include the Jewish people.

HEROD'S TRIAL (23:6-12). At the trial of Herod, religious authorities are only mentioned in 23:10 where "the chief priests and scribes stood by, vehemently accusing him." This verse is unique to Luke, a return to his previous designation for the Sanhedrin. This is the last time that the scribes are mentioned in Luke's Gospel.

PILATE'S SECOND TRIAL (23:13-15). Luke's nomenclature for the religious leaders completely changes at the second trial before Pilate. Luke states that Pilate called together "the chief priests and *the rulers* and the people." This pericope is also unique to Luke. A number of observations may be made:

1) This is Luke's fullest description so far of those present at the trials of Jesus, including both the Jewish religious establishment and the Jewish people.

2) Luke has changed his designation within the Sanhedrin from scribes to rulers. The referent of rulers in 23:13 seems to be the scribes, the only other members of the Sanhedrin in the trials of Jesus referred to by Luke. The referent may also include the elders, but they are noticeably absent during the Lukan trials of Jesus. It may also be a general term that refers to the leaders in the Sanhedrin besides the chief priests. Luke will not refer to scribes again, and will speak of chief priests once more in 24:20. He will, however, refer to rulers again: in 23:35, at the foot of the cross, where the rulers will scoff at Jesus and say, "He saved others; let him save himself, if he is the Christ of God," and in

116

24:20. If the rulers are leaders of the Pharisees, then it is the Pharisees who taunt Jesus in 23:35.[26]

3) The use of "the people" (*laós*) in 23:13 indicates that Luke wants to implicate the Jewish nation in bearing responsibility for the death of Jesus. There are various views as to the role of the people (*laós*) in the death of Jesus in Luke. J. Kodell concludes that

"Luke . . . does not deny the fact that the Jewish nation was guilty in the death of Jesus, but he presents the guilt as softened by ignorance, and does not in the least consider the Jewish people cursed or rejected. The lion's share of the blame falls on the Jewish leaders, carefully distinguished from the people as a whole."[27]

Kodell finds it difficult to explain Luke 23:4-5 and 23:13 in view of his thesis. Rejecting the argument that there is a corruption in the text in 23:13, i.e. that *"tous árchontas kai ton laón* was substituted for the original *tous árchontas tou laoú,"*[28] Kodell argues that Luke 23:4-5 and 23:13 must be taken together and explained in this way:

"Tradition told Luke that the people of Jerusalem were involved in the condemnation and death of Jesus (see Acts 2,23; 3,17; 10,39; 13,27); but while affirming this in his Passion account, he

---

[26]Cf. the parallels in Matthew 27:41, where "the chief priest, with the scribes and elders, mocked him," and Mark 15:31, where "the chief priests mocked him to one another with the scribes . . . ." In both cases, the Sanhedrin is mocking Jesus. Luke's "rulers" may be shorthand for the Sanhedrin. Cf. also Luke 14:1 where Jesus went to dine at the house "of a ruler who belonged to the Pharisees." Luke 14:3 indicates that those invited to the house of this ruler of the Pharisees besides Jesus were lawyers and Pharisees. Scribes are not mentioned in this context, but, as I observed, many of the leaders of the Pharisees were scribes. Scribes and Pharisees return to the Lukan vocabulary in 15:2 in the introduction to the three parables. Although it is difficult to press a reference to the scribes in 14:1, Luke may refer here to a member of the Sanhedrin. Ellis, *The Gospel of Luke*, 193 supports this: *"ruler:* a Sanhedrin member who belonged to the Pharisees or a leader of the Pharisee party" (emphasis Ellis).

[27]Kodell, "Luke's Use of *Laos*," 343.

[28]Ibid., 332.

plays down their culpability, still leaving the impression that the leaders bore most of the guilt."[29]

A number of exegetes do not consider the people (*laós*) as innocent of the death of Jesus as Kodell does. Concerning the role of the people in the trials of Jesus, J. Neyrey concludes that "in each case, Luke has suggested the broadest possible Jewish representation of the Jews in keeping with his interest in presenting Israel's formal rejection of God's prophet."[30] The theme of rejection by Israel is foreshadowed in Luke 4 in the sermon at Nazareth and now finds fulfillment here in the trials of Jesus. Tyson confirms Neyrey's thesis in his analysis of the theme of acceptance and rejection of Jesus:

"But when we come to the scenes of Jesus' trial, death, and resurrection (Luke 22:47–24:53), we find that, although Jesus is not without some popular support, the crowd as a whole is lined up with his opponents, who are led by the chief priests. With them, they insist before Pilate on Jesus' guilt (23:4-5, 13-14), call for the release of Barabbas (23:18), call for Jesus' crucifixion (23:21,23), and stand around watching it (23:35)."[31]

Since I argued that the rejection of Jesus is part of Luke's Christology, I support the position that the people (*laós*) are implicated in the death of Jesus along with the religious authorities. This makes Luke 23:13 a pivotal verse for Luke and climactic in his portrayal of the opposition of Jesus. It is closely related to Luke 24:19-20, where Jesus' failure to live up to the lower expectations of the disciples and the people (Jesus as a prophet mighty in deed and word before all the people) causes disillusionment and allows the people to consider joining forces with the chief priests and rulers in their condemnation of Jesus that led to his crucifixion. Luke has purposely portrayed the people as rejecting Jesus because Jesus does not meet their messianic expectations. Thus, both 23:13 and 24:19-20 serve as accurate summaries of the opposition of Jesus in his trials and after his resurrection.

[29]Ibid., 333.
[30]Neyrey, *The Passion*, 81.
[31]Tyson, *The Death of Jesus*, 34.

The referent throughout Luke 23:18-25 is the group that Pilate called together in 23:13, the chief priests, rulers, and the people. Neyrey shows five places within the second trial of Jesus before Pilate where the Jewish religious leaders and crowds of 23:13 consciously *choose* the death of Jesus, a unique Lukan accent.[32] Luke has shaped the trials of Jesus so as to implicate these three groups in his death. The only other reference to the rulers (*árchontes*) in the passion narrative is in 23:35 where they are distinguished from the people (*laós*). Here the attitude of the rulers is still portrayed by Luke as hostile, but it is difficult to discern the attitude toward Jesus of the people who are portrayed as observers. Luke sets the stage here for their reaction in 23:48: "And all the multitudes who assembled to see the sight, when they saw what had taken place, returned home beating their breasts." A separation between the rulers and the people is reinstated by Luke after they witnessed the crucifixion. Although the people were implicated in the death of Jesus, Luke is quick to demonstrate their sorrow at their crime.

Who are the rulers in Luke 24:20? This brings us back to the original question: Who are the rulers in Luke 24:20, and why are they mentioned?[33] The possibilities include the elders, the scribes, or even a synonym for the chief priests. In any case, it most likely refers to leaders of the Sanhedrin, as the evidence above suggests. Since the chief priests have been included within the verse, the possibilities are reduced to the elders or the scribes. The closest referent to Luke 24:20 is the group called together by Pilate in

[32]Neyrey, *The Passion,* 83 writes: "Luke draws special attention to them as *choosing*:

1. They choose Barabbas and reject Jesus (23:18).

2. Their shouting prevails, *choosing* (*aitoúmenoi*) Jesus to be crucified (23:23).

3. Pilate gave sentence that their *choice* (*aítēma*) be granted (23:24).

4. He released Barabbas, whom they *chose* (*ētoúnto*, 23:25a).

5. And he handed Jesus over *to their will* (*tô thelēmati autôn,* 23:25b)" (emphasis Neyrey). In his analysis of *laós* in the Jerusalem narrative, Kodell does not discuss this pericope.

[33]With reference to "ruler" in Luke 18:18, Fitzmyer, *X-XXIV,* 1198 offers a helpful hermeneutical principle in determining the referent for "ruler": "Its [*archōn*] specific sense in Palestinian (or other) society can only be gained by the context."

23:13 ("the chief priests and the rulers and the people"), and the rulers who are mocking Jesus at the cross in 23:35. The reader of Luke would have observed how carefully the evangelist has constructed the four trial scenes of Jesus so as to pinpoint those responsible for his death. Throughout the trials, the chief priests and scribes (later called leaders) gather the support of the people, condemning Jesus to death and calling for his crucifixion. Thus, it seems reasonable to conclude that the rulers in 24:20 are scribes, who, I have argued, are Pharisees.[34]

Matthew confirms this in 27:62 by referring to "the chief priests and the Pharisees" within the Jerusalem narrative who appear before Pilate after Jesus' death to urge him to seal the tomb. Matthew has no difficultly associating the Pharisees with the chief priests in connection with the death of Jesus, although he is more apt to associate the chief priests with the elders (Matt 27:1, 3, 12, 20) or the scribes and the elders (27:41).[35] Luke could simply be referring in 24:20 to the other leaders of the Sanhedrin besides the chief priests, but it appears as if the evangelist wants the reader to make a more specific association. *If these rulers are Pharisaical scribes, the reader could conclude that the Emmaus disciples considered the chief priests, Jesus' opposition in Jerusalem, and the Pharisaical scribes, Jesus' opposition outside of Jerusalem, to be responsible for his death.*

This conclusion does not necessarily contradict Tyson's assertion that "the Pharisees disappear as Jesus approaches Jerusalem and are totally absent from the scenes that describe his arrest, trial,

[34]Fitzmyer's principle applied to "ruler" in Luke-Acts supports this assertion. In Luke 8:41, the referent is difficult to determine; in Luke 14:1, a Pharisee is called a leader; in Luke 18:18, the closest referent is the Pharisees in 17:20, reinforced by the parable of the Pharisee and publican in 18:9-14; and in Luke 23:13, 35 and 24:20, I argued that the leaders are Pharisaical scribes. The two references in Acts pertinent to this discussion offer no serious difficulties. In 3:17, the referent seems to be the religious leaders in Jerusalem. In 4:1-8, Luke describes a meeting of the Sanhedrin. In 4:1 he refers to representatives of the temple authorities; in 4:5 to the Sanhedrin.

[35]Cf. Mark 15:1, which gives a broad description of "chief priests, with the elders and scribes," but goes on in 15:3, 10, 11 to use only the "chief priests" as representative of Jesus' opposition. In 15:31, he includes the scribes with the chief priests. These observations in Mark are consistent with my findings in Luke.

and crucifixion.''[36] Luke may very well be preparing the reader to view the Pharisees in a more favorable light since they will be treated favorably by him in Acts. As Tyson himself says, ''the description of Pharisees in Acts can best be described as positive.''[37] The reader, however, is very much aware of the opposition the Pharisees gave to Jesus during his ministry outside Jerusalem. It would be unreasonable not to include their accusations against Jesus in the overall plot against him, especially since so much time is devoted to their interaction with him during Jesus' ministry. For Luke, it is not helpful to accuse them by name, since they will be significant to the emerging Christian community in Acts. However, in keeping with Luke's methodology of forcing the reader to read back into the Gospel for clues to the motifs he brings to completion in Luke 24, the evangelist must include the Pharisaical opposition to Jesus in the overall opposition of the Jewish religious authorities represented by the Sanhedrin. The reason for this will be forthcoming in the next two chapters when the charges against Jesus will be evaluated in the context of Jesus' teaching and table-fellowship during his ministry outside Jerusalem.[38]

THE JUDGMENT OF DEATH — *paradídōmi*

The second step in determining the Christological perspective of the Jerusalem authorities is to identify the charges the opponents of Jesus brought against him that led to his death. Luke 24:20 necessitates such a decision since it reads, ''and how our chief priests and rulers delivered him up to be condemned to death (*eis kríma thanátou*), and crucified him.'' ''Condemned to death'' (*eis kríma thanátou*) suggests a judicial setting in which a sentence of condemnation is being handed down on the basis of the decision of a court.[39] In any judicial decision, charges are made. In the trial of Jesus, it is critical to determine the charges against Jesus.

[36]Tyson, *The Death of Jesus*, 72.
[37]Ibid., 71–72.
[38]Cf. W. R. Farmer, *Jesus and the Gospel* (Philadelphia: Fortress Press, 1982) 36–48 on the teaching of Jesus against the Pharisees in the context of table fellowship.
[39]Cf. Bauer, Arndt, and Gingrich, *Greek-English Lexicon*, 451 who classify Luke 24:20 under the category of ''*judicial verdict* . . . mostly in an unfavor-

"To deliver him up" (*parédôkan*) also suggests a judicial setting, especially when one traces its use in Luke's Gospel. An analysis of *paradídômi* helps establish a relationship between the death of Jesus and the table fellowship matrix. This is especially significant since *paradídômi* became a technical term in Eucharistic liturgies because of Paul's use of it in 1 Corinthians 11:23 (*paredídeto*—a passive that suggests the agency of God).[40] The context of the Last Supper was the betrayal of Jesus into the hands of sinful people, a fact that confronted the disciples on their walk to Emmaus and caused their sorrow. The betrayal of Jesus in the context of the meal in Luke 22 will soon become the basis for their hope in the context of the new meal they will eat with Jesus at Emmaus in Luke 24. The betrayal of Jesus and the meal of Jesus are inextricably entwined.

The following references in Luke's Gospel are significant to my investigation of the death of Jesus in relationship to the table fellowship matrix and the charges against Jesus that led to his death.

Luke 9:44

In the second Lukan passion prediction, Jesus states that "the Son of man is to be delivered (*paradídosthai*) into the hands of men." This is a reference to arrest and trial in Luke 22–23. The passive voice of this present infinitive suggests that Jesus is being delivered up according to the plan of God.[41] This is in keeping with Luke's theology of the death of Jesus. The referent for "the hands of men" is uncertain.

---

able sense, of the *sentence of condemnation,* also of the *condemnation* and subsequent *punishment* itself . . . *death sentence*" (emphasis BAG). Cf. also F. Büchsel, *kríma, TDNT* III 942 n. 5.

[40]Cf. Jeremias, *Eucharistic Words,* 112–113 on 1 Corinthians 11:23 in the section, "The development of a Christian liturgical language:" "The following 'in the night when he was delivered up' is also liturgical, for it is not a mere chronological statement. The verb 'delivered up,' used absolutely, refers to an action of God; the passive is thus a circumlocution for the divine name, as in Rom 4.25. We are to understand it as 'on the night when God delivered him up,' and we cannot fail to hear the echo of Isaiah 53" (emphasis Jeremias).

[41]Cf. Marshall, *The Gospel of Luke,* 394.

Luke 18:32

In the third Lukan passion prediction, *paradídōmi* is also used in the passive: "for he will be delivered (*paradothēsetai*) to the Gentiles." This is a much fuller prediction that mentions Jerusalem as the city of destiny, the fulfillment of Scripture, the various sufferings that will go along with the betrayal (mocked, shamefully treated, spit upon, scourged, killed) and the resurrection. The passive voice is again in force. Luke replaces "into the hands of men" with "the Gentiles," suggesting the involvement of Pilate and the Roman authorities. This is a direct reference to the trials of Jesus and the charges that are evaluated by Pilate in connection with Jesus' arrest. Only Luke has two trials before Pilate. The relationship between Pilate, Herod, and the Jewish religious leaders is significant in determining the charges against Jesus.

Luke 20:20

The context is the plot of the scribes and chief priests to arrest Jesus "so as to deliver him up (*paradoúnai*) to the authority and jurisdiction of the governor." Luke has now moved from a general reference in 18:32 ("the Gentiles") to a specific reference in 20:20 ("the governor"). The presence of the scribes and chief priests foreshadows Luke 24:20. Luke uses a result clause (*hôste* with the infinitive *paradoúnai*) to express the intentions of the religious authorities. The absence of the passive here shows how the scribes and chief priests have become active participants in the plan of God, acting on his behalf in seeking Jesus' death.

Luke 21:12, 16

paradídōmi is used here to foreshadow the persecution of the apostles as the Christian Church emerges in Acts. This is the first suggestion we have seen that the trials of Jesus are proleptic of the trials of his disciples. The Emmaus disciples are unaware that their recitation of Jesus' deliverance into the hands of the chief priests and rulers foreshadows their own deliverance.[42]

---

[42]Cf. Neyrey, *The Passion*, 87–88 on Luke 21:12-15 as programmatic for the narrative in Acts: "What binds Jesus' trials with the trials of the Church in Acts is not just the conscious fulfillment of Jesus' prophecies in Acts. In Luke's Gospel, Jesus himself is the archetype and model of the Church's experience, and so the essential items of the prediction are dramatized in Jesus' own story."

Luke 22:4, 6

All the references in Luke 22 that speak of Jesus' betrayal are centered in the plot of Judas and the Jewish religious authorities. The first two references to betrayal in Luke 22 refer specifically to Judas' plotting with the chief priests and captains because Satan has entered into him (22:3).

Luke 22:21, 22

paradídōmi is used twice by Luke in these two verses, occurring within the context of the Supper itself, coming right after the words of institution in Luke 22:20: "This is my body. . . . This cup which is poured out for you is the new covenant in my blood." Jesus announces here his knowledge of the betrayal to the apostles. There are a number of significant themes in Luke 22:21-22 that are related to my investigation:

1) The betrayal of Jesus has now been reduced to the person of Judas. The plot of the chief priests, scribes, captains, and Satan in 22:1-6 has been located in the person of Judas. Judas is an important person in Luke, especially since Luke gives the fullest account of Judas' role of betrayal.[43]

2) Jesus' knowledge of the preordained necessity of his death is indicated by his words in 22:22: "For the Son of man goes as it has been determined" (*katá to hôrisménon*). Jesus is referring to his journey to Jerusalem, the city of his destiny. The use of *to hôrisménon* suggests the preordained plan of God for Jesus, especially from his use of this word in Luke-Acts.[44]

3) Luke 22:21-23 contains the "characteristic elements of a fare-

---

[43]Ibid., 20: "The story of Judas serves several functions: (a) as agent of Satan (22:3), Judas indicates that the forces of evil rose up against God's Holy One, indirectly attesting to Jesus' closeness to God and his innocent suffering; (b) his role is the fulfillment of Scripture (Acts 1:16); thus his treachery is not outside God's knowledge or control; (c) Judas functions as a foil to Peter and to the faithful followers of Jesus."

[44]Cf. Fitzmyer, *X-XXIV*, 1410: "Luke writes *kata to hôrismenon*, lit. 'according to that (which has been) determined,' i.e. by God (theological passive . . .). For the Lukan use of *horizein*, see Acts 2:23; 10:42; 11:29; 17:26,31. In four of these passages the reference is to God's will. With this phrase Luke has related the betrayal of Jesus by Judas to the Father's plan of salvation-history. This plan provides the background for the necessity of Jesus' suffering and death. Recall 13:33."

well speech.''[45] Within the table fellowship matrix, the genre of a farewell speech is significant.

Luke 22:48

Luke 22:48 marks the actual deliverance of Jesus into the hands of his enemies. The betrayer now meets the betrayed. The betrayal is by means of a kiss. The confrontation is like that between God and Satan. Tyson observes that for Luke, ''Judas' . . . role in Luke 22 is that of isolating Jesus from the crowd . . . of driving a wedge between the crowd and Jesus.''[46] Luke's use of ''to draw near'' (êggisen) in 22:47 points again to Jesus' preordained destiny as it is connected with the Last Supper.

Luke 23:25

Luke uses paradídômi from 22:4 to 23:25 to provide the framework for the passion narrative. The narrative that began in 22:4, with the plot of Judas to deliver Jesus to the chief priests and captains, concludes with the trial of Jesus in 23:25 when Pilate delivers Jesus over to the will of the chief priests, the rulers, and the people. The next step is death by crucifixion. Luke 23:25 is the culmination of the betrayal that was anticipated in 9:44, 18:32, 20:20, and 22:4, 6, 21, 22, and partially realized in 22:48. The referent in Luke 24:20, therefore, is to all these passages that find their completion in 23:25. The phrase ''delivered up to their will'' is a significant Lukan phrase since it fully implicates the chief priests, the rulers, and the people mentioned in 23:13. It serves as the final indictment of Israel in the death of Jesus.[47]

Luke 24:7

The two occurrences of paradídômi in Luke 24 mark it not only as a significant passion word, but also as part of the passion formula

[45]Neyrey, The Passion, 17–18 gives a detailed analysis of these elements as they relate to Luke 22:21-23.

[46]Tyson, The Death of Jesus, 121.

[47]Sanders, The Jews in Luke-Acts, 81 concludes on the Jews in Luke-Acts: ''By the end of Acts the Jews have become what they from the first were; for what Jesus, Stephen, Peter and Paul say about the Jews—about their intransigent opposition to the purposes of God, about their hostility toward Jesus and the gospel, about their murder of Jesus—is what Luke understands the Jewish people to be in their essence'' (emphasis Sanders).

that will be used of Jesus in Acts 3:13, a programmatic text for the proclamation of the kerygma in Luke's second volume, and for the deliverance of the apostles into the hands of their persecutors in Acts 8:3; 12:4; 21:11; 22:4; 27:1; and 28:17. As the first of three passion statements in the final chapter of the Gospel, Luke 24:7 occurs within the story of the empty tomb. The angels call the women to "remember how he told you while he was still in Galilee" (24:6). The reader, like the women, is encouraged to recall what Jesus said in Galilee in the first passion prediction in Luke 9:22, for the angels ask the women to remember "that the Son of man must be delivered (*paradothênai*) into the hands of sinful men." The reader might also remember Luke 9:44 and 18:32, those passion statements that speak of Jesus' deliverance into the hands of his enemies. Thus, the betrayal of Jesus, i.e. his death and the charges that led to his death, is recalled by the reader as he confronts Luke 24:7.

In *24:20* the Emmaus disciples will use the same language as the two angels in 24:7: Jesus was delivered (*paradídômi*) and crucified. The reader of 24:20 will not only return to the previous pericope and observe the same language, but he will also observe it throughout Luke's Gospel as passion language, confirming the methodological approach of Luke that calls for the reader to read back into the Gospel from the perspective of the final chapter.

Conclusions on paradídômi

There are a number of conclusions to be drawn from my observations about *paradídômi*:

1) It is part of the vocabulary of the passion, and could even be considered a technical term for Jesus' betrayal, suffering, and death. Luke uses it in his passion predictions (9:44; 18:32), in the plots of the Jewish religious authorities and Judas to put Jesus to death (20:20; 22:4, 6), in predictions of the disciples "passion" in the Church (21:12, 16), in Jesus' recognition of his destiny during the Last Supper (22:21-22), in the actual entrance into the passion with Jesus' arrest (22:48) and his crucifixion (23:25), and in reflections about what was prophesied and what took place in Jesus' passion (24:7, 20). A simple "remembrance" of Luke's use of

paradídōmi would recall for the reader the passion of Jesus and the charges that were filed against him leading to his passion.

2) The use of the passive voice in Luke 9:44; 18:32; 21:16; and 24:7 suggests the agency of God who is ultimately responsible for delivering Jesus to his death according to his preordained plan of salvation (cf. also Luke 22:21-22). The necessity of Jesus' death may be seen in the passion predictions themselves (by Luke's use of *dei*), but the necessity of Jesus' death according to God's plan is a major Lukan perspective on the death of Jesus.

3) Luke first narrows the agent of betrayal from "the hands of men" (9:44) to "the Gentiles" (18:32) to "the scribes and chief priests" (20:20) to "Judas" who has been entered by "Satan" (22:4, 6, 48), and then he broadens the responsibility to implicate all of Israel, "the chief priests and the rulers and the people" (23:25). Jews, Gentiles, and Satan are all responsible for Jesus' death in accordance to the way determined by God (22:22).

4) The methodology of reading back into the Gospel from the perspective of Luke 24 is suggested by Luke's use of *paradídōmi* in 24:7 and 20. Such a reading of Luke will acquaint the reader with the reasons for Jesus' death.

Chapter 9

Lukan Meals and Meal Metaphors— The Galilean Ministry

My investigation thus far has identified the opposition of Jesus that delivered him up to death on the basis of certain charges drawn up within a judicial setting. The next step is to determine the exact nature of those charges. In the following two chapters I will argue that *Jesus' table fellowship* is one of the reasons he is put to death by the chief priests, his antagonists in Jerusalem, and the Pharisees (the rulers in 24:20), his antagonists outside Jerusalem. This was first suggested by R. Karris in *Luke: Artist and Theologian*.[1] Karris' study is important for this chapter on Lukan meals. He has compiled a list of all the references to food in Luke's Gospel.[2] His awareness of the intricate and extensive structure of the food motif must be brought to bear upon the table fellowship matrix.

Although table fellowship is a category under Luke's food motif, it is not synonymous with it. I will accent different aspects of Luke's table fellowship, particularly as they relate to the Emmaus meal and the eschatological dimension of the table fellowship. Table fellowship is just one expression of Luke's sensitivity to the role of food as a means of communicating God's faithfulness to his creation. But table fellowship must not be restricted to what is expressed around a table. Much of the teaching of Jesus includes table metaphors that reflect his view of table fellowship and the

---

[1]See Karris, *Luke: Artist and Theologian*, 47–78. In his chapter "The Theme of Food" he states on p. 47: "My major point in this chapter is that in Luke's Gospel Jesus got himself crucified by the way he ate."

[2]Ibid., 48–52 for an exhaustive list of the food imagery in Luke. Cf. also Flender, *St. Luke: Theologian of Redemptive History*, 81 on Luke's table settings.

eschatological kingdom.[3] In my discussion of the table fellowship matrix, some Lukan references to food will be considered, especially as he uses them to illustrate the eschatological fellowship. These references to food are part of the teaching of Jesus and serve as illustrations within his teaching.[4]

From the perspective of Luke 24, the table fellowship of Jesus consists primarily in his teaching at the table, much of which involves table metaphors. The actual eating itself, particularly as it involves those with whom Jesus eats, is also a form of teaching.[5] Neither the teaching itself nor the eating itself is of greater importance than the other; both must be considered together as one-and-the-same activity. When one sits down at a table with friends, one talks and one eats; both activities are integral to table fellowship.[6] Table fellowship reveals something about the participants of

[3]Cf. E. Lohmeyer, *Lord of the Temple* (Edinburgh and London: Oliver and Boyd, 1961) 79–80: "The gospel of the Kingdom is so full of sayings concerning meals, eating and drinking, hungering and thirsting, that there is not *one* element of it which is not expressed somewhere in terms of a meal-metaphor. The blessing of this Gospel message, the challenge, the commandments, the promise, all are comprehended in this meal context and in the corresponding custom. . . . This meal is both metaphor and reality, both parable and event; it reveals in the word what the act adumbrates, and sets forth in the act what the word by implication promises. Here we have the centre, around which all Jesus' words and work revolve and in virtue of which they have unity. The meal takes place here and now, and yet remains in the nature of an eschatological message. The mystery of the meal explains the present and uncovers the coming fulfillment. In it there is brought together and interwoven all that the existence and the coming of the Kingdom of God involve" (emphasis Lohmeyer).

[4]Cf. P. Minear, *Commands of Christ: Authority and Implications* (Nashville: Abingdon Press, 1972) 180 who states that for Luke "table fellowship as interpreted by table talk constituted the gospel"; and Dunn, *Unity and Diversity*, 162: "We must note also *the eschatological significance* of Jesus' fellowship meals. That is, we must set Jesus' practice of table-fellowship within the context of his proclamation" (emphasis Dunn).

[5]Cf. Feeley-Harnik, *The Lord's Table*, 167: "Jesus repeatedly emphasizes the difficulty of explaining his gospel in words, and indeed, most of the time his disciples do not understand what he is saying until he finally speaks to them in food."

[6]The unique character of this juxtaposition of teaching and eating was suggested by the classic liturgical formulation of word and sacrament. Both Karris, *Luke: Artist and Theologian*, 71–72 n. 7 and Neyrey, *The Passion*, 11

that fellowship, particularly the host at the table. The table fellowship of Jesus reveals something about who he is, therefore it has a direct relationship to Lukan Christology. As Karris has pointed out also, table fellowship has something to do with Jesus' death, a position that connects it with the eschatological kingdom. An investigation of the significance of Jesus' table fellowship in Luke's Gospel begins with Jesus' teaching at the table.[7]

1. LUKE 5:27-39 — THE FEAST WITH LEVI THE TAX COLLECTOR

The feast with Levi the tax collector is the first meal in Luke's Gospel and is programmatic for all other meals, introducing the major themes that will be associated with Luke's table fellowship

---

quote from anthropologist Feeley-Harnik's seminal study on food and teaching in the OT and NT. Neyrey synthesizes Feeley-Harnik's observations in his analysis of Luke 22:14-38 on p. 11: "These statements rest on the basic principle: as God gives food to the covenant people, so God gives Torah-instruction to them. Bread/food are a clear and unmistakable symbol of Torah-instruction. . . . Food and instruction are *interchangeable* symbols, *replicating* each other. In other words, a meal is a perfect setting for teaching, as Wisdom in the Old Testament or symposia in Greek literature indicate" (emphasis Neyrey). See D. E. Smith, "Table Fellowship," 614–17 and Bösen, *Jesusmahl*, 87 for a discussion of the Greek symposium tradition in Luke's Gospel as a precedent for Jesus' teaching at the table, his "table talk." My study will view teaching in Luke's table fellowship more from the perspective of Jewish food symbolism than from the Greek symposium.

[7]A number of studies focus specifically on Lukan meals. Cf. Davis, "The Significance of the Shared Meal," a redactional critical study on Lukan messianic banquet motif; Wanke, *Eucharistieverständnis*; Smith, "Table Fellowship," 613–638; Guillaume, *Luc interprète*, 139–144 who divides Lukan meals into four categories: 1) meals with sinners (5:29-30, 33-35); 2) meals with Pharisees (7:36-50; 11:37); 3) meals with friends (10:38-42); and 4) the multiplication of loaves (9:12-17); Bösen, *Jesusmahl*, 78–108; and Esler, *Community and Gospel*, 71–109 who concentrates exclusively on Acts, taking a look at the table fellowship between Jews and Gentiles from both a social science and theological perspective. Like Feeley-Harnik, Esler discusses on pp. 73–76 Jewish purity laws in light of the views of anthropologists Mary Douglas and Edmund Leach. He states his purpose on p. 72: "The result of this analysis will be to show that a theme [table fellowship] which most writers on Luke regard as a minor one of mainly theological interest, actually has an all-important social significance as the central arch in the symbolic universe which Luke creates to legitimate the sectarian separation of his community from Judaism."

130

matrix.[8] The community invited to share in the table fellowship of Jesus is made up of the outcasts of society, the tax collectors and sinners.[9] These sinners receive the blessings of the kingdom of God because they are poor, as Luke's first beatitude announces in 6:20, "Blessed are you poor, for yours is the kingdom of God." In his Lukan theology of poverty, J. Navone describes the poor:

"The tax-gatherers, the Gentiles and the sinners like Mary Magdalen, who could purchase a costly ointment for Jesus, were not economically poor. And yet they were poor in the sense that they recognized their poverty before God; they were *receptive* of His Messiah, of His salvation, of the forgiveness of their sins. And for all these divine benefits repayment was impossible."[10]

This table fellowship with sinners characterized the essence of Jesus' whole ministry, and was at the center of his controversy with the religious establishment, particularly the Pharisees. As Navone goes on to say about Luke's theology of poverty:

". . . in Luke's theology, the poor were all those whom the religious leaders of Israel at the time of Christ considered, for one reason or another, as hopelessly excluded from the kingdom of God. They were the marginal men living on the fringes of Jewish society precisely because they deviated from the religious ideals of the Pharisees. Luke shows that social and economic poverty actually fostered the receptivity requisite for the acceptance of the Messiah."[11]

[8]Cf. Tannehill, *Narrative Unity*, 103–139 in his chapter "Jesus' Ministry to the Oppressed and Excluded": "Beginning in 5:17 the narrator demonstrates special interest in Jesus as the proclaimer of the release of sins by taking a diverse group of stories related to this theme and artfully connecting them, even though they are separated by other material." Many of these pericopes also form the table fellowship matrix.

[9]Cf. J. Navone, "The Lucan Banquet Community," *The Bible Today* 51 (December 1970) 155–161. Dillon, *From Eyewitnesses*, 245–246 describes the "suggestive combination of *forgiveness* and *houseguest relationship with the lowly . . . .*" (emphasis Dillon).

[10]J. Navone, "The Parable of the Banquet," *The Bible Today* 14 (November 1964) 927. Also J. Jeremias, *New Testament Theology: The Proclamation of Jesus* (New York: Scribner's, 1971) 108–121 on the poor in the Gospels; Tannehill, *Narrative Unity*, 64–65, 127–132 on the poor in Luke.

[11]Navone, "The Parable of the Banquet," 928.

The question of who was and who was not a sinner was a major one in Jerusalem society at that time. Both J. Jeremias in *Jerusalem in the Time of Jesus* and G. Feeley-Harnik in *The Lord's Table: Eucharist and Passover in Early Christianity* give a detailed description of those considered to be ethnically pure Israelites according to lines of descent based on the genealogies of Ezra, Nehemiah, and the Chronicles. The purpose of this was to determine who was worthy to engage in table fellowship with them. Anyone not worthy of commensalism was considered a sinner, and the categories of sinner were long and detailed. Feeley-Harnik summarizes it this way:

"Despite the concern with descent, however, there were many categories of people in Jewish society who deliberately, by nature, or through ignorance did not conform to the ideal of the law. In addition to Jews of mixed or illegitimate origin, these included the 'sinners,' the members of despised trades such as tax collectors, herdsman, peddlers, or tanners, the physically deformed, the *am ha-arez* or mass of the population, Samaritans, and, to a certain extent, women. Sinners were comparable to gentiles in their lack of observance of the the law, as Paul suggests when he speaks of 'we . . . who are Jews by birth, not Gentile sinners' (Galatians 2:14)."[12]

The feast with Levi the tax collector takes place in this society and embraces all these themes. This sets the stage for my interpretation of Luke's table fellowship matrix. Luke 5 and 7 will be discussed first as an example of table fellowship and then compared with the meal at Emmaus.

a. Table Fellowship

The first Lukan meal includes two sections: 1) the activity of Jesus where he calls Levi and eats with him; and 2) the teaching of Jesus in the parables about fasting and table fellowship. It func-

[12]Feeley-Harnik, *The Lord's Table*, 42. See also Jeremias, *Jerusalem in the Time of Jesus*, 269–380 in "Part Four: The Maintenance of Racial Purity"; Esler, *Community and Gospel*, 78–80 on the pagan evidence supporting the Jewish refusal to table fellowship with Gentiles, pp. 80–84 on the Jewish sources, and pp. 89–93 on the table fellowship in Mark and Matthew (Mark supports table fellowship between Jews and Gentiles; Matthew is more reluctant).

tions literarily within Luke's Gospel as an introduction to the whole table fellowship matrix of Luke. The step-parallelism of Luke 1-2 concerning John the Baptist and Jesus is continued here, and will be completed in Luke 7:18-35.

Luke has shaped his material in a number of ways to highlight the table fellowship of Jesus with sinners and to reflect this equation between the table fellowship of Jesus and the messianic new age that comes with Jesus.

1) Among the Synoptists (cf. Matt 9:9-17; Mark 2:14-22), only Luke introduces this second controversy with the Pharisees by using the expression "after this" (*kai metá taúta*), a clear connection with the preceding material, particularly the immediate context of Luke 5:17-26 in the cure of a paralyzed man, the first controversy with the Pharisees.[13] I. H. Marshall describes the connection in this way: "A story in which the authority of Jesus to forgive sins has been demonstrated is fittingly followed by the present narrative in which he is shown welcoming sinners and (it is implied) bestowing upon them a forgiveness expressed symbolically in fellowship at table."[14]

2) Luke alone uses the phrase "a tax collector, named Levi," emphasizing his character as tax collector, (i.e. sinner), and Jesus' meal with Levi as a meal with sinners.

3) Only Luke says that Levi left everything behind, reflecting Luke's theme that the proper use of possessions is to be rich towards God by recognizing one's poverty before God. The rich young man in Luke 18:18-30 illustrates the same point, a pericope that ends in 18:30 with the eschatological promise of eternal life in the age to come.[15]

---

[13]Cf. Carroll, "Luke's Portrayal of the Pharisees," 607-612 on 'Pharisees and Plot Development in the Gospel' [Luke].

[14]Cf. Marshall, *The Gospel of Luke*, 217. Forgiveness through table fellowship is a major Lukan motif. Cf. Dunn, *Unity and Diversity*, 162: "For the oriental, table-fellowship was a guarantee of peace, trust, brotherhood; it meant in a very real sense a sharing of one's life. Thus, table-fellowship with tax collector and sinner was Jesus' way of proclaiming God's salvation and assurance of forgiveness."

[15]Cf. Marshall, *The Gospel of Luke*, 219 who interprets this "leaving behind" as one that "stresses his [Levi's] decisive break with his old life (aorist participle) followed by his continuing life of discipleship (imperfect indicative)."

133

4) Only Luke says that Levi gave a great reception (*dochên megá-lên*) for Jesus himself, whereas Matthew and Mark use participial phrases to indicate that "as he *sat at table* in the house, behold, many tax collectors and sinners came and *sat down* with Jesus and his disciples" (Matt 9:10). Luke's language emphasizes the character of this meal as a "great feast," reflecting the table fellowship language of Luke, e.g. 14:13 (*dochên*); 14:16 (*deípnon méga*); and 22:12 (*anágaion méga*).

5) "Luke remodels the text to indicate clearly that it was Levi who acted as host to Jesus."[16] Therefore it is a gross sinner, a tax collector, who sets the table for Jesus.

6) Luke does not use "sinners" (*hamartôloí*), as do Matthew and Mark, but says: "and there was a large company of tax collectors and others sitting at table with them." The Pharisees clearly regard the company as sinners (5:30).

7) Luke describes the religious leaders who witnessed this table fellowship of Jesus eating with sinners as "the Pharisees and their scribes." Matthew has only Pharisees; Mark has the scribes of the Pharisees. Only Luke says they were grumbling (*egógguzon*),[17] linking this meal with the parables of Luke 15: "Now *the tax collectors and sinners* were all drawing near to hear him. And *the Pharisees and the scribes murmured* (*diegógguzon*), saying, 'This man receives *sinners* and *eats with them*'" (15:1-2). Luke's use of scribes (i.e. the lawyers) and *goggúzô* may imply that the complaint is about his disciples eating with such unclean people.[18]

8) All three evangelists quote the Pharisees and/or scribes as addressing Jesus' disciples about their eating habits. Only Luke speaks of the *drinking* habits of *Jesus and his disciples*: "Why do *you* [disciples and Jesus] eat and *drink* with tax collectors and sinners?" Matthew and Mark refer to *Jesus' eating* habits, not the disciples', e.g. "Why does *your teacher eat* with tax collectors and sinners?" (Matt 9:11). The reference to eating and drinking gives

[16]Ibid., 219.

[17]Cf. Thayer, *A Greek English Lexicon of the New Testament* (New York: American Book Company, 1886) 120 on *goggúô*: "to murmur, mutter, grumble, say anything in a low tone."

[18]It also connects it with the meal with Zacchaeus in Luke 19:7: "And when they saw it they all murmured, 'He has gone in to be the guest of a man who is a sinner.'"

134

Levi's meal the character of a feast, a fuller description of the table fellowship of Jesus.

9) Only Luke has "to repentance" (*metánoian*) in 5:32, a word that is characteristic of his Gospel. Matthew uses *metánoia* and *metanoéô* seven times (3:2, 8, 11; 4:17; 11:20, 21; 12:41) and Mark three times (1:4, 15; 6:12). Luke uses it fourteen times (3:3, 8; 5:32; 10:13; 11:32; 13:3, 5; 15:7 (twice), 10; 16:30; 17:3, 4; 24:47). Luke's use of "I have not come" (*ouk elêlutha*) instead of "I came not" (*ouk êlthon*—Matt and Mark) suggests that Jesus' ministry is ongoing: "I am come," i.e. it lasts into the present.[19] His acceptance of the first invitation to dine with tax collectors and others is to invite them "to repentance."[20]

10) Matthew [and Mark] use the disciples of John to question Jesus concerning his fasting practices. In Luke, however, the Pharisees and their scribes ask the questions. Matthew and Mark focus on fasting in their questions to Jesus,[21] recalling the old age, of which John the Baptist is the paradigm in his ascetic lifestyle of not eating and not drinking. In contrast to the fasting and prayers of the disciples of John and the Pharisees, Luke mentions the disciples of Jesus who simply feast. Luke's reply to the Pharisees is that the disciples of Jesus recognize the presence of the bridegroom in their midst by engaging in table fellowship. They are therefore worthy of the title "wedding guests." Eating and drinking is the proper behavior at a feast, a characteristic of the new age, implying that "the present time is thus likened to a wedding, and the period of Jesus' ministry is seen in terms of the messianic banquet."[22] The disciples of Jesus, therefore, cannot be compelled to fast (Luke 5:34).

[19]Cf Fitzmyer, *I-IX*, 592; Marshall, *The Gospel of Luke*, 220–221.

[20]Esler, *Community and Gospel*, 39ff. claims that in Acts "there are three conversion accounts where table-fellowship is given considerable prominence, in addition to the Cornelius narrative" (Acts 18:1-11; 16:11-15; and 16:25-34). One of Esler's conclusions on p. 42 is that "the meaning of the mission to the Gentiles is not primarily that they have become an object of evangelistic endeavour instead of the Jews, but *that table-fellowship in Christ's name may now be established between them and the Jews*" (emphasis mine).

[21]Mark even has an introduction where he says the disciples of John and the Pharisees were fasting.

[22]Marshall, *The Gospel of Luke*, 222. Cf. also J. Pieper, *In Tune With The World*

11) In 5:36, Luke introduces two parables by saying that Jesus told them a parable, indicating that the two stories have one and the same point: *the message* of the parables of the new garment and the new wine is the arrival of the new age in Jesus. These are Jesus' first parables; they discuss the breaking in of the new age in Jesus; they are eschatological;[23] and they occur within the context of Jesus' table fellowship.[24]

12) All three evangelists use *palaíos* to refer to the old patches and wineskins, and Luke has *kainós* for the new garments and wineskins, *néos* for the new wine. The distinction between *néos*, "new in time" [*neuf*] and *kainós*, " 'new in nature' [*nouveau*] (with an implication of 'better')" suggests the dual nature of the messianic new age that breaks in with Jesus.[25] It is both a present reality (*néos*) and an eschatological one (*kainós*).[26] Matthew and Mark call the piece from the new garment "unshrunk cloth" (*hrákous agnáphou*); Luke describes it as "new garment" (*himatíou kainoú*). Therefore, Luke is the clearest of the evangelists to express the

---

(Chicago: Franciscan Herald Press, 1963) a classic study on theories of festivity.

[23]Cf. F. Hauck, *parabolê*, TDNT Abridged 775–776: "While rabbinic parables expound the law, the parables of Jesus are mostly eschatological (although not apocalyptic). Most Jesus' parables are interwoven into a didactic context."

[24]Luke also introduces other significant meal metaphors and parables by *parabolê*, particularly Luke 14:7, the parable of the Great Banquet, and the three parables of Luke 15 which conclude with the feast for the Prodigal Son. Other Lukan meal parables introduced by *parabolê* are 8:4, 9, 10, 11; 12:16; 12:41; 13:6; 20:9, 19; 21:29.

[25]J. Behm, *kainós*, TDNT Abridged 388: "*kainós* denotes the new and miraculous thing that the age of salvation brings. It is thus a key teleological term in eschatological promise: the new heaven and earth in Rev. 21:1; 2 Pet. 3:13, the new Jerusalem in Rev. 3:12; 21:2, the new wine in Mk. 14:25, the new name in Rev. 2:17; 3:12, the new song in Rev. 5:9, the new creation in Rev. 21:5 . . . God's saving will is worked out in the promised new covenant that Jesus has now set up (Lk. 22:20; I Cor. 11:25; Heb. 8:8ff.; 9:15) . . . . The fact that the old and the new cannot be mixed (Mk. 2:21-22) [parallel Luke 5:36-39] stresses the element of distinctiveness."

[26]Cf. J. Behm, *néos*, TDNT Abridged 628: "Unlike *kainós*, *néos* does not have an eschatological content in the NT. It refers to the new reality of present salvation. The new wine of Mk 2:22 [Luke 5:37-38] represents the unheard of element in the person and message of Jesus (cf. Mt 12:6, 41-42; Lk 4:21; Mk 10:6ff.)."

now/not yet tension of the age of salvation Jesus brings. The *new-in-time* wine (*néos*) of the present age *must be* (Luke's unique use of the verbal adjective *blêtéon*) compatible with and stored in the *new-in-nature* wineskins (*kainoús*) of the age to come. Both the wine and the wineskins are from Jesus, the bringer of the new age. For Luke, the comparison in this parable is not simply between the compatibility of the old and the new,[27] but between present and future, or the presence of the future symbolized by the new wine in the new wineskins. In the table fellowship of Jesus, not only is the new incompatible with the old, but the future eschatological blessings of the new age (*kainós* as quality) are brought forward to the present and tasted in the new wine (*néos* as a present in time reality).

13) What are we to make of 5:39? "And no one after drinking old wine (*palaión*) desires new (*néon*) for he says, 'the old is good.'" Luke is the only evangelist who adds this. There is general agreement that Luke's inclusion of this verse is to support his understanding of the parable and sum it up in an ironical saying. Thus Marshall writes: "The verse expresses the viewpoint of those who are content with the old, because they think it is good, and make no effort to try the new. It is thus an ironical comment on the Jews who refused to taste the 'new wine' of the gospel which was not hallowed by age."[28]

There is one nuance that is not brought forth by the commentators. Humanly speaking, for a Jew and a Pharisee, old wine is qualitatively better than new wine, and one who has tasted of the old, aged wine would never prefer new wine. But contrary to what is normal and expected, the kingdom is hidden in new wine, a paradox that demonstrates the radical nature of the kingdom. The table fellowship of Jesus is like new wine: it breaks old barriers by including sinners and tax collectors; it bears the character of a wedding, a foretaste of the messianic feast in which the bridegroom is continually present; it brings forward into the present the eschatological blessings of salvation.[29] In order to taste the

[27]Both Marshall, *The Gospel of Luke*, 227–228 and Fitzmyer, *I-IX*, 601–602 stress the idea of compatibility.
[28]Marshall, *The Gospel of Luke*, 228.
[29]Cf. Tannehill, *Narrative Unity*, 174.

new wine, one must radically break with the past by repentance. This is the essence of Jesus' table fellowship. The fact that Levi the tax collector is able to embrace this, and the Pharisees are not, sets up the bitter controversy between Jesus and these Jewish religious authorities that will ultimately culminate in his death. Luke hints at this rejection unto death in 5:35: "The days will come, when the bridegroom is taken away from them." Table fellowship, then, becomes emblematic of Jesus' kingdom and his teaching, an expression of the new age of salvation that he will accomplish on the cross.

b. A Comparison with the Meal at Emmaus

Although there are no linguistic or stylistic similarities between Luke 5:27-39 and 24:13-35, there are thematic parallels that are theologically significant. The table fellowship of Jesus in Luke 5:27-39 contains three significant elements that will characterize his table fellowship throughout his ministry, particularly his meal with the Emmaus disciples.

1) It is a table fellowship with sinners, i.e. it is an inclusive event.[30] This will be the theme of Luke's table fellowship matrix throughout his Gospel (e.g. Luke 15:1-2; 19:1-10) culminating with the Emmaus meal where Jesus also eats with sinners.

The Pharisees of Luke 5:27-39 reject the table fellowship of Jesus because it does not conform to their religious expectations—they would prefer the old age to the new one that comes with Jesus. Since the new age comes through suffering and death, any rejection of that suffering and death is a rejection of the new age. Inasmuch as the Emmaus disciples were unable to confess the second phase of Lukan Christology in which the suffering and rejected prophet is placed in the hands of the chief priest and rulers and is crucified, they fell into the category of sinners, since they had lost their messianic hope as it was focused in Jesus (24:21).[31] Thus, the

---

[30]Neyrey, *The Passion*, 8–9 states that "meal in Luke's Gospel are *inclusive events*" and lists as a subcategory "*saints eat with sinners*" (emphasis Neyrey). Cf. also Dunn, *Unity and Diversity*, 162: "But *Jesus' table fellowship was marked by openness, not by exclusiveness*" (emphasis Dunn). The inclusivity of Jesus' table fellowship will become a critical part of my discussion of this matrix.

[31]Cf. Neyrey, *The Passion*, 9: "Although the Emmaus disciples are not ex-

Emmaus disciples are no different than the Pharisees in that they reject the new age because they reject the death of Jesus through which the new age comes.

2) It is a table fellowship where Jesus teaches about the kingdom. Table fellowship with Levi the tax collector provided an occasion for Jesus to relate two parables about the kingdom that showed the incompatibility of the old and new ages. This is the first point that Jesus wishes to make, but it will not be fully understood until, during the meal at Emmaus, he "interprets to them [the Emmaus disciples] in all the scriptures the things concerning himself" (24:25-27), namely, the necessity of Christ suffering before entering into his glory. This is the didactic section of the Emmaus meal that is Christological at base. The opening up of the Scriptures by itself does not open up the eyes of the Emmaus disciples, for this comes with the breaking of the bread. It is a combination of both teaching and eating that opens their eyes and thus makes the meal at Emmaus *a revelatory process* as to who Jesus is and what he came to do.

3) The table fellowship is itself an expression of the new age. On Luke 5:27-39, E. C. Davis writes: "The entire section under study is steeped in the atmosphere of Messianic invitation to the Banquet of the New Age."[32] The feast with Levi the tax collector is characterized as an eschatological meal: it is described in terms of the messianic banquet in which Jesus is the bridegroom; it is joyous where fasting is inappropriate, and eating and drinking are critical to the nature of feast; it is reconciling where those who partake of it have come in repentance (5:32); it is a meal of the new age where new garments are worn and new wine is drunk. The meal at Emmaus is the culmination of the eschatological meals of Jesus because it occurs after Jesus' death and resurrection *and* his insti-

___

actly apostate sinners, they had lost hope and left the group: nevertheless, Jesus eats with them (24:29-35)."

[32]Davis, "The Significance of the Shared Meal," 66. Cf. also Dunn, *Unity and Diversity,* 16: "In his own ministry Jesus embodied this forgiveness and acceptance of the end-time kingdom, particularly in his table-fellowship. These gatherings, from which Jesus excluded no one, even open sinners, expressed the heart of his message, for they were the foretaste of the messianic feast of the new age (Luke 14.13,16-24)."

tution of the Last Supper where he connects the new age and his death in the context of a meal. As Jerome Neyrey says:

"Meals are a prime symbol of *election, forgiveness, and eschatological blessing*. . . . The sign of Zacchaeus' conversion is his eating with Jesus (19:5-7). And reconciliation for the Emmaus disciples is the meal shared with Jesus (24:30-35)."[33]

2. LUKE 7:18-35 — THE BRIDEGROOM AND THE ASCETIC

The link between Luke 5:27-39 and 7:18-35 is evident when they are both placed within the table fellowship matrix. Further, a comparison of Luke 7:18-35 with the parallel in Matthew 11:2-19 also shows that the differences are significant for Luke's table fellowship. Traditionally this section of Luke has been divided into three,[34] but for the purposes of my study, it will be divided into four because of the unique Lukan material in 7:29-30 that highlights his table fellowship matrix. The analysis of Luke 7:18-35 will be based on the findings of Luke 5.

a. Table Fellowship

1) *Luke 7:18-23 The question of John and the answer of Jesus.* The question of John to Jesus and Jesus' response is not, in and of itself, a table fellowship matter. It is a Christological one, but as we have already seen, Christology is often expressed in terms of table fellowship. At first, Matthew appears to signal his Christological intentions more than Luke:

Matthew 11:2   "Now when John heard in prison about *the deeds of the Christ*. . . ."

Luke 7:18   "The disciples of John told him of *all these things*."

Matthew refers to Jesus' previous activity as "the deeds of the Christ" (*ta érga tou Christoú*), whereas Luke refers to them in a general way with "all these things" (*perí pántôn toútôn*). There is some question as to whether this passage refers to Jesus as per-

[33]Neyrey, *The Passion*, 9 (emphasis Neyrey). Cf. also Tannehill, *Narrative Unity*, 218: "Eschatological fulfillment, and specifically sharing in God's reign, is repeatedly pictured in terms of a festive meal in Luke."

[34]Cf. Marshall, *The Gospel of Luke*, 287–304; Fitzmyer, *I-IX*, 662–682; and Ellis, *The Gospel of Luke*, 119–120.

forming messianic work. Is "he who is to come" (*ho erchómenos*) in 7:19 a messianic title, or does it refer, as J. Fitzmyer suggests, to *Elias redivivus*, or to a manifestation of the Isaianic figure who brings eschatological blessings?[35] It is unclear what Fitzmyer and his supporters mean by a messianic title, especially when they describe what Jesus is saying here in traditionally messianic and eschatological terms, e.g.:

"Rather than understanding his mission as that of a fiery reformer of the eschaton, Jesus sees his role as the embodiment of the divine blessings promised to be shed on the unfortunate of human society by Isaiah. . . . Luke 7:22 is to be understood as an echo of the quotation of Isa 61:1, as presented by Luke in 4:18 [which Fitzmyer also does not understand messianically]. . . . Implicit in the whole passage is the idea of fulfillment. The OT promises of bounty and blessings on human beings, associated with the eschaton, are now seen to be begun in the activity of Jesus himself. His deeds and preaching, witnessed by the two disciples of John, already concretize what was promised as eschatological blessings."[36]

A messianic interpretation of Luke 7:18-23 seems necessary in light of the Lukan context. The antecedent of "all these things" includes all the preaching, teaching, and miracles of Jesus since the start of his ministry in Nazareth in Luke 4:16.[37] If Luke 7:18-23 is seen in light of Luke 4:18, as Fitzmyer suggests, then according to the interpretation I offered of 4:18, the deeds of Jesus that are reported to John the Baptist are to be understood as part of the first phase of Lukan Christology where the teaching of the Messiah takes precedence over his miracles. The miracles are significant, however, in that they point to the eschatological blessings of the Messiah that come when the new age breaks in, as Isaiah prophesied. This is why Luke inserts a restatement of the question to Jesus and Jesus' response in 7:20 that "in that hour he cured many of diseases and plagues and evil spirits, and on many that were blind he bestowed sight."

[35]Fitzmyer, *I-IX*, 666 rejects a messianic interpretation, but lists those who consider it messianic.
[36]Ibid., 664–665. Cf. also Tannehill, *Narrative Unity*, 64, 79–82, especially on the relationship between 4:18-19 and 7:22.
[37]Cf. Fitzmyer, *I-IX*, 665.

By highlighting the miracles, the fulfillment of the Old Testament is affirmed and the teaching of Jesus is given a messianic imprimatur, stressed by Luke's "what you have *seen* and *heard*" as opposed to Matthew's "what you *hear* and *see*." When John's disciples see the works of Jesus, they should interpret messianically both the Old Testament prophecies and the teaching and preaching of Jesus since his sermon in Nazareth. Thus Luke's purpose in the Nazareth episode is reiterated here.

Luke 7:23 anticipates the rest of this passage by introducing the theme of this section: the acceptance and rejection of Jesus and John. What is critical to both Luke and Matthew is the question of Jesus' identity—is he the Messiah? Here in Luke 7:18-23, the response points to Jesus' messianic deeds, and whether or not they offend (*skandalisthê*) a person. The *scandal* comes from identifying Jesus with the particular idea of the Messiah prophesied in the Old Testament.[38] In Luke 4:16-30, this identification was part of the offense that led his hometown of Nazareth to react in violent rejection. Their problem, like John's and his disciples, was a Christological one. They looked for Jesus to come in judgment, citing Isaiah 61:2b, "the day of vengeance of our God," and not just Isaiah 61:2a, the proclamation of "the year of the Lord's favor." But Jesus brings judgment only in his death, and not as John and his disciples expected. Instead, Jesus comes performing miracles, teaching about the kingdom of God, and announcing forgiveness. This is how Jesus fulfilled Isaiah 61 and other messianic prophecies—release from captivity and bondage. Thus, Luke 7:18-23 allows for a Christological interpretation of Luke 7, demonstrating that Christology is a fundamental part of Luke's table fellowship matrix.

2) Luke 7:24-28 The witness of Jesus about John. The significance of Luke 7:24-28 for Luke's table fellowship matrix is again Christolog-

---

[38]Cf. Dunn, *Jesus and the Spirit*, 60–61: ". . . the stumbling block is Jesus' proclamation of the presence of God's eschatological grace and the 'not just yet' of his final judgment; the ones who might stumble are those who have believed the warnings of the Baptist . . . he himself, not just his preaching, was the stumbling block . . . . Jesus had clearly not simply proclaimed the presence of the end-time kingdom, he had proclaimed its presence in himself, or, more precisely, in *his own* ministry" (emphasis Dunn).

ical, reiterating John's role as the precursor in a subordinate role to Jesus the Messiah in God's plan of salvation. A number of Lukan themes are illustrated here by John's ministry.

John is the hinge between the phases of salvation history as first suggested by Conzelmann, i.e. the period of Israel comes to a conclusion with John's ministry and the period of Jesus commences with the preaching of John. John was the last of the Old Testament prophets, but he is the greatest prophet in that he announces the new era of salvation that comes in Christ.[39] John's *new age preaching* conforms to the parables of Luke 5:27-39, but John is not part of the new age since "even the most insignificant member of the kingdom ranks above the messenger who prepared the way for it."[40]

Since John is, according to 7:27, the forerunner of Jesus as Malachi 3:1 announces, he prepares Jesus' way to Jerusalem, giving Luke's geographical perspective Old Testament backing. The way to Jerusalem is the way to the cross, and thus, in the witness of Jesus about John, Luke introduces the second phase of his Christology: the rejection of the Messiah. As Luke 7:18-23 paralleled Luke 4:14-21, now 7:24-28 parallels 4:22-30, setting the stage for the final section of Luke 7 where the people of this generation reject wisdom's children, John and Jesus.

Thus, Luke 7:24-28 continues Luke's Christological perspective by emphasizing John's function in the breaking in of the new era of salvation. As the precursor of Jesus who is rejected, John prepares the reader for the second phase of Lukan Christology, Jesus' rejection by crucifixion. Ironically, John's question as to whether Jesus is "he who is to come" receives a first phase answer of wondrous deeds, but John should be able to recognize that in his preparations for the messianic new age, rejection was fundamental both to his ministry and to that of the Messiah. Jesus points this out to the Emmaus disciples on the basis of Old Testament prophecy, in Luke 24:26-27.

3) *Luke 7:29-30 The people who accept and reject God's plan of salvation.* Both Matthew and Luke insert their own material at this

[39]Cf. O. Linton, "The Parable of the Children's Game," *New Testament Studies* 22 (1975-76) 178.
[40]Marshall, *The Gospel of Luke*, 293.

point in the narrative. The Matthean addition of 11:12-15 further develops the rejection phase of Jesus' messiahship as John foreshadows it with the violence that occurs against him in his imprisonment and execution. John announces the kingdom and prepares its way, although the violence he suffered in no way brings the kingdom of God into existence. John merely anticipates the violence unto death Jesus suffered on the cross through which the kingdom becomes present.[41] Thus, Matthew continues to emphasize the relationship between John and Jesus in salvation history.

Luke takes a different perspective that fits well into his Christology. Luke 7:29-30 is his editorial comment upon John the Baptist and the reaction of the people and religious authorities to the ministry of John. It expands the prophet Christology of Luke 7:11-17, showing that both John and Jesus are in line with rejected Old Testament prophets like Elijah and Elisha as Luke 4:22-30 developed. Luke's editorial comments in 7:29-30 demonstrate the polarization that now exists between the religious authorities and the people.

The two groups in 7:29-30 are "all the people (laós) and the tax collectors" and "the Pharisees and the lawyers" (lawyer is a synonym for scribe). "All the people" is a Lukan expression that signifies all of Israel, a significant phrase because it occurs in Luke 24:19, "a prophet mighty in deed and word before God and all the people." According to Luke 7:29, to accept Jesus is to declare God righteous (edikaíōsan), an unusual use of dikaióō. It is usually God who declares people righteous, not vice versa. A manifestation of this acceptance (this declaring God righteous) is to be baptized with the baptism of John. The meaning here is clarified in the next verse when the rejection of Jesus is explained: "the Pharisees and the lawyers rejected the purpose of God (tēn boulēn toú theoú) for themselves, not having been baptized by him." To declare God righteous is to accept his plan (boulē)[42] of salvation as it is manifested in the baptism of John. The ministry of John involved both a "preaching a baptism of repentance for the forgiveness of

---

[41]Cf. Schweizer, Matthew, 263.
[42]Cf. Tannehill, Narrative Unity, 176.

sins'' (3:3) and the baptism itself, a ministry whose purpose is described by Luke (3:4-6) in the words of Isaiah 40:3-5.

The baptism of John prepares for messianic salvation, a theme Luke accents by adding Isaiah 40:4-5 to Matthew's Isaiah 40:3. The Isaiah prophecy sums up the content of the belief of those who accept God's plan of salvation as they hear it from the preaching of John, allowing them to recognize that Jesus is this Messiah *as they observe his messiahship in his table fellowship.* E. E. Ellis describes the content of this belief based on Isaiah 40:3-5:

"The Isaiah passage begins a section in which the Exodus is a basic motif. Its immediate reference is to the Babylonian exile. The application to John's eschatological message by the New Testament arises from the conviction that these earlier 'redemptions' prefigure the future exodus of Israel from the realm of death to the kingdom of God. The Baptist is the herald or 'voice' of this messianic deliverance."[43]

It is significant that in the description of the ministry of John the Baptist only Luke among the evangelists describes tax collectors and other sinners coming to be baptized by John (Luke 3:10-14). This exclusive Lukan material sets up Jesus' table fellowship and informs Luke 7:29. In order to understand what these tax collectors believed that allowed them to "justify" God, Luke's description of the ministry of John in Luke 3 needs to be considered. Obviously, the Pharisees and lawyers reject the plan of God because they reject John's interpretation of his role as precursor to the Messiah. If they reject John, they must also reject Jesus.

Thus, Luke 7:29-30 draws the lines between Jesus and his opponents. It is a Christological debate that revolves around God's plan of salvation through the message of John and Jesus. Jesus will go on to explain in 7:31-35 that as a Christological problem, it is also a question of table fellowship.[44]

4) Luke 7:31-35 The judgment of Jesus upon those who reject God's plan. The interpretation of Luke 7:18-35 reaches it climax in this fourth section. By means of a parable (7:31-32), its interpretation

[43]Ellis, *The Gospel of Luke,* 89.
[44]Cf. Tannehill, *Narrative Unity,* 177; Carroll, "Luke's Portrayal of the Pharisees," 609.

(7:33-34), and a concluding wisdom-saying (7:35), the theme of this section is brought to completion: the acceptance and rejection of Jesus and John as God's eschatological messengers, his children of wisdom. This concluding section is significant for Luke's table fellowship matrix for the following reasons:

a) Jesus is portrayed as addressing his opponents concerning their rejection of him. The metaphors used by him are ones that fit easily into the vocabulary of table fellowship: weddings and funerals, eating and drinking, gluttons and drunkards. There is a problem of interpretation in attempting to identify the opponents of Jesus in the parable, the "men of this generation." Are they the children who propose the games or those who refuse to play the games? As many have indicated, the introduction to the parable suggests the former, but traditional interpretations of this passage opt for the latter.[45] Ultimately, both interpretations point to the same thing. Marshall gives the position that most logically fits the language of this passage: "The first group may be a picture of the Jews who tell the ascetic John to dance and the joyful Jesus to mourn. Neither John nor Jesus will satisfy them."[46] The thrust of both interpretations is the rejection of John and Jesus by the religious authorities, those who reject "the purpose (boulē) of God for themselves."

O. Linton's discussion of this passage focuses on this rejection, maintaining that the Pharisees never demanded "anything extraordinary, only that John and Jesus should behave according to normal Jewish practice."[47] His view is that Jesus deviated from normal Jewish practice, the point of Luke 5:27-39 where Jesus and his disciples do not fast as the Pharisees and John's disciples do. But the real offense of Luke 5 is that Jesus eats with tax collectors and sinners, the very essence of Jesus' interpretation of this parable in Luke 7. Jesus is attacked for the way he eats and drinks, especially since he claims that his way is from heaven.[48] John is

---

[45]Linton, "The Parable of the Children's Game," 172–179 offers the most detailed arguments for both positions and has raised the argument to a new and different level.

[46]Marshall, The Gospel of Luke, 300–301.

[47]Linton, "The Parable of the Children's Game," 175.

[48]Ibid., 177.

attacked for preaching repentance and fasting.[49] Both Jesus and John are attacked for their different notions about feasting and fasting. The verdict against them is negative because they do not follow normal Pharisaical customs. Thus the charges against Jesus are beginning to be formulated by the Pharisees on the basis of his table fellowship.

b) The rejection of Jesus is Christological, fulfilling the second phase of Lukan Christology, the rejection of the prophet. This rejection points ahead to the passion predictions that begin in Luke 9, and to the cross where Jesus is rejected by the religious authorities because of his public teaching, his public works, *and his public table fellowship*. The reference to the passion of Jesus is suggested here by Jesus' use of the title "Son of Man"—the title Jesus uses in all Lukan passion predictions (Luke 9:22; 9:44; 18:34); in the context of the Last Supper referring to the passion (Luke 22:22, 48);[50] and in the passion statement in Luke's resurrection narrative (Luke 24:7).[51] The *character* of Luke's literary composition is to use "Son of Man" within his passion material.

c) The description Jesus uses with reference to his table fellowship is "a glutton and a drunkard, a friend of tax collectors and sinners." Jeremias writes that the phrase "a glutton and a drunkard," "is derived from Deut 21.20 and stigmatizes [Jesus] on the strength of this connection as 'a refractory and rebellious son', who deserved to be stoned."[52] Jeremias' observation is very pertinent, since immediately following Deuteronomy 21:20 comes a passage classically applied to crucifixion:

"And if a man has committed a crime punishable by death and he is put to death, and you hang him on a tree, his body shall not remain all night upon the tree, but you shall bury him the same day, for a hanged man is accursed by God; you shall not defile

[49]Note that Luke 7:33 adds *árton* and *oínon* to Matthew 11:18, emphasizing the character of the meal (cf. Luke 5:27-39).

[50]Note the similarity in concept between Luke 22:22 (*kata to hôrmisménon poreúetai*) and 7:30 (*tên boulên toú theoú*). Cf. Neyrey, *The Passion*, 18.

[51]Cf. Tannehill, *Narrative Unity*, 220–221.

[52]Jeremias, *Parables*, 160. Cf. also Marshall, *The Gospel of Luke*, 302: "The description resembles that of the unruly son in Dt. 21:20 MT who is to be stoned; thus a proverbial expression for apostasy is being applied to Jesus."

your land which the Lord your God gives you for an inheritance"
(21:22-23).

Although Deuteronomy 21:22-23 does not function significantly
in the Gospels as an Old Testament reference to Jesus' crucifixion,
Luke uses it in Acts 5:30 to describe the crucifixion of Jesus when
Peter accuses the Jews of Jesus' death: "The God of our fathers
raised Jesus whom you killed by hanging him on a tree." Even
more significant is Luke's use of this phrase from Deuteronomy
21:22-23 in Acts 10:39. He begins with Jesus' anointing of the
Holy Spirit in baptism, describes his rejection by the Jews as "put
to death by hanging on a tree," and includes a table fellowship
reference in 10:41 concerning those who are able witnesses of his
resurrected body, those "who ate and drank with him after he
arose from the dead." Paul quotes Deuteronomy 21:22-23 as an
explicit reference to the crucifixion in Galatians 3:13 as a demonstration of the curse of God upon Jesus: "Cursed be every one
who hangs on a tree."

Jesus himself recognizes the charges against him and the conse-
quences of those charges according to the Torah, for his table fellowship with tax collectors and sinners places him in a category
worthy of condemnation according to Old Testament law. Thus,
within Luke's table fellowship matrix, one finds the theme of
Jesus' fulfillment of Old Testament prophecy.[53]

d) In the final wisdom saying, Luke connects 7:29-30 and 7:31-35
by means of "to justify" (*dikaióô*). Just as those who are baptized
by John declare God righteous because they have accepted the
plan of God as it is manifested in John, so now divine *Wisdom*
(either Wisdom personified[54] or Wisdom as "the rightness of
God's plan"[55]) is vindicated by her children, (Jesus, John, and
their disciples)[56] *because they are rejected*. The focus here is on the
rejection of God's eschatological prophets who come preaching a

[53]Feeley-Harnik, *The Lord's Table*, 63–72 discusses the context of Deuteronomy 21:22-23, and the rebellious son, the glutton, and drunkard in Deuteronomy 21:18-21, in its relationship to Jesus.

[54]Fitzmyer, *I-IX*, 681.

[55]Marshall, *The Gospel of Luke*, 303.

[56]The identity of wisdom's children is difficult. Are they John or Jesus or
their disciples? Both interpretations yield the same meaning.

148

message that is contrary to the message of the Pharisees.[57] This message is scandalous and unpopular, hidden in the preaching of repentance by John the ascetic and the preaching of the kingdom by Jesus the bridegroom. The rejection is both from the message itself, *and* because the message takes place in the context of *a table fellowship with tax collectors and sinners.* The children of wisdom are all those who are willing to accept God's righteous plan as it is manifested in the ministries of John and Jesus. They turn out to be the most unlikely members of Palestinian society—tax collectors and sinners. For the Pharisees and the other religious authorities, *this is the great scandal,* and thus the coming of the new age through John and Jesus is hidden from them.[58] As Linton concludes:

"John proclaims the Kingdom and therefore he calls to repentance, and that includes fasting. Jesus brings the new era with wondrous works (Matt. xi. 2-4; Luke vii. 22-33) and there is no time for fasting. Also in this connection there is a time for mourning and a time to rejoice. But the timetable is different. This is hidden from 'this generation.' They do not understand 'the signs of the time' but keep to old-established rules and insist that John and Jesus observe them. When John and Jesus do not follow these exhortations they can see no reason for that. But the 'children of Wisdom' know better."[59]

b. A Comparison with the Meal at Emmaus

As Luke's table fellowship matrix expands, he elaborates upon the themes that he has already established, pointing toward the completion of those themes in Luke 22 and 24. Therefore, the table fellowship of Luke 7:18-35 contains many of the same elements found in Luke 5:27-39 as it relates to the meal at Emmaus and the eschatological kingdom.

[57]Matthew replaces Luke's "all her children" with "by her deeds" in 11:19, thereby framing this section with the messianic deeds of Jesus (11:2—"the deeds of the Christ"). The messianic deeds of Jesus are integral to this passage, and Matthew's message seems to be that Jesus (Wisdom) is vindicated by his table fellowship with sinners, one of his central messianic deeds.

[58]Cf. Farmer, *Jesus and the Gospel,* 36–40 on Pharisaical attitudes concerning table fellowship.

[59]Linton, "The Parable of the Children's Game," 178.

1) It is a table fellowship with sinners, i.e. it is an inclusive event. Jesus' discourse in Luke 7 elucidates the distinctions between his table fellowship and the expectations of the Pharisees. The table fellowship of Jesus is a major contributor to the charges brought against him that lead to his death. *All the people* in Luke 7:29 and 24:19 accept him as the prophet of the new age, but "our chief priests and rulers delivered him up to be condemned to death, and crucified him" (24:20). One reason for Jesus' rejection and crucifixion, the very issue discussed by the Emmaus disciples in 24:19ff., is that his table fellowship with tax collectors and sinners placed him outside the circle of observant Jews.

2) It is a table fellowship where Jesus teaches about the kingdom. Although the word "kingdom" is not used in this passage, the content of the kingdom is described in the images employed. It is like a wedding, but the guests reject the invitation to join in—"we piped to you, and you did not dance." It is like a feast, but the invited guests criticize those who go—"the Son of man has come eating and drinking; and you say, 'Behold, a glutton and a drunkard, a friend of tax collectors and sinners!' " The use of the title "Son of Man," and the reference to table fellowship point forward to Emmaus. The reader of Luke could make a connection between Luke 7, Luke 24:7, and the Emmaus narrative through the table fellowship and passion matrices.

3) The table fellowship is itself an expression of the new age. Luke continues here what he began in chapter 5—to describe the ministry of Jesus in terms of the messianic banquet in which Jesus the bridegroom comes eating and drinking. Again the images of feast and fasting predominate as descriptions of the new and old ages. In this sense, the table fellowship of Jesus is eschatological because he is the Messiah who is the host at the messianic feast. The two Lukan Christological phases are present in Luke 7:18-35 in the response to John. Just as the miracles of Jesus are a sign that the new age has come, so also the table fellowship of Jesus is a sign of the new age which will be celebrated and perfected in the Last Supper, the meal at Emmaus, and the early Christian meals.

3. LUKE 7:36-50 — THE ANOINTING OF THE FEET OF JESUS AND THE FORGIVENESS OF A SINFUL WOMAN

The connection between Luke 7:18-35 and 7:36-50 is more obvious than many commentaries suggest.[60] The common ground is table fellowship. As the second Lukan meal, it will include, and elaborate upon, many of the Lukan table fellowship motifs.

a. Table Fellowship

1) The first link between Luke 7:18-35 and 7:36-50 is the theme of the acceptance and rejection of Jesus. In both passages, the categories of people are sinners and Pharisees; the criteria for the acceptance or rejection is Christology. The response of these two kinds of people is paralleled: the sinful woman accepts Jesus and receives his forgiveness; the Pharisees reject Jesus by questioning his ability to impart forgiveness (7:49).

2) The second link is the context of table fellowship. Luke's second meal mentioned is his first with a Pharisee.[61] In Luke 5, Jesus dines with a sinner, Levi the tax collector; the nature of the meal is a feast in honor of Jesus and on the occasion of Levi's conversion. In Luke 7, Jesus dines with a Pharisee at his invitation because he is a prophet (7:39) and a teacher (7:40). It is also a special meal because Jesus reclines (*kateklíthê*), a posture only practiced at festive banquets (cf. 9:14-15; 14:8; and 24:30).[62]

---

[60]Cf. Fitzmyer, *I-IX*, 684. However, Tannehill, *Narrative Unity*, 118 notes that three quest stories appear in Luke 5 and 7, and three in Luke 17, 18, and 19, another link between certain pericopes in the table fellowship matrix.

[61]J. Neusner, "Two Pictures of the Pharisees: Philosophical Circle or Eating Club," *ATR* LXIV:4 (1982) 525–538 concludes 535 that "the Pharisaic groups did not conduct their table-fellowship meals as rituals." Cf. also E. S. Steele, "Jesus' Table-Fellowship with Pharisees: An Editorial Analysis of Luke 7:36-50, 11:37-54, and 14:1-24" (Ph.D. diss., Notre Dame, 1981); and Carroll, "Luke's Portrayal of the Pharisees," 604, 607, 610–612 on Pharisaical table fellowship. See Lietzmann, *Mass and the Lord's Supper*, 622–625; Jeremias, *Eucharistic Words*, 29–31; R. Otto, *Kingdom of God and Son of Man* (London: Lutterworth, 1943) 278–280; G. Dix, *The Shape of the Liturgy* (New York: The Seabury Press, 1982) 50–70; and Davis, "The Significance of the Shared Meal," 21–23 on the related topic of the *haburah* meal. The *haburah* meal contributes to the religious and cultural milieu of Jesus' table fellowship as a Jewish ritual meal, but it is difficult to determine any direct influence.

[62]Cf. Fitzmyer, *I-IX*, 688. Jeremias, *Parables*, 126 reinforces my contention

3) There is another, more subtle link between Luke 5 and 7. Jesus' forgiveness of the woman's sins elicits a question from the Pharisees in 7:49: " 'Who is this, who even forgives sins?' " This is similar to the question in 5:21 by the Pharisees immediately preceding the feast which Jesus eats with Levi where the forgiveness of sins was the issue. Note the similarities in language here:

Luke 7:49 "Then those who were at table with him began to say among themselves, 'Who is this, who even forgives sins (*hamartías aphíêsin*)?' "

Luke 5:21 "And the scribes and Pharisees began to question, saying, 'Who is this that speaks blasphemies? Who can forgive sins (*hamartías apheínai*) but God only?' "

These similarities suggest that in both Luke 5 and 7 the issue is the forgiveness of sins. In Luke 5, Jesus demonstrates his power to forgive sins by healing the paralytic, causing a controversy among the Pharisees and teachers of the law. Then he shows his continuing interest in sinners by immediately joining the feast with Levi, ending with 5:32: "I have not come to call the righteous, but sinners *to repentance.*"

In Luke 7, Luke reverses the order. He begins first with the teachings about the breaking in of the messianic age in Jesus, causing a controversy with the Pharisees, the target of his teachings.[63] Jesus is then invited by a Pharisee to dine with him, and while sitting at the table, a sinful woman comes to Jesus, greets him with signs worthy of a most honored guest,[64] and receives

---

that teaching and eating go together: ". . . the meal to which the Pharisee invited Jesus is clearly a banquet (*kateklíthê*, v. 36); it is in honour of Jesus, since Simon is allowing for the possibility that Jesus may be a prophet, and that with him the departed Spirit of God has returned, bringing the New Age. Since it was a meritorious act to invite travelling teachers, especially if they had preached in the synagogue, to a sabbath meal (cf. e.g., Mark 1.30f.), we may at all events infer that before the episode which the story relates took place, *Jesus had preached a sermon which had impressed them all, the host, the guests and an uninvited guest, the woman*" (emphasis mine).

[63]Cf. Jeremias, *Parables*, 124.

[64]The Lukan additions complement his theme of table fellowship with sinners. He alone calls her a sinner and records her reaction. Her tears indicate her repentance (cf. 5:32), and her acts of love towards Jesus indicate that she

the forgiveness of her sins. Here forgiveness occurs in the context of table fellowship and flows out of it.

The irony, however, is that the Pharisees sitting at the table with Jesus do not receive the forgiveness of their sins. Forgiveness is for the sinful woman who is *not* at the table, with whom the Pharisees are *not* in fellowship. Table fellowship does not *guarantee forgiveness*, as Jesus teaches in Luke 13:26-27: "Then you will begin to say, 'We ate and drank in your presence, and you taught in our streets.' But he will say, 'I tell you, I do not know where you come from; depart from me, all you workers of iniquity.'" Only Luke preserves this saying. Here he states the criteria for accepting Jesus—it is not merely a matter of accepting his table fellowship, listening to his teaching, or eating and drinking in his presence. One must show signs of love. Both Luke 5 and 7 point out that the Pharisees do not receive the forgiveness of their sins. It is sinners who receive forgiveness because they accept Jesus and his table fellowship.[65]

Luke 7:47 is a most difficult verse: "But he who is forgiven little, loves little." In other words, is the woman forgiven because of her great love, or does she love because she is forgiven? The critical consensus is in support of the latter. She comes to Jesus because she believes that he will forgive her sins, and her demonstration of gratitude and love is her response to Jesus' forgiveness. Therefore, as Jeremias says,

"Hence it is conclusively established that in the much-discussed phrase in v. 47a, forgiveness comes first, as is shown unequivocally by v. 47b and by the parable, and this implies that *hóti* in v. 47a indicates the evidence of forgiveness: 'Therefore I say to you that God must have forgiven her sins, many as they are, since she displays such deep thankfulness (grateful love); he to whom God forgives little, shows little thankfulness (thankful

---

considers him the Messiah who can forgive her sins. The Lukan theme of hospitality is highlighted by the contrasting hospitality between Simon the Pharisee and the sinful woman. The kissing of the feet may be contrasted to the kiss of Judas in Luke 22:47-48, the sign of betrayal. Both acts acknowledge that Jesus is the Messiah (cf. John 12:3).

[65]Cf. Fitzmyer, *I-IX*, 583, 692 who comments on *aphéôntai* as a theological passive in 5:20 and 7:47.

love).' The story therefore implies that *Jesus in his sermon had offered forgiveness.*"[66]

Although the text does not confirm Jeremias' contention that this sinful woman heard a sermon from Jesus in which he offered forgiveness, it does acknowledge that she is responding to a *teaching* of Jesus in which forgiveness is offered. She heard it either directly, which seems likely, or by word of mouth. The relationship here is between *teaching about forgiveness*, the offer of forgiveness, and the response of love and gratitude, a practical application of the truths of Luke 5 and 7.

In Luke 5, Jesus offers forgiveness to the paralytic in 5:20, he *teaches* about the Son of Man's authority to forgive sins in 5:20-24, and he heals the paralytic in 5:24 as a proof that his teaching about forgiveness is with authority. Levi the tax collector responds to *the teaching about forgiveness* in 5:27-39 by giving a feast for Jesus where his teaching may be expanded to show the all-encompassing forgiveness of Jesus for sinners.[67]

In Luke 7, the relationship is even clearer. The *teaching about forgiveness* occurs in 7:28-35 where the one who accepts the plan of God accepts John the Baptist as the precursor preaching repentance and Jesus as the coming one preaching forgiveness. The offer of forgiveness comes to the sinful woman, the paradigm of a sinner in Luke's table fellowship matrix in 5:17-39 and 7:18-35. The response is again from the woman that signals her belief that Jesus is the prophet spoken of by Simon the Pharisee in 7:39.[68]

Luke's use of prophet in 7:39 teases the reader into considering its meaning in relation to 7:16. In calling Jesus a prophet, does the Pharisee consider this a visitation of God to his people? Jeremias' remarks quoted above suggest this possibility, especially if Jesus had preached a sermon in which he claimed that his miracles indicated that the messianic age had dawned. A precedent exists in Jesus' sermon in Nazareth where he teaches this very thing. Luke's organization of the material in chapter 7 also suggests this possibility (i.e. the raising of the widow's son at Nain and the

[66]Jeremias, *Parables*, 127 (emphasis mine). Cf. also Tannehill, *Narrative Unity*, 117–118.
[67]Luke's editorial *kai metá taúta* in 5:27 links together 5:17-25 and 5:27-39.
[68]Cf. Tannehill, *Narrative Unity*, 106.

declaration that this is a prophet, God's visitation to his people; the discussion with John's disciples about the miracles of Jesus; the demonstration of the plan of God in the ministries of John and Jesus; and Jesus' table fellowship in which he teaches and offers the forgiveness of sins). Simon the Pharisee observes that the progression of events suggests Jesus is the eschatological prophet of the new age. He does in fact call Jesus a teacher (7:40), "a title revered in contemporary Palestine."[69] Simon's difficulty with God's plan is that it includes sinners, the reason behind the Pharisees' rejection of Jesus.

Thus, the parable of the two debtors is lived out in the lives of the Pharisee and the sinful woman. She owes the great debt and is forgiven, thus showing great gratitude in contrast to Simon the Pharisee. The motive here is her faith in God's plan as it is manifested in John and Jesus, even though she is a horrible sinner. Thus Jesus says to her: "Your faith has saved you; go in peace," two favorite Lukan themes already enunciated in 5:20 ("and when he saw their faith he said, 'Man, your sins are forgiven you' "). Jesus' concern for sinners within his table fellowship is to show that "only the poor can fathom the full meaning of God's goodness."[70] The sinners and tax collectors receive the salvation and peace of God because they accept God's plan in Jesus and his table fellowship.

b. A Comparison with the Meal at Emmaus

The parallels between Luke 5 and 7 suggest further elaboration upon the table fellowship themes already established.

1) It is a table fellowship with sinners, i.e. it is an inclusive event. At stake in Luke 7:36-50 is the manner in which Israel receives Jesus: like this sinful woman, with the same open hospitality Jesus showed, or like the Pharisee, with hostility and rejection?[71] It is Jesus' attitude to the woman that leads to the charge of blasphemy by the Pharisees that culminates in his death. At this meal

---

[69]Fitzmyer, *I-IX*, 690.

[70]Jeremias, *Parables*, 127.

[71]The inhospitable character of Pharisee meals with Jesus is reflected in Luke 11:38 and 14:1. In all three meals with the Pharisees, Jesus is treated as an outsider within the religious establishment.

in Simon's house, the forgiveness of sins and Jesus' table fellowship are inextricably entwined.

2) It is a table fellowship where Jesus teaches about the kingdom. Parables again provide the vehicle for Jesus' teaching about the kingdom. Although the word "kingdom" is not used in this passage, the content of the kingdom is described—the forgiveness of sins. The focus of the parables of Luke 5:36-39 and 7:41-42 is on forgiveness, for Jesus brings a kingdom in which sinners receive the forgiveness of their sins. Luke's summary of Jesus' Galilean ministry in 8:1 echoes the content of Luke 5-7: "Soon afterwards he went on through the cities and villages preaching (*kêrússôn*) and bringing the good news of the kingdom of God (*euaggelizómenos tên basileían*)." The good news of the kingdom refers to the kingdom parables of Luke 8, *and* the parables of Luke 5 to 7. The transition from Luke 7:47-50 to 8:1-3 hinges upon the forgiveness of sins, the essence of Jesus' teaching about the kingdom as it is expressed in Jesus' table fellowship. The meal at Emmaus will connect this teaching with the suffering and death of Christ.

3) The table fellowship is itself an expression of the new age. Jeremias' comments about the expectations of Simon the Pharisee suggest that this meal with Jesus resulted from Jesus' preaching/teaching about the presence of the new age in him. Jeremias includes this parable under the category of "God's Mercy for Sinners":

"They [a second group of parables] are those which contain the Good News itself. The gospel in the true sense of the word does not only say that God's day of salvation has dawned, that the New Age is here, and that the Redeemer has appeared, but also that salvation is sent to the poor, and that Jesus has come as a Saviour of sinners."[72]

4. LUKE 9:10-17—THE FEEDING OF THE FIVE THOUSAND

As the Gospel moves towards its climax in Jerusalem, Lukan meals become more messianic and eschatological. The feeding of the five thousand is the climax of Jesus' Galilean ministry, just as the Last Supper is the climax of his Jerusalem ministry, and the

[72]Jeremias, *Parables*, 124.

meal at Emmaus is the climax of his post-resurrection appearances.[73] The Emmaus meal reflects both the feeding of the five thousand and the Last Supper, serving as the climax for Luke's table fellowship in his Gospel and the beginning of the table fellowship of the Church in Acts. *These are the three most significant meals in Luke's Gospel,* functioning literarily as fitting conclusions to the major sections of Jesus' ministry.[74] By chapter 9, the table fellowship of Luke is fully developed. Thus, there is no need in the final four pericopes to make a subdivision between table fellowship and a comparison with Emmaus.

The observations in chapter two about the similarities between the feeding of the five thousand and the Emmaus meal are instructive, suggesting a number of thoughts about Lukan table fellowship:

a) Luke 9:10-17 must be considered within the context of Luke 9. The chiasmus between Luke 9 and 24 supports the thesis that Jesus' table fellowship is *ecclesiological* (9:1-6; 24:44-49—the incorporation of the Twelve/Eleven into the ministry of Jesus); *Christological* (9:7-9; 24:36-43—the identity of Jesus); *passion-centered* (9:18-22; 24:25-27—passion predictions and statements); *orderly and participatory* (9:23-27; 24:13-24—the order of the kingdom is suffering before glory, the cost of discipleship); and *resurrection-directed* (9:28-36; 24:1-12—the goal of the passion). The feeding of the five thousand is, as Ellis suggested, the climax of Jesus' Galilean ministry because, within the context of Luke 9, it serves as the great act of Jesus that elicits the climactic responses of Peter's confession and Jesus' prediction of his passion.[75] As such, it thrusts the table fellowship motif into the center of one of Luke's most critical chapters, suggesting that table fellowship is essential to understanding Lukan Christology.[76]

[73]Davis, "The Significance of the Shared Meal," 72 n. 71 makes a similar observation.

[74]Cf. Wainwright, *Eucharist and Eschatology,* 28–29 on the "messianic significance" of the feeding miracles in the Gospels.

[75]Ellis, *The Gospel of Luke,* 138. Fitzmyer, *I-IX,* 764 rejects such a claim and sees the confession of Peter and the passion prediction as climactic. Both are possible if Luke 9 is a unit.

[76]Cf. Tannehill, *Narrative Unity,* 218–219.

b) Luke 9:10-17 has an Old Testament precedent that anticipates Luke's intentions in the Emmaus narrative where the fulfillment of the Old Testament Scriptures is a major theme. As I. H. Marshall states:

"But the stress on the OT background of the incident is there; what God did through Moses and Elisha in OT times, feeding the people with manna in the desert (Ex. 16; Nu. 11) and a hundred men with barley loaves and grain (2 Ki. 4:42-44), he now does again plenteously through Jesus."[77]

The relationship between the feeding of the multitudes and the manna feedings has been drawn in detail, particularly with respect to the feeding miracle in John 6 and the manna references.[78] But for Luke more than the other Synoptics, 2 Kings 4:42-44, a proto-type of Jesus' feeding miracle, is as significant an Old Testament allusion as Exodus 16. Not only is Jesus like the great prophet Moses, who feeds his people in the wilderness (9:12), but he also continues the prophetic line as Elisha did.[79] This is consistent with Luke's Christology, for in his Nazareth sermon he compares Jesus to Elisha and Elijah, examples of Old Testament rejected prophets. These prophetic alignments indicate that the Old Testament promises are coming true in Jesus Christ. The table fellowship be-tween God and his people, foreshadowed in the prophets Moses and Elisha, has now reached its fulfillment in the ministry of Jesus, who feeds the multitudes in the wilderness with abundant bread.

c) Luke alone stresses the teachings about the kingdom of God in 9:11. In Luke 24:6, the women are asked to recall what Jesus said in Galilee, i.e. in Luke 9. Jesus spoke prophetically in Luke 9 because he taught about the kingdom of God (9:11) and made the first prediction of his death (9:22). In Luke 24:32, this same pro-phetic speaking is granted to Jesus' words on the road to Em-

[77]Marshall, *The Gospel of Luke*, 357.

[78]See Ellis, *The Gospel of Luke*, 138–139.

[79]Cf. H. D. Hummel, *The Word Becoming Flesh* (St. Louis: Concordia Publishing House, 1979) 143, on 2 Kings: "Far more to the point is the parallelism between many of Elisha's and Jesus' miracles: raising the dead, *multiplying food*, controlling nature, etc. . . . miracles cluster about signal interventions of Yahweh in the life of His people" (emphasis mine).

maus: "Did not our hearts burn within us while he talked to us on the road, while he opened to us the scriptures?" The opening up of the Scriptures on the road revealed from the prophetic writings (Luke 24:25: ". . . all that the prophets have spoken") that the Christ must "suffer these things and enter into his glory" (24:26). In other words, as Jesus speaks prophetically about the kingdom and the necessity of his death in Luke 9 and 24, he exhibits his continuity with the prophets of old. This prophetic speaking is part of the Lukan fulfillment of Scripture.

Luke also emphasizes the complementarity between the teaching and miracles of Jesus. The three evangelists differ concerning the activity of Jesus immediately preceding the feeding miracle. Matthew 14:14 states that "he had compassion on them, and healed their sick"; Mark 6:34 says that "he had compassion on them, because they were like sheep without a shepherd; and he began to teach (*didáskein*) them many things."[80] Only Luke 9:11 has both healing and teaching: "and [he] spoke[81] (*elálei*) to them of the kingdom of God, and cured those who had need of healing." Luke shapes his narrative to include both Jesus' teaching and healing, with teaching taking precedence. In effect, the kingdom of God consists of the Messiah teaching, healing, and feeding his people as was promised by the prophets of old.

d) The language of the feeding miracle is the language of the institution narrative in Luke 22:19 and the meal at Emmaus in 24:30.[82] G. Wainwright points out the common language between

[80]Cf. Dillon, *From Eyewitnesses*, 106 who, on the basis of Luke's adaptation of Mark 6:34 in Luke 9:11, compares Luke's agenda in 9:11-17 (teaching and eating) with Luke 24:35 and the meals of Acts: ". . . Lk redefines the dominical *didáskein* prefacing Mk's miracle (6:34) as a *laleín perí tês basileías toú theoú* (Lk 9,11), the very same instructional program that was to mark the appearances (and meals!) of the risen Christ according to Acts 1,3f."

[81]Cf. Fitzmyer, *I-IX*, 766: "Or 'continued to speak,' since the verb is impf. . . . This is a Lucan redactional addition about the content of Jesus' teaching; Mark 6:34 ends merely with, 'he taught them many things.' Luke clearly wants to relate the coming miracles to Jesus' kingdom-preaching."

[82]G. H. Boobyer, "The Eucharistic Interpretation of the Miracles of the Loaves in St. Mark's Gospel," *JTS* 3 (1952) 162–3 argues that "the vocabulary alone, then, in Mark 6:35-44 and 8:1-9 can supply no sure ground on which to base eucharistic interpretations of the incidents described there." What is remarkable here is not the specific words used by the evangelists, but the

the feeding miracles in the Gospels and the institution narratives. Inserted in Wainwright's schema is the language in common with Emmaus:

1. Jesus took (*labôn/elaben*): Matt. 14:19; 15:36; 26:26; Mark 6:41; 8:6; 14:22; Luke 9:16; 22:19; [24:30]; John 6:11; I Cor. 11:23.
2. Bread (*tous artous/arton*): Matt. 14:19; 15:36; 26:26; Mark 6:41; 8:6; 14:22; Luke 9:16; 22:19; [24:30]; John 6:11; I Cor. 11:23.
3. He looked up to heaven (*anablepsas eis ton ouranon*): Matt. 14:19; Mark 6:41; Luke 9:16.
4. He blessed/gave thanks (*eulogêsen/eulogêsas/eucharistêsas*) Matt. 14:19; 15:36; 26:26; Mark 6:41; 8:6; 14:22; Luke 9:16; 22:19; [24:30]; John 6:11; I Cor. 11:24.
5. He broke (*klasas/eklasen/kateklasen*): Matt. 14:19; 15:36; 26:26; Mark 6:41; 8:6; 14:22; Luke 9:16; 22:19; [24:30, 35]; John 6:11; I Cor. 11:24.
6. He gave (*edôken/edidou/dous/diedôken*): Matt. 14:19; 15:36; 26:26; Mark 6:41; 8:6; 14:23; Luke 9:16; 22:19; [24:30]; John 6:11.
7. The crowds/the disciples ate (*ephagon/phagete*): Matt. 14:20; 15:37; 26:26; Mark 6:42; 8:8; Luke 9:17; cf. I Cor. 11:26.[83]

This meal language binds these three passages together, setting the stage for interpreting the feeding of the five thousand as a prefigurement of the Last Supper, and the Last Supper as the precedent for the table fellowship of the early Christian community. The messianic and eschatological context of the feeding miracle confirms the significance of the miracle in the table fellowship matrix and its relation to these other two Lukan meals.

e) The lack of reaction of the crowds to the miracle in all three Synoptic accounts (as compared to John 6:14-15) tips off the reader to look for a reaction somewhere else. In Luke, the reaction comes

---

constellation of the vocabulary within a messianic and eschatological context. Cf. Tannehill, *Narrative Unity*, 219; Dillon, *From Eyewitnesses*, 149–150.

[83]Wainwright, *Eucharist and Eschatology*, 35–36 also draws the following conclusion about the relationship between the feeding miracles and the Eucharist: ". . . when the patristic church saw a relation between the feedings and the eucharist it was maintaining a relation which had certainly been seen retrospectively by the primitive church from the viewpoint of its own eucharistic experience, and *which had indeed (we would judge) already been seen by Jesus*" (emphasis mine). Also Tannehill, *Narrative Unity*, 289–290.

in the Christological confession of Peter who, in response to the questions of Jesus as to his identity, *and the miracle of the feeding of the five thousand,* declares that Jesus is "the Christ of God" (9:20).[84]

Luke ties this confession of Peter in 9:20 to Jesus' passion prediction in 9:21 (*ho de . . . eipôn*). By so doing, he links the passion of Jesus as the Christ with the table fellowship which has evoked this confession. The Messiah, who comes in fulfillment of the Old Testament promises to feed the people of Israel, is the one who suffers, dies, and on the third day rises again. These ideas will become more explicit in the context of the Last Supper occurring on the night in which he was betrayed, and for Luke, in the context of that first Easter morning when the crucified one, risen from the dead, walks with the Emmaus disciples, opens the Scriptures for them, teaches them about the necessity of suffering, death, and resurrection in fulfillment of Scripture, and breaks bread with them. This opens their eyes to his identity as "the Christ of God" crucified and risen. Thus the miracle of the feeding of the five thousand both prefigures the Lukan table fellowship that will find completion in Luke 22 and 24 and introduces the *two major elements of that fellowship: 1) teaching about the passion of Jesus from the Messiah himself, and 2) eating with the Messiah in his kingdom.*

f) The Lukan petition for daily bread in the Lord's Prayer in 11:3 is a commentary on the feeding miracle of Jesus and the Lukan table fellowship matrix. The debate over the hapax legomena "daily (*epioúsion*) bread" is well known.[85] Wainwright gives con-

---

[84]Cf. Tannehill, *Narrative Unity*, 218–219.

[85]Wainwright, *Eucharist and Eschatology*, 30–34 has perhaps the best treatment of this in its depth and clarity. See also S. A. Falcone, "The Kind of Bread We Pray for in the Lord's Prayer," *Essays in Honor of Joseph P. Brennan*, ed. R. F. McNamara (Rochester, N.Y.: St. Bernard's Seminary, 1976) 36–59; J. Jeremias, *The Lord's Prayer* (Facet Books, Biblical Series 8; Philadelphia: Fortress, 1973) 23–27; J. J. Petuchowski and M. Brocke, *The Lord's Prayer and Jewish Liturgy* (New York: Seabury, 1978); B. Orchard, "The Meaning of *ton epiousion* (Mt 6:11= Lk 11:3)," *BibTrans* 3 (1973) 274–282; J. Hennig, "Our Daily Bread," *TS* 4 (1943) 445–454; A. Baker, "What Sort of Bread Did Jesus Want Us to Pray For?" *NB* 54 (1973) 125–129; and M. Black, "The Aramaic of *ton arton hêmôn ton epiousion* (Matt vi.11 = Luke xi.3)," *JTS* 42 (1941) 186–189.

vincing evidence that many Church Fathers considered this petition to be both an eschatological and Eucharistic reference in which the disciples petition the Father to "give us already now the bread of the future age."[86] Wainwright argues that an eschatological interpretation is consistent with an understanding of the other petitions in the Lord's Prayer:

"The bread for which we pray is *at the one and the same time* both earthly bread to meet the hunger and need of the present day, and also the future bread which will satisfy the elect in the eschatological kingdom and is already given to us in anticipation— miraculous feedings of the crowds were, in sign and reality, present experiences of the future messianic meal at which those who now hunger will be satisfied."[87]

If this is a legitimate interpretation of this petition for bread, then the feeding of the five thousand becomes not only a messianic meal, but a meal in which the Messiah is giving substantial food to his people *in abundance*. Every one present at the meal was satisfied, and each disciple gathered his own basket of leftover bread (9:17), "twelve baskets of broken pieces." The leftover bread is a sign that the abundant new age is present among the crowds in the person of Jesus.[88] When Jesus instructs his disciples

[86]Wainwright, *Eucharist and Eschatology*, 32 who cites the following Church Fathers as evidence for this position: Origen, Athanasius, Jerome, Cyril of Alexandria, Peter Chrysologus, and John Damascene.

[87]Ibid., 34 (emphasis Wainwright). Wainwright notes on p. 168 n. 113 that Jeremias, *Prayer*, 25–27 also argues for this interpretation. Jeremias' intent is to argue that "for Jesus, earthly bread and the bread of life are not antithetical. . . . The bread which he [Jesus] proffered when he sat at table with publican and sinners was everyday bread, and yet it was more: it was bread of life. The bread which he broke for his disciples at the Last Supper was earthly bread, and yet it was more: his body given for many in death, the gift of a portion in the atoning power of his death. *Every meal his disciples had with him was a usual eating and drinking, and yet it was more: a meal of salvation, a messianic meal, image and anticipation of the meal at the consummation, because he was the master of the house*" (emphasis mine).

[88]The number 12 may carry eschatological significance here, supporting an interpretation of the feeding of the five thousand as a foretaste of the eschatological banquet. McHugh, *The Mother of Jesus*, 423–424 argues that in the Apocalypse "the number 12 is never used of earthly realities, but only of

162

to pray for bread, they know that he has provided and will continue to provide the earthly bread and the bread of the future age. Table fellowship with Jesus is a foretaste of the future eschatological meal; or as Wainwright puts it, "the meals of Jesus during His ministry were signs of the coming feast in the kingdom: they were a throwing forward into the present of the first part of the future feast."[89]

g) There is only one significant difference between the feeding miracle and the other passages we have considered in Luke's meal motif: there is no opposition from the religious establishment. This is also true of the Last Supper and the Emmaus meal. These three meals are portrayed in Luke as non-controversial *as they are being acted out*. In and of themselves, they are manifestations of a pure table fellowship *now* that foreshadows the joy, the abundance, and the peace of a table fellowship *not yet*. In fact, any controversy that arises during these three meals is not between Jesus and his opponents but between Jesus and his disciples. In all three meals, the identity of Jesus is not in question for the reader, but the disciples are only able to recognize Jesus as the crucified and risen Messiah when he reveals himself in the breaking of the bread after the resurrection. This now introduces a theme hinted at in the discussion of the parables of the new garment and new wine (and brought to the forefront in the Emmaus meal), namely, that table fellowship is a primary means of Lukan *revelation* that Jesus is the Messiah who comes to offer his life through death as bread for the world (cf. 24:21—"he was the one to redeem Israel").[90]

---

heavenly things . . . the number 12, however, is reserved for the fullness of perfection which will not pass away . . . one could say that it is this number which marks the city as God's New Jerusalem."

[89]Wainwright, *Eucharist and Eschatology*, 30. Cf. Tannehill, *Narrative Unity*, 238–239 on the connection between the kingdom (11:2) and the bread (11:3). Some manuscripts of Luke's version of the Lord's prayer make this association more directly than Matthew's (6:10-11).

[90]Davis, "The Significance of the Shared Meal," 74 emphasizes *revelation* throughout his thesis. He explains on pp. 77–78 the content of this revelation: "For Luke the Banquet *is* now—in the feeding of the five thousand, in the meals of the outcasts—for those who see. True, it is more perfectly revealed later, but even this takes place for Luke in the early Church. This is not to say that Luke has no futuristic eschatology; on the contrary, he merely em-

This could not become a significant theme until the first passion prediction occurs in Luke 9. Thus, Luke 9 functions as climactic in the development of Luke's passion theology and his table fellowship matrix.

---

phasizes the *present* aspect without taking from future elements" (emphasis Davis).

Chapter 10

Lukan Meals and Meal Metaphors— The Journey to Jerusalem

Between the feeding of the five thousand and the discourse of Luke 14, many Lukan meals and meal metaphors contribute to the development of Luke's table fellowship matrix. They are significant, though not highlights within Luke's thematic structure.

THE LUKAN MEALS

Luke 10:7-9, 17-20, 21-24

The instructions of Jesus to his seventy disciples in Luke 10:7-9 point out the continuity between the table fellowship of Jesus and that of the disciples. Only Luke has the command to "remain in the same house, eating and drinking what they provide, for the laborer deserves his wages; do not go from house to house." This may refer to table fellowship with those who are ritually unclean, i.e. do not go from house to house looking for food that is ritually clean. In the same context they are told to heal the sick and say "the kingdom of God has come near to you" (10:9). The kingdom of God is near in the ministry of the disciples because they bring with them the table fellowship of Jesus—his teaching, healing, and eating.[1] Luke 10:17-20 describes the success of the mission of the seventy in eschatological terms, and 10:21-24 seems to resemble Jewish wisdom sayings concerning eschatological secrets.

Luke 10:38-42

The meal with Mary and Martha in Luke 10:38-42 emphasizes the significance of the teaching activity of Jesus within his table

---

[1]Marshall, *The Gospel of Luke*, 421 suggests a parallel to 1 Corinthians 10:27 and the problem of Christian table fellowship with Gentiles.

fellowship; his word is the good portion that will not be taken away. As Davis comments:

"Luke is possibly seeking to correct any tendencies to take the shared meal fellowship, which is under the motif of the Messianic Banquet, in too literal a fashion. It is the communion with the Messiah through the Messianic Banquet of the New Age which is important, not the actual physical meal itself."[2]

Luke 11:37-54

The second meal of Jesus with the Pharisees in Luke 11:37-54 continues their controversy, resulting in harsh words by Jesus to the Pharisees, lawyers, and scribes in the form of woes. There is a close connection here with Luke 7:18-35 and its Wisdom sayings, for just as in Luke 7, Jesus and John are Wisdom's representatives, rejected by the Pharisees, so in Luke 11, all the prophets and apostles "from the blood of Abel to the blood of Zechariah" (11:51) have been persecuted and killed by Israel. Thus, Luke 11:53-54 brings the controversy to a crisis as the lawyers and Pharisees begin plotting against Jesus.[3]

THE LUKAN MEAL METAPHORS

Luke 12:13-48

After Luke 12:1, the meal metaphors in Luke 12:13-48 contrast the meal of this present age with the age to come. Anxiety over food in this age fails to recognize the significance of Jesus' eschatological table fellowship. Table fellowship with Jesus is portrayed by Luke as both a present and future reality. D. E. Smith perceives a literary theme of luxury expressed in negative terms with eschatological overtones:

"The luxurious meal functions as a symbol for the debauchery of 'this age,' which is due to be condemned in the future judgment. These texts thus function both as a warning and as an assurance to the faithful. They are assured that those who feast luxuriously

[2]Davis, "The Significance of the Shared Meal," 80.
[3]Cf. D. E. Smith, "Table Fellowship," 623 on Luke 11:37-41 and the symposium tradition illustrated in Luke 14; also Tannehill, *Narrative Unity*, 180–182.

166

now will eventually be judged, and they are warned lest they fall into the same trap."[4]

Luke 13:22-35

The Lukan meal parables and sayings of Luke 13:22-35 provide the context for the material of Luke 14. Following immediately upon Jesus' *teaching* in a synagogue on the Sabbath (13:10), a Sabbath healing controversy (13:11-17), and two parables "stressing the inevitable growth of the kingdom and its active power"[5] (13:18-21), Luke begins a section about those who will be received into the kingdom of God, introduced by the question in 13:23: "Lord, will those who are saved be few?" E. E. Ellis entitled Luke 13:22–16:13 "Teachings of Messiah: Who Will Enter the Kingdom?" He points out that the principle of reversal is operative here, and that Jesus' words are directed against the Jewish religious authorities.[6]

The teachings about acceptance and rejection of the kingdom take place as Jesus is journeying (*poreían poioúmenos*) toward Jerusalem (13:22). Jerusalem now asserts itself as both the place of destiny (13:31-35) and the place for feasting (13:26-30—cf. the Last Supper). The setting for these teachings in 13:22-30 is the eschatological table fellowship of Jesus, where "men will come from east and west, and from north and south, and *sit at table in the kingdom of God*" (13:29).

Luke 13:29 is *the* classic statement on the nature of Jesus' eschatological table fellowship.[7] This feast is a time of joy because of the consummation of the kingdom, and a time of sorrow because of the judgment upon those who do not accept the coming of God's messianic kingdom in Jesus. Those rejoicing at the

[4]Smith, "Table Fellowship," 624–626. Smith points to other illustrations of this in Luke 17:26-29; 21:34; and 6:24-25. The classic illustration of this is the parable of the rich man and Lazarus in 16:19-31. See also Tannehill, *Narrative Unity*, 240, 249–251 who on p. 249 notes that "imagery which points to the eschatological banquet appears repeatedly in Luke 12–15 (see 12:37; 13:28-30; 14:15-24; 15:22-32)."

[5]Fitzmyer, *X-XXIV*, 1019.

[6]Ellis, *The Gospel of Luke*, 187.

[7]See Guillaume, *Luc interprète*, 147–148, 154 on Luke 13:29 and the universality of Luke's eschatological table fellowship.

eschatological table fellowship of Jesus in the kingdom of God will include the patriarchs, Abraham, Isaac, and Jacob, the prophets, and the Gentiles from east and west, north and south.[8] Those excluded are all members of Israel who say "we ate and drank in your presence, and you taught in our streets,"[9] but who then reject Jesus' messiahship. This is Luke's reversal of roles motif where the last will be first and the first will be last (13:30); for who appears more fit for the kingdom than the Pharisees and the other religious luminaries, and who appears more unfit than the unclean Gentiles? But as Luke's Gospel unfolds, the Pharisees, who oppose Jesus during his ministry and bring charges against him that lead to his death, befriend him in 13:31, never appear as his opponents during his trial and crucifixion, and become foundational for the Church by the end of Acts.[10]

OLD TESTAMENT AND INTERTESTAMENTAL PRECEDENTS

A discussion of table fellowship in Luke 14 necessitates a brief consideration of the possible Old Testament and intertestamental precedents for the Lukan themes of table fellowship and the eschatological kingdom. In *Eucharist and Eschatology*, Wainwright states:

"The Old Testament sets the scene for our understanding of the eschatological significance of the eucharistic meal. Israel shared the idea common to many religions that eating and drinking, especially in a cultic setting, is a means of appropriating divine blessings."[11]

Wainwright's four Old Testament categories are possible precedents to Lukan table fellowship, namely *the meal at the making of*

[8]Cf. Marshall, *The Gospel of Luke*, 568 on the identity of these people from the four points of the compass as Gentiles.

[9]Ellis, *The Gospel of Luke*, 187 calls them "proud, religious Judaism."

[10]Tyson, *The Death of Jesus*, 72. See also Tannehill, *Narrative Unity*, 109–110 on the "sayings and parables of reversal."

[11]Wainwright, *Eucharist and Eschatology*, 19. He discusses these precedents under the two categories of "1. The Old Testament Preparation," and "2. The inter-testamental period." See also Davis, "The Significance of the Shared Meal," 1–46 on "Religious Meals in the Old Testament and in Judaism"; and I. H. Marshall, *Last Supper and Lord's Supper* (Grand Rapids: Eerdmans, 1980).

168

the covenant at Mount Sinai (Exod 24), sacred meals in places of sacri-fice (Gen 31:54; Exod 18:12; 1 Sam 9:11-14; Deut 12:5-7, 17-18; 14:23, 26; 15:20; 27:7), the wisdom literature (Prov 9:1-6; Ps 23:5; Cant 5:1), and the feeding and feasting in the future salvation (Isa 25:6-9; 48:21; 49:9f.; 55:1-2, 5; 65:13; Ezek 34:13f., 23, 25-31; Zech 9:16-17).[12] The Passover is the most likely Old Testament prece-dent, particularly due to the "strong eschatological expectation, and that messianic, attached to the Jewish passover at the time of Jesus."[13] The enthronement feast is another possible precedent,[14] as is suggested by Isaiah 25:6-8,[15] the meals that celebrate the coronation of a king (1 Sam 11:15; 2 Sam 15:11-12; 1 Kgs 1:9, 25; 1 Chr 29:21-22), and the enthronement Psalms (47; 93; 95; 96; 97; 98; and 99).[16] All these Old Testament meal precedents contribute to the religious and cultural milieu of Lukan table fellowship, but it is difficult to discern any direct influence.

[12]Wainwright, Eucharist and Eschatology, 19–21.

[13]Ibid., 23. Wainwright places this in the intertestamental period because of the messianic expectation associated with the feast at the time of Jesus.

[14]See S. Mowinckel, He That Cometh (New York: Abingdon Press, 1954) 80ff. on enthronement feasts. Davis, "The Significance of the Shared Meal," 32–33 places it under the category "The Apocalyptic Feast: Messianic Age and Its Banquet"; also R. de Vaux, Ancient Israel, Volume 2: Religious Institutions; trans. J. McHugh (New York: McGraw-Hill Book Company, 1961) 504–506.

[15]Cf. F. Delitzsch, Isaiah (Grand Rapids: Eerdmans Publishing Company, 1976) 439 on Isaiah 25:6-8: " 'This mountain' is Zion, the seat of God's pres-ence, and the place of His church's worship. The feast is therefore a spiritual one. The figure is taken, as in Ps. xxii. 27 sqq., from the sacrificial meals con-nected with the shelâmim (the peace-offerings) . . . . The thing symbolized in this way is the full enjoyment of blessedness in the perfected kingdom of God" (emphasis Delitzsch). See also E. J. Young, The Book of Isaiah, Volume II (Grand Rapids: Eerdmans Publishing Company, 1969) 191: "As in ancient times (1 Sam. 11:15; 1 Kings 1:9,19,25) it was customary after a coronation to sacrifice and to celebrate a sacrificial meal, so also after the Lord takes up His reign in Jerusalem, there is to be a festal meal. It is the Lord, however, who provides the banquet, for all is of His grace. He who makes the feast is desig-nated the LORD of hosts, a phrase which recalls 24:23, where it is stated that the LORD of hosts reigned."

[16]See S. Mowinckel, The Psalms in Israel's Worship, Volume I (New York: Abingdon Press, 1962) 106–192; and A. Weiser, The Psalms (Philadelphia: Westminster, 1962) on the enthronement Psalms.

In the intertestamental period, the Qumran literature stands out as the most likely precedent, particularly *Manual of Discipline* 1 QS vi, 2-8, and *Rule of the Congregation* QSa ii, 11-22.[17] There are parallels between the table fellowship of Jesus and the sacred meals of Qumran. Like the Old Testament precedents, the Qumran sacred meals probably describe the kind of table fellowship Jesus engaged in. But it is difficult to determine any direct influence of Qumran upon Jesus' table fellowship.[18] The significant difference between the sacred meals of Qumran and the table fellowship of Jesus is a Christological one. Though K. G. Kuhn does not comment on the relationship between the Qumran and Gospel meals, he does describe the relationship between the Qumran meals and the Lord's Supper in terms that also apply to the table fellowship of Jesus in Luke:

"Whether the church understood the meal [Lord's Supper] in this way or that way [as either meal fellowship with their Master or as meal of eschatological joy], the person of the historical Jesus and his redemptive role is of central significance for the religious meaning of the meal. In the Qumran texts we find no trace of such an ultimately redemptive significance of an historical person. Thus the person of Jesus and his redemptive significance, i.e., *the christology*, is the decisively new fact of Christianity. This becomes

[17]Wainwright, *Eucharist and Eschatology*, 21-25 suggests a number of other categories such as *"the abundance of food"*—4 Ezra 8:52-54; II Baruch 29:5; *"the new manna"*—Exodus 16:4, 15; Psalm 78:24f.; Nehemiah 9:15; Wisdom 16:20; 4 Ezra 1:19; II Baruch 29:8; Midr Qoh I,9; *"the future (messianic) feasting"*—Ethiopian Enoch 62:13-16; and Qumran *Interpretation of Psalm 37*, 4QpPs, 37 II, 10-11; *Rule of Interpretation*, 1QSa II,11-22 (emphasis Wainwright).

[18]K. G. Kuhn, "The Lord's Supper and the Communal Meal at Qumran," *The Scrolls of the New Testament*, ed. K. Stendahl (New York: Harper, 1957) 65-93 describes on p. 87 the influence of Qumran on the New Testament meals: "The abiding significance of the Qumran texts for the New Testament is that they show to what extent the primitive church, however conscious of its integrity and newness, drew upon the Essenes in matter of practice and cult, organization and constitution. The daily meals of the Essene Community are certainly analogous to the daily meal of the Jerusalem church." Cf. also M. Burrows, *More Light on the Dead Sea Scrolls* (New York: The Viking Press, 1955) 93: "It is as though Jesus and they [Qumran] drew water from the same spring but carried it in different vessels."

especially clear in comparison with Essene Judaism, as it is now known through the Qumran material, no matter how great the similarities and even the dependence of Christianity upon the Judaism of the Qumran texts may be and actually is."[19]

F. M. Cross in *The Ancient Library of Qumran and Modern Biblical Studies* describes the meal in the *Rule of the Congregation* in eschatological terms: "The common meal of the Essenes is hereby set forth as a liturgical anticipation of the Messianic banquet." On the basis of the heightened apocalyptic environment at the time of Jesus, Cross ties together the enthronement feast on the mountain in Isaiah 25, the sacred meals of Qumran, and the New Testament:

"By Hellenistic and Roman times the eschatological banquet and its associated themes became frequent in apocalyptic writing, and are amazingly frequent in the New Testament [he includes Luke 13:28f.; 14:15-24; and 22:30 among his references]. It comes as no surprise, therefore, to discover these motives were at home among the Essenes."[20]

5. LUKE 14:1-24 — SABBATH HEALING, MEAL ETIQUETTE, AND THE BANQUET PARABLE

a) Luke 14:1-6—Sabbath Healing

The Lukan banquet parable is introduced by Luke's third and last Sabbath miracle of healing. The setting of Luke 14 is a meal at the house of a ruler of the Pharisees in which Luke weaves together three passages in order to bring forth one particular point about the table fellowship of Jesus.[21] By using a unique expression, the purpose clause "to dine" (literally "to eat bread"—*phageín árton*), Luke 14:1 immediately suggests another meal set-

[19]Kuhn, "The Lord's Supper," 78 (emphasis mine). L. F. Badia, *The Dead Sea People's Sacred Meal and Jesus' Last Supper* (Washington: University Press of America, 1979) 40 agrees with Kuhn that the difference between the meals of Jesus and the Qumran meals is Jesus.

[20]F. M. Cross, *The Ancient Library of Qumran and Modern Biblical Studies* (New York: Doubleday, 1958) 90–91.

[21]Navone, "The Parable of the Banquet," 923–924 explains the context of Luke 14 in terms of its fulfillment of the messianic banquet prophesied in Isaiah.

ting for the teaching of Jesus, the sixth of nine meals in Luke (cf. 5:29-37; 7:36-50; 9:10-17; 10:38-42; 11:37-54; *14:1-24*; 19:1-10; 22:7-38; 24:13-35). Although "to eat" (*esthíô*) and "bread" (*ártos*) are sometimes found in the same context (Luke 4:2-4; 9:13-17; 15:16-17; 22:15-19), there are only four places where they are used together (Luke 6:4; 7:33; 14:1; and 14:15). Luke 7:33, discussed above, and 14:1, 15, the subject of the present discussion, are clearly part of the table fellowship matrix.

The other reference in Luke 6:4 comes from the first Sabbath controversy in Luke concerning both the unlawful picking and eating of corn plucked from a grainfield in 6:1-5, and the healing of the man with the withered hand in 6:6-11. Luke 6:4 is part of the table fellowship matrix for two reasons: first, it is part of Jesus' Sabbath controversy with the Pharisees, and second, it is a controversy over the eating of bread. Wainwright affirms this in his remarks about the parallel in Mark 2:23-28:

"H. Riesenfeld gives a Eucharistic flavour to this theory that the cornfield episode of Mark 2:23-28 and parallels is a sign of the dawn of that eschatological sabbath which is characterized by the messianic 'bread' or 'feast'. When the gospel accounts of Jesus' words about the incident of David eating the showbread are contrasted with the LXX text at 1 Regn. 21:7, then the differences point to a eucharistic intent in the gospel texts: David, the prototype of the messiah, replaces Abimelech as subject of the action, and the typically eucharistic verbs *lambánein* (Luke 6:4), *didónai* (Mark 2:26; Luke 6:4), and *phageín* (Mark 2:26; Luke 6:4; Matt 12:4; cf. Matt 26:26) appear together in the same context (just as they do in the accounts of the miraculous feedings) in a way which the Old Testament account would not suggest. If Riesenfeld is right, then the evangelists at least, if not Jesus himself, saw a relationship between the eucharist and the cornfield episode."[22]

Luke 6:4 fits into the language pattern of 9:16, 22:19, and 24:30. It includes four out of the six words that make up the language of the institution narrative: "to take" (*lambánein*), "to give" (*didónai*), "to eat" (*phageín*), and "bread" (*árton*) (the two missing words are

[22]Wainwright, *Eucharist and Eschatology*, 36–37 who refers to H. Riesenfeld, *Jésus transfiguré* (Copenhagen: Munksgaard, 1947) 318–324.

"to bless/give thanks [*eulogéô/eucharistéô*] and "to break"
[*kláô/kataklÃ¡ô*]). This language suggests a connection between
Luke's Sabbath theology and his table fellowship matrix. If, after
the resurrection, Sunday replaces the Sabbath as the eschatological
day in Luke's time sequence, then Jesus' declaration in Luke 6:5
that "the Son of man is Lord of the Sabbath" demonstrates that
he is ushering in the new age of messianic salvation.

By teaching in the synagogue on the Sabbath in Luke 6:6, [7:36],
13:10, and 14:1, Jesus foreshadows his teaching on the road to
Emmaus on Sunday, the eschatological day. Luke 14:1-6, then, not
only marks Luke 14 as part of Luke's meal motif, but it begins the
process of tying together many Lukan themes under the table fellowship matrix. The healing on the Sabbath is a Christological act
that suggests, in the context of this banquet, that Jesus is the Lord
of the Sabbath.[23]

b) Luke 14:7-14—Meal Etiquette[24]

The meal setting continues as Jesus now tells two parables that
deal with meal etiquette at the eschatological table fellowship.[25]

[23]See Navone, "The Parable of the Banquet," 924. See Davis, "The Significance of the Shared Meal," 57–58 on Luke 14:1-4 as "a scene of revelation" because of the significance of the Sabbath healing in a meal setting; and
Tannehill, *Narrative Unity*, 174–176, 182–183 on Luke 6:11ff. and 14:1-6 as a
"type-scene" of Jesus' relationship with Pharisees and scribes.

[24]See D. E. Smith, "Table Fellowship," 618–620, 621–622 on Luke 14:7-24
from the perspective of the Greek symposium tradition. On p. 619 he observes some of the literary themes in Luke 14 as compared to Plutarch's *Table
Talk*: (1) "the subject of the discourse is introduced with a brief anecdote
relating to the actual choosing of positions by the participants"; (2) "the motif
of the late-arriving guest whose proper position at table has already been
taken"; (3) "the discussion then goes on to question the custom of ranking
on the basis of other criteria derived from table fellowship ethics." He also
comments on p. 619 that "friendship and pleasure are two of the most common ethical categories in the traditional philosophical discussions of ethics (or
etiquette) at the table." But Smith cautions on p. 620 that "Luke's relationship to Plutarch should not be overemphasized. Luke is clearly not writing a
philosophical dialogue, nor is it probable that he is relying on Plutarch for his
images. Rather, the similarities in the accounts of the two authors suggest
that both are utilizing a literary motif that derives from popular literature in
general and symposium traditions in particular." See Smith p. 614 n. 5 for a
bibliography on the symposium motif.

[25]Luke's use of *kataklinô* in 14:8 connects this meal parable with other signifi-

The key statements that give this passage its eschatological thrust are Luke 14:11 and 14:14. The major themes are *the humility* of those who "sit at table in the kingdom of God" (13:29) and *the reversal of roles* for those who are members of this kingdom (13:30). This parable, told while Jesus is at table with his Pharisaic opponents, reinforces the themes of Luke's table fellowship motif in Luke 5:29-37 and 7:18-50—*the table fellowship of Jesus is with sinners, i.e. it is an inclusive event.* It teaches the same principle of repentance and acceptance of the messianic kingdom of God in Jesus. Luke illustrates this further in the parable of the Pharisee and the publican in 18:9-14, concluding with the same logion in 18:14 as 14:11.

Humility is a mark of the messianic age in the teaching of Jesus, who becomes a paradigm of this humility both in his instructions on table fellowship with the outcasts of society in 14:12-14, and in his humble suffering and death upon a cross, just prophesied in 13:31-35. This humility illustrates once again that *the table fellowship of Jesus is where he teaches about the kingdom and is itself an expression of the new age.* The kingdom does not belong to the Pharisees, but to these outcasts and sinners, for wherever Jesus is sitting at table with these humble, repentant, believing sinners, there is the kingdom of God. Those who *now* sit at table with Jesus will be rewarded at the resurrection of the just to sit at table at the messianic feast, the very thrust of the next parable in Luke 14:15-24. In essence, they are both the same table, expressing the eschatological tension of the present and future realities of the kingdom of God.

Once again, the parabolic teaching of Jesus *at the table of the Pharisees* becomes a lightning rod for charges against him that will lead to his death. In Luke 14, Jesus opposes their Sabbath laws and reinforces the differences between his table fellowship and theirs. Jesus' offer of God's forgiveness and fellowship to repentant sinners at the table provoked the Pharisees and led to a crisis in the religious establishment of Israel. The table, then, is a place for fellowship, but also a place of controversy that leads to a bloody end.

---

cant Lukan meals (7:36; 9:14, 15; and 24:30), forming another connection between this meal/meal metaphor and the meal at Emmaus.

c) Luke 14:15-24—The Banquet Parable

The pivotal verse for Luke 14:1-24 is the beatitude in 14:15: "Blessed is he who shall eat bread in the kingdom of God." This is a response to the first two passages on Sabbath healing and meal etiquette that leads into the third passage on the banquet parable, the climax of Luke 14:1-24. This beatitude illustrates the significance of this banquet parable and links together a series of beatitudes in Luke's Gospel that illustrate the pervasive nature of Luke's table fellowship matrix.

Lukan Beatitudes.

LUKE 6:20-26. The beatitudes and woes of Luke describe those who accept membership in the kingdom and those who reject it. They both have an eschatological thrust, and a concern for the outcasts in society, particularly the poor and the hungry. The poor play a significant role in Luke in Jesus' messianic proclamation of the kingdom (4:18; 7:22; 14:13, 21; and 19:8), for the poor are an object of his forgiveness—theirs is the kingdom of God (6:20).[26]

The hungry represent all those who are oppressed in this life and hunger *now* for satisfaction (the poor, maimed, lame, and blind). They will be filled and satisfied in the age to come at the messianic banquet, the very point of the banquet parable in 14:15-24. Fitzmyer points out that "the second part of this beatitude alludes to the Old Testament motif of the eschatological banquet (cf. Isa 25:6-8; 49:10-13; Ps 107:3-9)."[27] The expectation of satisfaction for the people of God at the eschatological banquet of the Messiah is clearly expressed in Psalm 107:9: "For he satisfies him (*echórtase*) who is thirsty, and the hungry he fills with good things."

The feeding of the five thousand is the fulfillment of this very thing, "and all ate and were satisfied" (*echortasthêsan*—9:17), the

---

[26]See Dunn, *Jesus and the Spirit*, 55 on the relationship between the Beatitudes and Isaiah 61. He also on pp. 60–61 states: "As the beatitudes confirm, the blessedness of the end-time is most clearly expressed in Jesus' gospel for the poor. (The 'gospel' here for Jesus would be his announcement that the poor share in God's kingdom [Luke 6.20], that *God's forgiveness and acceptance was for them and was already expressed in the openness of his table-fellowship to 'tax-collectors and sinners')*" (emphasis mine).

[27]Fitzmyer, *I-IX*, 634. See also Navone, "The Lucan Banquet Community," 155-156 on the Old Testament background.

same language used of the hungry in 6:21: "Blessed are you that hunger now, for you shall be satisfied" (*chortasthêsesthe*).[28] The satisfaction and abundance at the feeding of the five thousand is a proleptic manifestation of the complete satisfaction and abundance the hungry will receive at the messianic banquet, whereas the woes emphasize that those who are full in this life will be hungry in the age to come. It is difficult not to see these words directed against the religious establishment of Israel.

LUKE 7:23. "And blessed is he who takes no offense (*skandalisthê*) at me."

This is a Christological beatitude, where the offense comes from identifying Jesus with the Messiah prophesied in the Old Testament. The offense extends beyond this Old Testament messianic identification to seeing the table fellowship of Jesus as proleptic of the eschatological banquet.

LUKE 10:23. "Blessed are the eyes which see what you see!"

This third beatitude is the response of Jesus to the seventy after their ministry of eating, healing, and saying "the kingdom of God has come near to you" (10:9). They are blessed as eyewitnesses who have seen and heard, the very instructions Jesus gave to John's disciples in 7:22 to show that he was the Old Testament Messiah that he spoke of in his sermon at Nazareth. In their mission activity, the disciples proclaim that the kingdom of God is near *in word and deed, in teaching and eating.* The beatitudes of Luke 7:23 and 10:23 are linked by their Christological and table fellowship themes, and thereby are linked with Luke 24:19 where the Emmaus disciples have seen and heard Jesus, "a prophet mighty in *deed and word*," but who fail to confess him as the crucified and risen one until the risen Christ opens up the Scriptures to them and interprets the things concerning himself.[29]

---

[28]Guillaume, *Luc interprète*, 146–147, 153 understands Luke 6:21 as the first announcement of the eschatological accent in Luke's table fellowship matrix. Cf. also Tannehill, *Narrative Unity*, 218.

[29]Cf. Dillon, *From Eyewitnesses*, 270: "Only when wondrous fact and interpreting word coincided in the conclusive self-disclosure of the Easter Christ did the messianic enigma dissipate and the messianic salvation become accessible. Such is the indispensable partnership of fact and word (Lk 24,19), of seeing and hearing (Lk 7,22; 10,23f.), hence of *narrative* and *sayings* traditions,

LUKE 11:27-28. "As he [Jesus] said this, a woman in the crowd raised her voice and said to him, 'Blessed is the womb that bore you, and the breasts that you sucked!' But he said, 'Blessed rather are those who hear the word of God and keep it!' "

This beatitude is part of Luke's word motif and raises the teaching of Jesus to a new level. It recalls both Mary's canticle in Luke 1:48, "For behold, henceforth all generations will call me blessed," and the words of Jesus immediately following the parable of the sower when he states that his true mother and brothers "are those who hear the word of God and do it" (8:21). Accepting the word (teaching) of Jesus is the measure by which one will know that he is blessed, a word that is central to the table fellowship matrix and to the testimony that Jesus gives to the Emmaus disciples about the centrality of his death and resurrection in the Old Testament.[30]

LUKE 12:37, 38, and 43 contain beatitudes from the parable of the doorkeeper and Jesus' response to the parable that points to the blessedness of those faithful of God who participate in the marriage feast at the end of time. The crux of the parable is watchfulness while the master is away to be prepared for him when he comes. But the twist to the parable is that if they are prepared, the master will "gird himself and have them sit at table, and he will come and serve them." This reverses the normal practice, emphasizing the very nature of Jesus' table fellowship—it is marked by his humility. Luke will expand this theme in the farewell discourse at the Last Supper in 22:24-27 during a dispute among the disciples concerning "which of them was to be regarded as the greatest" (22:24). Jesus' response in 24:27 is that the greatest is not the one who sits at the table, but the one who serves, and that he, Jesus, is with them "as one who serves" (*ho diakonôn*).[31]

LUKE 14:15. "Blessed is he who shall eat bread in the kingdom of God!"

---

which must constitute both the credentials of the Easter witness and the content of the Easter message" (emphasis Dillon).

[30] Cf. J. Navone, "Lucan Joy," *Scripture* 19–20 (1967–68) 56.

[31] Cf. Davis, "The Significance of the Shared Meal," 115–116 who suggests that ". . . in Acts a continuation of Christ's humility may be seen in the meals of the Church. . . ."

This unique Lukan beatitude is a summation and culmination of all previous beatitudes because it focuses squarely on the blessings of God in the table fellowship of Jesus. Luke 14:14 already anticipates this state of blessedness for those who invite the poor, the maimed, the lame, and the blind to sit at table with them. The ultimate blessedness is to eat bread in the kingdom of God. The banquet parable that follows is merely a commentary on this beatitude and the beatitudes that lead up to it.[32]

Lukan Banquet Theology. The parable of the banquet in Luke 14:15-24 is a high point in Luke's banquet theology. Here Jesus presents his table fellowship as the fulfillment of the Old Testament banquet prophecies. As Navone writes:

"The significance of this chapter [14] derives from the prophetic and wisdom literature of the Old Testament, which had developed the banquet theme as an expression of the perfect happiness which God has in store for his faithful at the end time. . . .

"The eschatological banquet symbolized the accomplishment of God's plan of salvation. It is doubtful that any of Jesus' Jewish hearers would have been unaware of the banquet theme and its significance. Jesus himself employed the wedding banquet as a symbol of ultimate happiness (Mt. 22,1-14 = Lk. 14,16-24; Mt. 25,1-13 = Lk. 12,35-38).

"Jesus' banquets were a realization of the messianic and eschatological prophecies; and at the same time they are only the beginning of the ultimate realization of these prophecies. They promise more; they are signs of the beginning of the eschatological banquet."[33]

The Lukan shaping of the parable emphasizes those who reject the invitation of the host of the banquet and those who are invited in their stead. The table fellowship of Jesus is an act of judgment. In this respect, this parable is directed against the Pharisees. D. O. Via writes:

[32]Cf. Smith, "Table Fellowship," 627 on Luke 14:15, and Tannehill, *Narrative Unity*, 89, 128–130, 183–185, 218 the theme of the messianic banquet in Luke's table fellowship matrix.

[33]Navone, "Lucan Joy," 54–55 who discusses the Old Testament banquet motif in Isaiah 25:6; 55:1-3; 65:3-7; and Proverbs 9:1-6.

"Luke, then, represents structurally the exclusion of the excuse makers as dominant, but in content he emphasizes the gracious inclusion of the poor. Form and content are in some tension rather than enforcing each other as they usually do in the narrative parables."[34]

Via rightfully recognizes a tension, but mistakenly suggests that the tension between form and content is not reinforcing. Luke's table fellowship matrix accents the tension between those who are excluded, the Pharisees and religious establishment of Israel, and those who are included, the tax collectors and sinners, the poor and maimed and blind and lame.

Luke's concern for the disenfranchised has already been traced (Luke 4:16-30; 5:27-39; 7:22, 34, 36-50; 9:10-17; and 14:7-14). Included among the outcasts of society are *the Gentiles*, for in the eyes of the Pharisees, Gentiles were the personification of the outcast and sinner. Luke certainly anticipates here, and throughout the development of his table fellowship matrix, the mission to the Gentiles in Acts.[35] This parable told in the presence of the Pharisees is the final blow to any expectations they had about the table fellowship of Jesus embracing their particular religious perspective. It confirms for them that Jesus is guilty of blasphemy and deserving of death, a view expressed by them in Luke 15:1-2: "This man receives sinners and eats with them."[36] This parable reiterates that Jesus' table fellowship is *with sinners, i.e. it is an inclusive event.*

But the parable itself goes beyond simply expressing this tension between those excluded and included at the banquet. There is also the tension between the present and future reality of the messianic feast. This eschatological feast is both a future event and one already realized in the ministry of Jesus. P. H. Ballard writes:

[34]D. O. Via, "The Relationship of Form to Content in the Parables: The Wedding Feast," *Int* 25 (1971) 177–178.

[35]Cf. Dillon, *From Eyewitnesses*, 202: "The 'great banquet' parable, which climaxes the dominical instruction in the meal scene of Lk 14, becomes in its Lucan version an allegory of the two-stage Christian *mission*: to the despised and disinherited of Judaism, then to the Gentile outsiders" (emphasis Dillon).

[36]Cf. Feeley-Harnik, *The Lord's Table*, 109–110 on the reversal of roles in the eschatological feast.

"The imagery of the supper was recognized as an eschatological image of the Kingdom of God. Part of the events of the last time will be the final sorting out of Israel so that the true faithful will be seen for what they are and the rest cast aside. Jesus seems to have laid great emphasis in word and action on table fellowship as demonstrating the already present eschatological activity of God. *Thus the invitation to the great feast was in fact the call to enter into a new age.*"[37]

Ballard reaffirms that the table fellowship of Jesus is *where Jesus teaches about the kingdom which is itself an expression of the new age.*[38] Jesus' table fellowship with sinners in the Gospel prepares for the full expression of this fellowship at the Last Supper with his disciples, where *in the meal itself* he will give his flesh and blood, and in the revelatory meal at Emmaus, where *in the breaking of the bread* the crucified and risen Christ will be made known to them.[39]

6. LUKE 15:1-2, 11-32 — MEALS WITH SINNERS AND THE PRODIGAL SON[40]

The parables of Luke 15 follow closely upon the meal parables of Luke 14. Luke 15:1-2 places the three parables in a meal context by combining parabolic words with parabolic actions, signaling the significance of the parable of the prodigal son for table fellowship. As Jeremias writes:

[37]P. H. Ballard, "Reasons for Refusing the Great Supper," *JTS* 23 (1972) 347 who also argues that Deuteronomy 20:5-7 and 24:5 have a bearing upon this parable (emphasis mine).

[38]Cf. also P. J. Bernadicou, "The Lukan Theology of Joy (Revisited)," *ScEsp* XXX/1 (1978) 62–64 on themes in Luke 14 as they relate to table fellowship.

[39]Navone, "Lucan Joy," 56 also accents the present reality of this eschatological table fellowship as a fulfillment of Old Testament prophecy that combines teaching (word) and meal (banquet). In Luke 14:34-35, there is another table fellowship reference in the covenant of salt. Cf. Feeley-Harnik, *The Lord's Table*, 85–86 who draws a comparision between the word for covenant and the verb "to eat."

[40]Many have suggested a new name for the parable to emphasize the centrality of the father's grace as opposed to the repentance of the prodigal son (cf. Jeremias, *Parables*, 128 suggestion: "the parable of the Father's Love"). However, the title of "prodigal son" has the weight of tradition, highlighting an essential element of table fellowship. Jesus, the model of the Father's love, eats with sinners, symbolized by the prodigal son.

"Jesus did not confine himself to spoken parables, but also performed parabolic actions. His most significant parabolic action was his extension of hospitality to the outcasts (Luke 19.5f.) and their reception into his house (Luke 15.1-2) and even into the circle of his disciples (Mark 2.14 par.; Matt. 10.3). *These feasts for publicans are prophetic signs, more significant than words, silent proclamations that the Messianic Age is here, the Age of forgiveness.*"[41]

a. The parable of the prodigal son is an apologetic parable told against the Pharisees and scribes.[42]

The parable of the prodigal son is Jesus' apologetic statement to the Pharisees, justifying his style of table fellowship, i.e. *"that in his actions the love of God to the repentant sinner is made effectual."*[43] Luke's introductory remarks in 15:1-2 clearly draw the lines between the tax collectors/sinners and Pharisees/scribes, suggesting that in the third parable of Luke 15, the prodigal son represents all repentant tax collectors and sinners, and the older brother represents all unrepentant Jewish religious authorities, particularly the Pharisees and scribes.[44] The charges formulated against Jesus sum up the opinion of Jesus' opponents about his table fellowship thus far in the Gospel: "And the Pharisees and scribes murmured, saying, 'This man receives sinners and eats with them'" (15:2).

By singling out the Pharisees and scribes, Luke is preparing for the charges against Jesus in his trial, and the summation of those charges by the Emmaus disciples in 24:20. By listing the Pharisees first in 15:2, the only place where Luke makes this distinction, he signals their leadership in bringing charges against Jesus because of his table fellowship. Thus in Luke 15, the opponents of Jesus *outside Jerusalem*, the Pharisaic party, first state charges against Jesus based on his table fellowship, having gathered evidence by witnessing Jesus' table fellowship first hand from the beginning of that fellowship in Luke 5.

---

[41]Jeremias, *Parables*, 227 (emphasis mine).
[42]Ibid., 132.
[43]Ibid., 132 (emphasis Jeremias).
[44]Cf. Ellis, *The Gospel of Luke*, 196 and Feeley-Harnik, *The Lord's Table*, 70 on these same categories for the prodigal son and his brother.

b. The parable of the prodigal son reflects the significance of repentance for acceptance into the kingdom in Lukan table fellowship.

Luke has accented repentance in the table fellowship of Jesus in 5:29-32, 7:18-35, and 7:36-50. Now in this series of three parables in the Gospel of the outcast, the Lukan theme to forgiveness for the repentant sinner reaches its apex. Table fellowship with God is renewed through repentance, a fellowship that overflows with joy, expressing itself in gifts of love in the parable of the prodigal son: the kiss of forgiveness, the new robe of the new age, the ring of authority, and the shoes of a free man.[45]

The repentance of the prodigal son fuels the story and forces its climax. The prodigal son's repentance is signaled by his awareness of his situation at his own hands: "He came to himself," or "he came to his senses" (15:17).[46] Twice Luke repeats the words of repentance: "Father, I have sinned against heaven and before you; I am no longer worthy to be called your son . . ." (15:18-19, 21).[47] This profound act of repentance evokes the great response from the father when he sees his son return home. The repentance of the prodigal son becomes the prototype for all those who desire table fellowship with God in the eschatological kingdom. As Fitzmyer writes:

"The parable portrays the message of Jesus, the kingdom-preacher, especially with the Lucan stress on the divine willingness to accept the repentant sinner into that kingdom . . . . In the Lucan Gospel as a whole the story exemplifies the proclamation of the Lord's year of favor, which Jesus was sent to announce to the downtrodden (4:18-19) . . . .

"Thus chap. 15 ends with its proclamation of the mercy of a loving father made manifest to the repentant sinner, no matter how gross the sinful conduct has been. It identifies Jesus himself as the incomparable herald of that proclamation. He turns, more-

[45]Jeremias, *Parables*, 130.

[46]Cf. Fitzmyer, *X-XXIV*, 1088.

[47]Ibid., 1089 where Fitzmyer claims that "the expression is simply a paraphrase of an Old Testament confession . . . see Ex 10:16; 1 Sam 7:6; 24:12; Deut 1:41." If so, then the Old Testament character of the story places it within Luke's table fellowship matrix that fulfills Old Testament precedents.

over, to consort and dine with 'toll-collectors and sinners' because such persons can find acceptance with God himself.''[48]

c. The parable of the prodigal son explicitly connects the Lukan theme of joy in the new age with the Lukan table fellowship matrix.[49]

Luke 14 and 15 form the core of Luke's theology of joy, but the banquet discourses of Luke 14 prepare for the expression of that joy at the feast in Luke 15:11-32. The beatitude of Luke 14:15 "indicates that the hearer understood Jesus' allusion to the joy of the eschatological feast,''[50] but it is still an allusion.

The parable of the prodigal son, however, explicitly connects joy with the eschatological kingdom and Lukan table fellowship. The first two parables of Luke 15, with the theme of the joy of God at the repentance of a sinner, is in anticipation of the fullest expression of that theme in the feast of celebration when the prodigal son returns home repentant. The vocabulary of this section is filled with the Lukan motif of joy: "rejoice/joy" (*chairô/chará*) in 15:5, 7, 10 and 32; "rejoice with" (*sugchaírô*) in 15:6 and 9; "make merry" (*euphraínomai*) in 15:23 and 32; and "music and dancing" (*sumphônía kai chorôn*) in 15:25. Luke 15:32 is the climax of the Lukan vocabulary of joy where "to make merry" (*euphraínomai*) is linked to the divine necessity (*dei*) of feasting in the kingdom of God when a sinner repents. As Fitzmyer suggests on 15:32: "The use of the impf. of *dei*, 'it is necessary,' echoes the Lucan use of it as an expression of an aspect of salvation-history; that may be hinted at here too.''[51] Luke's use of *dei* in 15:32 may be part of

[48]Ibid., 1085-1086.
[49]See P. J. Bernadicou, "Programmatic Texts of Joy in Luke's Gospel," *TBT* 45 (December, 1969) 3098-3105 on the Lukan theme of joy whose subtitle aptly applies to this thesis: "JOY results from the experience of salvation (soteriology), come through Jesus Christ (Christology), incorporating one into the lasting community of friendship with the Father (eschatology) through the power of the Spirit"; also Bernadicou's "Biblical Joy and the Lucan Eucharist," *TBT* 51 (December, 1951) 162-171 (subtitled "Joy in the presence of God is basic to biblical religion. It finds its fullest expression in the Eucharistic celebration"), and "The Lukan Theology of Joy (Revisited)," 57-80; and Navone, "Lucan Joy," 49-62.
[50]Bernadicou, "The Lukan Theology of Joy (Revisited)," 59. Cf. also Jeremias, *Parables*, 180.
[51]Fitzmyer, *X-XXIV*, 1091.

Luke's passion vocabulary (9:22; 13:33; 17:25; and 24:7, 26, 44). The necessity for celebration and joy at table (*euphranthênai de kai charênai édei*) is the death and resurrection of Jesus (cf. Luke 22:20; 24:26).[52]

The joy at the feast in Luke 15 is merely a parabolic telling of the joy of the disciples in Luke 24 as they return to the temple praising God (Luke 24:52-53). The Lukan vocabulary for joy permeates Luke 24 ("joy" [*chará*] in 24:41, 52; "blessing" [*eulogéô*] in 24:30, 50, 51, 53). *True celebration at the table of Jesus comes to the Emmaus disciples after he teaches them, breaks bread with them, and is revealed to them as the risen Lord.*[53] What Davis says about the parables of Luke 15 holds true for Emmaus as well: "Once again Luke presents the New Age as an invitation to fellowship (*sugkaleî*) which is rejected by the leaders, but accepted by the outcasts."[54]

7. LUKE 19:1-10—THE MEAL WITH ZACCHAEUS

The final Lukan meal outside Jerusalem "brings to an end that part of the Lukan travel account which has been called the 'Gospel of the Outcast.' "[55] Luke has located this story at the end

[52]Cf. Bernadicou, "The Lukan Theology of Joy (Revisited)," 76 on the purpose of Luke 15: "But in revealing to us the Father's gentleness with sinners, Jesus also tells us the secret of his own mission. His earthly life is but the witness of God's merciful and saving love for men. Ultimately he would show by his death on the cross how God, in the excess of his love, has even sacrificed his only Son in order to save his children from the slavery of sin. We cannot separate God's love, as it is taught in the parable, from the concrete witness given it by Jesus' own attitude and manner with sinners. While teaching us how God acts, Jesus also provides us with the key to the mystery of his saving life and death."

[53]Cf. Tannehill, *Narrative Unity*, 293, 298–301.

[54]Davis, "The Significance of the Shared Meal," 70. Davis also comments on pp. 69–70: "In these three parables this theme of the New Age—salvation and joy—are present possessions of the repentant. That Luke intends references to the Banquet and its Age is seen not only in the total context, the shared meal as an introduction, the feast of the stories, and the permeating theme of joy, but also in the elaborate details of the return of the prodigal son. The bestowal of the new robe is a symbol of the New Age, as is the forgiveness stressed in the closing verses of the chapter."

[55]Fitzmyer, *X-XXIV*, 1218.

of Jesus' journey to Jerusalem to bring to conclusion the themes of Jesus' Galilean ministry and the travel account. The symmetry of Luke's structure is evident by beginning and ending the table fellowship of Jesus *outside Jerusalem* with a meal with a tax collector and a sinner.[56] Just as the feast with Levi the tax collector was programmatic for all other Lukan meals by foreshadowing the themes of Luke's table fellowship, so now this meal with Zacchaeus completes Luke's matrix by illustrating its major themes.[57] Luke 19:10 is climactic for Jesus' activity at the table where he teaches and eats with sinners: "For the Son of man came to seek and save the lost."[58] The following points on 19:1-10 summarize the major themes of Luke's table fellowship matrix:

a) It is a table fellowship with sinners, i.e. it is an inclusive event.

Luke's description of Zacchaeus the tax collector in 19:2 is similar to his description of Levi in 5:27 and recalls Luke's references to tax collectors:

Luke 5:27 ". . . a tax collector, named Levi, sitting at the tax office . . . ."

Luke 19:2 "And there was a man named Zacchaeus; he was a chief tax collector, and rich."

In 5:27, Luke emphasizes Levi's character as "tax collector," i.e. sinner, highlighting Jesus' table fellowship *with sinners*. In 7:29 and 7:34, Luke again places the tax collectors in the center of Jesus' table fellowship as those who accept him as the Messiah prophesied in the Old Testament. In 15:1-2, the murmuring Pharisees lay down a charge against Jesus that sums up their

[56]See Davis, "The Significance of the Shared Meal," 72.

[57]Cf. J. O'Hanlon, "The Story of Zacchaeus and the Lukan Ethic," *JSNT* 12 (1981) 8 on the following similar components between the feast with Levi and the meal with Zacchaeus: "invitation, immediate response, meal, murmuring, seeking the lost unto repentance." Cf. also Tannehill, *Narrative Unity*, 107–108, 112–113, and 122–125 on 19:1-10 as a quest story.

[58]Cf. Fitzmyer, *X-XXIV*, 1221: "v. 10 sums up . . . the soteriological message of the entire travel account—and the Lucan Gospel." Cf. also W. P. Loewe, "Towards an Interpretation of Lk 19:1-10," *CBQ* 36 (1974) 321-331 on Luke 19:1-10 as a conclusion to the program Luke laid down in 4:16-30 in the Nazareth sermon and in 6:12-49 in the Sermon on the Plain.

opinion of his table fellowship: "This man receives sinners and eats with them."[59]

The opposition of the Pharisees to the tax collectors comes to a head in Luke 18:9-14 in the unique Lukan parable of the Pharisee and the publican. Although this parable does not figure in Luke's table fellowship matrix as a meal or a meal metaphor, it affirms what the reader already knows—Jesus' ministry is characterized by bringing sinners to repentance (he who humbles himself),[60] a direct attack against the self-righteousness of the Pharisees (he who exalts himself). It may be linked with the parables of Luke 15 in Luke's "parables of mercy—about God's mercy shown to a sinner who stands before him and acknowledges his own worthlessness."[61]

The parable itself is directed against those who fit Jesus' assessment of Pharisaic attitudes: ". . . some who trusted in themselves that they were righteous and despised others" (18:9). It addresses two major questions within the context of this parable: in 17:21, Jesus answers a question concerning the coming of the kingdom (17:20) by saying "the kingdom of God is in the midst of you"; in 18:8, Jesus answers the question concerning whether the Son of Man will find faith on the earth with the parable of the Pharisee and the publican in 18:9-14. The kingdom is present in the ministry of Jesus,[62] particularly in the ministry of Jesus at table with tax collectors and sinners. The Son of Man will find faith on the earth in those who accept God's plan as it manifests itself among sinners who repent and join the table fellowship of Jesus.

---

[59]The grumbling of the those who disagree with Jesus' table fellowship with sinners and tax collectors is another link between Luke 5:30 (egógguzon), 15:2 (diegógguzon), and 19:7 (diegógguzon). O'Hanlon, "The Story of Zacchaeus," 16 observes that "the Exodus background to the murmuring supplies the key to Luke's thought here." This is another indication of Jesus' table fellowship fulfilling Old Testament precedents.

[60]The conversion of the sinner and his reception at the table of Jesus is one of the key links between Luke 18:9-14 and 19:1-10.

[61]Fitzmyer, X-XXIV, 1184.

[62]Marshall, The Gospel of Luke, 655. Ellis, The Gospel of Luke, 211 writes that entós humôn "refers to the presence of the kingdom in the eschatological powers manifested in Jesus' person and acts." Cf. Luke 11:20.

Luke's final use of "tax collector" in 19:1 is to call Zacchaeus a chief tax collector (*architelônês*). This is the only use of this word in the New Testament and all of Greek literature.[63] It is the key to understanding this story "as an internal sign of the culminating, paradigmatic character of the pericope."[64] As chief tax collector, Zacchaeus' response to Jesus represents the response of all tax collectors and sinners.

But Zacchaeus is also described by Luke as rich. The proper use of possessions is a Lukan theme[65] that affects his table fellowship matrix in connection with Luke's "theology of poverty." A concern for riches dominates the context of this pericope (Luke 16:13, 14, 19-31; 18:18-30). This concern for possessions has also appeared in those pericopes associated with Luke's table fellowship matrix (7:22ff.; 14:12ff.). Zacchaeus represents all outcasts in society from the perspective of the Pharisees because he is a tax collector and sinner. But from the perspective of Jesus, he is an outcast because he is rich (Luke alone in 16:14 calls the Pharisees "lovers of money"), the very thing Jesus speaks against throughout his teaching in Luke (6:24, 27-35; 7:22; 12:15-21; 14:12-24; 16:10-15, 19-31; 18:18-30; 21:1-4). Thus, Zacchaeus becomes an object of salvation from the religious perspective of both the Pharisees and Jesus.[66]

[63]See Liddell and Scott, *A Greek-English Lexicon*, 253.

[64]Loewe, "Towards an Interpretation of Lk 19:1-10," 331.

[65]See L. T. Johnson, *The Literary Function of Possessions in Luke-Acts*, SBL Dissertation Series 39 (Missoula: Scholars Press, 1977); R. J. Karris, "Poor and Rich: The Lukan *Sitz im Leben*," in *Perspectives on Luke-Acts*, ed. C. H. Talbert (Macon: Mercer University Press, 1978) 112-125; M. D. Guinan, *Gospel Poverty: Witness to the Risen Christ, A Study in Biblical Spirituality* (New York: Paulist Press, 1981); W. Pilgrim, *Good News to the the Poor: Wealth and Poverty in Luke-Acts* (Minneapolis: Augsburg, 1981); J. Dupont, "The Poor and Poverty in the Gospels and Acts," *Gospel Poverty: Essays in Biblical Theology* (Chicago: Franciscan Herald, 1977); W. E. Nickelsburg, "Riches, The Rich, and God's Judgment in 1 Enoch 92-105 and the Gospel according to Luke," *NTS* 25 (1978/79) 324-344.

[66]Cf. Loewe, "Towards an Interpretation of Lk 19:1-10," 322-323 on *ploúsios* in Luke. O'Hanlon, "The Story of Zacchaeus," 20-21 includes in his discussion the very texts that make up the table fellowship matrix, i.e. 4:18; 6:20; 7:22; 14:13, 21; 18:22; and 19:8.

b) It is a table fellowship in which Jesus teaches about the kingdom and by which the new age itself is expressed.

In the story of Zacchaeus, the teaching of Jesus at the table about the kingdom is the means by which that kingdom comes. The present reality of salvation "today" in the life of Zacchaeus is the climax of the story in 19:9-10 when Jesus announces "Today (*sêmeron*) salvation (*sôtêría*) has come to this house, since he also is a son of Abraham. For the Son of man came to seek and save (*sôsai*) the lost."

In Luke 19:3, Zacchaeus is seeking to see who Jesus is. As W. P. Loewe says: "Thus Zacchaeus, in his eagerness to see who Jesus was, was seeking the kingdom of God."[67] Zacchaeus' desire to see Jesus may indicate that he has heard the preaching of Jesus about salvation and the kingdom, and wants to see for himself if it is true. His activity of climbing the sycamore tree is unusual for someone of his position, suggesting that the preaching of Jesus has reached him and spurred him to action.

Zacchaeus may be anxious to see who Jesus is, based on Jesus' preaching; but it is Jesus who calls Zacchaeus just as he called Levi. Jesus' invitation in 19:5 contains the salvific vocabulary of Luke's Gospel: "Zacchaeus, make haste and come down; for I must (*dei*) stay (*meínai*) at your house today (*sêmeron*). The use of *dei* in connection with *meínai* suggests the significance of *the presence of Jesus* in order for salvation to come to that house today (*sêmeron*). This anticipates the Emmaus meal in 24:29 where Luke uses "to stay" (*ménô*) twice to indicate the presence of Christ at the meal at Emmaus. Although the story of Zacchaeus makes no explicit references to a meal or to the act of eating, Luke's use of "to stay" (*meínai*) and "to be a guest" (*katalúsai*) strongly suggest that Jesus has eaten a meal with Zacchaeus at his home. To spend the night at someone's house necessarily implies that a meal would be eaten.[68]

[67]Loewe, "Towards an Interpretation of Lk 19:1-10," 331. Cf. Herod's desire to see Jesus in Luke 9:9, anticipating Jesus' question of the disciples in 9:20: "But who do you say that I am?"

[68]Some even see in *statheís* in 19:8 that Zacchaeus is standing up from reclining at the table. Cf. Ellis, *The Gospel of Luke*, 221; M.-J. Lagrange, *Evangile selon saint Luc* (Études bibliques; Paris: Gabalda, 1921; 8th ed. 1948) 489; and Marshall, *The Gospel of Luke*, 697.

Luke 19:9 is also filled with the Lukan vocabulary of salvation: "Today (*sêmeron*) salvation (*sôtêría*) has come to this house; since he also is a son of Abraham." "Today" (*sêmeron*) and "salvation" (*sôtêría*) are significant in the Lukan vocabulary to announce the presence of the kingdom of God in the person and ministry of Jesus which is itself an expression of the new age.

"Today"—sêmeron. In *Luke 2:11*, the angel announces that "today" salvation will come in the baby, a Savior, Christ the Lord. Fitzmyer writes: "This is the first occurrence of the adv. *sêmeron*, which will figure prominently in the rest of the Lucan Gospel (4:21; 5:26; 12:28; 13:32, 33; 19:5, 9; 22:34, 61; 23:43). It often has the nuance of the inaugurated eschaton, and is to be so understood proleptically here."[69] In *Luke 3:22*, manuscript D and other important witnesses include Psalm 2:7, "Thou art my beloved Son; today (*sêmeron*) I have begotten thee," considered by some commentators to be the preferred reading.[70] It sets Jesus' baptism apart as the beginning of his ministry of salvation (cf. Acts 13:32-33). In *Luke 4:21*, Jesus announces that the messianic acts of salvation from Isaiah are now fulfilled "today" in their hearing, i.e. in his person and his activity as God's anointed one. In *Luke 5:26*, the people respond to the healing of the paralytic and the pronouncement by Jesus that "the Son of man has authority on earth to forgive sins" by saying: "We have seen strange things today" (*sêmeron*). This suggests that in Jesus' healing and authority to forgive sins, the people have seen "the extraordinary character of the new dimension in human life that comes with Jesus' power and authority."[71] This forgiveness is now demonstrated in Jesus' first Lukan meal with Levi the tax collector and sinner in 5:29-32. In *Luke 23:43*, Jesus announces to the thief on the cross "today (*sêmeron*) you will be with me in paradise."[72]

[69]Fitzmyer, *I-IX*, 409.

[70]Ibid., 485: "They [Grundmann, Harnack, Klostermann, Leaney, W. Manson, Moffatt, Streeter, Zahn] retain it on the principle of *lectio difficilior*, thinking that it was eliminated by copyists who harmonized the Lucan text with that of Mark 1:11 or Matt 3:17 or eliminated it for other (doctrinal) reasons."

[71]Ibid., 586.

[72]Cf. R. H. Smith, "Paradise Today: Luke's Passion Narrative," *CurrTM* 3 (1976) 326-327 on Luke's use of pairs to teach about the kingdom that links

The announcement that "today" paradise belongs to the penitent thief sums up Luke's use of *sêmeron*, emphasizing the present reality of future eschatological blessings. R. H. Smith writes:

"Hades continues to embody all the dark and unpleasant features associated with the Hebrew Sheol, while Paradise sparkles with the brilliance of the Garden planted by God (Gen. 2 and 3; 13:10; Ezek. 28:13; 31:8; 36:35; cf. Is. 51:3; Joel 2:3). It contains the tree of life and enjoys the living water and is the place where the righteous will feast at the banquet of salvation on living bread in fellowship with God.

"In response to the penitent, giving more than he asked, Jesus solemnly declared, 'Truly, I say to you, today you will be with me in paradise.' The criminal did not have to wait any more than the tax collector had to wait to go down to his house justified (18:14) or any more than Zacchaeus had to wait for salvation; it came to his house in his fellowship with Jesus 'today' (19:9). By means of the repeated utterance of 'today' in his gospel (2:11; 3:22; 4:21; 13:31-33; 19:5, 9; Acts 13:32-33) Luke does not intend to describe the words so qualified as belonging to past history. Luke is rather addressing his readers and saying to them that they 'today' stand confronted with the same affirmations and offers by means of the word of his testimony."[73]

In view of Luke's use of *sêmeron*, the force of this word in Luke 19:5 and 9 becomes evident. The presence of Jesus at the table of Zacchaeus means that *today* salvation has come to this house. This Lukan usage embraces the Old Testament understanding of *sêmeron* as meaning "fulfillment, revelation, whether as salvation or disaster."[74] Thus, "today" the era of God's salvation is present in Zacchaeus' house, embracing God's salvific acts in Israel's past, and God's present and future salvific acts in the work of Jesus, God's Messiah. The word *sêmeron* signals the climax of the table fellowship matrix outside Jerusalem.[75]

23:43 with the table fellowship matrix (7:36-50; 10:38-42; 15:11-32; 16:19-31; 18:9-14; 19:1-10).

[73]Ibid., 329-330. Cf. also Tannehill, *Narrative Unity*, 125-127, 198-199 on Luke 23:39-43.

[74]E. Fuchs, *sêmeron*, TDNT VII 271.

[75]Cf. also J. Drury, *Tradition and Design in Luke's Gospel* (Atlanta: John Knox

"Salvation"—sôtêría. This climax is further suggested by Luke's use of *sôtêría* in 19:9 and *sôzô* in the final logion in 19:10: "For the Son of man came to seek and to save the lost." The word *sôtêría* and its derivatives are part of Luke's vocabulary of salvation. His is the only Synoptic Gospel to refer to Jesus as "Savior" (*sôtêr*— Luke 1:47; 2:11; cf. Acts 5:31; 13:23), and he alone uses the two nouns for "salvation" (*sôtêría*—Luke 1:69, 71, 77; 19:9; cf. Acts 4:12; 7:25; 13:26, 47; 16:17; 27:34; and *sôtêrion*—Luke 2:30; 3:6; cf. Acts 28:28). "To save" (*sôzô*) is also more common in Luke (seventeen times and thirteen times in Acts) than in Matthew (fifteen times) and Mark (thirteen times).[76]

Salvation is linked by Luke to the passion of Jesus in the context of Luke's first passion prediction (9:22) in 9:24. Note the similarities between Luke 9:24 and 19:10:

Luke 9:24   "For whoever would *save* his life will *lose* it; and whoever *loses* his life for my sake, he will *save* it."

Luke 19:10 "For the Son of man came to seek and *to save the lost.*"

The Lukan principle of reversal of roles is in full force. The kingdom of God comes with the death and resurrection of Jesus, and those who are to be saved lose their life and identify with the kingdom by following Jesus in a cruciform life. In Luke 13:22-30, "those who are saved" (13:23), "sit at table in the kingdom of God" (13:29), where in the reversal of roles "some are last who will be first, and some are first who will be last" (13:30).[77]

The significance of *sôtêría* is heightened by its association with the forgiveness of sins.[78] The connection is made by Luke in the ministry of John the Baptist (1:77—"to give knowledge of salvation

---

Press, 1976) 70-71 on "today." He notes that some manuscripts include *sêmeron* in 24:21.

[76]Cf. Tannehill, *Narrative Unity*, 87 who notes a connection between *sôzô* and miracles of healing (Luke 6:9; 8:36, 48, 50; 17:19; 18:42).

[77]The combination of miracle/table fellowship links together Luke 13 and 19. Cf. O'Hanlon, "The Story of Zacchaeus," 7: "As a 'son of Abraham,' Zacchaeus is also the counterpart of the bent woman of Luke 13:10-17 who is a 'daughter of Abraham.' "

[78]Ibid., 17 on the relationship between the themes of salvation and forgiveness in Luke-Acts.

[*sôtēría*] to his people in the forgiveness of their sins''; cf. 3:3-6) and in the ministry of Jesus (7:47-50). "Forgiveness" (*áphesis*) occurs in the context of salvation preaching: in the programmatic sermon of Nazareth (4:18, twice) connected with "the acceptable year of the Lord,''[79] and in Luke's commissioning of the disciples in 24:47. The objects of salvation are the outcasts of society, the lost sinners (19:10).

Although "forgiveness" (*áphesis*) is not pronounced in Luke 19:1-10, the declaration of salvation "today" implies the forgiveness of sins within the table fellowship of Jesus.[80] All the key ingredients are here: the chief tax collector and sinner Zacchaeus, the table fellowship of Jesus, the declaration of salvation "today," and the summation of Jesus' table fellowship with sinners, "for the Son of man came to seek and to save the lost." The only thing missing is the reversal of roles.

W. P. Loewe, however, suggests that this may be found in Zacchaeus' status as a son of Abraham.[81] Salvation is by right of birth for a son of Abraham, but even those who claim Abraham as their father are not excluded from bearing fruits of repentance (Luke 3:8-9). The reversal of roles is evident in Zacchaeus' status as a son of Abraham *who is a tax collector/sinner.* Jesus eats with him and declares that salvation is present in his house, not because he is a son of Abraham, but because he is a repentant tax collector/sinner. Zacchaeus responds by bearing fruits of repentance (19:8). He is paradigmatic of all lost sinners who are saved by Jesus.[82]

[79]Cf. Fitzmyer, *I-IX,* 533 on 4:19 as a reference to "the salvific period now being inaugurated."

[80]Cf. Loewe, "Towards an Interpretation of Lk 19:1-10," 329: "From 18:35 on, Lk rejoins Marcan order to round off his journey narrative with a healing miracle and a discourse. Thus the narrative ends with final instances of the two major aspects of Jesus' ministry, miracles and preaching . . . . Jesus' miracles point to *aphesis* and the conferral of salvation. The meaning implicit in the miracle becomes explicit in Jesus' encounter with Zacchaeus." Cf. also O'Hanlon, "The Story of Zacchaeus," 15: "He [Zacchaeus] welcomes Jesus into his home joyfully for the proffered friendship is a sign of acceptance and even forgiveness (5:27-32; 7:36-50; 14:1-14; 15:1-10,11-32)."

[81]Cf. Loewe, "Towards an Interpretation of Lk 19:1-10," 326 and 330. Cf. also Tannehill, *Narrative Unity,* 124–125; Sanders, *The Jews in Luke-Acts,* 62–63, 207–208.

[82]Cf. O'Hanlon, "The Story of Zacchaeus," 18–19: "What it means to be

"In place of his riches, Zacchaeus has received the ultimate wealth, salvation, forgiveness of his sins (Jesus eats with sinners while they are still sinners but this fellowship brings about repentance) and that is 'good measure, pressed down, shaken together and running over' " (6:38).[83]

Thus, the meal with Zacchaeus brings to a close the Lukan meals and meal metaphors *outside Jerusalem*. Once again, the meals of Jesus serve as *revelatory events* of the salvation that Jesus brings with the forgiveness of sins. As Davis writes:

". . . *for Luke the meal is a scene of revelation*, especially to the repentant sinners (cf. 7:36-50; 5:29-32; as well as the contrast of the Pharisee's lack of perceptiveness in 7:36-50; 11:37-52; 14:1-6). Viewed from another angle, this passage [Luke 19:1-10] is the very focal point, the zenith in the meals of Jesus with sinners. It is the *revelation to the sinner* and his joyous response which is stressed here; the entrance of Zacchaeus into the New Age through the forgiveness and fellowship portrayed here. For this was indeed the hope of the Old Testament . . . it is not merely the invitation to the Messianic Banquet being emphasized here—it is even more a *demonstration of the joys* when the invitation is accepted."[84]

THE TEACHING OF JESUS AGAINST THE CHIEF PRIESTS IN JERUSALEM

These two chapters on Lukan meals and meal metaphors illustrate that *because of his table fellowship,* Jesus is put to death by the chief priests—his antagonists in Jerusalem—and the Pharisees (the rulers in 24:20)—his antagonists outside Jerusalem. Soon after the Zacchaeus story, the teaching of Jesus outside Jerusalem comes to

---

lost can be learned from the way Luke develops the concept in the parables of the Lost Sheep and the Lost Coin and fleshes it out in the portraits of the Prodigal Son and the Tax Collector of 18:9-14. The lost is anyone separated from that which gives identity, meaning and value to one's life. The lost is personified in the chief tax collector, Zacchaeus. He has sold his identity as a son of Abraham to the foreign oppressor and he has battened on his own people, literally robbing them (19:8c) to fill his own coffers. He has gone into his own far country. But the Son of man came to seek and to save the lost."

[83]Ibid., 21.

[84]Davis, "The Significance of the Shared Meal," 72 (emphasis Davis).

an end in Luke 19:44, and so does the opposition of the Pharisees. The last word from the Pharisees in Luke's Gospel is heard in 19:39: "Teacher, rebuke your disciples." This final opposition to Jesus by the Pharisees is the result of the people assigning to Jesus the messianic title "the Coming One" and designating him as "the King" in 19:38.[85] The Pharisees reject in Jesus the fulfillment of the messianic promises of the Old Testament, the very rejection Jesus experienced in Luke 4:16-30.

The major opposition to Jesus by the chief priests comes from his teaching against them in Jerusalem. When Jesus enters Jerusalem in 19:45, Luke portrays him as immediately entering into the temple for his final teachings in Luke 20-21 (cf. 19:47-48; 20:1; 20:9-18, 20-26, 41-44; 21:37-38). They are aimed against the Jerusalem religious establishment (20:1: "the chief priests and the scribes with the elders") and are interpreted by them as such (20:19-20). The temple is now a place of conflict, and, as J. Tyson says, "in Luke's writing, the rejection of Jesus by the chief priests, their refusal to recognize him as lord of the temple, and their refusal to grant him his rightful control of the temple led to his death."[86] Thus, Jesus' teachings will be the basis for his rejection by the Sanhedrin (19:47; 20:19), and the people's (*ho laós* as Israel) positive response to him (19:48; 21:38).

The chief priests and scribes set in motion the arrest of Jesus in 22:1-6 through Jesus' disciple Judas *"as the feast of Unleavened Bread drew near, which is called the Passover."*[87] Although four charges against Jesus may be discerned in his trials, it is the fourth charge in Luke 23:5 that directly affects the table fellowship matrix, namely *the teaching of Jesus*: "But they [Sanhedrin] were urgent saying, 'He stirs up the people, teaching (*didáskôn*) throughout all Judea, from Galilee even to this place'" (23:5).[88] Such a charge

[85]*Ho erchómenos* and *ho basileús* stand in apposition to one another.
[86]Tyson, The Death of Jesus, 110
[87]Cf. Fitzmyer, X-XXIV, 1366 on the significance of the change of locale between the temple (Luke 21) to Jerusalem, the place of the passion (Luke 22). The connection between the Passover (*páscha*) and the passion (*páschô*) is unavoidable. The meal as the place of betrayal is part of the Eucharistic tradition of the church as far back as Paul (1 Cor 11:23: "on the night when he was betrayed").
[88]See Catchpole, *The Trial of Jesus*, 72–152 on the charges against Jesus.

encompasses all of Jesus' teaching from his Nazareth sermon to his teaching in the temple, thus illustrating the Lukan geographical perspective. Jesus is rejected for his teaching at the table that he is God's anointed Messiah, present in the world to fulfill the Old Testament promises of salvation in the forgiveness of sins.

Tyson, *The Death of Jesus*, 129–133 describes the first three as: 1) Luke 23:2—Jesus is "perverting our nation;" 2) Luke 23:2—Jesus is "forbidding us to give tribute to Caesar"; 3) Luke 23:2—Jesus claims that "he himself is Christ a king." Cf. also Tannehill, *Narrative Unity*, 195: "The charge of perverting the people through his teaching is repeated three times in the trial scene (23:2, 5, 14) . . . thus what Jesus taught throughout his ministry ('beginning from Galilee to here,' 23:5) is an important cause of the religious leaders' rejection of him in Jerusalem."

Chapter 11

The Center Circle—The Teaching of Jesus

The table fellowship of Jesus, his teaching and his eating with outcasts and sinners, is one of the ways Luke teaches about salvation in the forgiveness of sins. In these final two chapters, I will focus on the colloquium of Jesus and the meal of Jesus at Emmaus, the two components of Lukan table fellowship.

I have yet to consider in full the significance of the resurrection for Luke's theology. In the Emmaus story, there is no mention of the resurrection until Luke 24:21 when it is hinted at by the reference to "the third day," which is expanded on in 24:22-24. Luke carefully calibrates his time so that Sunday, the first day of the week, the third day in the sequence of Jesus' passion, is also theologically significant as the eighth day, the first day of the new creation, the day of the resurrection, the eschatological day. Here in the transition from the old Sabbath observances to Sunday, the eschatological day, there is a new reckoning of time because of the earth-shattering events of *these days* in Jerusalem (24:18). According to Luke's time sequence, a new age has dawned, the eschaton has arrived, and the first celebration of that new era of salvation takes place at Emmaus.

As it is introduced into the Emmaus narrative, the resurrection is both subtle and significant. *It is the risen Christ who opens up the Scriptures and makes himself known in the breaking of the bread.* Is it significant that the risen Christ now intercedes for them? Is the resurrection in some way *a sign of fulfillment*—the fulfillment of the kerygma, of Scripture, and of Jesus' table fellowship?

THE PRELUDE TO THE KERYGMA OF THE COLLOQUIUM —
LUKE 24:21-24

The kerygmatic words of the colloquium in Luke 24:26 are unintelligible without a Christological prelude in Luke 24:21-24. This report of Jesus' embarrassing death by crucifixion, and the disturbing news of an empty tomb and a vision of angels, sets the stage for Jesus' teaching from the Old Testament Scriptures about the necessity of his suffering.

Luke 24:21 The Frustrated Hope of Redemption for Israel

Luke 24:21 introduces the two major thoughts of this section: the concept of the "redemption of Israel," (*lutroústhai ton Israêl*), and the concept of the resurrection "on the third day," (*trítên taútên hêméran*).

The Redemption of Israel. Luke introduces the concept of redemption into the narrative through the words of the Emmaus disciples: "But we had hoped that he was the one to redeem Israel" (*lutroústhai ton Israêl*). We may note first, that although "hope" (*elpízô*) is not part of Luke's salvation vocabulary in his Gospel,[1] his use of the word here in conjunction with "redemption" (*lutroústhai*) and the resurrection anticipates the connection between hope and the resurrection in Acts 2:26; 23:6; 24:15; and 26:6-8. It is significant that Luke ends both his Gospel and Acts with a reference to the hope of Israel. In Acts 28:20 Luke quotes Paul as stating "since it is because of the hope of Israel that I am bound with this chain."[2] Both the Emmaus disciples (Luke 24) and Paul (Acts 28) "naturally think in terms of the redemption of God's own people, Israel."[3] The reference in Acts 28:23 to Paul's expounding of the Scriptures to the Jews reminds the reader of Jesus' opening of the Scriptures to the Emmaus disciples in Luke 24:25-27 where the language is almost the same:

Acts 28:23   "And he expounded the matter to them from morning till evening, testifying to the kingdom of God and

---

[1]E.g. Luke 6:34; 23:8.

[2]Cf. J. Munck, *The Acts of the Apostles* (New York: Doubleday, 1967) 258: "The true motive force behind all these events was Israel's hope of the Messiah and *the resurrection of the dead* which had caused him to preach the Gospel all over the world and to gather the collection and take it to Jerusalem" (emphasis mine). Cf. also Haenchen, *The Acts of the Apostles*, 722: "Paul bears 'these chains' which the Jews see on account of the (Messianic) hope of Israel."

[3]Marshall, *The Gospel of Luke*, 895.

trying to convince them about Jesus both *from the law of Moses and from the prophets.*"

Luke 24:27   "And beginning *with Moses and all the prophets*, he interpreted to them in all the scriptures the things concerning himself."

Both Luke 24 and Acts 28 stress that the bringing of salvation to Israel is connected with Old Testament promises, and is thus the fulfillment of the *hope* of Israel.

Secondly, the expression "the one who was about to" (*méllô*) in 24:21 *is* part of Luke's salvation vocabulary. It occurs in many eschatological or passion contexts to suggest the impending accomplishment of God's salvific purposes in Jesus Christ (e.g. Luke 3:7; 9:31; 9:44; 19:11; 21:7; 21:36; 22:23). "To be about to" (*méllô*) links Luke 24:21 to these prophecies in Luke's Gospel and places Luke's use of "redemption" (*lutroústhai*) within the evangelist's motif of the redemption of Israel through the suffering and death of Jesus in fulfillment of the Scriptures.

Thirdly, the verb "to redeem" (*lutróomai*) occurs only once in the Gospel in Luke 24:21, and never in Acts. What does Luke mean by "the redemption of Israel," and what does Luke imply concerning the Emmaus disciples' understanding of the phrase? It appears as if Luke has a double meaning here, one for the reader, who would connect redemption with the cross, another for the Emmaus disciples, who cannot see the cross as a means of redemption.[4] Their concept of redemption was political, a freedom from Roman tyranny through a "messianic" deliverer (cf. Acts 7:35 where Moses is called by Luke as "ruler and deliverer" [*lutrôtên*]). For the Emmaus disciples, according to Old Testament

---

[4]Cf. Osborne, *The Resurrection Narratives*, 121–122: "Luke's emphasis here really centers on Jesus' mission. He will not accept the disciples' faulty role of political Messiah to 'redeem Israel' the way they expect him to. Instead he will follow God's sovereign plan which includes the way of suffering, death, and resurrection. The same misunderstanding occurs here as in Acts 1:6-8, where the Lord again refuses to accept the role of the political Messiah. Luke continues to build to the explanation of verses 26f. *'Redeem Israel' thereby speaks on two levels: Jesus would not 'redeem' in the way they expected but in the way sovereignly chosen by God, through passion and resurrection*" (emphasis mine).

standards, Jesus fits the messianic pattern as a "prophet mighty in deed and word," which should be enough to qualify him to redeem Israel. But they fail to see the other part of the Old Testament pattern, the messianic rejection, which is part of the process of Israel's redemption.[5]

However, by Luke's use of the noun "redemption" (*lútrôsis*) the reader is transported back to the infancy narrative in 1:68: "Blessed be the Lord God of Israel, for he has visited and redeemed (*lútrôsin*) his people"; and 2:38, "to all who were looking for the redemption (*lútrôsin*) of Jerusalem." Bock comments:

"Also, the redemption of Jerusalem in v. 40 (sic) is unique for the Old and New Testaments, though the concept seems to be drawn from Isa. 52.9. The term is taken as a virtual synonym for the 'consolation of Israel' found in Luke 2.25. In fact, these two ideas are fused together in Luke 24.21 . . . ."[6]

Other links between Luke 24 and the infancy narrative are the nation of Israel[7] and the visions of angels.[8]

Reading back to the infancy narrative from Luke 24 because of Luke's use of *lutroústhai ton Israêl* anticipates the hermeneutical principle in Luke 24:25-27 where the Old Testament shows the ne-

[5]Cf. Dillon, *From Eyewitnesses*, 128–132 who concludes on p. 132 that the Emmaus disciples missed "the *meaningful connection of the three elements*: wondrous deeds, rejection, redemption!" (emphasis Dillon). Cf. also I. H. Marshall, *Luke: Historian and Theologian* (Grand Rapids: Zondervan, 1970) 174 n. 1.

[6]Bock, *Proclamation from Prophecy and Pattern*, 86. Cf. also Tannehill, *Narrative Unity*, 35, 280–281.

[7]E.g. Luke 1:16, 54, 68, 80; 2:25; 2:32; and 2:34. In Luke's Gospel, Israel occurs only four times outside the infancy narratives and Luke 24 (4:25, 27; 7:9; and 22:30), although it is used fifteen times in Acts (1:6; 2:36; 4:10, 27; 5:21, 31; 7:23, 37, 42; 9:15; 10:36; 13:17, 23, 24; and 28:20). Dillon, *From Eyewitnesses*, 129 comments: ". . . the word 'Israel' does not function in his pages as a one-dimensional name of the people that rejected its messiah. Quite the contrary, the name *Israêl*, like the designation *laós*, forms a salvation-historical continuum which includes the adherents of Jesus and from which the Jews who reject him are excluded. This is why the celebration of Israel's 'redemption' and 'consolation' in the infancy narrative (Lk 1,68; 2,25.32) can still be a matter of Paul's kerygma at Acts 13,23 and his service in chains at Acts 28,20 . . . ."

[8]E.g. Luke 1:11-19; 1:26-38; 2:9-15; and 2:21.

cessity of the death and resurrection of Jesus. In Luke 1-2, the infant Jesus is seen as the hope, the consolation, the redemption of Israel.[9] The links between Luke 24 and the infancy narrative are created purposely to show that the redemption of Israel by Jesus the Messiah has been accomplished.[10] The words of these Old Testament saints form the foundation and background for understanding Jesus' words in 24:25-27.

"On the Third Day." I have already observed that Luke uses "on the third day" exclusively in his Gospel as a reference to the final day of the three day sequence in which Jesus rises from the dead. "On the third day" is used three times, in Luke 24:7, 21, and 46, to portray Sunday as the final, climactic day in salvation history. This was anticipated by Luke throughout his Gospel, reaching fulfillment in this final chapter (24:21) where it becomes a fundamental part of the Lukan kerygma that is to be proclaimed by the emerging Church in Acts (Luke 24:46).

There can be no doubt that "on the third day" is part of Luke's resurrection Christology, a reference to the resurrection occurring on the first day of the new creation, the eighth day, the eschatological day. This prepares the reader for the risen Christ opening the Scriptures to the disciples, and points the reader towards the eschatological day. The phrase is thus a necessary link to the next verses.

Luke 24:22-24—The Dilemma of the Empty Tomb

Luke 24:22-24 confirms the ignorance of the disciples. All the elements for grasping the truth are present, but their misunder-

---

[9]Cf. Fuller, *The Formation*, 110: "The word redeem (*lutrousthai*) is full of Old Testament associations, recalling the deliverance from Egypt and entry into the promised land, as also the return from the exile. In this case 19b and 21a [Luke 24] will belong to the same stratum of tradition, that of a Mosaic eschatological-prophet Christology (cf. also Acts 3:12-14 and 7:2-53)." Cf. Dillon, *From Eyewitnesses*, 131 n. 180: "*lutroún* and related nouns belong to the LXX vocabulary of redemption esp. (in the case of the verb) that of the Psalter and the Deutero-Isaiah."

[10]Cf. Esler, *Community and Gospel*, 19, 68 who on p. 69 concludes that "central to Luke's composition of a unique history, which encompassed the Jesus story and its sequel in Acts, was an ardent desire to present Christianity as the legitimate development of Judaism."

standing is acute. Having introduced the concept of the third day in connection with the hope of redemption in 24:21, the inability of the disciples to see the signs and grasp the truth in 24:22-24 is encapsulated in their final words, "but him[11] they did not see."

Thus, the combination of the frustrated hopes of redemption (24:21) and the dilemma of the empty tomb (24:22-24) sets the stage for the climax of the colloquium in 24:25-27, and is the perfect foil for Jesus' interpretation of the Scriptures in which the necessity of his suffering before his glory is expounded as the proper hermeneutical approach to Christology.

THE KERYGMA OF THE COLLOQUIUM — LUKE 24:25-27

The core of the colloquium is Luke 24:25-27, the first climax of the Emmaus meal, in which Jesus recalls for the Emmaus disciples the words of Moses and the prophets.[12] Here Luke unites the death and resurrection of Jesus to table fellowship with Jesus where, throughout the Gospel, forgiveness of sins has been offered. This first climax of the Emmaus story, and of the Gospel itself, accomplishes two aims for the Lukan reader: 1) in 24:26, the kerygma of the Gospel is forged into one simple statement, "Was it not necessary that the Christ should suffer these things and enter into his glory?" and 2) in 24:27, a scriptural foundation is provided for this kerygma, "And beginning with Moses and all the prophets, he interpreted to them in all the scriptures the things concerning himself." The following discussion will be a literary one, which keeps in mind the reader who is gradually coming to an understanding of who Jesus is and what he has accomplished in terms of God's plan of salvation.

Luke 24:25—The Disciples' Lack of Faith

The kerygma of the colloquium begins with Jesus' rebuke of the disciples' lack of faith in 24:25, bringing to a conclusion the Christology of the Emmaus disciples that is framed by their sad

[11]Both Marshall, *The Gospel of Luke*, 896 and Fitzmyer, *X-XXIV*, 1565 observe that *autón* is in an emphatic position at the head of this phrase. The Emmaus disciples are totally blind to the presence of Jesus in their midst.

[12]This is similar to the approach of the angels with the women in Luke 24:7. Luke also uses "Moses and the prophets" in 16:29-31.

expression in 24:17 and their foolishness and slowness of heart in 24:25.[13] Jesus' rebuke characterizes his perspective on their understanding of his mission and purpose as miscomprehension of prophecy and foolishness of unbelief.

Now the dialogue changes speakers. Luke shifts the focus of the dialogue so that Jesus changes his status from that of guest to that of teacher and host, a shift from the Christology of the Emmaus disciples to the Christology of Jesus.[14] From 24:18 to 24:24, the dialogue had been a one-way conversation—the Emmaus disciples presented their Christological understanding of Jesus as a mighty prophet who was condemned to death and crucified by the religious leaders of Jerusalem. This miscomprehension must be reversed by *the risen Christ* who will open up the Scriptures to demonstrate the necessity of the Messiah's suffering and resurrection. Jesus, now the speaker in the dialogue, is introduced by the emphatic "and he (*kai autós*) said to them."[15]

A Question of Faith. Within the framework of Luke 24, the rebuke of the Emmaus disciples by Jesus in 24:25 is parallel to the rebuke of the women by the angels in 24:5b-7—the addressees should not be slow to believe in the resurrection because of the prophecies of Jesus' death and resurrection. Whereas the women remembered Jesus' own prophecies in Galilee, the Emmaus disciples are to remember *both* the Old Testament prophecies as well as the prophecies of Jesus.[16] In either case the question is one of *faith*—faith to believe all that the prophets have spoken, *including the prophet Jesus* who on three occasions predicted his passion and resurrection. The women lacked faith to believe, but they recalled

[13]Dillon, *From Eyewitnesses*, 132–133 suggests that 24:17 and 25 "enclose what is spoken in between within the framework of the messianic passion-mystery."

[14]Cf. also Betz, "The Origin and Nature of Christian Faith," 36: "After verse 25 the role of the wanderer changes completely. While up to now he has pretended to be ignorant and has asked questions, from this point on he functions as the *teacher*" (emphasis Betz). Cf. also Dillon, *From Eyewitnesses*, 111.

[15]The intensive use of *kai autós* is Luke's favorite expression for Jesus in the Emmaus story, 24:15, 25, 28, and 31.

[16]See Dillon, *From Eyewitnesses*, 18–19, 132–133 who first suggested this parallel.

the passion prediction of Luke 9 and returned to the disciples, reporting these things to them (24:9). It is impossible to discern whether or not the women did this because they believed, but Luke tells us of the reaction of the Eleven and all the rest in 24:11: "but these words seemed to them an idle tale, and they did not believe them." This unbelief of the Eleven and all the rest is now focused in the unbelief of the Emmaus disciples who are "foolish men and slow of heart to believe."

The colloquium's accomplishment of its goal—faith in a suffering and rising Christ—serves as *preparation for the meal at Emmaus.* Jesus' rebuke of the disciples is a rebuke of their lack of faith in the Christology of rejection, suffering, crucifixion, and resurrection. Their lack of faith comes from not understanding the prophecies. But now *Jesus the teacher* opens the Scriptures so that their hearts, which are slow to believe (24:25), become burning (24:32).

The question of faith or lack of faith is simply another term for the Lukan themes of recognition vs. nonrecognition, open and closed eyes, comprehension and miscomprehension of passion facts. The evangelist moves from the surface memory to the deeper one, from physical seeing to the heart, from non-comprehension to faith. Access to the deeper memory comes from understanding *and* believing the prophets, a goal only *the risen Christ* can accomplish in the Emmaus disciples. As Dillon says:

"The veil of mystery is now to be lifted, according to divine determination, in the only way it could be lifted: by the personal presence and instruction of the risen Lord, who 'opens' the scriptures by showing their realization in himself . . . The 'things concerning Jesus of Nazareth' that the travelers could not grasp (v. 19) are now the focal point of the Easter exposition of all Scripture. No more than the events themselves could the Scripture by itself beget faith in the messiah's triumph; *only he can bestow that as his personal gift.*"[17]

This colloquium prepares the Emmaus disciples to receive the gift of forgiveness in the breaking of the bread, setting the pattern for all Christian dialogue within the worshipping assembly of early

[17]Ibid., 133 (emphasis Dillon). Cf. also Tannehill, *Narrative Unity,* 281–284 on the irony of Luke 24:17-25.

liturgical communities. *The personal presence and instruction of the risen Lord* is the significant element that sets this act of teaching apart from all other acts. Now that the third day has come and the resurrection has taken place, the followers of Jesus are able to believe all that the prophets have spoken because the first instruction comes from the risen Lord himself. The resurrection, then, is the pivotal event that makes faith possible by opening up the eyes of the disciples to the fulfillment of Scripture in Jesus of Nazareth. It is *the sign of fulfillment,* bringing to completion not only the kerygma of suffering before glory, but also the table fellowship where the teaching of the risen Christ prepares the Emmaus disciples for the meal of the risen Christ in Luke 24:28-30 by giving them faith to believe all that the prophets have spoken.

To Believe All that the Prophets Have Spoken. The foundation for the faith of the Emmaus disciples is the voice of the prophets, the first time in Luke 24 that this concept occurs. Luke introduces here what Fitzmyer calls "a major point in his theology,"[18] a point that will dominate the remaining kerygmatic statements in Luke 24 as the totality of the fulfillment of the Scriptures becomes progressively broader (24:27—"and beginning from Moses and all the prophets, he interpreted to them in all the scriptures the things concerning himself"; 24:44—"everything written about me in the law of Moses and the prophets and the psalms must be fulfilled"). The all-encompassing totality of the prophetic witness will be emphasized by Luke in 24:25-27 (v. 25—"*all* that the prophets have spoken"; v. 27—"*all* the prophets . . . in *all* the scriptures"). The reader is struck with the realization that the Old Testament Scriptures provide a prophetic witness that is, in its totality, Christological. According to Luke, the resurrection as a sign of fulfillment is possible because this is the major thrust of the Old Testament Scriptures.

This Lukan motif of the fulfillment of the Scriptures is not new to the reader who recognizes it as part of Luke's style throughout his Gospel and in Acts.[19] Luke anticipates this prophetic fulfillment in his Gospel by demonstrating that Jesus is *the last and*

[18]Fitzmyer, *X-XXIV,* 1565.
[19]Cf. Luke 18:31; 20:17; and 22:37; Acts 2:22-28; 3:13-18; 4:10-11; 8:30-35; 10:39-43; 13:26-41; 17:2-3; 26:22-23; and 28:23.

greatest prophet like unto Moses, the fulfillment of the prophetic line.[20]
In the programmatic text of Luke 4:16-30, the evangelist begins his
portrait of Jesus by developing a Christology that is embodied in
figures of the Old Testament like Elijah and Elisha. They served as
patterns of Christ, a pattern characterized by teaching,
miracleworking, and rejection.[21] The type of Christ *par excellence* is
Moses who, like all the prophets, teaches, performs miracles, and
is rejected by his own people. Throughout Luke-Acts, the evangelist engages in step-parallelism between Jesus, the greatest
prophet and the fulfillment of the prophetic tradition, and all who
stood in the prophetic tradition before him, such as Moses, Elijah,
Elisha, and John the Baptist. Jesus is different from all the
prophets because his crucifixion and resurrection usher in a new
era of forgiveness.

That forgiveness is the goal of Jesus' messianic mission is already proleptically present in Luke 1:77 in the ministry of *the
prophet* John who, in preparing the way of the Lord, gives
"knowledge of salvation to his people in the forgiveness of their
sins," and who, in 3:3, preaches "a baptism of repentance for the
forgiveness of sins." The proclamation of forgiveness reaches fulfillment in the messianic ministry of Jesus, a major thrust of
Luke's programmatic sermon in Luke 4:16-30 where forgiveness is
the essence of the kerygma the Messiah proclaims. Luke's use of
"forgiveness" (*áphesis*) in 4:18 and 24:47 links together the first
and last proclaimed words of Jesus and shows that forgiveness is
essential to Luke's portrayal of the teaching of Jesus as a proclamation of salvation, "*God's 'liberation' of men from sin's bondage.*"[22]

[20]Dillon, *From Eyewitnesses*, 138 remarks that "all the scripture of the Jews is
prophecy and Moses, its first and principal author, is likewise its first and
principal *prophet*" (emphasis Dillon).

[21]Ibid., 136 where Dillon observes that Luke handles Scripture in 4:16-30
and 24:13-35 in the same way: "The Emmaus dialogue and the temple sermon converge also in their characterization of the OT scriptures. They are
considered in both places globally as *prophecy,* and their authors are all
prophets . . . . It probably accounts for the fact that, in the gospel's programmatic episode at the beginning of the public ministry, Jesus' instruction at the
synagogue in Nazareth is based on a prophet's text rather than a pericope
from the Torah (Lk 4,17ff./Is 61,1f)" (emphasis Dillon).

[22]Ibid., 136 (emphasis Dillon).

Thus, when Jesus says to the Emmaus disciples "O foolish men and slow of heart to believe all that the prophets have spoken," he is not merely referring to prophetic passages in the Old Testament but is also pointing to the prophets themselves who embody in their lives (teaching, miracles, rejection) proleptic manifestations of Jesus' teaching, miracles, and crucifixion that bring to completion the prophetic tradition of the Old Testament. The Emmaus disciples are foolish and slow to believe because they did not *read*: 1) the lives of the prophets, 2) Jesus' interpretation of their lives in his ministry (e.g. Luke 4:16-30 and 7:18-35), and 3) the life of Jesus himself. Had they *listened* to the voice of the prophets, they would have understood the necessity of the Christ's suffering before entering into glory.

Luke 24:26—The Kerygmatic Formula

The kerygmatic formula of Luke 24:26, "Was it not necessary that the Christ should suffer these things and enter into glory?," reminds the reader in one simple, climactic statement of themes that Luke has developed throughout his Gospel.

First, the divine necessity of death and resurrection (*édei*) indicates the inexorable destiny of God's plan of salvation focused in Jesus the Messiah. However, Jesus' death and resurrection is no longer a goal, but is completely accomplished. Luke already used *dei* in Luke 24:6-7 where the women were asked by the angel to remember the passion prediction of Luke 9. This begins the process of asking the reader to look back into the Gospel to see how the evangelist has developed the kerygma. It is this methodology of "remembering" which invites the reader to "remember" how the infancy narrative speaks of the redemption of Israel in the child who is set for the fall and rising of many in Israel.

Second, the crucifixion and death of Jesus at the hands of the chief priests and rulers is now summarized in the phrase "that the Christ should suffer these things," the Christology of a suffering Messiah based on Isaiah 52-53. "Suffering" (*patheín*) has been part of Luke's passion vocabulary from the very beginning, in 9:22, 17:25, and 22:15. In fact, Luke 24:26 is the climax of the suffering Christology in Luke's Gospel, later to be used by Luke in 24:46 as a standard phrase in Lukan passion

206

theology and kerygmatic preaching for the crucifixion and death of Jesus.[23]

Third, the resurrection of the suffering Christ takes on new meaning by means of a new formula—"enter into his glory."[24] Luke reveals his understanding of the resurrection as encompassing not only the empty tomb, but also the ascension and the session at the right hand of the Father, Jesus' final eschatological destiny.[25] Jesus is already in the state of glory as he walks with the Emmaus disciples, for all things have been fulfilled. In conjunction with "on the third day" in Luke 24:21, "enter into his glory" completes Luke's resurrection theology and demonstrates that it is the sign of fulfillment of the Old Testament *and* Jesus' journey to Jerusalem.[26]

Fourth, the final element of the kerygma, the proclamation of repentance and the forgiveness of sins, although not occurring within this passion statement, will form a fundamental part of

[23]Ibid., 279: ". . . that Luke concentrates the messianic *mysterium* in the phrase *pathein ton christón* plainly implies that he found primary *salvational* significance there." Cf. Acts 1:3; 3:18; and 17:3.

[24]Ibid., 143: ". . . *eiselthein ktl.* should be understood as a resurrection statement, *but more*: an assertion of Jesus' *leadership* on the journey to everlasting life, which is also brought out by the title, *archêgós tês zôês*, that is accorded the risen One in Acts 3,15" (emphasis Dillon).

[25]Cf. Bock, *Proclamation from Prophecy and Pattern,* 116 on *éxodos* in Luke 9:31. The use of glory in 9:31-32, a unique Lukan contribution to the transfiguration account (cf. also 9:26), supports Bock's interpretation and relates directly to Luke 24:26. This interpretation also supports my contention that "the redemption of Israel" refers to the exodus event, showing that Jesus' eschatological deliverance is typologically located in Israel's redemption from Egypt. Cf. also *analêpseôs* in 9:51.

[26]Cf. Osborne, *The Resurrection Narratives,* 122: "Both 'third day' (v. 21) and 'enter into glory' (v. 26) emphasize resurrection as the fulfillment of prophecy, an emphasis which meshes well with Luke's total view of Jesus' ministry. The event was foreordained by God and foretold by the prophets, and, according to Luke, truly understood only within the context of the sacrificial meaning of his death. The other Gospel writers viewed the cross through the empty tomb, but Luke views the empty tomb through the cross. Christ's post-resurrection 'glory' is thus part of the passion and provides a transition to the proclamation of the early church." Unlike the passion formula, Luke returns to the familiar resurrection formula in 24:46, i.e. "on the third day rise from the dead."

Luke's last passion statement in 24:47, i.e. "and that repentance and forgiveness of sins should be preached in his name to all nations." The forgiveness of sins is included by Luke parabolically in the table fellowship of Luke 24:28-30, for table fellowship where forgiveness is offered is accompanied by the teaching of Jesus, in this case, teaching about his suffering and glory on the basis of the Old Testament.

Thus Luke's kerygmatic statement in 24:25-27 helps him to forge together the kerygma of a suffering and resurrected Christ, the forgiveness of sins, the fulfillment of Scripture, and the table fellowship of Jesus in the Emmaus narrative. If the reader has not "read back" into the Gospel thus far, these kerygmatic verses will press him to go back and see how these have been developed in the Gospel and the Old Testament. Luke's motif of *proclamation from prophecy and pattern* applies to the Old Testament and to the prophetic ministry of Jesus who patterned himself after the Old Testament prophets. W. Grundmann comments:

"As distinct from Mt., Lk. presents the story of Jesus between His birth and His crucifixion and resurrection as prophetic rather than Messianic action. Only the way through the cross to glory actualises the Messiahship proclaimed at the outset. Hence Lk.'s picture of the Messiah is decisively shaped by the crucifixion and the resurrection of Jesus."[27]

Luke 24:27—The Proof from Moses and the Prophets

The kerygmatic formula of Luke 24:26 receives a scriptural foundation from the evangelist in an editorial comment that expands upon the words of Jesus in 24:25 that demand faith in what the prophets have spoken. Luke broadens Jesus' reference to the prophets, adding "and beginning with Moses and all the prophets, he interpreted to them in all the scriptures the things concerning himself." The evangelist will expand this even further in 24:44: ". . . that everything written about me in the law of Moses and the prophets and the psalms must be fulfilled."

A common approach in Lukan studies is to read ahead into Acts

[27]W. Grundmann, *chríô ktl.*, TDNT IX 534. Cf. Reicke, *The Roots of the Synoptic Gospels,* 65-67 on a variation of this theme in the section "Life Setting in Baptism and the Eucharist."

for passages that illuminate the Gospel, e.g. Acts 2:22-36; 3:11-26; 4:5-12; 5:27-32; 10:34-43; and 13:26-41.[28] Such references from Acts suggest that early Christian preaching developed a rhythm between death and resurrection that expanded upon the kerygmatic formula of Luke 24:26. Christ's triumph and exaltation comes through suffering, death, and resurrection. *After the resurrection*, the Church boldly confessed in Acts what was laid down in Luke 24 as the foundation of the kerygma—death, resurrection, fulfillment of Scripture, repentance, forgiveness, mission. Thus before the Sanhedrin, Peter and the apostles proclaim: "The God of our fathers raised Jesus whom you killed by hanging on a tree. God exalted him at his right hand as Leader and Savior, to give repentance to Israel and forgiveness of sins. And we are witnesses to these things, and so is the Holy Spirit whom God has given to those who obey him" (Acts 5:30-31).

But what does Luke tell us about the kerygma *before the resurrection*? My methodology has not been to read ahead into Acts, but to read back into the Gospel to see how Luke developed the kerygma *in the Gospel*. In other words, how does the reader respond to Luke 24:25-27 on the basis of what Luke has said in chapters one to twenty-three? At Luke 24:27, several questions confront the reader: How is the Old Testament Christological, and how does it prophesy the suffering, death, and resurrection of the Messiah? Are there any clues in Luke's Gospel that enable the reader to go back into the Old Testament and find specific passages that speak of Christ's suffering, death, and resurrection? Or does Luke insist that if the reader really understood the agenda of the Old Testament, he would see that Jesus Christ is its center and its purpose?[29]

[28]Larkin, "Luke's Use of the Old Testament as a Key to His Soteriology," 328.

[29]See McHugh, "A Sermon for Easter Sunday," 92 who, in response to the numerous affirmations of Luke 24 concerning the resurrection in fulfillment of the Scriptures, asks: "Does this mean that, if we delve deep enough into the Old Testament, we shall discover texts predicting that the Messiah would rise from the dead? Hardly, for then our Lord's disciples, and no doubt many other Jews, would surely have noticed them too; and the disciples would never have been so sceptical when they first heard about Jesus' Resurrection. In fact, as St Luke tells us, their immediate reaction was to pour scorn on the

Luke's Hermeneutical Use of the Old Testament. The reader of Luke 24:25-27 might also ask: What did Jesus tell the disciples as he began from Moses and the prophets, interpreting to them in all the Scriptures the things concerning himself? Did Jesus go back and piece together proof texts that prophesy about Christ's death and resurrection? What passages might he have chosen? The reader would find it difficult to discover any such passages from reading the Gospel of Luke, for the evangelist does not cite any specific Old Testament passages that refer to the death and resurrection of Christ, with the exception of Isaiah 53:12 at Luke 22:37. As H. J. Cadbury said:

"In Luke the Scripture serves a more apologetic motive, being applied to that which is hard to understand, like the general proposition that Christ must suffer, rather than to the specific details. . . . There is an abundance of reference to the Scriptures in general. . . . Luke carries this idea beyond the death of Jesus. The resurrection also was predicted; its witnesses were chosen in advance. It is followed by the program of repentance and forgiveness of sins and, after an interval, by 'the restoration of all things' and the 'resurrection both of the just and unjust' and the 'judgment of the living and the dead.' To all these 'the prophets testify.' "[30]

Cadbury suggests the thesis that Luke uses the Old Testament as a means of "proving" that Jesus *must* (*dei*) suffer, die, and be raised, and that repentance and forgiveness of sins be preached in his name to all nations. This presents the question: How does

---

idea as a lot of nonsense (24:11), and to dismiss the testimony of the three holy women as a flight of fantasy, the product of a distraught imagination (*cf.* 24:10,22). Quite simply, the Old Testament did not predict that the Messiah, or anyone else, would rise from the dead on the third day; what then does it means to say that on the third day, Jesus 'rose again in accordance with the Scriptures'? We must find an answer to this question, *if only because our Lord insisted that if we really understood the Old Testament, we should see at once that it was only to be expected, it was inevitable, that he should be raised to life from the tomb*" (emphasis mine).

[30]Cadbury, *The Making of Luke-Acts,* 304. He also discusses on pp. 303–305 Luke's use of the Old Testament in a general way under the rubric of "divine necessity."

Luke use the Old Testament?[31] Perhaps most pertinent to this study of the Emmaus narrative is D. L. Bock's analysis of how Luke uses the Old Testament to interpret the death and resurrection of Jesus.[32] Luke does not cite specific prophecies in a proof text methodology, but weaves into the fabric of his narrative Old Testament allusions, ideas, and illustrations so that his Gospel begins to appear *to the reader* as a continuation of the Old Testament narrative, and therefore a continuation of the "history of the Redemption."[33] As Bock says of W. J. Larkin's assessment of Luke's hermeneutical method: "[Luke's] desire is to help the reader relive these events through a direct narrative presentation in Old Testament terms rather than to defend the events in apologetic (as Matthew does) through block quotation and editorial comment."[34]

Bock's methodological approach to Luke's use of the Old Testament is based on his survey of recent literature in this area. It answers three questions about Luke's hermeneutics. First, "how is the Old Testament used?" Bock gives seven different classifications: "(i) *typological-prophetic*[35] . . . (ii) *analogy* . . . (iii) *illustration*

---

[31]Cf. Bock, *Proclamation from Prophecy and Pattern*, 13–53 on "The Debate on Luke's Use of the Old Testament in Recent Study: Text, Sources, Purpose—Proof from Prophecy, and Hermeneutic." Cf. also Juel, *Messianic Exegesis*, 31–57 on "Biblical Interpretation in the First Century C.E."

[32]Bock, *Proclamation from Prophecy and Pattern*, 37–46 uses the following representative studies: Dupont, *The Salvation of the Gentiles* (New York: Paulist Press, 1979) 129–159; M. Rese, *Alttestamentliche Motive in der Christologie des Lukas* (Gerd Mohn: Gütersloher Verlagshaus, 1969); and W. Larkin, "Luke's Use of the Old Testament in Luke 22–23."

[33]J. Daniélou, "The New Testament and the Theology of History," *Studia Evangelica* I (1959) 25–34.

[34]Bock, *Proclamation from Prophecy and Pattern*, 45.

[35]The *typological-prophetic* category is the most important one for the Emmaus story. Bock, *Proclamation from Prophecy and Pattern*, 49 defines it in this way: "*Typology* or better *typological-prophetic* usage expresses a peculiar link of patterns with movement from the lesser OT person or event to the greater NT person or event. The link must be identifiable. In this usage *pattern and prophecy* is involved through appeal to the OT. By pattern and prophecy is meant that God's pattern of salvation is being reactivated in a present fulfilment. This fulfilment takes place both in accordance with messianic hope and promise and in accordance with the pattern of God's activity in salvation. It is the

. . . (iv) *a legal proof* . . . (v) *a proof passage* . . . (vi) *an explanatory or hermeneutical use* [that] specifically explains *the nature or significance* of an event . . . (vii) *prophetic* or *direct prophecy.*"[36] Second, "what does the New Testament presuppose?" This embraces promise and fulfillment, Christological, messianic, prophetic and eschatological concepts, law, non-prophetic history, or even a combination of these. Third, "why is the Old Testament used?" Bock's answer is the subtitle of his book, i.e. Luke's use of the Old Testament contributes to and helps shape his Christology.

Thus Bock's analysis affirms that Luke is not engaging in specifics and details, but in ideas and concepts based on a complex and diverse hermeneutical approach. The goal of this approach is to describe to the reader, on the basis of Old Testament prophecies and patterns, the theological significance of the person of Jesus Christ whose suffering, death, resurrection, and offer of forgiveness forms the core of the Lukan kerygma. Bock's concluding remarks summarize his position on Luke's use of the Old Testament:

"The stress of Luke's use of the OT for christology is not primarily in terms of a defensive apologetic. Rather Luke's use of the OT for christology involves the direct proclamation of Jesus. Jesus is the Christ promised in the Scriptures. It is more correct to call Luke's use of the OT for christology, *'proclamation from prophecy and pattern.'* By this phrase it is meant that Luke sees the Scripture fulfilled in Jesus in terms of the fulfilment of OT prophecy and in terms of the reintroduction and fulfilment of the OT patterns that point to the presence of God's saving work. In referring to OT patterns, we refer to what is commonly called typology, while noting that the patterns that occur refer to more than christology (see Luke 1.5-25). Sometimes both prophecy and pattern are seen together. Of these two basic categories of usage, prophecy fulfilled has the dominant role. . . . The proclamation of Jesus from prophecy and pattern sees the church on the offensive concerning Jesus. We believe this new phrase represents a better description

---

combination of these two elements that allows one to see the invocation of a prophetic OT appeal; hence the term typological-prophetic."

[36]Ibid., 49–50 (emphasis Bock).

of Luke's use of the OT for christology. . . . *'Proclamation from prophecy and pattern'* is the umbrella term that describes Luke's use of the OT for christology.

"This motif is not exclusively Lucan in as much as we have already shown that much of his actual material is traditional. However, what Luke has done is to emphasize this motif more explicitly than the other Synoptics *in its specific reference to the death, resurrection, and offer of forgiveness in Jesus* (Luke 24.44-47)."[37]

On the third day he rose again in accordance with the Scriptures. If Luke's hermeneutical method is not to cite proof passages from the Old Testament, but rather to see that Jesus is the final consummation of the pattern set by the prophets, how does Luke understand the necessity of Jesus' death and resurrection in fulfillment of the Scriptures? Bock states that "of these two basic categories of usage [prophecy and pattern], prophecy fulfilled has the dominant role." But is this true in connection with the death and resurrection of Christ? Is this not where pattern dominates prophecy, where the overall thrust of God's redemptive activity in the Old Testament, in conformity with his righteous plan of salvation, demands that God's innocent and righteous Messiah suffer an agonizing death and be raised on the third day? J. McHugh writes:

". . . *Suppose there were* a human being who was utterly without sin? What would have to happen 'according to the Scriptures'? Clearly, whatever happened to such a person would have to vindicate, not to undermine, the Old Testament teaching that God is always and in every action utterly just and righteous. Now if there is one thing the disciples had observed *before* Jesus died, it is that he was in every single deed and word faultlessly obedient to God his Father. They knew him intimately for more than two years, and had every opportunity to observe him; and their judgement was, that Jesus was completely without sin. That is why our Lord can chide them, on the day of his Resurrection, with not understanding the Scriptures, with not perceiving that it was inevitable that God would raise him from the grave. True, it had been necessary that he should first suffer and die and be buried, in

---

[37]Ibid., 274–275 (emphasis mine). Cf. also Tannehill, *Narrative Unity,* 284–289.

order that his obedience to the Father should extend, and should be seen to extend, over the whole span of earthly human existence. But once that was done, and seen to be done, it would have been utterly unjust if his body had been left to decay and corruption. The Resurrection of Jesus *had* to happen, if the teaching of the Old Testament about God was true.''[38]

The resurrection of Christ is the final consummation of all Scripture—*it is the sign of fulfillment.* Jesus fits the pattern of the prophets in his life and death and completes it. Deuteronomy 18:15ff. becomes the programmatic text in the Old Testament for Jesus' interpretation of the Scriptures as fulfilled in himself. As Bock suggests in his exposition of the transfiguration imperative "listen to him" in 9:35,[39] Deuteronomy 18 is Luke's source, and Moses is the one who sets the pattern for Jesus' rejection as well as his teaching and miracles:

"This use of Deuteronomy 18 as a call to understand God's plan as revealed in the prophet like Moses, Jesus, is present also in Acts 3.19-24. Its connection with teaching about Jesus' suffering and coming glory suggests that these points of Jesus' ministry

---

[38]McHugh, "A Sermon for Easter Sunday," 92 (emphasis McHugh). Cf. also M. Hengel, *The Atonement* (Philadelphia: Fortress Press, 1981) 41: "The suffering 'of the righteous' is to be integrated completely and utterly into the suffering of the Messiah. *The Messiah alone is the righteous and sinless one par excellence.* His suffering therefore has irreplaceable and unique significance" (emphasis Hengel); and Juel, *Messianic Exegesis,* 25–26, 102–103.

[39]Cf. G. Schrenk, *eklektós, TDNT* IV 189: "Common to the sayings in Lk. 9:35 and 23:35 is the fact that Christ in connection with His passion is called *ho uiós mou ho eklelegménos* at His transfiguration, just before entering the way of suffering [cf. Lk. 9:31: Moses and Elijah speak with Him about His *éxodos*] and then *ho christós tou theoú ho eklektós* as He hangs on the cross. The first saying is a declaration of the heavenly voice, the second a contemptuous doubting of His claim by His enemies. It is in Lk., who in 24:26,46 shows the passion to be a necessary point of transition to the glory, that this designation as the Elect is brought into connection with the suffering. He is the Elect, not merely in or in spite of His passion, but in His appointment thereto. The scorn of His adversaries proves that this Elect refuses to help Himself. Herewith His claim to be *eklektós* is shown to imply a complete break with human ideas of success. The electing divine will does not depend on appearances."

may not have been appreciated as a part of the OT hope about Messiah."[40]

Even the use of "to raise up" (*anastêsei*) in Deuteronomy 18:15 could be seen as an allusion to the resurrection of Jesus. Luke's phrase "beginning with Moses" suggests that we read back into the Gospel to see the evangelist's development of his Moses typology that sets the pattern *par excellence* for the progressive unfolding of those prophetic characteristics that will mark the Messiah, a pattern that may be seen in Abraham, David, Elijah, Elisha, John the Baptist, the future apostolic community in Acts, and in Israel itself.[41]

Jesus, therefore, is *the eschatological prophet*, the end of the ages, the fulfillment of all Scripture. He is *the teacher* who, at the table, completes the teaching of the prophets—he is *the miracle-worker* who, through his miracles and his presence at the table, before and after the resurrection, demonstrates the presence in the world of the new age of salvation, the fulfillment of the kingdom of God—he is *the rejected one* who, by his death on the cross, fulfills his own prophecy that "a prophet should not perish away from Jerusalem" (Luke 13:33). But the disciples or the people of Israel could not understand that Jesus was the fulfillment of Scripture until *after the resurrection*. As Dillon concludes: "Only at Easter could the properly *Mosaic prophecy* of Jesus be brought to light."[42]

Luke began the ministry of Jesus in his programmatic text of 4:16-30 where the fulfillment of Scripture was the issue that led to Jesus' rejection at Nazareth.[43] There, Luke quotes specific Old Testament texts to show how Jesus fulfills the messianic works of teaching and miracles. However, he cites no specific texts from the Old Testament to prove that Jesus' rejection is in fulfillment of the

[40]Bock, *Proclamation from Prophecy and Pattern*, 115.
[41]Cf. C. B. Caird, *Saint Luke* (Philadelphia: Westminster Press, 1963) 258.
[42]Dillon, *From Eyewitnesses*, 136.
[43]Ibid., 136–137. Dillon also makes the connection between Luke 24:27 and 4:18. He concludes that "Indeed, *the same Jesus who spoke out over the closed book to his kinsfolk and countrymen is also the speaker who announces the scriptures' fulfillment in the kerygma of the apostles.* The voice is the *eschatological prophet's* voice, Moses' counterpart, end and fruition of the prophets' line, bestower of the gift of *forgiveness* just as they *all* had foretold" (emphasis Dillon).

Scriptures. Instead he offers Elijah and Elisha as examples of rejected prophets. This is Luke's pattern throughout his Gospel: even John the Baptist's violent death is part of the pattern and sets the stage for Jesus' crucifixion. Luke does not give a separate account of John's death as do Matthew (14:1-12) and Mark (6:17-29), but simply reports in 9:9, in the mouth of Herod, that John was beheaded. This occurs in Luke 9 before Jesus predicts his own death and resurrection (9:18-22), and thus John's rejection serves as a type of Jesus' rejection. The reader will recall the step-parallelism between John and Jesus in the infancy narrative, and Luke's continuation of this step-parallelism in terms of Jesus' fulfillment of God's divine plan of salvation in Luke 7:18-35.

For Luke, Jesus is the ultimate righteous man of faith, not unlike the righteous saints in the Old Testament and the righteous saints in his own Gospel such as Zechariah, Elizabeth, Mary, Joseph, Simeon, and Anna.[44] For example, Zechariah and Elizabeth are "righteous (*díkaioi*) before God" (1:6), and Simeon is "righteous (*díkaios*) and devout, looking for the consolation of Israel" (2:25). Luke wants the reader to see his Gospel as a continuation of the Old Testament both in its content and its Septuagintal style. The plan of salvation, begun in the Old Testament, now continues to unfold in the history of Jesus, and the infancy narrative gives context to Jesus' life, showing that he is one with the Old Testament saints.[45]

Luke has read the Old Testament for his reader, and now the reader does not have to read back into the Old Testament as the evangelist did. From Luke's portrait of Jesus in the infancy narrative, the reader understands that Jesus is the righteous Messiah come to fulfill the promises to Israel of restoration and redemption (e.g. 1:32-35; 1:68-75; and 2:29-35).[46]

[44]Cf. Bernadicou, "Christian Community According to Luke," 208.
[45]Cf. J. McHugh, *The Mother of Jesus*, 24, 35–36.
[46]S. Ferris, *The Hymns of Luke's Infancy Narratives* (*JSNT*, Supplement Series 9, Sheffield, England: JSOT Press, 1985) 151–160 makes some observations about the theological significance of the hymns (the Magnificat, the Benedictus, and the Nunc Dimittis). In his final chapter he summarizes their significance under the heading of "promise and fulfilment" and "the restoration of Israel," both of which will become major themes in Luke-Acts. He concludes on p. 160: "But in using these hymns the Church takes up and

The uniqueness of Jesus comes from his perfect righteousness and innocence as the one who is without sin and does what no one else could do.[47] If one passes immediately from the infancy narrative to the passion narrative, Luke continues the same line of argument for Jesus' death and resurrection. There are no proof texts here, but clear allusions from the Old Testament, establishing a pattern that the reader sees reaching its climax in Jesus. By using Isaiah 53 and Psalms 22, 31, and 69 as background for understanding the nature of Jesus' suffering as a righteous man, Luke is able to present Jesus as the fulfillment of the Old Testament pattern of the suffering righteous Messiah.[48]

But what of that strange, last addition in Luke 24:44, "and in the psalms"? Bock speaks to this question:

"Jesus, in the entrusting of his spirit to the Father, follows the pattern of an innocent righteous saint and fulfils specifically the plan of God for *the* innocent sufferer. Luke 24.46 points to the climax of the Passion narrative. It is intended to have the reader see that though Jesus suffered, surely he was righteous, a key Lucan theme in Acts.

"The allusions from the Psalms point to the context in which Jesus suffered by the plan of God. He suffered in the pattern of innocent righteous saints in the hope that God would vindicate him and therefore validate his claims about himself. With the

---

declares anew its Jewish heritage. Just as Luke suggested, we in the Gentile Church are built on the foundation of pious Israelites who received the gospel with joy. We are built upon not only 'the foundation of the apostles and prophets' whose activities are recounted in Acts but also the humble sons and daughters of Abraham, whose worship still echoes in the hymns of Luke 1-2." Cf. also Bock, *Proclamation from Prophecy and Pattern*, 55-90 on "Luke's Old Testament Christology in the Infancy Narrative."

[47]Karris, *Luke: Artist and Theologian*, 79-119 in the chapter entitled "Luke 23 and Luke's Thematic Christology and Soteriology" describes Jesus "as the Innocently Suffering Righteous One." He comments on 23:32 and 22:37 on p. 95: "And these two verses are references to the innocently suffering righteous servant of Isaiah 53:12. As God's righteous one, Jesus obediently and lovingly goes along the path laid out for him by God. He wills to be with the outcasts of society during their darkest hours and thus embodies a God whose greatest longing is to be with his beleaguered creatures."

[48]Luke continues the language of "the righteous one" in the Acts sermons (3:14; 7:52; 22:14).

resurrection, Jesus' vindication occurred and all things were fulfilled so that now witnesses could be sent out with the message about Jesus as the suffering but raised Christ who can offer forgiveness of sins (Luke 24.44-47)."[49]

Luke prefers the declaration of the centurion to read "certainly this man was innocent" (*ontôs ho anthrôpos oútos díkaios ên*) in 23:47, as opposed to Matthew's "truly, this was the Son of God" (*alêthôs theoú huiós ên oútos*) in 27:54. God raises Jesus from the dead, not only because he is the Son of God, but because he is the only one who is truly innocent and righteous in fulfillment of Old Testament prophecy and pattern.[50] Thus, the resurrection in Luke is God's great vindication, *the sign of fulfillment*. The resurrection of Jesus "*had* to happen, if the teaching of the Old Testament about God was true."[51]

[49]Bock, *Proclamation from Prophecy and Pattern*, 148 (emphasis Bock). Tannehill, *Narrative Unity*, 193 suggests that "the specific Scriptures cited in Luke which prepare the reader to understand that Jesus' suffering will lead to glory are Pss 118:22 and 110:1." See Dillon, *From Eyewitnesses*, 205 on the inclusion of the Psalms in 24:44 because "they furnish the major Old Testament passages invoked by the Acts preachers as prophecy of the resurrection/exaltation: Ps 16,8-11 (Acts 2,25ff.), Ps 110,1 (Acts 2,34f.), Ps 118,22 (Acts 4,11), Ps 2,7 (Acts 13,33; cp. Ps 2,1-2 in Acts 4,25f.)"; and Juel, *Messianic Exegesis*, 89–117 on "Christian Interpretation of the Psalms."

[50]Cf. Dillon, *From Eyewitnesses*, 100–103 on Psalm 31, *óntôs*, and the relation between 24:34 and 23:47.

[51]McHugh, "A Sermon for Easter Sunday," 92.

Chapter 12

The Center Circle—The Meal of Jesus

The primary focus of the Emmaus narrative is *table fellowship*: the *teaching of Jesus* and *the meal of Jesus* that must be considered together as "*a single act*."[1] The teaching of Jesus functions as *preparation for* the meal of Jesus where reconciliation takes place, i.e. the proclamation of the kerygma from prophecy and pattern by the risen Lord prepares the Emmaus disciples for the recognition of the reality of the resurrection in the breaking of the bread.

What then is the climax of the meal at Emmaus? There are, in fact, two climaxes, the first preparatory of the second. The first climax is the teaching of Jesus that takes place in Luke 24:25-27 where the risen Christ opens up the Scriptures to the disciples. But this "climax" simply prepares for the greater climax where Jesus is recognized in the breaking of the bread in Luke 24:30-31. The significance of this distinction is that *the teaching together with the breaking of the bread form the climax of Luke's Gospel*. This is the first time a disciple of Jesus recognizes *by faith* that *Jesus is the risen, suffering Messiah prophesied in the Old Testament*. The teaching of Jesus in 24:25-27 creates burning hearts, preparing the disciples for revelation, but it is in the breaking of the bread in 24:30 that we have *the moment of revelation*.[2]

The question must be asked: Why does Jesus choose to reveal himself in the breaking of the bread?[3] This chapter will address

---

[1]Dillon, *From Eyewitnesses*, 154 (emphasis Dillon). Cf. Léon-Dufour, *Sharing the Eucharistic Bread*, 28: "The conclusion is unavoidable: the word of God was always joined to the shared meal"; also Marshall, *Last Supper*, 124–125.

[2]From the beginning, I have argued that the Emmaus meal is the climax of Luke's table fellowship matrix and the climax of his Gospel. The reason is given in this chapter, i.e. it is the moment of recognition that Jesus is the crucified and risen Messiah.

[3]This question was also posed by Dillon, *From Eyewitnesses*, 105: ". . . why was the *fractio panis* the moment? Why was it precisely that which

that question in light of the conclusions about the teaching of
Jesus discussed in the previous chapter. If we compare Luke 24
with the feeding of the five thousand, the climax of Jesus'
Galilean ministry, and the Last Supper, the climax of Jesus'
Jerusalem ministry, we see that at Emmaus Luke has *reversed the
order at the table* from eating/teaching to teaching/eating. This order
of "teaching, then eating" sets the pattern for the early Christian
meals in Acts. This dual aspect of the story is neatly phrased in
Luke's concluding verse for the meal at Emmaus in 24:35: "And
they expounded the things he taught on the road and how he was
known to them in the breaking of the bread" (my translation).

THE SETTING OF THE BREAKING OF THE BREAD — 24:28-29

The setting of the breaking of the bread in Luke 24:28-29 is
paralleled with the opening of the dialogue in 24:17-18. But although the *participants* are the same (Jesus, Cleopas, and the other
disciple), there are two marked differences between the setting of
the dialogue and the setting of the meal. First in terms of the
place, the dialogue occurs on the road in 24:17 whereas the meal
takes place after arriving at the village in 24:28. Second, in terms
of the *time*, the journey occurs during the day in 24:13, whereas
the meal at Emmaus comes at the close of the day in 24:29. This
leads to two obvious areas of discussion: the place of the meal in
24:28 and the time of the meal in 24:29. There is, however, a third
area as well, involving the invitation of Jesus to the meal by the
Emmaus disciples and his acceptance in 24:29.

The Place of the Meal—24:28

The place of the meal is closely tied to Luke's journey motif, for
24:28 is filled with Lukan vocabulary characteristic of the journey:
"So they drew near (*êggisan*) to the village to which they were
going (*eporeúonto*). He appeared to be going (*poreúesthai*) further. . . ." "To draw near" (*eggízô*) carries eschatological connotations in connection with both Luke's geographical perspective and

---

brought the decisive disclosure (*egnôsthê*)? Better still: what is the relationship
between the 'eye-opening' of the *fractio* and the 'scripture-opening' of the
journey (*ta en tê hodô*) in the scrupulous economy of Lk's narrative?"

his table fellowship matrix, e.g. 15:1, 25; 19:29, 37; 21:8, 20, 28, 30, 31; 22:1, 47. The parallels between 24:28 and 24:15 in the Emmaus narrative with respect to "drawing near" (*eggizô*) are significant, since both are associated with Luke's geographical perspective: 24:15—"to go with" (*suneporeúeto*); 24:28—"to go" (*eporeúonto* and *poreúesthai*).

In fact, the disciples' arrival at Emmaus signals the end of the journey and therefore the end of the teaching of Jesus. This also sets up the climax of the story in 24:30-31, and the climax of the whole Gospel.[4] When Luke tells us that Jesus "appeared to be going further," this confirms that a climax has been reached (cf. the hapax legomena *prospoiéô*, along with *porrôteron*). The reader can expect that when the disciples invite Jesus to dine with them, he will either accept or continue on his way. The pretense of going farther forces the reader to ponder these two options, a choice that is settled when Jesus accepts their invitation. Without the invitation, there would have been no meal and no revelation of Jesus to the Emmaus disciples.

But why at Emmaus? Luke's placement of the first post-resurrection meal *outside Jerusalem* is a significant part of his table fellowship matrix and his geographical perspective. The meals of the new age that are founded on the death and resurrection of Christ will now be celebrated as much outside Jerusalem as within Jerusalem.

The Time of the Meal—24:29

The time reference in Luke 24:29, "for it is toward evening and the day is now far spent," reminds the reader that other meals in Luke's table fellowship matrix occurred when the day was drawing to a close, particularly the feeding of the five thousand in 9:12-17 and the Last Supper in 22:14-38.[5] This connection with the other Lukan meals further suggests the climactic nature of the breaking of the bread at Emmaus.

---

[4]Cf. Fitzmyer, *X-XIV*, 1567 on the double use of *poreúesthai* in 24:28 as a reflection of Luke's geographical perspective. He concludes: "The goal of their walk is reached, but it is also the climax of the story."

[5]Navone, *Themes of St. Luke*, 27 claims other meals occurred at the close of the day, e.g. Luke 4:38-40; 5:29-38; 7:36-50; 11:37-41; 14:1-24; 24:36ff.

The Invitation to the Meal and Jesus' Acceptance—24:29

In 24:29, the verb "to stay" (*ménô*) occurs twice: in the invitation ("stay with us"—*meínon meth' hêmôn*), and in Jesus' acceptance of the invitation ("he went in to stay with them"—*tou meínai sun autoís*—an infinitive of purpose). The significance of Christ's presence at the meal has already been anticipated by Luke in the meal with Zacchaeus where Jesus says in 19:5, "for I must (*dei*) stay (*meínai*) at your house today," and in 19:9, "today salvation has come to this house." The meal with Zacchaeus reveals the *abiding presence* of God's salvation in the forgiveness of sins because of *the presence of Jesus* at the table with Zacchaeus. Just as it was necessary that Jesus stay with Zacchaeus, so it is necessary that Jesus now stay with the Emmaus disciples. But his presence at Emmaus is more significant, for he is now the risen Lord.

Luke's use of the preposition "with" (*metá* and *sun*) in connection with "to stay" (*ménô*) highlights the presence of Christ at the meal, for these two words belong to the vocabulary of the table fellowship matrix (Luke 7:36; 15:2, 29f.; 22:15, 21; and 24:29f.).[6] Further, "to go in" (*eisérchomai*) is used in 19:7 to describe the action of Jesus coming to Zacchaeus the sinner to bring salvation in the forgiveness of sins. In 24:29, "to go in" (*eisérchomai*) is followed by an infinitive of purpose (*tou meínai sun autoís*), underlining Jesus' intent to be present with the disciples at the meal at

[6]Cf. W. Grundmann, *sun-metá*, TDNT VII 796: "*sun* and *metá* are particularly important in connection with meals, for the meal creates fellowship, Lk. 15:29f.; 7:36. Jesus eats with publicans and sinners; His adversaries take offence at this, Mt. 9:10f.; Mk. 2:16; Lk. 15:2. Judas' betrayal is especially shameful as a breach of table fellowship, Mk. 14:18, 20; Lk. 22:21. Jesus had a particular desire for this fellowship (Lk. 22:15) and He looks forward to its restoration and fulfilment in the Father's kingdom, Mt. 26:29, cf. also 8:11; 25:10. The Emmaus disciples ask their unknown guest to have fellowship at table, Lk. 24:29f. The community regarded the Lord's Supper as fellowship with the Risen Lord and observed it in expectation of the coming meal in the kingdom of God. This is perfectly plain in the hymn appended to the letter to Laodicea in Rev. 3:20. This is an eschatological saying which is now fulfilled for the community in the Lord's Supper and which is addressed to the individual member (*eán tis akoúsê . . . eiseleúsomai pros autôn*) with a view of taking him up into reciprocal fellowship with Jesus and maintaining him in it: *deipnêsô met' autoú kai autós met' emoú*." Betz, "The Origin and Nature of Christian Faith," 37 observes the same reference to Rev. 3:20.

Emmaus. This was for him the ultimate reason for journeying with them. The urgent attempt by the disciples to prevent Jesus from going any further (*parabiázomai*—"urge strongly, prevail upon")[7] reinforces the presence of Christ at the table of the Emmaus disciples.

Thus the reader is invited to note the invitation and its acceptance. The stranger becomes first the guest and finally the host. The setting for the breaking of the bread is now in place.

THE BREAKING OF THE BREAD
AND THE RECOGNITION — 24:30-31

The climactic moment is reached in 24:30-31 when Jesus reclines with them, takes bread, blesses it, breaks it, gives it to them, their eyes are opened to recognize him, and he disappears from their sight.[8] Almost every word in these two verses is significant for the reader *within the context of Luke's Gospel as he comes to the climax of the Gospel*, for much of the vocabulary has already occurred in Luke 1–23 and will recur in Acts.[9]

The breaking of the bread in Luke 24:30 cannot be separated from the opening of the eyes, the recognition, and the disappearance in 24:31, for these two verses are linked grammatically as one complete thought. Taken together they describe the meal of Jesus

[7]Bauer, Arndt, and Gingrich, *Greek-English Lexicon*, 617. The only other use of this word in the New Testament is Acts 16:15, which some see as a parallel to Luke 24:29.

[8]Cf. Tannehill, *Narrative Unity*, 289: "Evidently recognition comes at this point because Jesus is assuming a role familiar to the disciples from meal fellowships previously shared."

[9]The meals in Acts are a topic for further study as Luke builds upon the table fellowship matrix of his Gospel in Acts. Cf. Esler, *Community and Gospel*, 71–109 on table fellowship in Acts, particularly Acts 10:1–11:18; 15; and 27:33-38; Dunn, *Jesus and the Spirit*, 182–188 on worship in Acts in which he discusses table fellowship and the teaching of the words of Jesus; Dunn, *Unity and Diversity*, 127–129, 163, 209; Robinson, "The Place of the Emmaus Story," 486, 490–493 on Acts 2:42-46; 20:7, 11; 27; Neyrey, *The Passion*, 16; Dupont, "The Meal at Emmaus," 117–120; Dillon, *From Eyewitnesses*, 105–108 (107 n. 109); Wanke, *Eucharistieverständnis*, 11–30; Tannehill, *Narrative Unity*, 290ff.; Bösen, *Jesusmahl*, 118–133; Davis, "The Significance of the Shared Meal," 141–178; Cullmann, *Worship*, 9–12; and P. H. Menoud, "Les Actes des apôtres de l'eucharistie," *RHPR* 33 (1953) 21–35.

at Emmaus. However, each verse needs to be treated separately. Thus, I will focus first on the action at the meal (24:30) and then on the revelation to the disciples that Jesus is the suffering Messiah risen from the dead (24:31).

Luke 24:30—The Action at the Meal

"And it came to pass (*kai egéneto*)
> when he was at table with them (*en tô kataklithênai auton met' autôn*)
>> taking the bread (*labôn ton árton*)
>> he *blessed* it and (*eulógêsen kai*)
>> breaking the bread (*klásas*)
>>> he *gave* it to them" (*epedídou autoís*)
>>>> (translation mine—main verbs in italics)

By diagramming Luke 24:30 in this way, the important relationships between the words of this verse are apparent. Note also that both verses 30 and 31 are governed by "it came to pass" (*kai egéneto*), a construction used by Luke to approximate a Biblical style. There is more to this than simply an imitation of a particular literary style, for this syntactical combination introduces significant passages in Luke 24. As suggested by Dillon and Wanke, the phrase *kai egéneto* is used in *Luke 24:4* "to evoke the atmosphere of the earthly appearance of heavenly beings, a particularly sacred occasion which the Old Testament always cloaked in numinous glow and solemn language."[10] In 24:4, the sacred occasion is the earthly appearance of the angels to announce the resurrection of Jesus to the women, the first of four heavenly appearances that point to Jesus as God's suffering Messiah risen from the dead.

In *Luke 24:15* the journey to Emmaus is introduced by the phrase "while they were talking and discussing together" (*kai egéneto en tô homileín autoús kai suzêteín*). The sacred person introduced into the narrative by *kai egéneto* is Jesus himself (*kai autós Iêsous*), the Messiah risen from the dead. The "numinous glow" that shrouds this introduction is the presence of the risen Christ. The parallel between 24:15 and 24:30 is not only in grammatical construction, but in the change of status of the participants in the

---

[10]Dillon, *From Eyewitnesses*, 21 and Wanke, *Die Emmauserzählung*, 29.

story. In 24:15, the Emmaus disciples are conversing with one another when Jesus comes and walks with them. But in 24:30, Jesus initiates the action of reclining with the disciples. Jesus has moved from being an ignorant stranger, to teacher, to guest, to host, whereas the disciples have moved from being hosts, to guests, to catechumens. They who once presented the *facts* of Jesus' death, now learn the *significance* of them from the stranger.[11]

Luke 24:51 may seem an unlikely candidate for comparison with pericopes in Luke's table fellowship matrix, but the same Lukan construction is used here, i.e. "while he blessed them" (*kai egéneto en tô eulogeín autón autoús*). Here, Jesus has fully assumed the position of authority in the post-resurrection appearances. As Jesus once blessed (*eulógêsen*) the bread at Emmaus, so now he blesses the Eleven as he departs. The blessing of the disciples by Jesus at his ascension may well be a hint to the reader that Jesus, when he is no longer with the disciples in a visible form, will be present with them in table fellowship wherever bread is blessed, broken, and given.[12]

Thus, the reader is alerted to see in Luke 24:30-31 the climax of the Emmaus story and the Gospel, for *it will come to pass* (*kai egéneto*) in the breaking of the bread that Jesus is recognized as the suffering, righteous Messiah risen from the dead.

A constellation of words appears in Luke 24:30 that is found in other Lukan meals.[13] The following verses demonstrate this:

7:36   ". . . and he went into the Pharisee's house, and sat at table (*kateklíthê*)."

---

[11]Dillon, *From Eyewitnesses*, 245 n. 52 notes that traveling missionaries imitated Jesus' action at Emmaus, i.e. moving from the status of guests to that of hosts.

[12]Cf. Fitzmyer, *X-XXIV*, 1588–1589 on 24:50-53: "Hence the 'ascension' is nothing more than this appearance of the risen Christ to his assembled disciples, in which for the last time he is visibly perceptible, as he takes his leave from them, gathered as the nucleus community. No longer will they behold him in this manner; hereafter he will be present to them not in visibly perceptible form, but in 'the breaking of bread' (v. 35) and through 'what my Father has promised' (v. 49; Acts 1:4-5; 2:31)."

[13]Cf. Tannehill, *Narrative Unity*, 290: "The careful repetition of this sequence of actions would not be necessary if it were not significant. It suggests an intention to recall previous occasions on which this occurred."

9:15-16 "And they did so, and made them all sit down (*katékli-nan*). And taking (*labôn*) the five loaves and the two fish he looked up to heaven, and blessed (*eulógêsen*) and broke (*katéklasen*) them, and gave (*edídou*) them to the disciples to set before the crowd."

14:8 "When you are invited by any one to a marriage feast, do not sit down (*kataklithês*) in a place of honor . . . ."

22:19 "And he took the bread (*labôn árton*), and when he had given thanks he broke (*éklasen*) it and gave (*édôken*) it to them, saying. . . ."

24:30 "When he was at table (*kataklithênai*) with them, he took the bread (*labôn ton árton*) and blessed (*eulógêsen*), and broke it (*klásas*), and gave it (*epedídou*) to them."

Luke 7:36 and 14:8 are included not only because of *kataklínô*, but because both pericopes are pivotal to Luke's table fellowship matrix as it teaches about God's eschatological kingdom.

In 7:36-50, we read of forgiveness in the context of table fellowship. In 14:8-24, we read that Jesus' table fellowship with the outcasts of society, "the poor, the maimed, the lame, the blind" (14:13), is a manifestation of the inclusive nature of God's eschatological table fellowship. But this table fellowship with sinners may be understood only in light of Jesus' humble suffering and death upon a cross.

In the Emmaus meal, the disciples are "the poor, the maimed, the lame, the blind" because they have misunderstood the passion facts and confessed a misguided Christology. They are restored to Jesus' table fellowship by Jesus himself, the one who opens their eyes when he breaks bread, creating in them faith to know his true identity. This revelation of Jesus is a sign of the presence of the eschatological kingdom where forgiveness is offered and received in the fellowship at the table. As the reader reaches the apex of the Emmaus meal at Luke 24:30, he will first recall the feeding of the five thousand in 9:15-16, and then the Last Supper in 22:14-38. (Cf. chapter IX, in which I made seven observations about the the relationship between the feeding of the five thousand and Luke's table fellowship, the meal at Emmaus, and the eschatological kingdom, all or some of which might have existed in the mind of the reader.)

Luke 22:14-38—The Last Supper

The institution narrative of the Last Supper in Luke 22:1-38 is of course the key to Luke's table fellowship matrix in his Gospel as it relates to the meals that precede it, and the Emmaus meal that follows it. It has been called the "private passion" of Jesus that serves as "an indispensable prelude to the 'public passion.'" Léon-Dufour has pointed out that there are "two major and overlapping themes: the inevitability of the death that already has Jesus in its grasp, and Jesus' consciousness of being free in the face of this death."[14] This focus on the death of Christ parallels the Emmaus meal where this private passion is interpreted by the risen Christ on the basis of the Old Testament Scriptures.

In order to draw significant parallels between Luke's account of the Supper and the Emmaus meal, some observations about the structure of Luke 22:1-38 must be made. Since Luke 22:1-13 is preliminary to the supper (a prologue to the meal)—dealing primarily with the plots of the religious leaders in Jerusalem (22:1-2), the betrayal of Judas (22:3-6), and the preparations of the meal (22:7-13)—this study will focus on Luke 22:14-38.

The Framework of the Last Supper

LUKE 22:14. 1) When the hour of the meal comes (*kai hóte egéneto hê hôra*), the reader is to connect the meal with the suffering of Christ and see it as the beginning of his passion, the first day of the three-day sequence, the day of preparation. At the same time, there begins the misunderstanding by the disciples concerning Jesus' death which continues until the risen Lord interprets the passion facts to the Emmaus disciples. When the passion mystery ends in Luke 24:33, the Emmaus disciples return to Jerusalem "that same hour" with burning hearts and open eyes, bringing the third day, the day of resurrection, to a close. The passion mystery is now clear to them. Luke therefore frames the passion/resurrection of Christ within "the hour" in 22:14 and 24:33.

2) Luke more than the other evangelists stresses that the Last Supper is an act of table fellowship. The first reference to table fellowship in the institution narrative occurs here in 22:14: "he sat at

[14]Léon-Dufour, *Sharing the Eucharistic Bread*, 186–187.

table (*anépesen*), and the apostles with him."[15] Luke uses *anapíptô* instead of *kataklínô*, each referring to the act of reclining at a festive meal. The matrix structure here, however, is not developed by identical wording, but in the action expressed, placing the Last Supper in continuity with other Lukan festive meals. Thus, those at the table with Jesus at the Last Supper and at the Emmaus meal engaged in the same act of reclining.[16]

3) The participants in the meal are the apostles. For Luke, the apostles and the Twelve are one and the same thing,[17] as he suggests in 6:13 where he chooses twelve (*dôdeka*) from the disciples (*mathêtai*) and calls them apostles (*apóstoloi*). In the account of the Last Supper all three words occur for those at the meal: *dôdeka* in 22:3, *mathêtai* in 22:11, and *apóstoloi* in 22:14. In Luke 24, the Twelve have become the Eleven (*éndeka*) and are described as apostles in 24:10 right before the Emmaus narrative. "Disciples" does not occur in Luke 24. The two Emmaus disciples are included in "all the rest" in 24:9, but not among the Eleven, a fact that is affirmed at the end of the story (24:33). The first eyewitnesses to the resurrected Lord and the first participants of the new meal in the new age are therefore contrasted with the participants at the Last Supper who are clearly the inner circle, the Twelve, the apostles.[18] This suggests that with the end of Jesus' earthly ministry, the scenario of the Gospel has changed, and that a new one is emerging in preparation for the Church's liturgical life in Acts.

---

[15]Neyrey, *The Passion*, 8 also lists five references to table fellowship in the institution narrative, the starting point of his discussion of Lukan table fellowship.

[16]*anapíptô* occurs at 11:37; 14:10; and 17:7; *kataklínô* is unique to Luke and occurs at 7:36; 9:14, 15; 14:8; and 24:30. The difference between these two words is slight: *kataklínô* has the sense of recline, whereas *anapíptô* has the sense of fall/lean back. Why Luke does not use *kataklínô* at the Last Supper is difficult to determine.

[17]Cf. Fitzmyer, *I-IX*, 254.

[18]Neyrey, *The Passion*, 12 claims that "it [22:14-38] is addressed to 'the apostles,' and it will have something specific to say about each of the individual apostles: (a) about Judas (22:21), (b) about Peter (22:31-34), and (c) about all of them (22:24-27,28-30,35-38)."

The Eschatological Significance of the Last Supper

LUKE 22:15-18. 1) The Last Supper, like the Emmaus narrative, is a dialogue between Jesus and his disciples, suggested by 22:15: "and he said to them."[19] The dialogue is dominated by Jesus, who is the speaker in 22:15, 17, 25, 34, 35, 36, and 38; the disciples address him in 22:33 (Peter), 22:35 (The Twelve), and 22:38 (The Twelve). The disciples engage in their own dialogue by discussing things among themselves in response to Jesus' words in 22:23. The Last Supper as a dialogue has the following significance.

a) The genre of dialogue emphasizes the relationship between Jesus and the disciples.[20] By means of Jesus' words and actions, a new community will be created as he gives himself to his followers in an eschatological relationship (22:16, 18). This new relationship also implies a new presence different from Jesus' presence during his earthly ministry, but one that is real nonetheless. The heart of this last meal in Luke 22 is the institution of this new *real presence*. The meal at Emmaus confirms that in the breaking of the bread, Jesus will make himself known to his people.[21]

b) The genre of dialogue suggests a consideration of Luke's institution narrative as a farewell discourse between Jesus, the dying leader (testator) and his disciples, the future leaders (testatees). This observation is now commonplace in Lukan scholarship,[22] but the clearest and most recent proponents of this position are J. Neyrey and X. Léon-Dufour. Neyrey delineates four elements of this genre in the farewell discourse: "1. *Prediction of Death* . . . 2. *Predictions of Attacks on Leader's Disciples* . . . 3. *Ideal Behavior Urged* . . . 4. *Commission* . . . ." Valuable as these insights are for reading the Last Supper as a farewell discourse, my analysis will focus

---

[19]See Léon-Dufour, *Sharing the Eucharistic Bread*, 60–62, 138–139, and 195–196.

[20]Ibid., 362 n. 22: ". . . here Jesus is in a reciprocal relation with his disciples."

[21]Ibid., 195–196.

[22]See Neyrey, *The Passion*, 194 n.2 and Léon-Dufour, *Sharing the Eucharistic Bread*, 339 n. 31 and 35 for a bibliography on Luke 22:14-38 as a farewell discourse. Cf. also W. S. Kurz, "Luke 22:14-38 and Greco-Roman and Biblical Farewell Addresses," *JBL* 104 (1985) 251–268; Tannehill, *Narrative Unity*, 263; Marshall, *Last Supper*, 80ff.

more on Jesus and the Christological character of the institution narrative than on the disciples and the pastoral character.[23]

Léon-Dufour presents Luke's account of the institution narrative as a farewell discourse by showing the relationship between the cultic and testamentary traditions, describing testament as a literary genre common to the Old Testament and Jewish apocryphal literature, particularly the *Testaments of the Twelve Patriarchs*. He discusses the various components and motifs of the testamentary tradition emphasizing that the farewell gathering sometimes takes place at a meal in a cultic context.[24] There is an eschatological dimension to this tradition from the perspective of the testator, for: "If I believe that eternity is present in time, does this not mean that the eternity which dwells in me wants to continue creating time?"[25]

c) The genre of dialogue links the Emmaus meal with the Last Supper. If the Last Supper is Jesus' farewell discourse to the twelve apostles, then the Emmaus meal is the first expression of a new relationship with other disciples. It is the first of many meals that the Church will celebrate in the time between the Last Supper and the eschatological meal at the parousia, every one of which involves both teaching (table talk) and eating (material communion).[26]

2) Although the literary genre may be that of testament, *the meal is the central event in the farewell discourse* (22:15-16: "I have earnestly desired to eat this passover [*toúto to páscha phageín*] with you before I suffer; for I tell you I shall not eat [*phágô*] it until it is fulfilled in the kingdom of God"). The reference here to the

---

[23]Neyrey, *The Passion*, 7-8: "As general as these features are, they do provide one important interpretative clue: in farewell speeches the focus of attention tends to be on the disciples addressed rather than on the speaker. So we should not be surprised if Lk 22:14-38 tells us more about Luke's view of the apostles, their commission, and the succession of leaders in the Church than about Jesus."

[24]Cf. Léon-Dufour, *Sharing the Eucharistic Bread*, 90-94 on testament as a literary form, and 230-232 for his outline of the Last Supper as a farewell discourse.

[25]Ibid., 93.

[26]In Acts, Luke lists the celebration of several meals to show the diversity of situations and places where they can be celebrated. Thus the Emmaus meal is solitary, but the first of many.

Passover raises the thorny question of whether or not this meal is a Passover.[27] The reader believes that it is a Passover or at least that it began as a Passover meal, with the atmosphere of a Passover, by Luke's numerous references to that fact (22:1, 7, 8, 11, 13, and 15). However, this is not a Jewish Passover but is the Passover of *Jesus*, as Léon-Dufour maintains (cf. 1 Corinthians 5:7 in *KJV*—"Christ *our* passover").

Jesus desires to celebrate this Passover with his disciples before he suffers. His first motive must have been to "unite himself in spirit with all of Israel as it celebrates the memory of its deliverance from Egypt."[28] Yet Luke's narrative is all about a meal "before I suffer" (22:15), about "my body which is given for you" (22:19), about "this cup which is poured out for you . . . the new covenant in my blood" (22:20). Jesus looks forward to eating a Passover with his apostles when "it is fulfilled in the kingdom of God" (22:16), and tells the same apostles to "do this in memory of me" (22:19). The past/present/future aspects are all present in Luke's narrative.[29] When Jesus breaks bread at Emmaus, we know that "it is fulfilled in the kingdom of God" (22:16).

3) Luke frames the Last Supper with the death of Jesus. At the beginning in 22:15, Jesus desires to eat the Passover with the disciples "before I suffer." At the end in 22:37, Jesus quotes Isaiah 53:12 to refer to his death. Both of these are predictions of Jesus'

---

[27]The literature here is vast. Jeremias, *Eucharistic Words*, 41–88 argues at length in favor of a Passover meal and directly responds to the many objections. See Jeremias and Léon-Dufour, *Sharing the Eucharistic Bread*, 382 for a bibliography on the Last Supper as a Jewish Passover. Léon-Dufour 306–308 dismisses Jeremias contention that the Last Supper was a Passover meal. He claims that although there was a Passover atmosphere, the Last Supper should be properly called the Passover of *Jesus*, not a Jewish Passover. Jeremias might agree with Léon-Dufour that the nature of this Passover meal is different from all previous Jewish Passovers and is, in a sense, the Passover of Jesus. See also E. Schweizer, *The Lord's Supper According to the New Testament* (Philadelphia: Fortress Press, 1967) 29–32 entitled "Was Jesus' Last Meal a Celebration of the Passover?" He seems to agree with Léon-Dufour on pp. 31-32: "a Passover meal could have received a completely new character from Jesus."

[28]Léon-Dufour, *Sharing the Eucharistic Bread*, 233.

[29]Ibid., 72 describes three successive periods, particularly the "inter-mediate period, the period of the sacramental meal" of which Emmaus is a part.

death, "a formal characteristic of farewell speeches,"[30] ac-
knowledging the divine necessity of Jesus' death according to
God's plan. Both the necessity of death, and death in fulfillment
of Scripture, are fundamental to Jesus' teaching on the road to
Emmaus.

4) The introduction of the death of Jesus into Luke's Passover
account coincides with the eschatological perspective in 22:16 and
18. The juxtaposition of table fellowship, death, and the eschatological kingdom will take on a new dimension when the risen
Christ breaks bread at Emmaus. Luke alone has two eschatological
references paralleling one another before the institution narrative
to set the entire meal in an eschatological context.

22:16 ". . . I shall not eat (phágô) it until it is fulfilled in the
kingdom of God" (en tê basileía toú theoú).

22:18 ". . . I shall not drink (píô) . . . until the kingdom of God
comes" (hê basileía toú theoú).

Both these verses, one about eating and the other about drinking,
state that Jesus will eat and drink in the kingdom of God. As
Neyrey summarizes:

"But what is this 'kingdom of God' in regard to Jesus: the parousia (see Mk 14:62)? his resurrection? According to Luke, Jesus' experience of the kingdom of God is his vindicating resurrection and
his establishment as Lord and Christ on David's throne (see Acts
2:36). Lk 22:16 and 18, then, should be seen as predictions of
Jesus' vindicating resurrection, balancing the predictions of his
death . . . in Luke's perspective, Jesus' reigning is not a remote
future event, realized only at the parousia as in Mt 25:31-46. Jesus
is recorded as saying in Lk 22:29 that God *has given* him a kingdom, which serves as the basis for his transference of authority to
the apostles. We are encouraged, then, to think of Jesus' passion,
death and resurrection as the context of Jesus' coming into his
kingdom."[31]

[30]Neyrey, *The Passion*, 12.

[31]Ibid., 13–14 (emphasis Neyrey). See also Marshall, *Last Supper*, 79–80 for
another perspective. Cf. Robinson, "The Place of the Emmaus Story," 486:
"In Jesus the Kingdom is made present, and the meal at Emmaus with Jesus

232

This fulfillment in the kingdom of God, as spoken of by Luke, is not necessarily reserved for the end of world history. On the contrary, the meal at Emmaus is the first meal after Jesus comes in the kingdom, and this table fellowship continues with the disciples in Acts (1:4; 2:42).[32]

The Words of Institution of the Last Supper
LUKE 22:19-20.

The longer and shorter text in Luke 22

The debate over the shorter text (22:19a) and the longer one (22:19b-20) in the Lukan institution narrative is long and complex.[33] Both textual traditions of Luke's institution narrative support "the breaking of the bread" as a technical term for Jesus' table fellowship.

1) If the shorter text is original, it may reflect the vocabulary of the early Christian communities ("the breaking of the bread" in 24:30 and 35; the phrase for significant religious meals in Acts 2:42, 46; 20:7, 11; 27:35).[34] Jeremias argues that the technical term "the breaking of the bread" for the Eucharist indicates that there are "traces of a celebration in one kind (*sub una*)," and "that celebration *sub una* not only was frequent in the earliest period but was actually the rule."[35] Léon-Dufour reconstructs the original words spoken in the upper room and concludes that "the text conforms in surprising fashion to assured historical data: 'Breaking of bread,' the early name for the eucharist, is given a solid basis."[36]

---

suddenly taking over as host is an *eikôn* of the Kingdom; the disciples are indeed now feasting at his table in the Kingdom."

[32]Cf. Wainwright, *Eucharist and Eschatology*, 37-38; P. Benoit, "Le récit de la Cène dans Lc. XXII, 15-20," *RB* 48 (1939) 357-393; and Smith, "Table Fellowship," 628-629.

[33]See Jeremias, *Eucharistic Words*, 139-159 on this issue and a bibliography.

[34]Cf. Tannehill, *Narrative Unity*, 290.

[35]Jeremias, *Eucharistic Words*, 115.

[36]Léon-Dufour, *Sharing the Eucharistic Bread*, 176. See also p. 360 n. 51 where he notes the liturgical references to communion under one kind and the scriptural texts he considers support this, i.e. Luke 22:19a (short text); John 6:32-35; Luke 24:35; Acts 2:42, 46; 20:7, 11; 27:35.

2) The command in the longer text in 22:19b to "do this in remembrance of me" is spoken of only in Luke among the Synoptics, *and only over the bread* and not over the cup, as Paul does in 1 Corinthians 11:24-25.[37] If the longer text is earliest, it too suggests that in Luke the bread recalls the whole meal, for in remembering the cultic action of Jesus at the Last Supper, it is sufficient to remember it by the title *the breaking of the bread*. Since Luke goes on to use this phrase for early Christian table fellowship at Emmaus and in Acts, the reader will recall that Luke placed the command of remembrance after the breaking of the bread.

The breaking of the bread

1) Bread itself is a significant metaphor for physical and spiritual existence. It may stand for all food, and even for all of creation (cf. Isa 55:1-3; Prov 9:1-6). The bread used at the Last Supper was unleavened bread. Jeremias discusses the midrash over the bread at the time of Jesus, asserting that it had an eschatological significance.[38]

2) What exactly was meant by "the breaking of the bread" in Luke-Acts? Scholars are generally agreed that it does not stand for the whole meal but simply describes the act of breaking bread that begins the meal.[39] If this is true, then how did the breaking of the bread become associated with the Eucharist? In Luke's Last Supper, the significance of the breaking of the bread is not the act itself, but the meaning that Jesus now invests in the act. He took the traditional Passover haggadah and made it his own. Jesus acts like an Old Testament prophet at the Last Supper:

"The exegetes agree that, taken as a whole, what Jesus said and did over the bread and the cup is a form of *behavior peculiar to the prophets* of the Bible. The latter often mime their message in gestures that are at once figurative and efficacious."[40]

[37]See Jeremias, *Eucharistic Words*, 115.
[38]Ibid., 59–60. Jeremias discusses on pp. 56–62 this midrash over the bread from an historical, allegorical, and eschatological perspective. Cf. also Feeley-Harnik, *The Lord's Table*, 72, 82–85.
[39]See Jeremias, *Eucharistic Words*, 119–120, especially n. 1; Losada, "El episodio de Emaús," 9–10 for a fine synopsis of the different arguments.
[40]Léon-Dufour, *Sharing the Eucharistic Bread*, 124 (emphasis Léon-Dufour).

234

Although the New Testament text never asserts this, many exegetes agree that Jesus spoke about himself during the haggadah as the sacrificial, Passover lamb in fulfillment of the Old Testament and the final fulfillment of the Exodus event. By calling the bread his body and the cup the new covenant in his blood, Jesus is now interpreting the Passover meal in terms of himself. As Jeremias says:

"Although an interpretation of the unleavened bread, and probably also of the wine, had already been given during the devotions, Jesus now interprets both again as he says grace, and this time in reference to his own person . . . *Jesus speaks of himself as a sacrifice.* It can be assumed with a high degree of probability that Jesus had prepared the way for this comparison of himself with the sacrifice earlier, in the passover meditation. It is certain that the interpretation of the passover lamb belonged to the passover *haggadah.* How did Jesus interpret the passover lamb? Since he interpreted the bread and wine in terms of himself, as the words of interpretation show, it is a likely assumption that in the preceding passover devotions he had *also interpreted the passover lamb in terms of himself.*"[41]

3) Although Jewish sources never used "the breaking of the bread" for the whole meal, the context of its use in Luke-Acts suggests that in early Christian usage it referred to the entire table fellowship between Jesus and the believing community in remembrance of all the meals that Jesus ate with the community. The act of breaking bread recalls in the minds of the disciples the Last Supper and all the meals they had with Jesus for, as Jeremias says, "at every common meal *the constitution of the table fellowship is accomplished by the rite of the breaking of bread.*"[42]

But the reader would recognize that this table fellowship at the Last Supper was memorable for a number of reasons, all of which would be recalled by the term "the breaking of the bread." First, it recalled the breaking of the bread by Jesus at the feeding of the

[41]Jeremias, *Eucharistic Words*, 221–222 (emphasis Jeremias). Cf. Marshall, *Last Supper*, 87–88 for a different view.

[42]Jeremias, *Eucharistic Words*, 232 (emphasis Jeremias); J. Behm, *kláō ktl.*, TDNT III 729–730; Léon-Dufour, *Sharing the Eucharistic Bread*, 22; and Cullmann, *Worship*, 14–15.

five thousand, which, in turn, recalled the manna in the wilderness. Second, the reader would recall the Lukan petition for daily bread in the Lord's Prayer in 11:3, a petition for the earthly bread of today and the eschatological bread of tomorrow. Third, the nature of Jesus' table fellowship throughout his ministry is to break bread with all kinds of people, whether sinners or Pharisees. Fourth, the unique Lukan beatitude of 14:15, "Blessed is he who shall eat bread in the kingdom of God," suggests that the ultimate blessedness of God is to eat bread in the kingdom of God. The reference to the eschatological kingdom in Luke 22:15-18 and the giving of his bread as body in 22:19 both indicate that the source of this blessedness will be in the table fellowship with Jesus. Bread thus takes on an eschatological significance. Jeremias writes:

"We can state this all the more confidently when we remember that to orientals the idea *that divine gifts are communicated by eating and drinking* is very familiar. Reference may be made to *the symbolic language of eschatology.* In apocalyptic and Talmudic literature as well as in the New Testament there are innumerable variations on the theme of the bread of life which satisfies all hunger; the tree of life, the fruit of which cures the sick; the heavenly manna, which will be the food of the redeemed in the world to come; the water of life—'for he that hath mercy on them shall lead them, even by the springs of water shall he guide them' (Isa. 49.10, cf. Rev. 7.17)—which is given freely and quenches all thirst for ever; the wine of the world to come which is kept for the children of the kingdom; the feast of salvation in the last days, which imparts salvation and life. 'Those who serve God unto death, will eat of the bread of the world to come in plenty.' 'Blessed is he that shall eat bread in the kingdom of God' (Luke 14.15). 'Blessed are they which are called unto the marriage supper of the Lamb' " (Rev. 19.9).[43]

The nature of Jesus' table fellowship
before, during, and after the Last Supper

Is there any difference between the table fellowship of Jesus with his disciples before the Last Supper, at the Last Supper, and

[43]Jeremias, *Eucharistic Words*, 233–234 (emphasis Jeremias).

after the resurrection?[44] Is the Last Supper or the Emmaus meal the first Eucharist? Is the Emmaus meal Eucharistic? Is there a difference?

1) As prophesied in Luke 22:16 and 18, Jesus engages in table fellowship with his disciples after his resurrection. Two of the three post-resurrection meals in the New Testament are in Luke 24: at Emmaus in 24:28-32 and at Jerusalem in 24:36-43,[45] (the other is in John 21:13).[46] In all these post-resurrection meals, it is bread (Luke 24:30; John 21:13) or fish (Luke 24:42-43; John 21:13) that make up the meal. There are no reports that Jesus drinks any wine, which may be cause to dismiss these post-resurrection meals of Jesus as Eucharistic. However, if "the breaking of the bread" is a technical term for table fellowship, then the fact that Jesus is not spoken of as drinking wine after the resurrection does not present a major stumbling block for considering those meals as part of Luke's table fellowship.[47] The New Testament does, in fact, use the bread metaphor in connection with Jesus' redemptive activity more than the wine, even though wine is a significant symbol in the Old Testament for God's salvific desire for his people.

[44]Cf. Léon-Dufour, *Sharing the Eucharistic Bread*, 113 on "three dimensions of memory": "(1) by means of the present cultic action (2) we go back to the Jesus who at a point in history manifested and made real the definitive presence of God the deliverer, and (3) who gives an everlasting salvation."

[45]An analysis here of Luke 24:36-53 goes beyond the confines of this study, especially in view of the exhaustive analysis by Dillon, *From Eyewitnesses*, 157–225. On p. 181 Dillon rightly notes the parallel between Luke 24:13-35 and 24:36-53 "with their symmetrical sequences of misapprehended appearance, revelation through word and meal, and departure of the apparition" (Dillon sees a close connection between the meal in 24:36-43, the teaching in 24:44-49, and the ascension in 24:50-53). Thus, Luke continues in 24:36-53 the Emmaus table fellowship of eating and teaching. Dillon also suggests on pp. 186–193 the establishment in 24:36-49 of a programmatic mission procedure of peace and table fellowship based on Old Testament precedents, foreshadowed in Luke 10, and realized in Acts. Cf. Fitzmyer, *X-XXIV*, 1574–1575; and Tannehill, *Narrative Unity*, 291.

[46]Cf. Dillon, *From Eyewitnesses*, 150–153, 186; Wanke, *Die Emmauserzählung*, 104f.; and Guillaume, *Luc interprète*, 137–139 on the relationship between the Emmaus meal and John 21.

[47]Cf. Cullmann, *Worship*, 14. Also Jeremias, *Eucharistic Words*, 207–218 on "Jesus' Avowal of Abstinence."

The only other references to Jesus' post-resurrection table fellow-ship are in Acts 1:4 and 10:41. In Acts 1:4 , the risen Lord speaks to the disciples just before ascension about the kingdom of God while he is eating with them (*sunalizómenos*).[48] He commands them to wait for the promise of the Father. The juxtaposition of teach-ing and eating is significant. In Acts 10:41, Peter narrates how God made the risen Christ manifest "not to all the people but to us who were chosen by God as witnesses, who ate and *drank* (*sunephágomen kai sunepíomen*) with him after he rose from the dead." This comes immediately after a strong kerygmatic state-ment in Acts 10:39-40 about the death and resurrection of Jesus ("They put him to death by hanging him on a tree; but God raised him on the third day . . ."). These references indicate that Jesus not only appeared to the disciples but continued the table fellowship that he began in his ministry of *teaching about the king-dom* (passion and resurrection) and *eating and drinking*.[49]

2) The Emmaus meal is the pivotal meal in the table fellowship matrix because it continues Jesus' pre-resurrection table fellowship and is paradigmatic for the table fellowship of the emerging Church. As an act of "the breaking of the bread" (24:35), it serves as the " 'connecting link' between the meals of Jesus with his dis-ciples and the Eucharistic repasts of the early Christian Churches."[50] To label it either as the first Eucharist or as an ordi-

---

[48]Cf. Liddell and Scott, *A Greek-English Lexicon,* 1694 on Acts 1:4: "eat salt with, eat at the same table with, Act. Ap. 1.4"; Bauer, Arndt, and Gingrich, *Greek-English Lexicon,* 791 offer the three alternatives, i.e. (1) "eat (salt) with" or (2) "bring together, assemble, pass. come together" or (3) the different form *sunaulízomai,* "spend the night with . . . be with, stay with"; Davis, "The Significance of the Shared Meal," 148–151; and Dillon, *From Eyewit-nesses,* 106 n. 106.

[49]Cf. Cullmann, *Worship,* 14–16 on the relationship between the post-resurrection meals and the early Christian meals. Cullmann states on p. 15: "If, then, the first appearances of the risen Christ took place during meals, we must take into consideration . . . the fact that *the first eucharistic feasts of the community look back to the Easter meals,* in which the Messianic Meal promised by Jesus at the Last Supper was already partly anticipated" (empha-sis Cullmann).

[50]Dillon, *From Eyewitnesses,* 105 who continues: "But this linkage of termi-nology only directs our attention to more important aspects of continuity in the meals. In both ministries, the Lord's and the church's, the 'breaking of

nary meal misses the point of its unique place in Luke's table fellowship matrix. These categories are too narrow and fail to take into consideration the broader matrix of table fellowship. Though every meal has its own significance, the Emmaus meal, due to its singular character as the first meal of the new age, differs from the meals that precede and follow it. To ignore the evangelist's careful shaping of the matrix by labeling everything as *the Christian Eucharist* is to miss the doctrinal significance of table fellowship. The same holds true if one labels the Emmaus meal as an ordinary meal. How ordinary could it be if the risen Christ is the one who teaches on the road, breaks bread, and reveals himself to be the crucified and risen Lord in fulfillment of the messianic promises of the Old Testament? Though most commentaries classify the Emmaus meal either as the Eucharist or as an ordinary meal, could it not be a unique meal within the table fellowship matrix that is Eucharistic even if it is not the first Christian Eucharist?[51]

The Emmaus meal is different from Jesus' meals with the disciples during his ministry, including the Last Supper, because Jesus had not yet experienced the passion and resurrection. The Last Supper of Jesus is different from all other meals, for it is here

---

the bread' is associated with the *instruction concerning his person and mission* of which he, the earthly Master, had established the prototype" (emphasis Dillon). Cf. also Tannehill, *Narrative Unity*, 290–291; Talbert, *Reading*, 230–231.

[51]Cf. Osborne, *The Resurrection Narratives*, 124: "Critics differ widely on the point, but whatever approach is accepted does not minimize the importance of Jesus breaking the bread precisely at the moment of recognition (vv. 31, 35), thus placing it at the critical point of the narrative. In terms of literary connections, the evidence favors the Luke 9 parallel (see Dillon, pp. 149f.); but as he [Dillon] admits, we cannot rule out eucharistic theology in the feeding pericope as well. On the whole, the technical use of the term in Acts suggests that any first-century reader would connect the term with the Eucharist. Wanke says ([*Die Emmauserzählung*] pp. 104f.) that though Luke's account definitely parallels the feeding miracle, it also definitely features the Eucharist in the recognition scene itself." One difficulty in calling the Emmaus meal the Eucharist is the absence of *eucharistéô* and the presence of *eulogéô*. Although the difference between "blessing" and "giving thanks" is insignificant (cf. Marshall, *Last Supper*, 41), one would expect Luke to use the same word in 24:30 he used in 22:19.

that he first speaks of "the new covenant in my blood." But the Emmaus meal is quite different from these pre-resurrection meals, since in the breaking of the bread, Jesus *for the first time* is recognized as the crucified and risen Messiah. The common bond between the Emmaus meal, the meals of Jesus during his ministry, the Last Supper, and the early Christian meals is that these meals are first and foremost *acts of table fellowship* where Christ is *present* in one form or another to *teach and eat* with his people. In this way, table fellowship is *revelatory*,[52] and the meal at Emmaus is the first revelation.

In reality, there is no difference between any of the meals of Jesus except their temporal relationship to the cross and the resurrection. At all these meals, Jesus is present—present to teach about the kingdom of God by teaching about his death—present to break bread and reveal his salvific and eschatological intentions. It is Eucharistic, even if it is not a formal Christian Eucharist, for the breaking of the bread is a sacramental action by which the present Christ is made known to the disciples. *The table fellowship is itself an expression of the new age.*[53]

3) The Emmaus meal sets the pattern for all Christian dining with God, and therefore is paradigmatic for Christian liturgy. It sets a liturgical pattern because it is an act of anamnesis.[54] Luke is the only evangelist to include the words for "remembrance" in his institution account, for Luke alone among the Synoptics records any post-resurrection meals between Jesus and his disciples in which the table fellowship of Jesus is remembered. According to Léon-Dufour, the call to remembrance at the Last Supper recalls God's covenant at creation and at the Passover. Remembrance takes place within the cultic worship of Israel where "what is celebrated is the great deeds of Yahweh that have marked the history of the chosen people." This is particularly true at the Passover where the haggadah at the meal was a recitation of God's

[52]The recognition theme is dominant in the Emmaus meal and will be highlighted in my forthcoming discussion of Luke 24:31.
[53]Cf. Neyrey, *The Passion*, 16. Cf. also Cullmann, *Worship*, 16–17 on the presence of Christ in the early meals.
[54]The following discussion of anamnesis is indebted to Léon-Dufour, *Sharing the Eucharistic Bread*, 102–116. Cf. also Jeremias, *Eucharistic Words*, 237–255.

redeeming activity in the exodus.[55] Note the parallelism between the call to remembrance in Exodus and the one in Luke:

Exodus 12:14   "This day shall be for you a memorial (*mnêmósunon*) day, and you shall keep it as a feast to the Lord . . ."

Luke 22:19   "Do this in remembrance (*anámnêsin*) of me."[56]

Remembrance takes place at the feast where liturgically the people of God recall the great acts of God's past salvation by recognizing the presence of God in their midst. Léon-Dufour asserts that in the act of remembrance, time becomes "the unfolding of eternity." Eternity now becomes present at the meal in the act of remembering the past, an eschatological event in which the future is anticipated because God is present in his saving acts.

"The God of Israel thus performs certain acts which of themselves, and not by reason of human imagining, control the flow of time; they have a dimension of eternity that makes them always present to those who remember them. Memory is time seen as a single whole; this applies to God as well as to human beings."[57]

Thus, the Emmaus meal is the fulfillment of Jesus' command "do this in remembrance of me" because it is *the first act of the breaking of the bread between Jesus and disciples after the Last Supper and the resurrection*. The whole action involved in the breaking of the bread is the antecedent of "do this," not simply the meal it-

[55]Léon-Dufour, *Sharing the Eucharistic Bread*, 105. He discusses on pp. 106–107 the significance of "the word" as a means of remembering in the cult.

[56]Léon-Dufour, *ibid.*, 110 points out this parallelism. Jeremias, *Eucharistic Words*, 244–249 has a different perspective than Léon-Dufour. He states on p. 249 that "(1) *eis anámnêsin* is said *for the most part in reference to God* and (2) it then designates, always and without exception, *a presentation before God intended to induce God to act*." Fitzmyer, *X-XXIV*, 1401 also sees a parallel to the Passover: "*Touto poieite* is a reinterpretation of the *anamnêsis* which the Passover meal itself was intended to be: 'that you may remember the day of your departure from the land of Egypt all the days of your life' (Deut 16:3d). As Jesus has substituted himself for the Passover lamb, so the memento of him is to replace the *anamnêsis* of the Passover itself."

[57]Léon-Dufour, *Sharing the Eucharistic Bread*, 109. On pp. 108–109 he discusses time in terms of remembrance in the section "Present and Past."

self or the consecrating words over the bread.[58] The Emmaus meal is not only reminiscent of the Last Supper, but is *an anamnesis of the entire table fellowship of Jesus.*[59] In a very real sense, it is more than a remembrance of *Jesus'* meals, for it is also an anamnesis of all the covenantal meals God celebrated with his people in the Old Testament, particularly the Passover meal. As an act of remembrance, the Emmaus meal is a continuation of the table fellowship of God with sinners.

Thus, in Luke's institution narrative, Jesus calls the disciples to break bread in remembrance of him. The Emmaus meal, as the first breaking of the bread between Jesus and his disciples after that Last Supper, ties together both memory and action.[60] The breaking of the bread as action at the table activates the deeper memory, allowing the Church "to descend to the inmost depths of memory . . . to (re)enter the presence of the Creator."[61]

---

[58]Ibid., 109: "The 'this' refers not to the entire meal taken at the Supper, but specifically to the actions and words over the bread and the cup"; Jeremias, *Eucharistic Words*, 250: ". . . *toúto* refers to the *rite of breaking the bread*, i.e. the rite of grace at table. To be exact, it is scarcely possible that the reference is to the normal table prayer—that would need no special instruction—it is rather to *the special grace by means of which the table fellowship of the Messianic community was established, which extolled the salvation activity of God and prayed for its consummation*, a prayer which Jesus himself used during his lifetime" (emphasis mine); Fitzmyer, *X-XXIV*, 1401 understands it as a reference to the action; Marshall, *The Gospel of Luke*, 804 says that "*toúto* will refer to the action of sharing of bread, since the meal came to be known as 'the breaking of bread,' perhaps together with the associated words"; and Plummer, *Gospel According to Luke*, 497–498 who gives a history of the interpretation of *toúto*.

[59]Cf. Dunn, *Unity and Diversity*, 163 (172) on the daily fellowship meals of Acts 2:42, 46 as "*the continuation of Jesus' fellowship meals*, for they were often conscious of his presence in their midst, particularly at the beginning (Luke 24.30f., 35; John 21.12-14; Acts 1.4; cf. Rev. 3.20), and the meals were almost certainly an expression of their eschatological enthusiasm (cf. Acts 2.46), and so, like Jesus' table-fellowship, a foretaste of the eschatological banquet" (emphasis Dunn). Cf. also Talbert, *Reading*, 229.

[60]Cf. Léon-Dufour, *Sharing the Eucharistic Bread*, 102. He explains on p. 105: "Memory and action are thus the two sides—the internal and the external—of the relationship between God and human beings. God saves human beings—which is certainly a 'memorable' action; when they remember this action, they renew their fidelity to the covenant."

[61]Ibid., 104.

4) The breaking of the bread at Emmaus is *in the presence of the risen Lord* who has now transformed time by his action at the cross, at the tomb, and now at the meal. There is a correspondence between Jesus' action at the Last Supper, at Emmaus, and at the early Christian meals. All of these are governed by the presence of Christ who in each case is remembered by the Church as the one who has suffered, died, and risen. Yet as Jeremias says: ". . . the death of the Lord is not proclaimed at every celebration of the meal as a past event but as an eschatological event, as the beginning of the New Covenant."[62] Table fellowship of teaching and breaking bread becomes the occasion for the presence of the eschatological kingdom because it is a celebration of the new covenant that is founded on Christ's death and resurrection.

The first celebration of this new covenant comes at Emmaus where the order is clearly established: teaching before eating, word before meal. In the feeding of the five thousand and the Last Supper, the order in Jesus' table fellowship is *eating before teaching* (9:10-17—eating; 9:18-22—teaching; 22:19-20—the meal; 22:21-38—teaching).[63] In Acts this same concern of teaching and eating will be present in the table fellowship of the Church (1:1-4; 2:42).[64] Luke's summary statement for the entire Emmaus meal in 24:35, "the things he taught on the road and how he was known to them in the breaking of the bread," lays the foundation for early Christian worship, which I will discuss shortly.[65]

The words over the cup in Luke 22:20

In the longer text, the second part of the words of institution in Luke 22:20 emphasizes the death of Christ in association with the meal: "this cup which is poured out for you is the new covenant in my blood."[66] The divine *dei* of God's plan demanded that God's righteous Messiah shed blood, as Jesus himself revealed to the Emmaus disciples in his teaching in Luke 24:25-27, on the

[62]Jeremias, *Eucharistic Words*, 253.

[63]Cf. Dillon, *From Eyewitnesses*, 105–108.

[64]Cf. Cullmann, *Worship*, 12–20; Tannehill, *Narrative Unity*, 291–292.

[65]Cf. D. E. Smith, "Table Fellowship," 629; Tannehill, *Narrative Unity*, 290–291; LaVerdiere, *Luke*, 285.

[66]Cf. Jeremias, *Eucharistic Words*, 218–237 and Léon-Dufour, *Sharing the Eucharistic Bread*, 137–156 on 22:20.

basis of the Old Testament in fulfillment of the covenant of blood in Exodus 24:6-8. Jesus completes a long line of suffering prophets who shed their blood in Jerusalem. He is God's "suffering just man" whose suffering and death ends the persecution of the Old Testament prophets and begins the martyrdom of New Testament apostles.[67] The emphasis in the Last Supper is on the drinking of the blood, an offense to the Jews, but the means by which the disciples will share in the life of Jesus.[68] To accept the cup and drink it, as he commanded, in memory of him, is to reaffirm one's faith that Jesus' suffering and death is the foundation of the new covenant; and it is after this new covenant is founded that Jesus enters into glory (cf. Luke 24:26: "Was it not necessary that the Christ should suffer these things and enter into his glory?"). As the Church now shares in the death of Christ in early Christian table fellowship, it is bound together as the new community, the body of Christ. The words over the cup bring the action at the meal to a close by focusing on the death of Jesus, the very topic in the teaching of Jesus at the table in the five dialogues with his disciples.[69]

[67]Cf. Léon-Dufour, *Sharing the Eucharistic Bread*, 143: "First, the verb 'shed' (Greek *ek-chinnó*) is used exclusively, at least in the New Testament, to describe the violent death of a human being. It is taken from the commandment in Genesis and is used above all of the death of martyrs and, more particularly, of persecuted prophets or the suffering just man. The same word is used in describing the death of Jesus and Paul. In saying that his blood will be shed Jesus thus shows that he is going wittingly to his death."

[68]Cf. Feeley-Harnik, *The Lord's Table*, 145-146: "By drinking the wine that is the blood, the participant 'cuts himself off from his kin' exactly as the law requires (Leviticus 7:27, 17:10-14). But by drinking 'the life of the flesh' (Leviticus 17:11), he acquires that life. The separation from kin that is synonymous with death is only the prelude to eternal life in Jesus Christ." Cf. Dunn, *Unity and Diversity*, 166-167 on Luke representing a tradition that "interpreted the last supper in terms of the new covenant" and thereby "the eschatological note predominates over the soteriological." Cf. also Cullmann, *Worship*, 14-15, 17-18; Léon-Dufour, *Sharing the Eucharistic Bread*, 234; and Jeremias, *Eucharistic Words*, 169-171.

[69]Cf. Feeley-Harnik, *The Lord's Table*, 116 who considers the accounts of the Last Supper to be "a kind of midrash on the life of Moses as depicted in the books of Exodus, Leviticus, Numbers, and Deuteronomy, beginning, in some instances, with Jesus' birth, and ending with his death. The midrash focuses on the covenant and the law that is its most important part, the sacrifice that

The Teaching of Jesus at the Last Supper—Luke's Five Dialogues. The five dialogues in Luke 22:21-38 form the teaching of Jesus at the Last Supper, particularly concerning the significance of his death.[70]

LUKE 22:21-23. Luke 22:21 indicates that the following dialogues take place while Jesus and the disciples are still at the meal ("But behold the hand of him who betrays me is with me on the table"). "The table" (*trapézês*) accents the table fellowship character of this meal, in contrast with Matthew and Mark's "dish" (*trúblion*).[71] Luke shifts the betrayal of Judas from the beginning of the meal to this first dialogue, an abrupt transition from Jesus offering his body and blood for his disciples. The two foci of Jesus' teaching are his betrayal and the presence of sinners at the table. Luke's placement of the betrayal of Judas after the meal may or may not suggest the "communion of Judas," but it reminds the reader that sinners are present at the Last Supper.[72]

The presence of Judas at the table as betrayer prepares the reader for the presence of the Emmaus disciples at the meal as unwitting, ignorant, and unfaithful sinners insofar as they are unable

---

ratifies the covenant, and the temple and priesthood established to carry out the sacrifice." On 129-130 she describes the passion narrative in the Gospels as a retelling of the passover haggadah because "his death and resurrection is the meal . . . the first cup of wine accompanies the kiddush. The second cup is offered in the garden of Gethsemane, the third immediately before the crucifixion, and the fourth, the one that the host finally takes, is offered at the end. The resurrection . . . is the afikomen. . . . The passion narrative is the passover haggadah. Jesus himself intones the Hallel" (emphasis Feeley-Harnik). Thus Feeley-Harnik concludes on p. 155 that "the last supper was another way of translating the complex imagery of the crucifixion into more manageable terms."

[70]Cf. P. Minear, "Some Glimpses of Luke's Sacramental Theology," 322-331 who for each dialogue provides a sequel later on in the passion story; Neyrey, *The Passion,* 17-48; and Marshall, *Last Supper,* 103.

[71]Cf. Léon-Dufour, *Sharing the Eucharistic Bread,* 235: "Luke uses the word 'table' here, instead of 'dish' as in Matthew and Mark, probably in order to emphasize the table fellowship and therefore the terribly contradictory situation of the traitor."

[72]Ibid., 235; Neyrey, *The Passion,* 17-18; on the "communion of Judas." Feeley-Harnik, *The Lord's Table,* 86 writes: "The worst kind of traitor is the traitor with whom one has shared food (Psalms 41:9; Obadiah 1:7; Matthew 26:21; Mark 14:17; *Luke 22:21;* John 13:18, 24-27)" (emphasis mine).

to accept a suffering and crucified Messiah (24:25—"O foolish men, and slow of heart to believe all that the prophets have spoken!"). I have already discussed Luke's use of "to betray" (*paradídomi*) in Luke 22:21-22 as a technical term for the Jesus' betrayal, suffering, death and resurrection, particularly in conjunction with "for the Son of man goes as it has been determined. . . ." (*katá to horisménon poreúetai*).

LUKE 22:24-27. 1) Luke 22:27 speaks of greatness in the kingdom of God in terms of table service ("For which is greater, one who sits at table, or one who serves?"), corresponding to Luke's principle of reversal (e.g. Luke 5, 7, and 14). Luke 13:29-30 is the classic statement of the principle of reversal: the sinners and Gentiles will sit at table in the kingdom of God; the Pharisees and other religious leaders will not. The axiom in 13:30, "some are last who will be first, and some are first who will be last," is a variation of 22:26, "let the greatest among you become as the youngest, and the leader as one who serves."[73]

2) According to Jewish society, certain categories of people did not observe the law, and thus were considered sinners by the Jewish religious establishment. One of the main categories was Gentiles. Table fellowship with Gentiles was scandalous, "for they ate unclean food that was furthermore likely to have been offered to idols."[74] The Gentile kings in 22:25 are an example to the apostles of the table fellowship of the rulers of this world. The normal practice of Gentile sinners is to seek to be the greatest and lord it over each other. The question the disciples ask in 22:24 ("which of them was to be regarded as the greatest") places them into the category of Gentile sinners[75] because they sit at table instead of serving (22:24-27), indicating they have not yet understood that the greater one is the one who serves (22:26). Even the Pharisees act like Gentiles in Luke 14:1-24 when they choose the places of honor.

[73]Cf. Tannehill, *Narrative Unity*, 227–228 on a foreshadowing of 22:24-27 in 9:46-48; and on 22:24-27 and related passages in Luke on pp. 254–257.

[74]Feeley-Harnik, *The Lord's Table*, 44.

[75]Cf. Minear, "Some Glimpses of Luke's Sacramental Theology," 327; Léon-Dufour, *Sharing the Eucharistic Bread*, 237.

246

However, Luke 22 stands in contrast to Luke 13 where the Gentiles are considered part of the eschatological table fellowship. They understand the nature of the kingdom: "some are last who will be first, and some are first who will be last" (13:30). To sit at the table of Abraham, Isaac, and Jacob, the disciples must be like the Gentiles in Luke 13, not like those in Luke 22.

3) The presence of the Gentiles here anticipates one of the major problems in the emerging Church of Acts and the Pauline epistles—the table fellowship between Jewish and Gentile Christians. In one sense, the significance of the table fellowship of Luke is that it prepares for the table fellowship vision of Peter and the conversion of Cornelius in Acts 10,[76] and the agreement between Paul/Barnabas and the Jerusalem Church at the apostolic council in Acts 15.[77] It also enlightens the controversy over table fellowship between Paul and Peter at Antioch in Galatians. The question of table fellowship with Gentiles is the question of table fellowship with sinners, the very issue addressed by Luke in his table fellowship matrix in the Gospel, and intimately associated with an acceptance or rejection of the death of Jesus.[78]

4) Luke 22:27 may be a parallel to Mark 10:45 and Matthew 20:28, the clearest statement of the atonement in Matthew and Mark:

Mark 10:45   "For the Son of man also came not to be served (*diakonêthênai*) but to serve (*diakonêsai*), and to give his life as a ransom for many."

Matthew 20:28 ". . . even as the Son of man came not to be served (*diakonêthênai*) but to serve (*diakonêsai*), and give his life as a ransom for many."

Luke 22:27   "For which is greater, one who sits at table, or one who serves (*ho diakonôn*)? Is it not the one

[76]Cf. Feeley-Harnik, *The Lord's Table*, 156–162 entitled "Peter's Vision" where she argues that "Jesus' sacrifice rescinds even this [Genesis 9:1-4] last restriction on food . . . ."

[77]Cf. Sanders, *The Jews in Luke-Acts*, 114–124, especially 119–121; Esler, *Community and Gospel*, 93–99.

[78]Cf. J. D. G. Dunn, "The Incident at Antioch (Gal. 2:11-18)," *JSNT* 18 (1983) 3–57 (responses 58–64); *Unity and Diversity*, 253–254; Farmer, *Jesus and the Gospel*, 50–63; and Esler, *Community and Gospel*, 87–89.

who sits at table? But I am among you as one
who serves (*ho diakonôn*).

The major difference between Luke and the other Synoptics is the
missing "to give his life as a ransom for many," causing many
commentators to suggest that Luke lacks any reference to the
atonement, to Christ's death as a sacrifice with a saving significance.[79] The common bond between these three passages, however, is the concept of service, *diakonéô,* that characterizes the
essence of Jesus' ministry. Luke has placed this saying here in the
dialogical teaching of Jesus at the Last Supper without the reference to the atonement because the reader knows that this reference
has already been made in the words over the bread, "This is my
body *which is given for you*" (*hupér humôn*—unique to Luke), and
over the cup, "This cup which *is poured out for you* (*hupér humôn*)
is the new covenant in my blood."[80] For Luke, the reference to

[79]Cf. Conzelmann, *The Theology of St. Luke,* 201. Cf. also D. E. Smith,
"Table Fellowship," 631: "I would suggest two reasons why Luke omits
Mark's reference to the death of Jesus at this point. The first is that the saying in Mark, especially the phrase 'the Son of man also came not to be served
but to serve' (Mark 10:45), is too limiting for the symbolism of servanthood.
In Luke, as we will see, one of the significant usages of the table service motif
is service offered to Jesus. Second, Luke seems to prefer ambiguity here, as in
other meal texts, in order that the symbolism may be capable of multiple interpretations. Thus, for example, Jesus is depicted as both host (22:17,19) and
servant (22:27) at the table." Cf. also Marshall, *Last Supper,* 98–99, 101–103;
Luke: Historian, 170–171.

[80]In discussing the sequel to this dialogue, Minear, "Some Glimpses of
Luke's Sacramental Theology," 327 writes: "When Jesus said, 'I am among
you as one who serves,' obviously he pointed to his death. The saying also
refers to this very occasion in which Jesus shares with them the bread and,
the cup." Cf. also Fitzmyer, *I-IX,* 220 on Luke's insertion in 22:19 as a
"sacrificial nuance": "Though Luke has for some inscrutable reason omitted
the Marcan saying about the Son of Man who had to give his life as a ransom
for many (Mark 10:45), he is the only Synoptist who has preserved the words
pronounced over the bread at the Last Supper as, 'This is my body *which is
given for you*' (22:19) . . . . Similarly, a sacrificial nuance of the death of Jesus
must be recognized in the covenant-blood spoken of in 22:20" (emphasis Fitzmyer); and Fitzmyer, *X-XXIV,* 1413–1414 who makes a similar observation on
Luke's longer text in 22:20. Neyrey, *The Passion,* 22 disagrees with this position, stating that there is "an absence of the Christological focus" with an
emphasis not "soteriological but pastoral; the focus is less on the speaker

the atonement and to service occur within the teaching of Jesus at the table, which he will fully explain in 24:25-27.[81]

LUKE 22:28-30.[82] Luke 22:30 connects eschatology and the table fellowship of Jesus with his disciples ("that you may eat and drink at my table in my kingdom"). This recalls for the reader the eschatological prospect of 22:16 and 18, the eschatological table fellowship of 13:29-30, and the beatitude of 14:15, "Blessed is he who shall eat bread in the kingdom of God!"

Does Luke see the fulfillment of this dialogue in the Emmaus meal? Comparing Luke to Matthew reveals that for Luke, the fulfillment of this prophecy may occur at an earlier point in time:

Matthew 19:28   "Truly, I say to you, *in the new world (en tê palig-genesía)*, when the Son of man shall sit on his glorious throne, you who have followed me will also sit on twelve thrones, judging the twelve tribes of Israel."

Luke 22:28-30   "You are those who have continued with me in my trials; as my Father appointed (*diatíthemai*) a kingdom for me, so do I appoint (*diétheto*) for you that you may eat and drink at my table in my kingdom, and sit on thrones judging the twelve tribes of Israel."

---

than on the apostles." He does not consider the relationship between 22:24-27 and 22:19-20 to be significant. C. H. Talbert, *Luke and the Gnostics: An Examination of the Lucan Purpose* (Nashville: Abingdon Press, 1966) 72-73 sees no evidence of the atonement here because he accepts the shorter text of Luke (22:19a).

[81]Cf. D. E. Smith, "Table Fellowship," 632: "Jesus' presentation of himself as host/servant at the Last Supper is thus seen as prefiguring his role as host/servant at the messianic banquet. This of course correlates quite well with the eschatological emphasis presented in the Last Supper pericope as a whole."

[82]Cf. Léon-Dufour, *Sharing the Eucharistic Bread*, 236 on 22:24-30: "The exhortation has two parts which correspond to the two aspects of the one mystery of Christ. Service to the brethren (22:24-27) corresponds to his death, and the prospect of coming glory which gives strength to the disciples of Jesus (22:28-30) corresponds to his resurrection."

Matthew seems to refer to the eschatological feast in the parousia by his expression "in the new world" (*en tê paliggenesía*). But Luke may be referring to Jesus' post-resurrection meals, beginning with Emmaus. Neyrey writes:

"The faithful apostles are commissioned to 'eat and drink at my table in my kingdom' (22:30a). Although there is a New Testament tradition of future eschatological life with Jesus as a messianic banquet, this is not the sense of the Lukan text here. Luke relates that Jesus continued to eat and drink with his apostles and close associates after his resurrection" (*Lk 24:30-35*, 41-43; Acts 1:3-4).[83]

The present tense *diatíthemai* indicates that the apostles will directly assume an eschatological leadership by presiding over the eschatological meal of the new age. The qualifications for such a position are perseverance with Jesus in his trials. It is only after the resurrection and Pentecost that the disciples are able to see themselves conforming to Jesus' statement that they continue with him in his trials.[84] The disciples will demonstrate their perseverance by making the cross and the resurrection (the center of Jesus' interpretation in 24:25-27 and the Church's proclamation in 24:44-49) an integral part of their proclamation of the kingdom, for which they too may suffer.

LUKE 22:31-34. After the general commissioning of the disciples, Jesus commissions Peter as leader of the disciples to strengthen them after the crucifixion causes them to stumble. Peter will also stumble, denying Jesus three times. His denial is the result of Satan's demand to have the disciples (*ho satanas exêtêsato humás—*

---

[83]Neyrey, *The Passion*, 27 (emphasis mine). Cf. also Léon-Dufour, *Sharing the Eucharistic Bread*, 240.

[84]Cf. Fitzmyer, *X-XXIV*, 1415 on 22:24-30 and its relationship to Emmaus: "There is yet another aspect of the Sayings of Jesus in this passage: He instructs his apostles to look for community with him *in glory* rather than distinction in earthly rank. Community in that sphere will depend not on who is greatest among them in mortal esteem, but on their perseverance with him in his trials. His words, in effect, foreshadow the coming passion, and more so the words that he will address to the disciples on the road to Emmaus, 'Was not the Messiah bound to suffer all this before entering into his glory?' (24:26)." Cf. also Tannehill, *Narrative Unity*, 268–270.

plural) in order to sift them like wheat. Jesus prayed for Peter (*perí sou̇—singular*) so that his faith (*hê pístis sou—singular*) may not fail. When Peter turns (*epistrepsas—singular*), he will strengthen the brethren (*toús adelphoús sou—plural*).[85] Peter is set apart as the leader of the disciples, *even though he will deny Jesus.* As a sinner, he will turn, repenting and receiving the forgiveness of sins promised in Jesus' table fellowship. The focus here is not on Peter's denial, but his return to faithfulness and his leadership in strengthening the disciples.[86]

When does this conversion and forgiveness of Peter take place? In Acts 1–11, Peter takes his place as leader in the Church and proclaims the gospel with boldness, strengthening the brethren because he was a witness to the resurrection. But is there an earlier moment of restoration by the evangelist? Peter appears once more in the passion narrative in 22:54-62 where he fulfills Jesus' prophecy and denies him three times. Otherwise, there is only Peter's appearance at the tomb (24:12) and the reference to Christ's appearance to Peter (24:34) that frame the Emmaus meal. Taken together, these two references form Peter's rehabilitation to his status as leader of the Church in fulfillment of Luke 22. *The risen Christ* has restored Peter, bringing about his repentance, conversion, and forgiveness. Thus, Luke 22:31-34 prepares the reader for the restoration of Peter in Luke 24.

LUKE 22:35-38. The focus of this final dialogue is Luke 22:37, the quotation from Isaiah 53:12 as the final passion prediction before Jesus is handed over by his betrayer to sinful people, the only place in Luke's Gospel where the Servant Song of Isaiah is quoted. The character of this passage fits within the passion vocabulary and content seen in other passion predictions and

---

[85]Cf. Minear, "Some Glimpses of Luke's Sacramental Theology," 327 concerning Luke 22:31-32: "The twelve, Peter; Peter, the twelve, strengthen the brethren. Yes, the fate of all is at stake in this dialogue."

[86]Cf. Neyrey, *The Passion*, 34: " 'Turn,' then, clearly has to do with sin, repentance and forgiveness *even after denial of Jesus* . . . . Luke, moreover, frequently speaks of the commissioning of the Church's leaders in the context of their sinfulness. In Lk 5:1-11, Peter confesses: 'I am a sinful man' (v. 8) to which Jesus replied: 'You will be catching men' (v. 10)." Cf. Tannehill, *Narrative Unity*, 264–265.

statements.[87] It describes the necessity of the death of Jesus in fulfillment of Scripture: "For I tell you that this scripture must be
fulfilled in me, 'And he was reckoned with transgressors'; for
what is written about me has its fulfillment." The use of *dei* places
it alongside the three passion statements in Luke 24:7, 26, and 44,
anticipating the teaching of Jesus in 24:25-27 and 24:44-49.[88] The
transgressors and the sword, a reference to the disciples, reiterates
that the Last Supper of Jesus is with sinners.[89]

CONCLUSIONS TO LUKE 22:14-38. Luke's narrative of the Last Supper, then, begins (22:15) and ends (22:37) with a reference to the
death of Jesus. The extended passion and resurrection narrative of
Luke is framed by two meals: the Last Supper—the final Passover
of the old age (Luke 22:14-38), and the Emmaus Supper—the first
meal of the new age (Luke 24:13-35). The dialogues between Jesus
and his disciples focus on the impending death of Jesus, and are
proleptic of future, eschatological eating and drinking with Jesus
because of the death of Jesus. Paul Minear offers this summary of
Luke's Last Supper dialogues:

"Thus far this [Last Supper dialogues] seems a rather bleak picture. What about the frivolity, the feasting, the rejoicing of the
earlier suppers? This picture, however, is not wholly dismal, for it
is in the very context of these dialogues that Jesus promises to
these transgressors that they will sit with him at his table in his

[87]Cf. J. F. Gormley, "The Final Passion Prediction: A Study of Luke 22:33-
38" (Ph.D. diss., Fordam University, 1974) 115–127. Neyrey, *The Passion,* 39
summarizes her position concerning 22:35-38 as a passion prediction like Luke
9:44-45 and 18:31-34 for the following reasons: "(a) a *prediction* is made . . .
(b) the passion is the *fulfillment* of scriptural *prophecies* . . . (c) the disciples *fail
to understand* Jesus . . ." (emphasis Neyrey). On pp. 142–156 Gormley
equates this pericope with Luke's motif of journey to Jerusalem and the missionary journey of the apostles. This corresponds to Luke's Emmaus journey
as well.
[88]Cf. Neyrey, *The Passion,* 38; Dillon, *From Eyewitnesses,* 205–206.
[89]Cf. Minear, "Some Glimpses of Luke's Sacramental Theology," 328–329:
"Their [the disciples] possession of the swords indicates their transgression.
'He was reckoned with transgressors' has its fulfillment in this very scene.
Two swords are enough to prove it. The swords become the two witnesses
which must be heard, according to Deuteronomy, before a man is judged
guilty. 'It is enough.' "

kingdom. He appoints them to thrones judging the twelve tribes of Israel (22:28-30).

"The continuity of ministry is here: 'You are those who have continued with me.' But this is continuity in his trials, in his temptations, temptations by the same tempter. Yet he has prepared for them a table in the midst of their enemies. He has eaten with them. In eating with them, he has pledged their health, their salvation: 'Take this cup and divide it among yourselves.'

"To Luke the symbolic center is taken by Jesus as the *diakonos*, fulfilling his *diakonia*. 'He was reckoned with transgressors.' Only so could his destiny be fulfilled. Not simply because transgression is an inevitable element in human life, but because transgression must be overcome before there can be joy and celebration. And how can it be overcome except by forgiveness? How can Jesus save transgressors except by eating with them?"[90]

THE CONCLUSION TO THE EMMAUS STORY

The reader comes to the conclusion of the Emmaus story at the moment of recognition, when Jesus breaks bread with transgressors. The purpose of Luke's Gospel, as stated in the prologue, was to give assurance to Theophilus concerning the things that he has been taught, and those things (the *ta* of Emmaus) have focused on the identity of Jesus as the suffering, righteous Messiah who was crucified and raised from the dead.[91]

I have attempted to show that table fellowship is one of the means by which the evangelist proclaims the arrival of the eschatological kingdom, the dawn of a new era. Table fellowship in Luke demonstrates that Christianity is a religion embracing both sinners and righteous, both Jews and Gentiles. Table fellowship reveals the most intimate nature of the kingdom of God, namely that God and humans have fellowship with each other through teaching and eating together. This is the basic, elemental stuff of human existence that all people of all times understand.[92] Jesus'

[90]Ibid., 329–330.

[91]Cf. Tannehill, *Narrative Unity*, 10.

[92]Cf. J. Jeremias, *Theology*, 115–116: "In the East, even today, to invite a man to a meal was an honor. It was an offer of peace, trust, brotherhood, and forgiveness; in short, sharing a table meant sharing life. In Judaism in particular, table-fellowship means fellowship before God, for the eating of a

lifestyle at the table is one of service, and he renders the ultimate service to humanity as God's innocent, suffering Messiah by giving up his life for the world and offering up that life at the table, for a table is the ultimate place of fellowship for those who will live together without end.[93] This table fellowship "reveals a God who wants to sit down at table with all men and women and will remove all obstacles, even that of death, which stand in the way of the accomplishment of that communion."[94] Table fellowship, then, is an act of communion and revelation, making known to the world a God who comes to teach about forgiveness through death and resurrection and to offer that forgiveness in the breaking of the bread.

Luke 24:31 and 24:35—The Recognition and the Faithful Response

The moment of recognition in 24:31 leads to the faithful response by the Emmaus disciples in 24:35. The similar language of 24:31 and 35 ties these verses together, with 24:31 preparing for and making possible 24:35.

The structure of Luke 24:31, the moment of recognition, reflects the structure of the Emmaus narrative itself. Both are chiastic, focusing on a central event and recapitulating the whole Gospel. Immediately following the center circle of the teaching of Jesus (24:17-27) and the meal of Jesus (24:28-30), Luke places another chiasm at the moment of recognition that emphasizes the climactic moment when the eyes of the disciples are opened to recognize him. The following two schematic diagrams highlight this:

---

piece of broken bread by everyone who shares in a meal brings out the fact that they all have a share in the blessing which the master of the house had spoken over the unbroken bread. Thus Jesus' meals with the publicans and sinners, too, are not only events on a social level, not only an expression of his unusual humanity and social generosity and his sympathy with those who were despised, but had an even deeper significance. They are an expression of the mission and message of Jesus (Mk 2:17), eschatological meals, anticipatory celebrations of the feast in the end-time (Lk 13:28f; Mt 8:11-12), in which the community of the saints is already being represented (Mk 2:19). The inclusion of sinners in the community of salvation, achieved in table-fellowship, is the most meaningful expression of the message of the redeeming love of God."

[93]Cf. Koenig, *New Testament Hospitality*, 115–116.
[94]Karris, *Luke: Artist and Theologian*, 80.

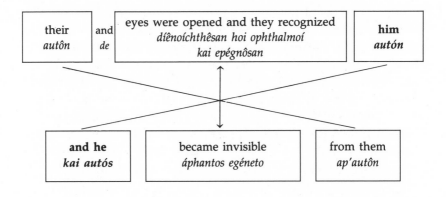

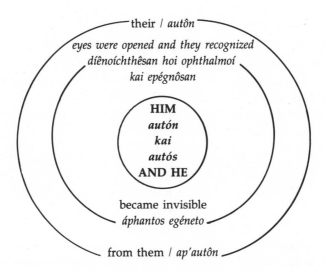

The chiastic structure suggests a number of observations about the moment of recognition:

The Outer Circle—The Emmaus Disciples. In the outer circle stand the Emmaus disciples: *their (autôn)* eyes are opened by God; Jesus disappears *from them (ap' autôn).* The moment of recognition is intended for the Emmaus disciples. They frame the scene of revelation, for although the story (and the Gospel) has been *about* Jesus, it is *for* the Emmaus disciples. The teaching about the passion facts on the basis of the opened Scriptures was for them; now the revelation in the breaking of the bread is for them. They represent the whole Church from Old Testament times to the parousia, and thus they are an icon of the eschatological community of saints who had waited for this moment of revelation and who have since remembered this moment as the climax of God's plan of salvation. The revelation of Christ to the Emmaus disciples in the breaking of the bread anticipates the Church's table fellowship where Christ is present in his suffering and resurrected flesh, which in turn represents the revelation of his face in glory (24:26; Acts 1:11).

The Center Circle—Jesus. The center of the chiasm is Jesus: "him; and he"—*autón kai autós*. This is the first time in Luke's Gospel that anyone sees and recognizes the risen Christ. Luke does not use the name Jesus (*Iêsoús*), but the intensive use of *kai autós* ("and he"). In the Emmaus story, it is Luke's most common term for Jesus (24:15, 25, 28, and 31), who is introduced to the story and departs from it by this phrase. By placing Jesus in the center of this verse, Luke places him in the center of the story. This great Christophany is an eschatological moment, the climax of the story and of the Gospel in which God's Old Testament plan of salvation is fulfilled.[95]

The Other Circle—The Moment of Recognition. The other circle of the chiasm describes the recognition by the words, "And their eyes were opened and they recognized him . . ." (*diênoíchthêsan hoi ophthalmoí kai epégnôsan autón*). This is familiar language for the reader both from the Emmaus story and from the Gospel itself. The opening of eyes in 24:31 is contrasted with their closing in 24:16 (the theological passive in both verses), and paralleling the opening of Scripture in 24:32[96] and the opening of their minds to understand the Scriptures in 24:45. The opening of the eyes characterizes this as *a recognition scene* that has *revelation* as its theme.[97]

[95]Cf. Fitzmyer, *X–XXIV*, 1568: "the goal of the story is reached."
[96]Cf. Tannehill, *Narrative Unity*, 279, 289; and Dillon, *From Eyewitnesses*, 149 who says that "the pathos established between *ekratoúnto* and *diênoíchthêsan* is Lucan dramaturgy in the service of Lucan theology."
[97]Cf. Davis, "The Significance of the Shared Meal," 107–108; Fitzmyer,

The word for recognition, *epiginôskô*, is part of the family of words that Luke uses as an alternative for "faith" (*pisteúô*). The reader would recall that this same word is used to describe the purpose of Luke's Gospel in the prologue in 1:4: ". . . that you may know (*epignôs*) the truth concerning the things of which you have been informed." In 24:18 a similar word, *ginôskô*, is used ironically by the evangelist, for when the Emmaus disciples ask Jesus, "Are you the only visitor to Jerusalem who does not know (*égnôs*) the things that have happened there in these days?," Luke shows that the disciples may know the passion facts, but they do not understand the meaning of those facts. The goal of the story is faith to believe (*toú pisteúein*) all that the prophets have spoken (24:25).[98] At the beginning of the story in 24:16, the disciples' eyes are kept from knowing Jesus; at the end of the story, this veil is taken away.[99] Faith as the goal of the colloquium is now unveiled in the breaking of the bread. Assurance (*aspháleia*) comes only when Christ interprets the passion facts and reveals himself in the breaking of the bread.[100]

X-XXIV, 1557–1558 on the revelatory motifs in the Emmaus narrative; and Robinson, "The Place of the Emmaus Story," 481–497 on the theme of recognition.

[98]Cf. Osborne, *The Resurrection Narratives*, 125: "Verse 35 anchors this newborn faith in the presence of the Lord expressed in both the Word and the bread. The symbols, in fact, point ahead to church worship; 'In the reading of Scripture and at the breaking of bread the Risen Lord will continue to be present, though unseen' (Dillon, pp. 100f.). The primary message here, however, is the awakening of faith."

[99]Cf. also Betz, "The Origin and Nature of Christian Faith," 39: ". . . the basis of faith is not the experience gained through fellowship with the historical Jesus, nor religious concepts inherited from Judaism, nor apocalyptic-eschatological expectations which would project a fulfillment into the future. Rather, according to the Emmaus legend, it is the presence of the crucified Jesus which makes Christian faith possible. Accordingly, Christian faith is in principle to be understood as faith in the resurrected Jesus of Nazareth."

[100]Cf. Feeley-Harnik, *The Lord's Table*, 90: "*Jesus provided his own test meals to prove the reality of the resurrection* to his doubting disciples by transforming breakfasts and suppers into sacrificial offerings (Luke 24:29-32; John 21:6-14)" (emphasis mine).

THE EXEGESIS OF "THE THINGS HE TAUGHT ON THE ROAD" (*ta en tê hodô*).

THE RECOGNITION "IN THE BREAKING OF THE BREAD" (*en tê klásei tou ártos*).

Luke brings the story to a close with the words: "And they expounded the things he taught on the road and how he was known to them in the breaking of the bread" (my translation).[101] Luke's use of "to expound" (*exêgéomai*) and "to make known" (*ginôskô*) remind the reader of the prologue, for *exêgéomai* is from the same family as *diêgêsis* ("narrative") in Luke 1:1, and *ginôskô* is from the same family as *epiginôskô* ("know") in Luke 1:4. The Gospel is described by Luke as "a narration (*diêgêsin*)[102] of the things (*pragmátôn*) which have been accomplished among us," inviting the reader to consider the development of the narrative that is to follow as a record and story of God's saving plan. Fitzmyer writes:

"The *pragmata* about which Luke writes can be compared to the 'facts' or 'happenings' that any historian would be interested in. But as the Lucan account unfolds, the reader learns that the 'events' are not being recounted merely as facts, nor even with the concern of a secular historian (ancient or modern). They are for Luke events of salvation-history, and the significance of them depends on the way one interprets the fulfillment mentioned. In the concrete, the 'events' refer not only to the deeds of the ministry of Jesus, his passion, death, burial, and resurrection, but also to the sequel to all this, the spread of the 'word of the Lord' from Jerusalem to the end of the earth in the activity of the chosen witnesses."[103]

As was observed above, the neuter *ta* is shorthand in Luke 24 for the three-day sequence of passion, death, and resurrection (cf. 24:18; 24:19; 24:27; and 24:35). At 24:35, the reader would understand that the time of fulfillment had come, the events of salvation-history had been accomplished, and the deeds of Jesus

[101]Cf. Dillon, *From Eyewitnesses*, 103, 108.
[102]Cf. Fitzmyer, *I-IX*, 173–174: "Luke's use of *diégésis* as the quasi-title of his work gives it not only a literary dimension, but alerts the reader to the historical implications of the story."
[103]Ibid., 292.

258

in his ministry of death and resurrection were complete. The passion facts at the beginning of the story and the journey (24:18) are now understood by faith, since the passion facts have been interpreted on the road. This highlights the journey motif of the Gospel and the Emmaus story.

But faith comes not only from understanding the passion facts, but also from recognizing Christ in the breaking of the bread. At the end of the journey, as the disciples sit at a table, Jesus is made known to them as the crucified and risen Savior. Luke's theological passive "was known" (*egnôsthê*) is in line with his passive in 24:16 (*ekratoúnto*) and 24:31 (*diênoíchthêsan*)—God alone closes and opens eyes. Knowing Jesus in the breaking of the bread is so important for Luke's purpose that he repeats it in 24:31 and 24:35. But what is most significant in the evangelist's summary is the complementarity of Jesus' exegesis of *"the things he taught on the road"* and the appearance *"in the breaking of the bread,"* of teaching and eating, of Word and Sacrament. These two synaxes form the foundation of Christian worship.[104]

The journey of the Gospel is recalled in the Emmaus journey.[105] The prologue and the Emmaus story frame the Gospel, for the things that make faith possible are assurance (*aspháleia*) in the catechetical tradition of the Church concerning the passion facts, and knowledge (*ginôskô*) of the presence of the crucified and risen one in the breaking of the bread. The disciples are now empowered to go out into the world in Acts armed with "the word and the bread . . . the means to mission."[106]

[104]Losada, "El episodio de Emaús," 9 concludes in his interpretation of the Emmaus story that "Scriptures and Eucharist appear as the indispensable elements for a total encounter with the Lord" (translation mine).

[105]Dillon, *From Eyewitnesses,* 113, 134.

[106]Osborne, *The Resurrection Narratives,* 124. He continues on pp. 124–125: "The word and the bread are the means to mission. Luke wants to show that the presence of the Lord in teaching and eucharistic fellowship empowers the church for participation in Jesus' mission to the lost (cf. Luke 19:10). Verse 32 graphically illustrates this point; the disciples' hearts 'burned within' them when Jesus 'opened the Scriptures' in the recognition experience. Mission is the result of this recognition as the disciples rush back to Jerusalem to tell the Eleven about the Risen Christ. Verses 33–35 tell about that triumphant return 'to Jerusalem.' Verse 33 combines both temporal ('at that same hour') and geographical ('to Jerusalem') factors. The result of recognition is mission; both

The Other Circle—The Moment of Disappearance. Just as the evangelist gives an account of the passion facts, so do the Emmaus disciples. They now proclaim the eschatological kingdom as present in table fellowship with God.[107] What surprises us is that Jesus, the moment he is recognized, disappears from sight (*áphantos egéneto*). Why would Jesus not stay with his disciples for the rest of the meal?

With the crucifixion and resurrection, the table fellowship of Jesus has been transformed, and therefore it is very appropriate for Jesus to disappear. He no longer reclines at table as he did during his ministry, for he is now present with the Church in a new way. The presence of Jesus at the Emmaus meal prepares the Church for his presence at the Eucharist.[108] Emmaus is the transitional meal between the historical meals, including the Last Sup-

---

are linked with the resurrection and Jerusalem as the starting point for the church's outreach." See also Dillon, *From Eyewitnesses*, 267 where he "choose[s] the *mission enterprise* as our focal point for distilling and refining the message of St. Luke that chapter 24 conveys." Dillon notes the mission's content, pattern, "witness" mandate, and recruits. Of special significance is his suggestion on pp. 278ff. that the "Lucan blending of christology and ecclesiology, drawing out the *missiological consequence* of the Master's path to glory through passion and death, contains the key to Luke's much debated theological appraisal of the death" (emphasis Dillon).

[107]Cf. Dillon, *From Eyewitnesses*, 154–155: "The 'breaking of the bread' is the sacramental action which renders the teaching Lord present to his congregation, disclosing to her the mystery of his person and laying upon her the burden of his own mission and destiny. As risen Lord, present in word and sacrament, he shows himself the *goal and meaning of all the scriptures*, and he imparts to his followers that ministry of the word which continues to unlock the secret otherwise hidden away in the sacred pages. *His voice* is what continues to be heard in that ministry of the word (thus Dt 18:15,18 can be invoked by his witnesses, Acts 3:22-23), for it is only *in personal encounter with him*, and from that perspective, that the whole mystery of God's plan of salvation is opened to the eye of faith.—That is, in the final analysis, the teaching of the Emmaus story. *It precisely forbids any ironical separation of the time of Jesus from the time of the Church*, as if the latter saw only an institutionalizing of what could no longer be a real presence of a living word!" (emphasis Dillon).

[108]See Tannehill, *Narrative Unity*, 290: "The presence of the risen Christ at Emmaus may also suggest that the meals in Acts go beyond fellowship among the believers to include communion with the risen Lord."

per, where he physically and visibly ate with his disciples, and the multiple, endless Eucharistic meals where he is present but not seen. Only in the Emmaus meal do the historical Jesus and the resurrected Christ have a common point of reference. The old covenant meals end and the final, eschatological meal is inaugurated.

The stranger who walked with them on the road, who became a guest at their home and then host at their meal, is a stranger no more. He is now the host who gives himself for food every time the Church gathers in fellowship around the table to celebrate the presence of the eschatological kingdom through the teaching of his words and the breaking of his bread.

Bibliography

Achtemeier, P. J. "The Lucan Perspective on the Miracles of Jesus: A Preliminary Sketch," *Journal of Biblical Literature* 94 (1975) 547-562.

Anderson, H. "Broadening Horizons: The Rejection at Nazareth Pericope of Luke 4:16-30 in Light of Recent Critical Trends," *Interpretation* 18 (1964) 259-275.

Arce, P. A. "Emmaús y algunos textos desconocidos," *Estudios Bíblicos* 13 (1954) 53-90.

Avanzo, M. "Jésus y la conducción de la communidad," *Revista bíblica* 37 (1975) 16-22.

Badia, L. F. *The Dead Sea People's Sacred Meal and Jesus' Last Supper.* Washington: University Press of America Inc, 1979.

Ballard, P. H. "Reasons for Refusing the Great Supper," *Journal of Theological Studies* 23 (1972) 341-350.

Barrett, C. K. *Luke the Historian in Recent Study.* London: Epworth, 1961.

_____. *The Gospel According to St John.* London: SPCK, 1967.

Bauer, W. and W. F. Arndt and F. W. Gingrich, *Greek-English Lexicon of the New Testament.* Chicago: University of Chicago, 1957.

Behm, J. *kainós,* TDNT Abridged 388-389.

_____. *kláô ktl.,* TDNT III 726-743.

_____. *néos,* TDNT Abridged 628.

Benoit, P. "Le récit de la Cène dans Lc. XXII, 15-20," *Revue Biblique* 48 (1939) 357-393.

_____. *The Passion and Resurrection of Jesus Christ.* New York: Herder and Herder, 1969.

Bernadicou, P. J. "Biblical Joy and the Lucan Eucharist," *The Bible Today* 51 (xxii, 1970) 162-171.

_____. "Christian Community According to Luke," *Worship* 44 (1970) 205-219.

_____. "Programmatic Texts of Joy in Luke's Gospel," *The Bible Today* 45 (xxii, 1969) 3098-3105.

_____. "The Lukan Theology of Joy (Revisited)," *Science et Esprit* XXX, 1 (1978) 57-80.

Betz, H. D. "The Origin and Nature of Christian Faith According to the Emmaus Legend," *Interpretation* 23 (1969) 32–46.

Black, M. "The Aramaic of *ton arton hêmôn ton epiousion* (Matt vi.11 = Luke xi.3)," *Journal of Theological Studies* 42 (1941) 186–189.

_____. *The Scrolls and Christian Origins*. New York: Scribner, 1961.

Blass, F. and A. Debrunner, *A Greek Grammar of the New Testament*. Trans. R. W. Funk. Chicago and London: The University of Chicago Press, 1961.

Bock, D. L. *Proclamation From Prophecy and Pattern: Lucan Old Testament Christology*. Journal for the Study of the New Testament, Supplement Series 12; Sheffield: JSOT Press, 1987.

Boobyer, G. H. "The Eucharistic Interpretation of the Miracles of the Loaves in St. Mark's Gospel," *Journal of Theological Studies* 3 (1952) 161–171.

Bornhäuser, K. *The Death and Resurrection of Jesus Christ*. (Bangalore, 1958).

Bornkamm, G. *présbus ktl..*, *TDNT* VI 651–683.

Bösen, W. *Jesusmahl, Eucharistisches Mahl, Endzeitmahl: Ein Beitrag zur Theologie des Lukas*. Stuttgart: Katholisches Bibelwerk, 1980.

Bovon, F. *Luke the Theologian*. Allison Park, Pennsylvania: Pickwick Publications, 1987.

Bowen, C. R. "The Emmaus Disciples and the Purposes of Luke," *Biblical World* 35 (1910) 234–245.

Brown, F. and S. R. Driver and C. A. Briggs, *A Hebrew and English Lexicon of the Old Testament*. Oxford: Clarendon Press, 1979.

Brown, R. E. *The Birth of the Messiah*. New York: Doubleday, 1977.

_____. *The Gospel According to John I-XII*. New York: Doubleday, 1966.

Bruce, F. F. *The Epistle to the Galatians*. Grand Rapids: Eerdmans, 1982.

Büchsel, F. *gínomai*, *TDNT* I 681–689.

_____. *kríma*, *TDNT* III 942.

Bultmann, R. *History of the Synoptic Tradition*. New York: Harper, 1963.

_____. *aphími, áphesis, paríêmi, páresis*, *TNDT* I 509–512.

_____. *gínôskô, gnôsis, epiginôskô, epignôsis*, *TNDT* I 689–719.

Burrows, M. *More Light on the Dead Sea Scrolls*. New York: The Viking Press, 1955.

Cadbury, H. J. "Lexical Notes on Luke-Acts: III. Luke's Interest in Lodging," *Journal of Biblical Literature* 45 (1926) 305–322.

_____. *The Making of Luke-Acts*. London: SPCK, 1958.

Caird, C. B. *Saint Luke*. Philadelphia: The Westminster Press, 1963.

Carroll, J. T. "Luke's Portrayal of the Pharisees," *Catholic Biblical Quarterly* 50 (1988) 604–621.

Catchpole, D. R. *The Trial of Jesus*. Leiden: E. J. Brill, 1971.

Combrink, J. B. "The Structure and Significance of Luke 4:16-30," *Neotestamentica* 7 (1973) 27-47.

Conzelmann, H. *The Theology of St. Luke.* New York: Harper, 1967.

Creed, J. M. *The Gospel According to St. Luke: The Greek Text, with Introduction, Notes, and Indices.* London: Macmillan, 1930.

Crockett, L. C. "Luke 4:25-27 and Jewish-Gentile Relations in Luke-Acts," *Journal of Biblical Literature* 88 (1969) 177-183.

_____. "The Use of the Old Testament in Luke: with Emphasis on the Interpretation of Isaiah 61.1-2" Volumes I and II. Ph.D. diss., Brown University; Ann Arbor: University Microfilms, 1966.

Cross, F. M. *The Ancient Library of Qumran and Modern Biblical Studies.* New York: Doubleday, 1958.

Cullmann, O. *Early Christian Worship.* London: SCM Press, 1953.

_____. *The Christology of the New Testament.* Philadelphia: Westminister, 1959.

Dahl, N. *The Crucified Messiah.* Minneapolis: Augsburg, 1974.

Daniélou, J. "The New Testament and the Theology of History," *Studia Evangelica* I (1959).

D'Arc, J. "Catechesis on the Road to Emmaus," *Lumen Vitae* 32 (1977) 62-76.

_____. *Les pelerins d'Emmaus.* Serie "Lire la Bible" 47; Paris: Editions du Cerf, 1977.

_____. "Un grand jeu d'inclusions dans 'les pelerins d'Emmaus,'" *La nouvelle revue théologique* 99 (1977) 143-156.

Davis, E. C. "The Significance of the Shared Meal in Luke-Acts." Ann Arbor: Xerox University Microfilms, 1967.

Delitzsch, F. *Isaiah.* Grand Rapids: Eerdmans, 1976.

Delling, G. *árchôn, TDNT* I 488-489.

De Vaux, R. *Ancient Israel.* Volume 2: Religious Institutions; trs. J. McHugh; New York: McGraw-Hill Book Company, 1961.

Dillon, R. J. *From Eyewitnesses to Ministers of the Word: Tradition and Composition in Luke 24.* Analecta biblica 82; Rome: Biblical Institute, 1978.

Dix, G. *The Shape of the Liturgy.* New York: The Seabury Press, 1982.

Dodd, C. H. "The Appearances of the Risen Christ: An Essay in Form-Criticism of the Gospels," *Studies in the Gospels: Essays in Memory of R.H. Lightfoot.* Ed. D. E. Nineham. Oxford: Blackwell, 1957, 9-35; reprinted, *More New Testament Studies.* Grand Rapids: Eerdmans, 1968, 102-133.

Drury, J. *Tradition and Design in Luke's Gospel.* Atlanta: John Knox Press, 1976.

Duesberg, H. "He Opened their Minds to Understand the Scriptures," *Concilium* 30 (1968) 111-121.

Dumm, D. R. "Luke 24:44-49 and Hospitality" in *Sin, Salvation, and the Spirit*. Ed. D. Durken. Collegeville: The Liturgical Press, 1979, 231–239.

Dunn, J. D. G. *Baptism in the Holy Spirit*. Philadelphia: The Westminster Press, 1970.

_____. *Christology in the Making*. Philadelphia: The Westminster Press, 1980.

_____. *Jesus and the Spirit*. Philadelphia: The Westminster Press, 1975.

_____. "The Incident at Antioch (Gal. 2:11-18)," *Journal for the Study of the New Testament* 18 (1983) 3–57.

_____. *Unity and Diversity in the New Testament*. London: SCM Press, 1977.

Dupont, J. "La parabole de la brebis perdue (Mt 18,12-24; Lc 15,4-7)," *Gregorianum* XLIX (1968) 265–287.

_____. "L'enfant prodique," *Assemblées du Seigneur* XXIX (1966) 52–68.

_____. "Les pèlerins d'Emmaüs (Luc xxiv, 13-35)," *Miscellanea biblica Bonaventura Ubach*. Scripta et documenta 1; Montserrat, 1953) 349–374.

_____. "The Meal at Emmaus," *The Eucharist in the New Testament*. Ed. J. Delorme. Baltimore and Dublin: Helicon Press, 1964, 105–121.

_____. "The Poor and Poverty in the Gospels and Acts," *Gospel Poverty: Essays in Biblical Theology*. Chicago: Franciscan Herald, 1977.

_____. *The Salvation of the Gentiles*. New York: Paulist Press, 1979, 129–159.

Ehrhardt, A. "The Disciples of Emmaus," *New Testament Studies* 10 (1963–64) 182–201.

Ellis, E. E. *Eschatology in Luke*. Philadelphia: Fortress Press, 1972.

_____. "Present and Future Eschatology in Luke," *New Testament Studies* 12 (1965–66) 27–41.

_____. "The Composition of Luke 9 and the Source of Its Christology," *Current Issues in Biblical and Patristic Interpretation: Studies in Honor of Merrill C. Tenney*. Grand Rapids: Eerdmans, 1975, 120–127.

_____. *The Gospel of Luke*. London: Thomas Nelson, 1966.

Esler, P. F. *Community and Gospel in Luke-Acts*. Cambridge University Press, 1987.

Falcone, S. A. "The Kind of Bread We Pray for in the Lord's Prayer," *Essays in Honor of Joseph P. Brennan*. Ed. R. F. McNamara. Rochester, N.Y.: St. Bernard's Seminary, 1976, 36–59.

Farmer, W. R. *Jesus and the Gospel*. Philadelphia: Fortress Press, 1982.

Feeley-Harnik, G. *The Lord's Table: Eucharist and Passover in Early Christianity*. Philadelphia: University of Pennsylvania Press, 1981.

Ferris, S. *The Hymns of Luke's Infancy Narratives*. Journal for the Study of the New Testament, Supplement Series 9, Sheffield, England: JSOT

Press, 1985.

Fitzmyer, J. "The Composition of Luke, Chapter 9," *Perspectives on Luke-Acts.* Ed. C. H. Talbert. Danville, Va.: Association of Baptist Professors of Religion, 1978, 139–152.

_____. *The Gospel According to Luke I-IX.* New York: Doubleday, 1981.

_____. *The Gospel According to Luke X-XXIV.* New York: Doubleday, 1985.

Flender, H. *St. Luke: Theologian of Redemptive History.* Philadelphia: Fortress Press, 1967.

Francis, F. O. "Eschatology and History in Luke-Acts," *Journal of the American Academy of Religion* 37 (1969) 49–63.

Friedrich, G. *kêrússô, TDNT* III 697–714.

Fuchs, E. *sêmeron, TDNT* VII 269–275.

Fuller, R. *The Formation of the Resurrection Narratives.* New York: Macmillan, 1971.

Geldenhuys, N. *Commentary on the Gospel of Luke.* Grand Rapids: Eerdmans, 1952.

Giles, K. "Present-Future Eschatology in the Book of Acts," *The Reformed Theological Review* XL-XLI (1981–82) 65–71, 11–18.

Gormley, J. F. "The Final Passion Prediction: A Study of Luke 22:33-38. Ph.D. diss., Fordham, 1974.

Goulder, M. D. *The Evangelists' Calendar.* London: SPCK, 1978.

Grassi, J. A. "Emmaus revisited (Lc 24,13-15 and Acts 8,26-40)," *Catholic Biblical Quarterly* 26 (1964) 463–467.

Grundmann, W. *sun-metá, TDNT* VII 766–797.

_____. *tapeinós, TDNT* VIII 1–26.

_____. *chríô ktl., TDNT* IX 527–580.

Guillaume, J. *Luc interprète des anciennes traditions sur la résurrection de Jésus.* EBib; Paris: Gabalda, 1979.

Guinan, M. D. *Gospel Poverty: Witness to the Risen Christ, A Study in Biblical Spirituality.* New York: Paulist Press, 1981.

Haenchen, E. *The Acts of the Apostles.* Philadelphia: The Westminster Press, 1971.

Hahn, F. *The Titles of Jesus in Christology.* London: Lutterworth Press, 1969.

Harris, R. L., G. L. Archer, and B. K. Waltke, eds. *Theological Wordbook of the Old Testament.* Chicago: Moody Press, 1980, I–II.

Hauck, F. *parabolê, TDNT* Abridged 773–776.

Hebblethwaite, P. "Theological Themes in the Lucan Post-Resurrection Narratives," *Clergy Review* 50 (1965) 360–369.

Hengel, M. *The Atonement.* Philadelphia: Fortress Press, 1981.

Hennig, J. "Our Daily Bread," *Theological Studies* 4 (1943) 445–454.

Hill, D. "The Rejection of Jesus of Nazareth (Luke iv 16-30)," *Novum Testamentum* 13 (1971) 161-180.

Horst, J. *oús, TDNT* V 543-558.

Huffman, N. "Emmaus among the Resurrection Narratives," *Journal of Biblical Literature* 64 (1945) 205-226.

Hull, J. M. *Hellenistic Magic and the Synoptic Tradition: Studies in Biblical Theology*, 2nd series, 28. London, 1974, chapt. VI.

Hummel, H. D. *The Word Becoming Flesh.* St. Louis: Concordia Publishing House, 1979.

Jasper, R. C. D. and G. J. Cuming, *Prayers of the Eucharist: Early and Reformed.* New York: Oxford University Press, 1980.

Jeremias, J. *Jerusalem in the Time of Jesus.* Philadelphia: Fortress Press, 1969.

_____. *Jesus' Promise to the Nations.* SBT 24; Naperville: Allenson, 1958.

_____. *New Testament Theology: The Proclamation of Jesus.* New York: Scribner's, 1971.

_____. *The Eucharistic Words of Jesus.* London: SCM Press, 1966.

_____. *The Lord's Prayer.* Facet Books, Biblical Series 8; Philadelphia: Fortress Press, 1973.

_____. *The Parables of Jesus.* London: SCM Press, 1963.

_____. *grammateús, TDNT* I 740-742.

_____. *parádeisos, TDNT* V 765-773.

Johnson, L. T. *The Literary Function of Possessions in Luke-Acts.* SBL Dissertion Series 39; Missoula: Scholars Press, 1977.

Juel, D. *Messianic Exegesis.* Philadelphia: Fortress Press, 1988.

Kaiser, W. C. *limmûd, TWOT* I 480.

Karris, R. J. *Luke: Artist and Theologian.* New York: Paulist Press, 1985.

_____. "Poor and Rich: The Lukan *Sitz im Leben*," in *Perspectives on Luke-Acts.* Ed. C. H. Talbert. Macon: Mercer University Press, 1978, 112-125.

Keck, L. E. and J. Martyn, eds. *Studies in Luke-Acts.* Philadelphia: Fortress Press, 1966.

Kittel G. and G. Friedrich, eds. *Theological Dictionary of the New Testament.* 10 vols.; Grand Rapids: Eerdmans, 1964-1976.

Kittel G. and G. Friedrich, eds. *Theological Dictionary of the New Testament.* Abridged in One Volume by G. Bromiley. Grand Rapids: Eerdmans, 1985.

Klosterman, E. *Lukas (Handbuch zum Neuen Testament,* ed. Lietzmann), 12 auflage. Tübingen, 1929.

Kodell, J. "Luke's Use of *Laos,* 'People,' Especially in the Jerusalem Narrative (Lk 19,28—24,53)," *Catholic Biblical Quarterly* 31 (1969) 327-343.

Koenig, J. *New Testament Hospitality*. Philadelphia: Fortress Press, 1985.

Kuhn, K. G. "The Lord's Supper and the Communal Meal at Qumran," *The Scrolls of the New Testament*. Ed. K. Stendahl. New York: Harper, 1957, 65–93.

Kümmel, W. G. *Promise and Fulfillment*. Naperville: Alec R. Allenson, 1957.

Kurz, W. S. "Luke 22:14-38 and Greco-Roman and Biblical Farewell Addresses," *Journal of Biblical Literature* 104 (1985) 251–268.

_____. "The Function of Christological Proof from Prophecy in Luke and Justin." Ph.D. diss., Yale University, 1976.

Lagrange, M.-J. *Evangile selon saint Luc*. Études bibliques; Paris: Gabalda, 1921; 8th ed. 1948.

Larkin, W. J. "Luke's Use of the Old Testament as a Key to His Soteriology," *Journal of Evangelical Theological Society* 20 (1977) 325–335.

_____. "Luke's Use of the Old Testament in Luke 22–23." Ph.D. diss., University of Durham, 1974.

LaVerdiere, E. A. *Luke*. Wilmington: Michael Glazier, 1980.

Leaney, A. R. C. *A Commentary on the Gospel According to St. Luke*. London: Adam and Charles Black, 1958.

Lee, G. M. "The Walk to Emmaus," *Expository Times* 77 (1965–66) 380–381.

Léon-Dufour, X. *Resurrection and the Message of Easter*. Trans. R. N. Wilson. London: Geoffrey Chapman Publishers, 1974.

_____. *Sharing the Eucharistic Bread*. New York: Paulist Press, 1987.

Liddell, H. G. and R. Scott, *A Greek-English Lexicon*. Revised by H. S. Jones and R. Mackenzie. Oxford at the Clarendon Press, 1968.

Liefeld, W. L. "Exegetical Notes: Luke 24:13-35," *Trinity Journal* 2 (1981) 223–229.

Lietzmann, H. *Mass and the Lord's Supper*. Leiden: E. J. Brill, 1979.

Linton, O. "The Parable of the Children's Game," *New Testament Studies* 22 (1975–76) 159–179.

Loewe, W. P. "Towards an Interpretation of Lk 19:1-10," *Catholic Biblical Quarterly* 36 (1974) 321–331.

Lohmeyer, E. *Galiläa und Jerusalem*. FRLANT 52; Göttingen: Vandenhoeck und Ruprecht, 1936.

_____. *Lord of the Temple*. Edinburgh and London: Oliver and Boyd, 1961.

Lohse, E. *Die Auferstehung Jesu Christi im Zeugnis des Lukasevangeliums*. BibS[N] 31; Neukirchen: Neukircherer-V., 1961.

_____. *sunédrion*, TDNT VII 860–871.

_____. *huiós Dauíd*, TDNT VIII 478–488.

Losada, D. A. "El episodio de Emaús: Lc 24, 13-35," *Revista bíblica* 35 (1973) 3–13.

Luce, H. K. *The Gospel According to St. Luke*. Cambridge: At the University Press, 1933.

Mackowski, R. M. "Where is Biblical Emmaus?" *Science et Esprit* 32 (1980) 93–103.

Marshall, I. H. *Last Supper and Lord's Supper*. Grand Rapids: Eerdmans, 1980.

_____. *Luke: Historian and Theologian*. Grand Rapids: Zondervan, 1971.

_____. "Slippery Words: I. Eschatology," *Expository Times* 89 (1977–78) 264–269.

_____. *The Gospel of Luke*. Grand Rapids: Eerdmans, 1978.

_____. "The Resurrection of Jesus in Luke," *Tyndale Bulletin* 24 (1973) 55–98.

McHugh, J. "A Sermon for Easter," *Clergy Review* LXXI (March, 1986) 91–93.

_____. *The Mother of Jesus in the New Testament*. Garden City, New York: Doubleday, 1975.

Metzger, B. *A Textual Commentary on the Greek New Testament*. London: United Bible Societies, 1975.

Meynet, R. "Comment etablir un chiasme: A propos de 'pelerins d'Emmaus,' " *La nouvelle revue théologique* 100 (1978) 233–249.

Michaelis, W. *kratéô*, TDNT III 910–912.

_____. *ophthalmós*, TDNT V 375–378.

_____. *páschô*, TDNT V 904–939.

Michel O. *telônês*, TDNT VIII 88–105.

Minear, P. *Commands of Christ: Authority and Implications*. Nashville: Abingdon Press, 1972.

_____. "Some Glimpses of Luke's Sacramental Theology," *Worship* 44 (1970) 322–331.

Moessner, D. P. *Lord of the Banquet: The Literary and Theological Significance of the Lukan Travel Narrative*. Minneapolis: Fortress Press, 1989.

Moo, D. J. *The Old Testament in the Gospel Passion Narratives*. Sheffield: The Almond Press, 1983.

Moule, C. F. D. "The Christology of Acts," *Studies in Luke-Acts*. Ed. L. E. Keck and J. Martyn. Philadelphia: Fortress Press, 1966, 159–185.

Moulton, J. H. and G. Milligan, *The Vocabulary of the Greek Testament*. London: Hodder and Stoughton, 1930.

Mowinckel, S. *He That Cometh*. New York: Abingdon Press, 1954.

_____. *The Psalms in Israel's Worship*. 2 Vols. Trans. D. R. AP-Thomas; New York: Abingdon Press, 1962.

Munck, J. *The Acts of the Apostles*. New York: Doubleday, 1967.

Navone, J. "Lucan Joy," *Scripture* 19-20 (1967–68) 49–62.

_____. "The Lukan Banquet Community," *The Bible Today* 51 (12, 1970) 155-161.

_____. *Themes of St. Luke.* Rome: Gregorian University Press, 1970.

_____. "The Parable of the Banquet," *The Bible Today* 14 (xi, 1964) 923-929.

Neusner, J. "Two Pictures of the Pharisees: Philosophical Circle or Eating Club," *ATR* LXIV:4 (1982) 525-538.

Neyrey, J. *The Passion According to Luke.* New York: Paulist Press, 1985.

Nickelsburg, W. E. "Riches, The Rich, and God's Judgment in 1 Enoch 92-105 and the Gospel according to Luke," *New Testament Studies* 25 (1978/79) 324-344.

O'Hanlon, J. "The Story of Zacchaeus and the Lukan Ethic," *Journal for the Study of the New Testament* 12 (1981) 2-26.

Orchard, B. "The Meaning of *ton epiousion* (Mt 6:11= Lk 11:3)," *The Bible Translator* 3 (1973) 274-282.

Orlett, R. "An Influence of the Early Liturgy upon the Emmaus Account," *Catholic Biblical Quarterly* 21 (1959) 212-219.

Osborne, G. R. *The Resurrection Narratives: A Redactional Study.* Grand Rapids: Baker Book House, 1984.

Otto, R. *Kingdom of God and Son of Man.* London: Lutterworth, 1943.

Palmer, H. "Just Married, Cannot Come," *Novum Testamentum* 18 (1976) 241-257.

Perrin, N. "The Use of *(para)didonai* in Connection with the Passion of Jesus in the New Testament," *Der Ruf Jesu und die Antwort der Gemeinde.* Eds. E. Lohse et. al. Göttingen: Vandenhoeck and Ruprecht, (1970) 204-212.

Petuchowski, J. J. and M. Brocke, *The Lord's Prayer and Jewish Liturgy.* New York: Seabury, 1978.

Pieper, J. *In Tune With The World.* Chicago: Franciscan Herald Press, 1963.

Pilgrim, W. *Good News to the Poor: Wealth and Poverty in Luke-Acts.* Minneapolis: Augsburg, 1981.

Platz, H. H. "Cleopas," "Clopas," *The Interpreter's Dictionary of the Bible,* I, 649-650.

Plevinik, J. "The Eleven and those with them according to Luke," *Catholic Biblical Quarterly* 40 (1978) 205-211.

Plummer, A. *Gospel According to St. Luke.* Edinburgh: T. & T. Clark, 1913.

Preisker, H. *eggús, eggízô, proseggízô, TDNT* II 330-332.

Puzo, F. "Marta y María: Nota exegética a Lc 10,38-42 y I Cor 7,29-35," *Estudios Eclesiásticos* 34 (1960) 851-857.

Reicke, B. *The Roots of the Synoptic Gospels.* Philadelphia: Fortress Press, 1986.

Rengstorf, H. *didáskô, TDNT* II 135-148.

Rese, M. *Alttestamentliche Motive in der Christologie des Lukas.* Gerd Mohn: Gütersloher Verlagshaus, 1969.

Riesenfeld, H. *Jésus transfiguré.* Copenhagen: Munksgaard, 1947.

Robertson, A. T. *A Grammar of the Greek New Testament in the Light of Historical Research.* Nashville: 1923.

Robinson, B. P. "The Place of the Emmaus Story in Luke-Acts," *New Testament Studies* 30 (1984) 481–497.

Rogers, B. B. *The Wasps of Aristophanes.* London: G. Bell and Sons, 1915.

Sabourin, L. "The Eschatology of Luke," *Biblical Theology Bulletin* 12 (1982) 73–76.

Sabugal, S. "La embajada mesiánica del Bautista (Mt 11,2-6 = Lc 7,18-23): Análisis histórico-tradicional," *Augustinianum* 13 (1973) 215–278; 14 (1974) 5–39; 17 (1977) 395–424.

Sanders, J. *The Jews in Luke-Acts.* Philadelphia: Fortress Press, 1987.

Schmidt, K. L. and M. A. *pároikos, paroikía, paroikéô, TDNT* V 841–853.

_____. *pároikos* [resident alien], *paroikía* [resident alien], *paroikéô* [to live as a resident alien] *TDNT* Abridged 788–790.

Schnider, F. and W. Stenger, "Beobachtungen zur Struktur der Emmausperikope (Lk 24, 13-35)" *Biblische Zeitschrift* 16 (1972) 94–114.

Schrenk, G. *archieréus, TDNT* III 265–283.

_____. *díkaios, TDNT* II 182–191.

_____. *eklektós, TDNT* IV 181–192.

_____. *entolê, TDNT* II 545–556.

Schraeder, H. H. *Nazarênós* [of Nazareth], *Nazôraíos* [Nazarene], *TDNT* Abridged 625.

Schubert, P. "The Structure and Significance of Luke 24," *Neutestamentliche Studien für Rudolf Bultmann.* Ed. W. Eltester. Berlin: Alfred Töpelmann, 1954, 165–186.

Schürmann, H. *Das Lukasevangelium: Erster Teil: Kommentar zu Kap. 1,1—9,50.* Herders theologischer Kommentar zum Neuen Testament III/1; Freiburg: Herder, 1969.

_____. *Der Einsetzungsbericht Lk 22,19-20* II. NTA 20/4; Munster: Aschendorff, 1955.

_____. *Der Paschamahlbericht Lk 22,(7–14)15–18* I. NTA 19/4; Munster: Aschendorff, 1953.

_____. "Die Gestalt der urchrislichen Eucharistiefeier," in idem, *Ursprung und Gestalt. Erörterungen und Besinnungen zum Neuen Testament.* Düsseldorf, 1970.

_____. *Jesu Abschiedsrede Lk 22,21-38.* III. NTA 20/5; Munster: Aschendorff, 1957.

Schweizer, E. *The Good News According to Luke.* Atlanta: John Knox Press, 1984.

_____. *The Good News According to Matthew*. Atlanta: John Knox Press, 1975.

_____. *The Lord's Supper According to the New Testament*. Philadelphia: Fortress Press, 1967.

_____. *sôma ktl.*, *TDNT* VII 1045-1094.

Sloyan, G. "The Holy Eucharist as an Eschatological Meal," *Worship* 36 (1962) 444-451.

Smith, D. E. "Table Fellowship As A Literary Motif in the Gospel of Luke," *Journal of Biblical Literature* 106 (1987) 613-638.

Smith, R. H. "History and Eschatology in Luke-Acts," *Concordia Theological Monthly* 29 (xii, 1958) 881-901.

_____. "Paradise Today: Luke's Passion Narrative," *Currents in Theology and Mission* 3 (1976) 323-336.

_____. "The Eschatology of Acts and Contemporary Exegesis," *Concordia Theological Monthly* 29 (ix, 1958) 641-663.

Stauffer, E. *eis*, *TDNT* II 420-442.

_____. *hina*, *TDNT* III 323-333.

Steele, E. S. "Jesus' Table-Fellowship with Pharisees: An Editorial Analysis of Luke 7:36-50, 11:37-54, and 14:1-24." Ph.D. diss., Notre Dame, 1981.

Suggs, M. J. *Wisdom, Christology, and Law in Matthew's Gospel*. Cambridge: Harvard University Press, 1970.

Sweetland, D. M. "The Lord's Supper and the Lukan Community," *Biblical Theology Bulletin* 13 (1983) 23-27.

Talbert, C. *Literary Patterns, Theological Themes, and the Genre of Luke-Acts*. Missoula: Scholars Press, 1974.

_____. *Luke-Acts: Perspectives from the Society of Bibical Literature Seminar*. New York: Crossroad, 1984.

_____. *Luke and the Gnostics: An Examination of the Lucan Purpose*. Nashville: Abingdon Press, 1966.

_____. *Perspectives on Luke-Acts*. Danville, Va.: Association of Baptist Professors of Religion, 1978.

_____. "Promise and Fulfillment in Lucan Theology," in *Luke-Acts: Perspectives from the Society of Bibical Literature Seminar*. Ed. C. Talbert. New York: Crossroad, 1984, 91-103.

_____. *Reading Luke*. New York: Crossroad, 1982.

Tannehill, R. *The Narrative Unity of Luke-Acts*. Philadelphia: Fortress Press, 1986.

Taylor, V. *The Passion Narrative of St. Luke: A Critical and Historical Investigation*. SNTSMS 19; ed. O. E. Evans; Cambridge: University Press, 1972.

Thayer, J. H. *A Greek English Lexicon of the New Testament*. New York:

American Book Company, 1886.

Thompson, G. H. P. *The Gospel According to Luke.* Oxford at the Clarendon Press, 1972.

Tiede, D. L. *Prophecy and History in Luke-Acts.* Philadelphia: Fortress Press, 1980.

Tyson, J. *Luke-Acts and the Jewish People.* Minneapolis: Augsburg, 1988.

_____. *The Death of Jesus in Luke-Acts.* University of South Carolina Press, 1986.

Via, D. O. "The Relationship of Form to Content in the Parables: The Wedding Feast," *Interpretation* 25 (1971) 171–184.

Von Rad, G. *Deuteronomy.* Philadelphia: The Westminster Press, 1966.

Wainwright, G. *Eucharist and Eschatology.* New York: Oxford University Press, 1981.

Walker, N. "After Three Days," *Novum Testamentum* 4 (1960) 261–262.

Wanke, J. *Beobachtungen zum Eucharistieverständnis des Lukas auf Grund der lukanischen Mahlberichte.* Erfurter theologische Schriften 8; Leipzig: St. Benno-Verlag, 1973.

_____. *Die Emmauserzählung. Eine redaktionsgeschichtliche Untersuchung zu Lk 24,13-35.* Erfurter theologische Studien 31; Leipzig: St. Benno-Verlag, 1973.

Weiser, A. *The Psalms.* Philadelphia: The Westminster Press, 1962.

Wilson, S. G. "Lukan Eschatology," *New Testament Studies* 15 (1968) 330–347.

Winter, P. "On Luke and Lucan Sources," *Zeitschrift für die Neutestamentliche Wissenschaft* 47 (1956) 217–242.

_____. "Some Observations on the Language in the Birth and Infancy Stories of the Third Gospel," *New Testament Studies* 1 (1954–1955) 111–121.

_____. "The Proto-Source of Luke 1," *Novum Testamentum* 1 (1956) 184–199.

Wojcik, J. *The Road to Emmaus: Reading Luke's Gospel.* West Lafayette, Indiana: Purdue University Press, 1989.

Young, E. J. *The Book of Isaiah, Volume II.* Grand Rapids: Eerdmans Publishing Company, 1969.

Zehnle, R. "The Salvific Character of Jesus' Death in Lucan Soteriology," *Theological Studies* 30 (1969) 420–444.

Ziesler, J. A. "The Removal of the Bridegroom: A Note on Mark II. 18-22 and Parallels," *New Testament Studies* 19 (1972–73) 190–194.

Biblical Index

Old Testament

Genesis

1	**41**
1:1–2:4a	41
1:2	41
1:3	41
2	190
2:3	41
3	**66–67**, 190
3:7	66
3:15	67
9:1-4	247 n. 76
15:13	76 n. 19
18–22	67 n. 27
31:54	169

Exodus

10:16	182 n. 47
12:6	37 n. 14
12:14	**241**
12:18-22	37 n. 14
16	158
16:4	170 n. 17
16:15	170 n. 17
18:12	169
24	169
24:6-8	244

Leviticus

7:27	244 n. 68
17:10-14	244 n. 68
17:11	244 n. 68
24:14	97 n. 41

Numbers

11	158

Deuteronomy

1:41	182 n. 47
12:5-7	169
12:17-18	169
14:23	169
14:26	169
15:20	169
16:3d	241 n. 56
18	214
18:15ff.	**214**
18:15-18	**7**
18:15	6, 7, 215, 260 n. 107
18:18-19	7
18:18	260 n. 107
20:5-7	180 n. 37
21:18-21	148 n. 53
21:20	147, 147 n. 52
21:22-23	148, 148 n. 53
21:23	8 n. 25
24:5	180 n. 37
27:7	169

Judges

21:16	63 n. 18

I Samuel

7:6	182 n. 47
9:11-14	169
11:15	169, 169 n. 15
24:12	182 n. 47

Subject and Author Index

Controversy dialogue, 70–71
Conzelmann, H., 74–75, 89, 94–95, 143
Cross, F. L., 171

Davis, E. C., 139, 163 n. 90, 166, 184, 193
Death of Jesus, xiii, 2–3, 5–6, 8–11, 12 n. 32, 13, 14–15, 18, 20, 22–25, 28, 36, 38, 41, 48, 52, 56, 62, 65, 71, 78, 82, 85–86, 94, 98, 100–102, 104, 106, 108, 110–111, 114, 116–128, 130, 138–140, 142, 144–145, 147–148, 150, 155–156, 158–159, 161, 163, 168, 174, 177, 179, 184, 191, 193–195, 197–198, 200–202, 206–207, 209–217, 221, 225–227, 229, 231–232, 238, 240, 243–248, 252, 254, 258–259
Delling, G., 111
Dillon, R., xiv–xv, 32 n. 17, 34 n. 1, 50, 53, 59, 102, 203, 215, 224, 237 n. 45
Disciples
  faith/recognition, 22, 29–30, 38, 47, 49–50, 79, 94, 202–204, 208, 219, 226, 244, 250–251, 254, 257, 259,
  incomprehension, 5, 9, 17, 20, 22, 24–25, 28, 38, 43, 45, 48, 50, 57–58, 58 n. 7, 64, 67–68, 70, 77, 81–83, 84, 86, 101, 104, 106, 108, 118, 122–123, 138–139, 142, 163, 176–177, 198–199, 200–202, 206, 215, 226, 227, 245–246, 252, 257
Dumm, D. R., 78 nn. 23, 24

Eighth day, 21, 21 n. 16, 39–41, 42 n. 28, 196, 200
Eleven, 2, 5, 16–18, 22, 26, 49, 53–54, 56, 81, 157, 203, 225, 228
Elijah, 6, 16, 55, 91, 96–97, 101, 106, 141, 205, 215
Elisha, 6, 91, 96–97, 101, 106, 158, 205, 215
Elizabeth, 105–107, 216
Ellis, E. E., 157, 167
Emmaus
  chiasm, 30–32,
    fifth circle, 55–56
    fourth circle, 57–58
    third circle, 59–64
    second circle, 64–68
    24:16 and 24:31a, 64
  Cleopas, 53, 72–75, 72 nn. 9, 11, 73 n. 12, 79, 82, 87, 220
  climax of Gospel, 10, 46, 63, 219, 219 n. 2, 221, 225, 240, 256
  climax of post-resurrection meals, 157
  dialogue content, 80–83
  dialogue participants, 72–79
  disappearance, 223, 260–261

Greek Word Index

eggízô, 60–63, 125, 220–221
elpízô, 197
en pásaia tais graphaís, 10
en tê hodô, 58, 82
enantíon, 105
epioúsion, 161–162, 161 n. 85
epiginôskô/ginôskô, 31, 64, 68, 82–83, 256–259
esthíô/éphagon, 160, 171–172, 230, 232
euaggelízô, 17, 91, 156
eucharistéô, 160, 172
eulogéô, 18, 160, 172, 184, 224–226
euphraínomai, 183–184
exêgéomai, 258
éxodos, 11, 21, 21n. 18, 207 n. 25

goggúzô/diagoggúzô, 134
grammateús, 111

ho erchómenos, 141, 194
hrêma, 81, 99
hupér humôn, 248

kai autós, 31, 63, 202, 224
kai egéneto, 48, 55, 59, 224–225
kai idoú, 21, 55–56, 55 n. 1
kainós, 136–137, 136 n. 25
katá to hôrisménon, 124
katalúô, 188
katêchêthês, 80–83
kêrússô, 12–13, 17, 91–92, 91 n. 23, 156
kláô/katakláô, 160, 173, 224, 226
klasmátôn/klásei, 18
klínô/kataklínô, 17, 18, 151, 224–226, 228
kratéô, 28, 64, 67, 259
kríma thanátou, 121

laléô, 17, 159
lambánô, 18, 160, 172, 224, 226
laós, 105, 107, 107 n. 57, 117–119, 144, 194
lógos, 70, 80–81, 99
lútrôsis/lutróô, 8, 197–199

méllô, 198
ménô, 188, 222
metánoia/metanoéô, 12, 135
mnêthête, 4–5, 22, 241

néos, 136–137, 136 n. 26

ophthalmós, 31, 64–65, 66, 256

paradídômi, 5, 8, 12, 24, 121–127, 246
pároikos/paroikéô, 75–77, 76 nn. 18, 19, 77 nn. 20, 22
páscha, 230
páschô/patheín, 12–13, 18, 24
pisteúo, 257
pléróô, 11, 13
poía, 85
poreían poioúmenos, 167
poreuómai/poreúesthai, 24, 58, 60 n. 13, 63, 220–221, 246
pragmeatôn, 81–82, 258
presbúteros/presbutérion, 111, 115

sêmeron, 188–190
skandalízô, 142
sôtêría/sôzô/sôtêr/sôtêrion, 61, 188–189, 191–193
stauróô/staurós, 5, 8, 12
sunalizómenos, 238

ta, 82–83, 84, 258
ta genómena, 82–83
ta legómena, 83
ta perí heautoú, 10
tê trítê hêméra, 5, 12, 18